PRAISE F

Home Baked

WINNER OF THE CALIFORNIA INDEPENDENT BOOKSELLERS
ALLIANCE'S GOLDEN POPPY AWARD FOR NONFICTION

A SAN FRANCISCO PUBLIC LIBRARY
"ON THE SAME PAGE" SELECTION

"A portrait of heroics, innovation, grit, and pot-baking in an epidemic (in this case, the AIDS crisis) . . . strikingly relevant . . . beautifully written."

Entertainment Weekly, "Books to Read in April"

"A raunchy and rollicking account of a vanished era told by someone who paid very close attention to her larger-than-life parents. I gobbled it up like an edible."

— Armistead Maupin

"A beautiful evocation of the Bay Area in the years before tech bros and big money changed the city . . . Under Volz's careful attention, all of it — the era, the place, and her own parents — is rendered clear, bright, and beautiful."

— *Paris Review,* staff pick

"I devoured this book! Sex, drugs, rock 'n' roll, a savvy business-woman, a social and medicinal revolution — what's not to love? This is a story Alia Volz was born to tell."

— Rebecca Skloot, best-selling author
of *The Immortal Life of Henrietta Lacks*

"An earnest yet comic memoir by the daughter of the owner of the Sticky Fingers bakery, purveyor of pot brownies and crusader for legalization."

— *New York Times*, "New and Noteworthy Audiobooks"

"[An] intensely personal portrait of an unconventional childhood, as well as a rigorously reported account of a kaleidoscopic time in San Francisco history, an era of exuberant highs and pitch-black lows."

— *San Francisco Chronicle*

"Intensively researched . . . timely."

— *Newsweek*

"[Volz] combines a journalist's eye for detail with a storyteller's sense of humanity . . . A sometimes-sad yet stirring love letter to San Francisco filled with profundity and pride."

— *Kirkus Reviews*

"A coming-of-age memoir like no other."

— *Shelf Awareness*, starred review

"[*Home Baked*] proves sometimes truth is stranger than fiction . . . Heartwarming, sharply witty . . . A touching story of eccentric families and the unusual bonds that bring people together."

— *Reader's Digest*, "The Best 14 Reads From the 2020 Quarantine Book Club"

"Volz has written a refreshing kind of family memoir — one that presents the messier truths of her family's life without pushing to create martyrs and villains . . . *Home Baked* will envelope you in its warm, generous heart."

— Chapter 16

"A spirited, rollicking ride full of the vibrant characters, neighborhoods, and rebel 'outsider' sensibilities that make [San Francisco] so special . . . [Volz is] wise enough to understand that the city will always be magic."

— *San Francisco Chronicle,*
"San Francisco: the eternal book subject"

"Alia Volz vividly portrays [San Francisco] in her delightful, heartfelt, nonfiction debut . . . *Home Baked* is part memoir, part ethnography, part lively history of a beloved city that Volz chronicles with tenderness and verve."

— Jenny Shank, *High Country News*

"In *Home Baked*, Alia Volz manages not only to write about her parents with clear-eyed compassion and empathy, but she also gives us a rich history of San Francisco in the 1970s and 1980s. As I read, her family and the city came alive for me: every person and street were vivid, complicated, tragic, and beautiful. I loved this engrossing, informative, funny, and heartbreaking book. Volz is a true talent."

— Edan Lepucki, best-selling author of
Woman No. 17, California, and others

"A hilarious, heartfelt, and unforgettable debut. I gobbled it up like a pan of fresh-baked brownies. Having come of age in the Bay Area when the Sticky Fingers operation was at its height, I devoured every last morsel of this evocative and occasionally heartbreaking tale, which is as much a deep dive into San Francisco's weird and fast-evolving weed scene as it is about Volz's unforgettable family. 'Eat it, baby!' was the bakery's motto; for Alia's wonderful book, I say 'Read it, baby!'"

— Julia Flynn Siler, best-selling author of *The White Devil's Daughters, The House of Mondavi,* and others

"Volz masterfully documents the history of San Francisco's LGBTQ+ and artist community in the 1970s and '80s."

— *Electric Literature*

"*Home Baked* is a deeply touching, funny, wise, and magical book. By telling her eye-popping family story and transporting her readers back to the kaleidoscope days of Northern California in the last quarter of the twentieth century, Alia Volz gives us not only an indelible memoir but also an intimate social history of the mom and pop marijuana business and how it revolutionized the world. With *Home Baked*, Volz joins the colorful parade of writers who have brought 'San Francisco values' fully to life, including Hunter S. Thompson, Armistead Maupin, Warren Hinckle, Diane di Prima, Richard Brautigan, Maxine Hong Kingston, Dave Eggers and Michelle Tea."

— David Talbot, best-selling author of
Season of the Witch and *The Devil's Chessboard*

"*Home Baked* hit me with the joy *and* sting of recognition. Here is a heroine I understand: a badass mom doing legitimate yet illegal work that provided for her daughter, but also shaped a community. This wonderfully written memoir delivers a world of risk and drugs and secrecy alongside heavy batches of love and wit and courage. Alia Volz deftly blends in social context with her coming-of-age story, concocting a fantastic history lesson on everything from marijuana laws to the AIDS crisis to the transformation of San Francisco, where she herself was home-baked. I loved this book, got high off its intoxicating allure; long after I read the last page, I couldn't come down."

— Bridgett M. Davis, author of
The World According to Fannie Davis

Home Baked

My Mom, Marijuana, and the Stoning of San Francisco

ALIA VOLZ

Mariner Books
Houghton Mifflin Harcourt
BOSTON   NEW YORK

First Mariner Books edition

hmhbooks.com

Library of Congress Cataloging-in-Publication Data
Names: Volz, Alia, 1977– author.
Title: Home baked : my mom, marijuana, and the stoning of
San Francisco / Alia Volz.
Description: Boston : Houghton Mifflin Harcourt, 2020. |
Includes bibliographical references.
Identifiers: LCCN 2019028706 (print) | LCCN 2019028707 (ebook) | ISBN
9780358006091 (hardcover) | ISBN 9780358007074 (ebook) |
ISBN 9780358315094 | ISBN 9780358316626 | ISBN 9780358505020 (trade paper)
Subjects: LCSH: Volz, Alia, 1977 — Childhood and youth. |
Mothers and daughters — California — San Francisco — Biography. |
Eccentrics and eccentricities — California — San Francisco — Biography. |
Bakers — California — San Francisco — Biography. | Cooking (Marijuana) |
Marijuana — Therapeutic use. | Children of divorced Parents — California —
San Francisco — Biography. | San Francisco (Calif.) — Biography.
Classification: LCC CT275.V5926 A3 2020 (print) | LCC CT275.V5926 (ebook) | DDC
979.4/61092 [B] — dc23
LC record available at https://lccn.loc.gov/2019028706
LC ebook record available at https://lccn.loc.gov/2019028707

Book design by Kelly Dubeau Smydra

Printed in the United States of America
DOC 10 9 8 7 6 5 4 3 2 1

Photograph and illustration credits can be found on page 433.

An alternate version of chapter 1 first appeared in essay form under the title "My Mother
the Ganja Dealer" on Narratively.com in 2014. Several chapters include parts of an essay
titled "In Any Light, by Any Name," first published by *Tin House* in 2014. Chapter 2
contains portions of the author's oral history with Shari Mueller, which first appeared in
Instant City in 2008. All written and used by permission of the author. All rights reserved.

For Doug and Meridy.

You kept me safe from the squares.

CONTENTS

On the Barge

When I was nine, my public elementary school participated in a program best known by the slogan, "D.A.R.E. to keep kids off drugs!" It was one of Nancy Reagan's pet projects, a prong of her Just Say No campaign. One afternoon per week, the entire fourth grade crowded into the cafeteria, where a uniformed policeman lectured us about the perils of narcotics like marijuana. We learned techniques for deflecting peer pressure and identifying and avoiding dealers. And we broke into groups to playact situations. I was careful to follow the program's script.

I knew how to keep a secret.

At home, there were giant black garbage bags of Mendocino shake crammed into the closet of our spare bedroom, along with pounds of fragrant, manicured buds sealed in gallon Ziplocs. My mom had operated Sticky Fingers Brownies — a massive, profoundly illegal marijuana-edibles business — since before I was born. Throughout my infancy, she and her partners distributed upward of ten thousand brownies per month; it was the first known business of its kind to operate at that scale in California. By the age of nine, I was helping my mom bake and individually wrap brownies on weekends. Sometimes I tagged along on deliveries after school.

We were the people the cop warned my class about.

By 1987, the year of my first D.A.R.E. lessons, AIDS was ravaging my hometown. People I loved as surrogate aunties and uncles were suffering gruesome, agonizing illnesses. Cannabis eased their discomfort and helped curb the deadly wasting syndrome. After-school deliveries had become tours of sickbeds.

I had been my mom's accomplice since I was in the stroller. Some of my earliest flashes of memory are from brownie runs back when San Francisco had a technicolor glow. I grew up believing that I was made of my hometown, that there was no difference between me and the place I was born.

My family's secrets sometimes isolated me from other kids, but secrets also act as a bonding agent between those in the know. I was never neglected like some hippie children were; I was fawned over, encouraged, welcomed into the conspiracy. An outcast at school, I was inner-inner circle within the Sticky Fingers world. The coolest of the cool kids.

And wherever we lived, the inner sanctum of the inner circle was my mom's king-size bed, nicknamed the "barge." Many customers became trusted friends. She'd invite them aboard, and they'd sprawl sideways or belly down and converse for hours — unpacking relationship troubles, planning career changes, swapping stories. Equal parts therapist's couch, executive boardroom, and ladies' lounge, the barge was a place for sharing and intimacy. It was also where my mom counted stacks of hundreds and fifties.

I can still see her enveloped in a miasma of pot smoke, blue-green-amber eyes gleaming with her latest anecdote or an old favorite. And then flopped over on her back, wheezing with laughter and slapping the covers. I remember how the barge trembled with a good punch line, and how steady it felt when you were down and needed reassurance.

There have been countless barges over the years — from mattresses so well-worn they were permanently imprinted with my mom's shape to hotel beds that carried us for a night or two. Wherever my mom "gets horizontal" for a heart-to-heart talk with someone she loves, that's the barge. It's a state of mind as much as a place.

That's where this book began. Sometime around 2007, I started taping my mom's best stories on a handheld cassette recorder. At first, I was just archiving for myself. But as she unspooled the yarns of Sticky Fingers, I became curious about how her contribution to cannabis history fit into the broader legalization movement and the story of my hometown, even my country. I wanted to understand the historical moment and social pressures that created the secretive world I grew up in. And to know why she risked her freedom — and my safety — to blaze trails in this illegal industry during the drug war.

To find out, I barged with my godmother and then my dad, both of whom helped build the business. The conversations began with people close to my heart, but the circle soon widened exponentially; it's the nature of drug dealing to radiate outward. The Sticky Fingers crew guided me to former customers, who brought their friends into the project. Some came to me, and others I had to hunt. Several people have passed away in the years since we talked, leaving me with staticky recordings of their memories. A hollow silence remains in place of the voices of our many friends lost long ago to AIDS.

Since beginning my recordings, I've conducted hundreds of hours of interviews with cannabis farmers, dealers, customers, activists, artists, business owners, city officials, and law enforcement — all of whom were somehow touched by this family-run pot-brownie business. I've sought to corroborate their memories with historical records, archival research, and contemporary news sources. All scenes and conversations are re-created with guidance from the original participants. Throughout, I've hoped to retain the sweetness of our early conversations. My "interviewing," if I must call it that, is relaxed and informal, as close to barging as I can manage.

Before I could spell my own name, I understood that I came from an outlaw family. If I ever revealed what my parents did for a living, I knew that they could go to prison and I could become a ward of the state. Whenever adults asked, I said my folks were professional artists — a true statement, though incomplete.

As of this writing, California is among eleven states (plus D.C.) to authorize the recreational use of cannabis for adults. Thirty-five states permit varying degrees of medicinal use, and another two states allow controlled preparations of CBD. Only Idaho and Nebraska still practice total prohibition. Marijuana laws are shifting so quickly that the landscape will likely be different by the time this book is printed. This sea change began in my lifetime; it began in my hometown of San Francisco, among my mom's close friends and associates; it began with a plague and the bravery and determination of those who fought for what their bodies needed.

The statute of limitations expired on my family's crimes years ago. The federal government still classifies marijuana as a Schedule 1 narcotic — more tightly controlled than cocaine or pharmaceutical opioids — but no one is going to do time because of this story. I'm writing with the consent and collaboration of those involved.

I vividly remember my mom dissuading me from taking a "cola" bud the length of my forearm to kindergarten show-and-tell. Now, as I enter my forties, I'm eager to break the silence I grew up with. I can finally bring Mom's home-baked brownies to share with the rest of class.

PART I

1

Eat It, Baby!

MAIL CONTAINS DRUG, YOUNG WOMEN SEIZED reads a 1969 headline from the *Milwaukee Journal*. Below, in grainy black-and-white, floats Meridy Domnitz's mug shot. My mom, twenty-one years old, already making a name for herself.

In the photo, she looks more pathetic than criminal. Her head is cocked to the right, forehead contorted into an expression of woe. Her frizzy hair has gone renegade from a sideways ponytail, and she's wearing what appears to be a paisley kurta. The mug shot beside my mom's stands in contrast. It belongs to her cousin's wife, Patty Abrams. Patty is all dimples and teeth, like it's her school picture.

This article details my mom's first dalliance with the wrong side of the law; by the time she had me nearly a decade later, the dealer persona had taken center stage.

A trail of brownie crumbs leads to the day when my mom stopped being a good girl: October 18, 1967, a chilly autumn afternoon with a wool-gray sky.

On her way to class at the University of Wisconsin-Madison, Meridy heard shouts breaking out between the frigid gusts coming off Lake Mendota. She rounded Bascom Hall and walked right into the Dow Chemical protest.

As Mer gleaned that morning, the company that gave the world

Saran Wrap was also the US government's sole manufacturer of napalm, which bonded with and quickly liquefied human flesh when exploded in a bomb, causing gruesome injury and death. Dow representatives were in the Commerce Building trying to recruit from the student body. Protesters jammed the building. The overflow — around a thousand people — grouped in the quad, pumping signs that read DOW SHALT NOT KILL and MORALS NOT BOMBS. A visiting contingent from the San Francisco Mime Troupe tooted bugles and rattled tambourines.

Mer had grown up on a tranquil, elm-lined street in Milwaukee. She was a daddy's girl through and through. With the McCarthy witch hunts in mind, her dad had sent her to college with a warning about protests. "Be careful who you run with," Bill had said. "And don't sign your name on anything." She kept her head down and her hair ironed. Now, by pure accident, she'd landed in the center of the action. Hugging her books to her chest, she slipped into the crowd. Mer had never been to a rock concert before, let alone a massive demonstration. She felt transported by the warm exhales of proximal humans, their mingled sweat, and unified spirit.

Thirty-five of Madison's finest arrived decked out in riot gear, some with their badges removed. They threaded into the crowd in a narrow phalanx, a long black snake, helmets gleaming. The police thrust into the Commerce Building and unleashed pandemonium with their billy clubs. One thing about head wounds: they gush. Students scrambled out of doors and windows, blood streaming down their faces. Once the hall had been cleared, cops let loose on the kids in the quad. Mer jittered around the periphery while protesters fought back with shoes, bricks, and books, sending thirteen policemen to the hospital together with sixty-three students. She had been raised to trust police, but they were bludgeoning college kids; it didn't look right.

A class period had ended, swelling the crowd with passersby, when the first canisters hit the ground, catching Mer in a billow-

Meridy in her "total square" days.

ing cloud of tear gas. Her eyes were still stinging when she got back to her dorm that night and flipped on the television. There she was on the evening news. Her hair was in a stiff flip, and she wore mustard-yellow Bermuda shorts and knee-high socks her mother had picked out at a department store. Her first thought: *Oh God, what if my parents are watching?* Second thought: *I look like a total square.*

She was mortified. At the same time, it was kind of thrilling. She knew what side she wanted to be on.

The next day, Mer borrowed bell-bottoms from her roommate and joined about two thousand people below the campus statue of Abraham Lincoln. Protesters had outfitted Abe with a gas mask. It was a much larger crowd, with as many straight-looking students as longhairs. Homemade signs announced the new theme: POLICE BRUTALITY: KILL IT BEFORE IT MULTIPLIES!

Madison was a tranquil midwestern city ringed by dairy farms and factories; it had been voted Best Place to Live in America in a nationwide poll. A few small antiwar protests had taken place, but the Dow riot seemed to transform it overnight. Student groups called a moratorium on classes. Speeches drowned out lectures; organizing usurped homework. Madison suddenly became one of the most politically active campuses in the United States. The nicest kids, wearing the crispest creases, called themselves radicals. It wasn't Berkeley, but almost.

Later that week, one of Meridy's cousins who lived in Madison made Grass-A-Roni (Rice-A-Roni cooked with pot butter) and they danced around the apartment to an Otis Redding 45. It was Mer's first taste of marijuana.

She liked it.

Mer morphed. She went from Dionne Warwick and Johnny Mathis records to the Rolling Stones and Jimi Hendrix. From setting her hair in juice-can rollers to au naturel curls, the bigger the better; Indian kurtas; and no bra. She dug oil paints and politics; she dug LSD, mushrooms, grass, amphetamines, and heroin; she dug Jung, Ginsberg, and Marcuse; she read tarot cards and consulted the *I Ching*.

The middle-class counterculture split into two general camps: hippies and radicals. They were tines of the same fork. Both rejected prescribed ideals; both loathed cops. But their priorities differed. Mer was a hedonist at heart, so she rowed merrily, merrily down the hippie stream.

Meridy arrived at her parents' door for summer break, 1969, decked in hippie regalia: fringed leather vest, cowboy boots, oversize necklace, hair frizzed out in a tongue-in-socket halo. Her mother, Florence, was a sober, dictatorial first grade teacher with a mean streak; as a child, Mer had often worn long sleeves to hide bruises.

Seeing Mer's new hippie look, Florence scowled. "What's the matter with your hair?"

Bill, a former tavern owner, doubled up in laughter. In many ways, he was Florence's opposite: tough but charming, always ready with a joke. While he didn't exactly understand hippies, he saw them as more ridiculous than threatening.

Mer planned to stay in Milwaukee until fall, but definitely not with her parents. She took a flat on the Eastside with a nurse whose boyfriend dealt reefer smuggled in from Nogales. He stored the pot in an oak trunk in the girls' living room. In exchange, Mer and the nurse could smoke their fill.

The trail takes a sharp turn here.

One of Meridy's cousins — I'll call him Nathan — had moved to California, where he attended UC Berkeley and intermittently dealt pot. He'd married a Native American woman, Patty, and together they had a son. In August 1969, Patty brought her four-month-old baby to Milwaukee to meet the family. She and the baby stayed at Mer's apartment, and the two women bonded over mushroom tea.

In classic hippie-dippie fashion, Patty had arrived without plane fare back to California. So Nathan mailed a special package through the USPS: a kilo of weed for Patty to sell. He sealed the 2.2-pound brick of grass in plastic, boxed it, wrapped it in butcher paper, and addressed it to his infant son. *With love, Dad.*

Mer wasn't involved in the scheme, but she did know about it. On August 21, she and her friend Sue planned to rent horses at Big Cedar Lake. The package had arrived by then and was waiting at the post office. As an afterthought, Mer offered Patty a lift to the post office to save her and the baby a sweltering trip on the bus — fully aware that they were about to collect a package of marijuana.

Mer and her friend waited in the car while Patty went for the box. The post office occupied the ground floor of the Milwaukee Federal Building, an ornate Gothic structure festooned with gargoyles. In the late summer afternoon, its spires cast knifelike shadows down the avenue.

Patty emerged balancing a large box in one arm and the baby in the other. The baby started to squall, so Mer hustled to help with the package.

As Meridy stooped to get back into the car, she felt the unmistakable sensation of a gun barrel pressed to the back of her head. The unnaturally loud click of the hammer being cocked.

I've heard my mom tell the story of her 1969 bust countless times.

When she gets to this part, her voice drops into a menacing growl. "All right, ya goddamn hippie. You're under arrest for interstate transportation of narcotics."

Meet Patrolman Robert Buxbaum: crewcut, Ban-Lon shirt, razor-sharp creases in his slacks.

In my mom's version, Buxbaum is her nemesis, the comic-book villain. The evil super cop determined to vanquish her. "The guy got a sadistic kick out of scaring us," she says, still outraged decades later. "Three unarmed women and a crying baby. Did he think we were going to resist arrest? He didn't have to hold a gun to my head, for Chrissake. Then he cocks the hammer! I thought he was going to kill me."

Buxbaum herded the women and baby into the Federal Building and down a seemingly endless corridor to a bare room empty but for a long table. He placed the sealed package in front of Meridy, and said, "Open it."

Mer was terrified. She felt sure that if she opened that package she was going to prison, so she gambled, hoping to buy a little time. "That's not addressed to me," she said, her heart pinballing around her chest. "Isn't it illegal to open someone else's mail?"

Buxbaum's jaw twitched.

The patrolman tried to intimidate Sue and Patty into opening the box, but they followed Mer's lead. The proper addressee slept in Patty's arms, saliva bubbling on his lips, hands balled beside his cheeks. He wouldn't be opening mail for years.

Mer watched Buxbaum's face rinse through deeper shades of pink. "He was really losing it," she tells me. "You could just see his blood pressure going up."

Finally, the patrolman sliced into the box himself. The dusky scent of Mexican gold bud wafted through the room.

A female officer performed the strip searches and found the girls' orifices vacant of drugs. Mer's wicker purse, however, was more interesting.

My mom's purses have always been cornucopias of random crap. The cop who sifted through her belongings would've pulled out coconut oil, makeup, art supplies, toothpicks, jewelry, and countless scraps of paper. Plus four seeds, three joints, two roaches, and a partridge in a pear tree.

Today, though marijuana remains a political hot topic, it's been decriminalized for certain controlled uses in most states. As of 2019, Wisconsin remains strict; the only permitted cannabis is nonpsychoactive CBD prescribed for medical conditions. Still, getting caught with an old roach isn't likely to land someone in the big house anymore. But back then, one could do hard time for any amount of pot.

Since 1930, the Federal Bureau of Narcotics had been inundating the American public with antipot propaganda under the guidance of booze prohibitionist Harry J. Anslinger. Lurid coverage of bud-induced crimes and propaganda films like *Reefer Madness* riled the public's fear of the "killer weed." One article Anslinger wrote himself began:

> The sprawled body of a young girl lay crushed on the sidewalk the other day after a plunge from the fifth story of a Chicago apartment house. Everyone called it suicide, but actually it was murder. The killer was a narcotic known to America as marijuana, and to history as hashish. It is a narcotic used in the form of cigarettes, comparatively new to the United States and as dangerous as a coiled rattlesnake.

This purported deadly viper had been used medicinally for at least three thousand years in Asia and Africa. It had been an important pharmaceutical component in the United States since the mid-1800s. According to the *New York Times*, twenty-nine out of thirty members of the American Medical Association disagreed with claims about the dangers of cannabis in a survey taken at the beginning of Anslinger's crusade. Furious, Anslinger systematically targeted pro-cannabis doctors with threats and ultimately bullied the AMA into reversing its stance. In 1941, he strong-armed the *United States Pharmacopeia and Formulary* into purging cannabis from its pages — where "Indian hemp" had previously been listed as a remedy for more than one hundred ailments.

Antipot legislation gradually populated the books at both federal and state levels, but recreational marijuana use only increased.

There's no such thing as bad publicity.

Jazz and blues musicians composed songs about "tea"; the Beats wrote odes and great rambles under its effects. Weed was driven underground but never stamped out. Smugglers brought it up from Mexico and farmers grew it in the backwoods. It was alcohol prohibition all over again. Then rock 'n' roll happened, and hippies passed joints to the white middle class. By the late sixties, America's youth was smoking dope as a rite of passage.

Enter Richard Nixon. Blustering with law-and-order rhetoric, he harnessed the fears and frustrations of the "silent majority" toward what historian Dan Baum calls the "lawless wreckers of their own quiet lives — an unholy amalgam of stoned hippies, braless women, homicidal Negroes, larcenous junkies, and treasonous priests." The Nixon administration swiftly identified drug criminalization as a powerful weapon to wield against its foes.

Decades later, Nixon's chief legal advisor, John Ehrlichman, admitted as much in a 1994 interview with Baum in *Harper's Magazine*.

The Nixon campaign in 1968, and the Nixon White House after that, had two enemies: the antiwar left and black people . . . We knew we couldn't make it illegal to be either against the war or black, but by getting the public to associate the hippies with marijuana and blacks with heroin, and then criminalizing both heavily, we could disrupt those communities. We could arrest their leaders, raid their homes, break up their meetings and vilify them night after night on the evening news. Did we know we were lying about the drugs? Of course we did.

Nixon claimed that drugs were "decimating a generation of Americans," but the facts didn't support him. As Baum points out, more people died from falling down the stairs in 1969 than from all drug use. Eighteen times as many people lost their lives to cirrhosis of the liver, a condition associated with alcoholism. Marijuana has never caused a single known death.

Antipot laws were rooted not in science, medicine, or sociology, but in politics and racism. Sentences varied dramatically and could be extreme. Black Panther Lee Otis Johnson got hit with a thirty-year prison sentence for passing a joint to an undercover cop at a party in 1968. A white, twenty-year-old University of Virginia track star named Frank LaVarre got twenty years for possession of three pounds of marijuana in 1969 — the same year Mer and Patty were busted with 2.2 pounds. LaVarre was later pardoned by a different judge after a heartbreaking portrait in *Life* magazine. In the days before mandatory sentencing, the courts had ample discretion to mete out punishment according to personal beliefs. Mer faced potentially life-crushing charges.

Meridy used her one phone call to contact her dad. Bill was not a pot smoker and surely didn't approve of the jam his daughter had gotten herself into, but he played it cool. "Just keep your mouth shut," he told her. "Don't say word one until I get down there with the lawyer."

Meanwhile, the booking officer was pressing Mer for basic information. He struck her as kind, maybe sympathetic, but she couldn't give him her address. There was the oak trunk full of Mexican weed that she and her roommate were storing in their living room. Plus, they each had their own stashes of LSD, mescaline, peyote, speed, or whatever the drug du jour was. Mer thought it would be a matter of time before the police figured out her address.

So she lied. "My dad can't get a lawyer," she told the nice cop, scrunching her eyebrows. "Couldn't I have one more call? I don't know what I'll do . . ." When she started sobbing — easy to do as she was genuinely terrified — he gave in.

Mer phoned her apartment. "I've been arrested for possession of marijuana," she said. "Take care of things." Picking up the signal, her roommate rushed from room to room gathering and flushing drugs.

Mer's dad had once owned the Loop Super Bar in downtown Milwaukee near the police station. After catching his nephew embezzling funds, Bill lost his bar and went to work at a local tavern until he slipped two disks in his spine lifting a keg of beer. Mer was thirteen when her dad went on disability permanently. Still, Bill kept friends on both sides of the law and friends who bridged the gap between. With Mer and Patty facing serious charges, he called on an old lawyer pal, Milton Bordow, to represent both girls.

Bordow was slick — a fast walker, smooth talker, and natty dresser. A man who knew how to work the system. He argued that because the package was addressed to someone else — the baby — and because Buxbaum had opened the box himself, the subsequent search and seizure was illegal. In a December 3, 1969, hearing, Bordow petitioned for dismissal.

"I don't buy that, by golly," the judge snapped. "He gets a report and two women pick up a package. They're both involved in the handling of a package of marijuana. It was found to contain marijuana. In a further search of this defendant, [he] actually found more marijuana on her person. Motion to dismiss denied."

By golly. Did people really talk like that? The transcript reads like a moralistic 1950s crime drama. Court dates slogged on through a slushy winter, derailing Mer's studies. Instead of returning to Madison to resume classes, she languished at her parents' house in Milwaukee. One evening, she noticed an unmarked car across the street and recognized Buxbaum in the front seat, about as subtle as Joe Friday on *Dragnet.* She told the lawyer, but he seemed unsurprised; he figured Buxbaum was hoping to patch the holes in his case. Mer's job was to stay home and give him nothing to use.

She watched television. The trial of eight young activists charged with conspiring to incite violence at the 1968 Democratic Convention in Chicago dominated local news. Courtroom drawings depicted Bobby Seale chained to his chair in view of the jury, silenced by tape covering his mouth and fabric tying his jaw shut. Photos showed Abbie Hoffman and Jerry Rubin wearing judicial robes and cocky smiles, hot to heckle the judge. Protesters flooded the streets outside the courthouse, facing down cops wielding well-worn billy clubs. Stuck watching the country convulse on her parents' black-and-white Motorola, Mer felt utterly isolated.

Bordow used antipot propaganda to his clients' advantage, portraying them as well-behaved young ladies who'd become temporarily confused under the deleterious effects of the Devil's lettuce. No Abbie Hoffman, Mer put on an act of innocence, dressing for court appearances in a blue church dress with a Peter Pan collar, her curly hair wrestled into braids. Buxbaum never missed a hearing. Even when his presence wasn't required, she remembers him always being there, sitting bolt upright in the front of the gallery.

Mer's mother was barely speaking to her and never once came

to court, but her dad accompanied her every time — which was a treat. They'd sit together and dream up tortures for Buxbaum. Bill would whisper, "I'll serve him a cow-piss gimlet." And Mer would whisper back, "We'll put his balls in a blender." They'd end up in fits from trying not to giggle in the courtroom.

Ultimately, Bordow got the matter transferred to another judge — one who saw things his way. Buxbaum had broken the chain of custody and blown the case. On March 20, 1970, the complaints were ruled "defective."

Case dismissed.

The story might have ended there, but Patrolman Buxbaum was just getting started. He seemed to take the loss personally. He had screwed up his own case by opening the package, and perhaps he resented Mer for manipulating him into a rookie mistake. Maybe he couldn't stand getting bested by a hippie, a young woman at that. Or maybe he really did think Meridy was a criminal mastermind who must be stopped. Whatever the reason, he nursed a grudge.

A week after the judge's decision, Bill received a call from a friend at the station. "Be sure your kid keeps her nose clean. Buxbaum's not done with her. He's fishing for a new warrant."

"No kidding," Bill said. "He's right across the street."

Buxbaum had been staking Mer out for months, but after he lost the case, it got worse. If Mer borrowed her dad's Malibu to go to the grocery store, Buxbaum would show up behind her, not even trying to blend into traffic. Mer thought about confronting him, but she was afraid; the memory of his gun barrel against her head remained fresh.

Mer couldn't go on dates or relax with friends because she might jeopardize them by bringing a policeman along. She intended to transfer to the Milwaukee campus to finish her degree, but what if he tailed her to school? It was humiliating. She felt trapped. The harassment dragged on for months.

But he was a cop. What could she do?

Then, in the depths of winter 1970, Bill came into Mer's bedroom where she was drawing. "Get this," he said, already laughing. "Buxbaum was bending over to put a traffic cone in the street, and he got hit by a truck — right in the *tuchus*. The putz is dead!"

Mer dropped her charcoal pencil, suddenly unmoored. A release of pressure so unexpected that she felt she might go flying around the room like an open balloon. She was free.

I first heard the story of Mom vs. Patrolman Buxbaum on the barge. I was a kid; I don't know how old. She was telling the story to a customer, but I was hanging around as usual. When she got to the part where the evil cop gets hit in his derriere, the barge rocked with laughter.

It became one of my favorite stories. There's comfort in a tried-and-true ending, in the familiar moment when the bad guy meets his demise. The huntsman eviscerates the wolf. Gretel shoves the witch into the oven. The good guy wins, which means the good guy will always win.

When you grow up knowing that the cops could show up at any moment to drag your parents to prison, the death of an officer with a hard-on for hippies is what passes for a happy ending.

Although, for my family, this ending was also a beginning.

My mom took the demise of her nemesis as a cosmic green light. She would soon move to San Francisco, launch a high-profile magic-brownie business, and spend the next quarter century dealing large quantities of marijuana. And while it's impossible to be sure, I suspect that none of this — San Francisco, Sticky Fingers Brownies, me — would've happened without Buxbaum. The way he hounded my mom and was then suddenly wiped out of her life as if by the hand of some god. A sense of invincibility buoyed her throughout her illicit career.

In reality, Buxbaum wasn't killed in the car accident as my mom believed. When I unearth his obituary, I learn that he sur-

vived the accident — barely — and ultimately died of cancer in
1999. Whether this discrepancy arose through confusion on Bill's
or Mer's part, I don't know. Either way, Buxbaum was injured
gravely enough to keep him on disability until his death almost
thirty years later. The effect on my mom's life was the same. Buxbaum fucked with her and paid a heavy karmic price; she charged
forth, overconfident and unscathed.

Truth is untidy. There are no good guys, not really. No bad
guys either. Robert Buxbaum's obituary describes him as a "loving father," "dear grandpa," and "beloved brother." He sounds like
a family man, not a supervillain — just someone who might have
taken his job too seriously. He survived a terrible accident and
undoubtedly suffered during his years on disability and his battle with cancer. But what interrupted his life made mine possible. When the accident got him out of my mom's way, she popped
like a champagne cork. That energy propelled her into the next
phase.

When I ask my mom if she learned any lessons from her 1969
bust, her answer is pure bluster: "Yeah," she says. "Don't get
caught."

In 1971, the War on Drugs officially began. Describing drug abuse
as "America's public enemy number one," Nixon announced a
"new, all-out offensive."

Months before, Congress had ratified the Comprehensive Drug
Abuse Prevention and Control Act of 1970 as part of a massive om-
nibus crime bill. Buried among its pages were major curtailments
to civil rights. Narcotics agents could now conduct no-knock raids
(breaking down doors unannounced); preventative detention became an option for arresting suspects *before* they committed a
drug crime; and witnesses could be jailed indefinitely for refusing
to testify in drug cases.

The new legislation created a scheduling system that ranked

drugs according to their health risks, addictiveness, and medicinal value. It also mandated that a blue-ribbon committee evaluate the cannabis threat once and for all. With this investigation pending, marijuana was temporarily placed in Schedule 1 — the category reserved for drugs with the highest abuse potential and no accepted medical use.

Nixon packed the committee with his drug-hawk cronies. "I want a goddamn strong statement on marijuana," he told his chief of staff in 1971. "I mean one on marijuana that just tears the ass out of them." But the chairman he'd appointed, a retired Republican governor of Pennsylvania, took his job seriously. Raymond Shafer commissioned more than fifty research projects and conducted extensive hearings with scientists, community leaders, doctors, students, and law enforcement, recording thousands of pages of transcripts. When the report arrived in 1972, it was 1,184 pages long.

It was not what Nixon had in mind.

Shafer, a law-and-order man, had been shocked to learn that the facts about cannabis didn't support the rhetoric. The report, *Marihuana: A Signal of Misunderstanding*, described a substance that caused neither physical addiction nor a marked tendency to graduate to harder drugs nor the violent behavior depicted in antipot propaganda nor serious damage to the body or brain. The danger, the report concluded, was political, stemming from the perception of marijuana as "fostering a counterculture that conflicts with basic moral precepts." The commission asked if criminal punishment for cannabis might be causing more harm to society than the drug itself. Instead of tearing the ass out of pot advocacy, the report recommended decriminalization.

Nixon allegedly refused to read beyond the first few pages. His administration buried the report and continued its alarmist rhetoric. Marijuana's "temporary" Schedule 1 status — categorizing cannabis as one of the most dangerous substances in the United States — quietly became permanent.

A mighty wind sailed westward across the lakes and cornfields of the Midwest. San Francisco worked magic on young imaginations. As an old Gold Rush saying had it, "The country tipped sideways, and all the loose screws rolled to California." San Francisco twinkled on the periphery: the Paris of America; Sodom, Gomorrah, *and* Cockaigne crumbled and rolled into a spliff; a rock 'n' roll paradise where hashish tarred the streets, LSD tabs grew on bushes, and it snowed PCP all year round.

During the 1967 media blitz dubbed the Summer of Love, some 100,000 people had descended on Haight-Ashbury. Kids camped in Golden Gate Park or crowded into communes, overloading the already run-down neighborhood. No sooner had the hippie party burned out than San Francisco began teetering under another mass influx from the fringe. By the mid-1970s, the chief of police estimated that 140,000 homosexuals were living in San Francisco, with eighty more arriving every week to join a burgeoning community where it was reputedly safe — even chic — to be gay.

One by one, in pairs or in clusters, Meridy's Wisconsin friends rode the slipstream west until there was hardly anyone left. After finishing her degree, she spent months backpacking in Europe and Africa, then twiddled her thumbs again in Milwaukee until it seemed there was nothing left to do but book a flight to San Francisco.

I picture my mom on an airplane in 1975, forehead pressed to the window, hoping for a first glimpse of her new home. She wouldn't know that the airport lies beyond city limits, situated such that you can never quite see San Francisco until you're inside it.

One of Mer's art professors from Madison helped her land a part-time gig illustrating children's books for the Rockefeller

Foundation. It wasn't a lot of money, but as long as she kept her expenses down, she could scrape by. She felt giddy with possibility. There was much fun to be had in freewheeling San Francisco — sans parents, sans Buxbaum. But it was more than that. She sensed something impending, a transformation. A new Meridy stepping out into the fabled city.

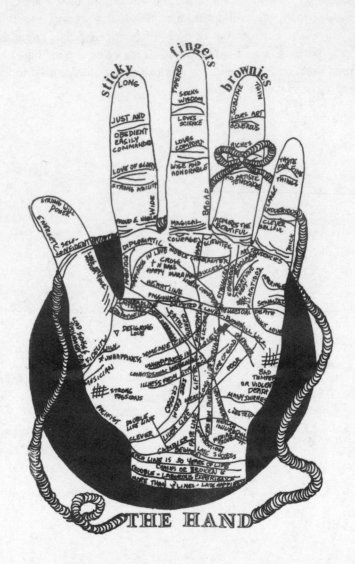

THE HAND

2

The Hand

At sixty-eight, my mom got initiated into the Santeria religion. After having her street clothes cut from her body with scissors, she kneeled naked in a shower stall, eyes closed, while the priestess, (called a *madrina*, or "godmother") bathed her in holy water and chanted in Yoruba. More kneeling followed, sometimes with arms extended crucifix-style to hold burning candles. My mom, who has bad knees, nearly fainted. At the end, she received her *elekes*, beaded necklaces in the colors and patterns associated with the five primary orishas. She left the botánica clothed entirely in white, hair sheathed in a white turban with hunks of coconut tucked into the folds. Since then, she has put on her *elekes* every morning with a prayer and wrapped them in a blessed cloth before bed every night. She makes offerings to the orishas on an altar in her home. But she's casual, forgoing animal sacrifice and the abstentions more serious initiates sometimes undertake.

My mom also uses the *I Ching*, a Chinese divination method nearly four thousand years old. She's handy with tarot cards and astrology, too. Occasionally, she observes aspects of the Judaism she grew up with. And she adores Christmas — mostly for the paganlike adoration of evergreen trees, the dreamy lights, the exchange of gifts. Some might call this dabbling, but I think of her more like a witch at a cauldron using a pinch of this, a dash of that.

When I ask my mom what triggered her fascination with the occult, her answer is circular. "That's easy. It's because of my Pisces moon in the fourth house of my astrological chart." For her, the interest feels so natural that it might be written in the stars. She has always been unusually sensitive to tacit signals and subtle shifts in energy (a helpful quality for an outlaw). But sensitivity comes with a price; she is thin-skinned and easily hurt. Believing in magic gives her a taste of control and methods for harnessing her natural vulnerability as a tool.

I don't live in a magical world, not like my mom and her friends. But I have to respect that this is her way of operating. The magic has changed flavor over the years, but it's always been there — part of my mom's every major decision. This is as true today as it was back in 1975 when she arrived in California and soon found herself at the helm of a mobile bakery that would grow into a massive underground operation.

But it started small. And it started with magic.

Meridy landed in San Francisco on the day Patty Hearst was arrested.

Nineteen months before, the heiress had been dragged out of her apartment in Berkeley by members of the Symbionese Liberation Army, a bizarre terrorist group operating under the slogan, "Death to the fascist insect that preys upon the life of the people." Two months later, Hearst reappeared as an SLA convert, robbing a bank with a sawed-off shotgun. On September 18, 1975, the day Mer arrived, FBI agents swarmed two safe houses, including the one where Patty was hiding. Four days after the arrests, another female radical fired two shots at President Gerald Ford as he exited the St. Francis Hotel on Union Square, missing his head by inches. The would-be assassin later said she'd been inspired in part by Patty and the SLA. The astonishing case of the heiress turned kidnapping victim, self-proclaimed revolutionary, terrorist, fugitive, and frail penitent would keep the press enthralled for many moons.

Mer felt bewitched by the sheer physical beauty of San Francisco, its geographic undulations and tumbling fog banks and improbably frilly Victorians. She settled in a tiny garden apartment on a steep block of Potrero Hill, which she shared with a former roommate from Milwaukee. Having grown up in a flat, muted stretch of the Midwest — among its endless gray winters and icy lakes — Mer had rarely seen the ocean. Now that she lived on a roughly seven-by-seven-mile peninsula surrounded on three sides by fragrant, churning seawater, she couldn't imagine ever wanting to leave.

Still, it wasn't easy. A peculiar darkness seemed to well up from within San Francisco, reminding Mer of a graceful image painted over an ugly one. In what was historically known as a "wide-open town," excess could become poisonous and often did. Mer, now twenty-eight years old, had always carried her own darkness: a penchant for melodrama, obsessiveness, and periods of depression; a singularity of vision that left her blind spots exposed; a vulnerability that no amount of magic could shield; and an unquenchable yearning — for a grand romance, artistic greatness, her Yellow Brick Road.

The people she met in her first weeks all came from somewhere else. But if Mer idly wondered where the locals were, it didn't hold her attention for long. In that way, she was like most everyone who traveled west hoping to reinvent themselves and ended up reinventing the West. She had spent time on Brady Street in Milwaukee (sort of a midwestern Haight-Ashbury minus the fame), so she wasn't shocked by the grittiness. But nothing prepared her for her first Halloween on Polk Street.

In Milwaukee, Halloween was a children's holiday. Not here.

Cross-dressing had been illegal in San Francisco since the Barbary Coast days. Cops routinely rousted transgender folks, drag queens, and other nonconformists. Halloween had offered a night of reprieve from arrests and police harassment — that is until paddy wagons showed up at the stroke of midnight to clear the streets. The antiquated law against wearing "dress not belonging to his or her sex" had just been stricken from the books in 1974, the

year before Mer's arrival, allowing the gender-bending Halloween party of 1975 to carry on past the witching hour. Newspapers
would later estimate the crowd on Polk Street at fifty thousand.

This was decades before initialisms like LGBTQ+ helped draw
awareness to a spectrum of gender and sexuality. Mer, who'd never
even seen anyone do drag, was awestruck by the expressiveness.
There were glamorous queens, bearded "genderfuck" queens, car-
toonish queens, queens on roller skates, and queens from outer
space. Drag kings, too: debonair women in tuxedos and top hats or
wearing facial hair and leathers. People flashed breasts and cocks
and bare asses. Everything seemed so much *more* here. Not just
a robot, but a multigendered sex-slave robot with blinking lights
and sound effects. Not just Little Bo Peep, but Little Bo Peep on
stilts trailed by a herd of half-naked sheep. Party buses nosed
through the throng delivering revelers from one barroom costume
contest to the next. People seemed limited only by their imaginations. It was unbridled, sexy, glittering, challenging, free.

Meridy soon reconnected with people from the old Milwaukee
crowd who'd preceded her to California. She had met Donald
Palmer on a summer day in Milwaukee shortly before her bust.
They'd cruised around the Eastside in her dad's Malibu convertible, filling the back seat with lilacs plucked from strangers' gardens and delivering fresh bouquets to friends all over town. Donald
was a foxy hippie with brunette curls, eyelashes a yard long, and a
rich, sonorous laugh. He was the first gay person with whom Mer
became close. At first, she nursed a crush and, in her ignorance of
homosexuality, hoped Donald might learn to love her. He eventually disabused her of the notion in a heart-to-heart talk. After that,
Mer marched with him in some of the first appearances of the Gay
Liberation Front in Milwaukee antiwar protests. In spring 1976, after a falling-out with her first roommate, Mer moved in with Donald and three other people in San Francisco's Western Addition.

The neighborhood teetered between wreckage and construction. Weed-choked lots alternated with half-constructed buildings. The San Francisco Redevelopment Agency had targeted this primarily black area for mandatory demolition, tearing into it with wrecking balls and bulldozers. By the agency's own reckoning, it displaced nearly five thousand families and nine hundred businesses, and razed some 2,500 Victorians in that neighborhood. Thousands of new housing units rose during the seventies and eighties, most to be rented at high market value while displaced families languished on low-income waiting lists.

In this atmosphere of frustration and disenfranchisement, a white pastor named Jim Jones preached to some eight thousand worshippers, mostly from local black families. Emphasizing sobriety, racial equality, communal living, and elder care, the Peoples Temple thrived in the ruins of this once-vibrant jazz district known as the Harlem of the West. Liberal politicians courted Jones for his remarkable ability to mobilize his congregation — though not without consequences.

In the 1975 mayoral election, George Moscone had squeaked into power by a narrow margin. His rival, John Barbagelata, was antiunion, antihippie, and antigay. The *New York Times* described him as "nervous, driven and crochety." But Barbagelata struck a chord with voters who thought their city was being overtaken by radicals. The race ended with a runoff that Moscone won by 4,315 votes. Barbagelata demanded a recount, which he financed with his own money. When that didn't change the results, he accused Moscone and other liberals of election fraud — via the Peoples Temple.

Barbagelata believed that Jim Jones and his congregation had stolen the election for the liberals by casting multiple votes under dead people's names. He vowed to expose the defrauders.

Mer watched the election scandal with half an eye. She liked the dashing new mayor with his Italian good looks. Moscone had grown up poor in San Francisco, raised by a single mother. He had street smarts and true-blue populist appeal, a mayor for the people — and he was rumored to smoke the occasional joint. He had been the California state senate majority leader before moving back to what he called the "greatest city in the world" to run for mayor, a post he said he'd wanted since childhood. During his senate years, Moscone had coauthored a bill decriminalizing sodomy and oral sex between consenting adults in California — a felony before then — earning the undying appreciation of the gay community. He'd also ushered in the Moscone Act, which knocked possession of less than one ounce of marijuana down from a felony to a misdemeanor, earning the undying appreciation of stoners like Meridy.

Late spring 1976, one of Mer's new roommates introduced her to a petite strawberry blonde from St. Louis named Shari Mueller. It was Shari who would soon get Mer and the other Wisconsinites involved in dealing marijuana brownies.

Shari was into her own kind of magic. In her version of the story, it was the Universe that inspired her to start selling pot brownies in the first place, and it was the Universe that eventually told her to give the business to my mom.

When she and Mer met, Shari was saving up to move to the Findhorn Ecovillage — a New Age commune in Scotland that worshipped nature spirits and grew abnormally large produce, including forty-pound cabbages that made international news. Looking back, Shari says, "I'd set my intention with the Universe at earning $10,000. Once you set an intention, you're supposed to let it go but keep your eyes open for what comes along."

Shari had started selling homemade breads and muffins out of a picnic basket on Fisherman's Wharf. Her best customers were the street artists who sold crafts to passersby; they couldn't leave their wares unattended to get breakfast so the baked goods were welcome. Shari had been at this for a few weeks when a jeweler asked if she'd consider adding some magic to her basket.

Shari tried to brush him off. "I kind of gave up drugs years ago," she said. "I wouldn't even know where to get the stuff anymore."

"Don't worry about that part," he said. "There's no back-alley kind of stuff to go through here."

Shari, who was nowhere near her savings goal, said she'd think it over. That night, she went into a meditative state.

"Look," she said to the Universe. "I need your advice here. If you want me to make marijuana brownies, let all the doors open. And if I'm not supposed to do this, whup me upside the head and make it real clear."

The following weekend, the jeweler handed Shari a paper bag of fragrant pot. "This is a gift," he said. "You can mess around with it in your kitchen. If you decide you don't want to do it, give whatever's left back. No strings attached."

Free marijuana seemed like a clear-enough sign to Shari, so she came up with a recipe. To distinguish the magic brownies from the regular ones, she put a cashew nut on top and carried them in a pouch over her shoulder rather than in the basket with everything else. The concept of selling drugs made her uncomfortable, so she invented a persona to handle the sales: the Rainbow Lady. Where Shari was a little shy, the Rainbow Lady was bold. She wore long gauze dresses in royal purple or kelly green beneath a hooded indigo-velvet cape, and placed a large rainbow pin over her heart.

Shari priced the regular brownies at a quarter apiece and sold the magic brownies for a dollar each. Her income shot to around $300 per weekend, a tidy sum in 1976.

One afternoon, a patrol cop asked to buy a brownie.

"Oh, sure," Shari said, handing him one from the basket. "That's twenty-five cents."

"Don't you have some with nuts?"

Okay, Shari thought, *this is a test*. She closed her eyes and quickly asked the Universe, *What am I supposed to do?* She sensed that it was all right. The best course of action would be to give him what he asked for without making a fuss. *Maybe,* she thought, *he just wants to make his job more fun.*

She extracted a marijuana brownie from her pouch. The policeman paid and went on his way.

After that, the cop became a regular, sometimes buying several at a time. Shari wondered if he might be sharing them with other policemen so they could all get high without putting themselves in jeopardy.

Then there were the cabbies. Shari sometimes took taxis to the wharf and began tipping the drivers with magic brownies. After the first couple of weeks, she'd call dispatch and have multiple cars show up at her door.

Meanwhile, Mer was living on illustration work. Between the children's books and side gigs designing posters for rock concerts, protests, and a catalogue for a company that made glass bongs, she could usually get by. Occasionally, she rolled out a rug and gave tarot readings on Fisherman's Wharf. But she hit a slow patch and was falling short of rent. Since Shari seemed to know a lot of people through her mobile bakery, Mer called to ask if she might have a lead on a way to generate fast cash. Shari said she would meditate on it.

Ten minutes later, Mer's phone rang.

"A cup of coffee," Shari said.

"Huh?"

"I have to admit, I'm a bit befuddled myself. I asked the Universe, *How is Meridy going to pay her rent?* And the next thing I know, I'm seeing this giant hand coming out of a puffy white cloud holding a cup of steaming coffee. I thought maybe you'd know what it meant."

Both women fell quiet.

"Oh, I know!" Shari said. "You can come out with me on Saturday and sell coffee to the street vendors. I know everyone will love it."

It struck Mer as an odd idea, but she happened to know where to get supplies. Her roommate Donald worked at a coffeehouse called the Haven. Mer knocked on his bedroom door and explained Shari's proposal. All they needed, she said, were basic coffee supplies. It took a little wheedling, but late that night, Donald let Mer raid the Haven's stockroom.

On Saturday, while Shari peddled her baked goods, Mer trailed behind, tugging coffee urns in a red wagon. Back then, you couldn't walk to the end of any given block and buy an upside-down iced soy macchiato and a low-fat coffee cake in a waxed baggie. It would take Starbucks another two decades to spread like chicken pox throughout San Francisco.

Meridy peddling tarot readings.

Mer cobbled together rent that month, so she began dragging herself out of bed before dawn every Saturday to follow the Rainbow Lady.

Nineteen seventy-six was the bicentennial, not only of the United States as an autonomous nation, but also of San Francisco as a colonial conquest. In 1776, the Spanish military claimed the peninsula's tip for its northernmost outpost. Almost simultaneously, Franciscan missionaries agreed that a lush lagoon six miles inland was a primo site for proselytizing the Ramaytush Ohlone people who'd fished its contributing creek for millennia. The ensuing two hundred years were violent, convoluted, and famously sordid. The name San Francisco didn't take until 1847; for a stretch, the settlement was called Yerba Buena, after the "good herb" that blanketed the bayside hills. The moniker refers to a species of feral mint, but it's bound to make stoners smile.

San Francisco has had dozens of colorful names and nicknames. But the most enduring one is simple, dating to the Gold Rush and the following half century, when this was the only urban metropolis on an otherwise rural and unruly frontier. Even today, to locals, San Francisco is the "City," capitalized.

July 4, 1976, was planned as a traditional two hundredth birthday party in the City: a flag-flapping parade through Golden Gate Park, a viewing of naval vessels and pleasure boats in the bay, a railroad and steam engine display, an Americana arts and crafts show, and a fireworks to-do at Candlestick Park. The Emporium advertised a patriotic blowout, featuring discounts on Crock-Pots and leisure suits. There would be antiestablishment rallies and the usual toots and bangs of fireworks, church bells, whistles, air horns, gun salutes, and drunks.

For her part, Meridy planned to stay in, take 150 micrograms of blotter acid, and draw. Her roommates were out so she had the flat to herself. She dropped her LSD at noon and the day expanded delightfully. The walls disintegrated into cheese curds, revealing the inside of white, where all colors shivered as one. Mer recorded the images in her sketch pad.

An hour or several hours into her trip, an alarm clock sounded. Time to wake up? The telephone? Mer eyed the phone. It stopped ringing. She turned back to her drawing and the ringing resumed. When she focused on the phone, it stopped. Was this a game? Was the telephone company pranking her for not paying the bill?

She picked up the receiver. "Stop it."

"Mer, it's Shari."

"Oh, hey, man, what's happening? I thought you were the telephone."

Shari giggled, an elfish twitter. "Look, I'm calling because I have a proposition for you." She explained that she had reached a crossroads. The magic brownies were generating more income than she'd ever made. And she was having fun. Despite not doing drugs herself, Shari found selling them intoxicating; the risk gave her a rush. She had met her goal of $10,000, then exceeded it — and still didn't want to leave; she was toying with the idea of staying. Then the Universe spoke to her again: *You made a commitment to yourself and to the Universe that you were going to Findhorn. Now you want to go back on your word? Things are not going to work out for you if you do that.* "The time has come for me to go," Shari said. "I'd like you to take over the business. I want you to have it."

"All?"

"Whole."

Meridy saw herself balancing on a brink. Below yawned an abyss; above gaped the blind sky. If she jumped, would she sprout feathers or would she plummet? "I'll ring you back, Shari," she said. "Let me think about that."

Mer hung up and set aside her drawing materials. The air throbbed in an ecstatic LSD warble. Practically speaking, the timing was good for marijuana brownies. In the wake of Watergate, Nixon's War on Drugs had lost favor in the polls. His successor, Gerald Ford, took a less strident approach toward cannabis, and that attitude filtered down to the state level. When the Moscone Act took effect in January 1976, California became the fifth state to decriminalize possession of small quantities of marijuana for personal use. Of course, selling marijuana remained a felony, as did possession of the multiple ounces needed to make brownies. Still, it was a move away from prohibition.

Did Mer consider this factor? Did she carefully weigh potential prison time against the stress of her unstable income? Not at all. Her decision would come down to three brass coins jingling in her palm; the *I Ching* would guide her actions.

Mer had been introduced to the *I Ching* in Madison by the same cousin who got her stoned the first time. Also known as the *Book of Changes*, the *I Ching* described a world in an unending state of flux. Rather than a rigid moral code, it offered guidance in riding life's ever-changing currents. To use the book for divination, you meditated on a question while rolling three specialized brass coins in one hand. Then you dropped them and recorded how they landed. The result of six throws, called a *hexagram*, corresponded to one of sixty-four passages — each composed of the Image (a metaphor for the present situation), the Judgment (how one should act in that situation), and the Lines (short passages predicting how the situation would evolve into its next phase). Mer loved the mutability and flow. Although the whole smorgasbord of hippie oracles appealed to her, the *I Ching* became her enduring favorite. She'd consulted it so frequently in the first years that she knew most of the thick book by heart.

Mer focused on grounding herself, imagining tree roots reaching from her body through the floor into the earth below. Her brass *I Ching* coins were greasy and smooth from use. Jingling them in one hand, she repeated a question in her mind: *What are the effects of running this bakery?*

Mer cast her coins onto the table six times. The progression led her to a passage titled, "14. *Ta Yu*/Possession in Great Measure." It was one of the *I Ching*'s most fortuitous hexagrams, promising

"supreme success" and "possession on a grand scale." The hexagram was too clear to second-guess.

"Wonderful!" Shari said when Mer called her back. "I know
you'll have fun with it. I'll write out all of my recipes, and we can
get together and go over them."

Mer felt power sparking through her fingertips. She spent the
evening scheming, her acid-charged brain chasing possible futures. She wanted to invent a street persona; the Rainbow Lady
was taken, and besides, Mer saw herself with more of a rock 'n' roll
edge. If she was going to run a bakery, she'd do it her way.

3

If All the World's a Stage

A friend gives my mom a sack of Puerto Rican *pasteles* to bring to a dinner party. *Pasteles* are made from stewed meat enveloped in masa paste and wrapped in a banana leaf, similar to Mexican tamales. The heating directions couldn't be simpler: drop the *pastel* into boiling water, then fish it out after five minutes. I find my mom in the kitchen, looking small and lost, dangling a *pastel* over a pot of still water.

"Isn't that supposed to be boiling?" I say.

"It is boiling," she answers, her tone mildly defensive. "Look, bubbles."

The water is tepid at best, the tiniest of bubbles swirling to the surface. That's right: my mom is sixty-nine years old and has never learned how to boil water. Through much of my childhood, we subsisted on Lean Cuisine, Cup O' Noodles, and takeout, which we habitually ate on the barge while watching TV. She struggled with her weight, undergoing "miracle" diets and medical fasts, none of which involved cooking whole foods. I never went hungry as a kid, but the kitchen was like uncharted territory on a medieval map.

My mom lives alone in Desert Hot Springs. How she keeps herself alive is something of a mystery, though I know it involves Safeway rotisserie chicken and a nearby strip-mall burrito shop. Faced with a refrigerator of raw ingredients, she might very well starve.

I help her get the water going and hang around, intending only to supervise, but I end up heating the *pasteles* myself. Sucking people into her projects without their noticing is one of my mom's superpowers.

I exact my revenge by telling our friends at dinner that my mom can't boil water. She laughs, her face reddening and bunching like a Christmas apple doll. "It was boiling!" she yells. "It was, I tell you, it *was!*"

This same woman took the reins of a do-it-yourself bakery on July 4, 1976.

She lay in bed the next morning, working out the tendrils of her acid trip. What had sounded like a righteous plan on 150 micrograms seemed impossible hungover. The idea of assembling the Rainbow Lady's zucchini bread made the bed spin. She would have to call Shari back and tell her no thank you.

But the hexagram had been unequivocally positive; for a business venture, you couldn't top "Possession in Great Measure" with no changing lines. If her belief in the *I Ching* was genuine, she had to follow through. Sipping coffee in bed, Mer realized that the only way she'd be able to do this was to get someone to do it for her.

When she heard her roommate Donald puttering in the kitchen, she shuffled out to make her pitch. "How about you bake?" she said, after explaining the Rainbow Lady's offer. "I'll handle sales. We'll split the profits fifty-fifty."

"Do I look like Betty Crocker to you?"

"You made those chocolate chip cookies that one time," Mer said. "They were good!"

Donald cocked one eyebrow. "Darling, a chimpanzee can make chocolate chip cookies."

"But can a chimp make pot brownies?"

This was something Mer counted on: Donald loved drugs. He

particularly enjoyed heroin, so much so that he wound up on people's shit lists for minor thefts and other dishonesties when he got strung out. A problematic friend — and a questionable choice for a business associate — but one who was usually up for an adventure.

Later, when the Rainbow Lady dropped off a box of recipes written on index cards, Mer feigned confidence. "Don't forget to write from Findhorn!" Back inside, she placed the box on Donald's pillow.

Though by no means an expert in the kitchen, Donald knew these recipes weren't written in unbreakable code. He agreed to try, beginning with modest goals: bran muffins, regular chocolate brownies, and magic brownies.

While Donald was dusting himself from ringlet to toe ring in flour, Mer made a general nuisance of herself. She chattered at his back, rolled joints on the cutting board, filed her long fingernails, and tossed *I Ching* hexagrams at the kitchen table. No question was too grand or too trivial for the oracle. *What are the effects of adding ginger to the bran muffins?* Jingle, jingle, jingle.

When Mer quipped that Donald's bran muffins looked like "mini cow pies," he frisbeed the mixing bowl into the sink and stomped down the hall to his room. Mer frowned at the wreckage — eggshells overflowing from the compost bucket, chocolate caked to the double boiler, an epic heap of pans and bowls and utensils in the sink — and lay her head on the table.

A bakery. What was she thinking?

She cleaned the mess slowly, hoping that Donald would come back to take over again.

He didn't.

A couple of days later, a semimiracle happened. Another transplant from Milwaukee, a costumer named Barbara Hartman, quit her job on a production of *The Wiz* over a tiff with the wardrobe

The girls: Barb and Mer.

mistress. She was freshly unemployed. And she was a monster baker.

Barb was tall and Germanic, with wheat-blonde hair and an apple-cheeked smile. She had grown up on the east side of Milwaukee, near the lakefront. Her mother, who'd borne nine children, saw baking as an inexpensive way to feed her brood. On icy winter afternoons, Barb would slog home from school to find fresh strudel cooling on the counter. She'd learned to bake in the most natural way; it was something she did from the heart.

Barb's ubiquitous companion in those days was a shaggy gray long-legged mutt named Boogie, a canine genius and literal party animal. (He once disappeared for a week, then reappeared on Barb's doorstep wearing a birthday hat and tie.) In 1976, Barb and Boogie were living with another costumer in the Glen Park neighborhood. Their apartment had a spacious kitchen with a sweet view of the sunny side of town. A carpenter friend had recently

built her a bread table near the window with cooling racks overhead.

Barb joined the mobile bakery and flourished in her new role.
Each Friday, she flipped through her recipe books to choose a special for the weekend. She made cranberry-banana bread, carrot
cake with raisins and nuts, cinnamon buns, and, of course, magic
brownies. An early riser, she relished mornings spent mixing
dough as sunrise splashed across the City or relaxing on her sofa
enveloped by the aromas of childhood with Boogie's muzzle on
her lap.

Donald was relieved to get out of baking, but he liked handling the
pot. Mer was buying bricks of Mexican gold from the same wharf
hippie who'd supplied the Rainbow Lady. The bricks came riddled
with tiny brown seeds that exploded under heat, exuding a foul
odor. Donald would do a little cocaine or Benzedrine and sit at the
kitchen table for hours picking apart the bricks to hunt for seeds.
It was slow, obsessive work, a project he could lose himself in. He'd
then crumble the pot into smaller pieces, run it through a blender,
and pass the powder through a sifter before handing it off to Barb
to work her kitchen-goddess magic.

Barb melted butter in a double boiler, added the powdered
weed, and simmered the mixture for half an hour, periodically
skimming foam. She added the cannabis ghee to melted chocolate, eggs, sugar, baking powder, and flour. Voilà: magic brownies.

Saturday mornings, Mcridy and either Barb or Donald would set
up the coffee and baked goods on a card table at Aquatic Park on
Fisherman's Wharf. Hundreds of craftspeople gathered on the
concrete bleachers to mill and gossip while waiting for booth as-
signments. The park descended from there to a narrow beach and
a semicircular pier with a postcard view of the Golden Gate Bridge
ablaze in international orange.

Fisherman's Wharf had been a bustling working-class waterfront since shortly after the Gold Rush. From 1895 on, the briny stench clashed with rich aromas from the Ghirardelli chocolate factory. In the mid-1960s, the Ghirardellis sold their San Francisco factory to a real estate developer who restored the red brick buildings around landscaped courtyards and converted the space into a shopping plaza. A second mall — the Cannery — opened catty-corner in a dormant fruit packing plant.

Shoppers didn't rush to the new malls all at once; the area still reeked of fish oil. But a path had been cut and more entrepreneurs followed. A young Cantonese immigrant named Thomas Fong turned a nearby grain mill into a wax museum with more than two hundred celebrities and a chamber of horrors. In the early seventies — after a nineteen-month occupation of Alcatraz Island by a group of American Indian activists asserting their right to disused federal land — the US government decided to rebrand the former maximum-security prison as a tourist attraction. The Red and White Fleet offered the first Alcatraz cruise in 1973. Souvenir shops specializing in ESCAPED INMATE T-shirts mushroomed throughout the area followed by upscale boutiques and art galleries. The blue-collar seaport morphed into one of the most visited tourist traps in the world.

Hippies began selling crafts on the waterfront around 1970; they were not welcome. Merchants fretted that the peddlers' shaggy outfits would mar the district's new image. Police cracked down, making arrests, so the craftspeople pooled their funds to hire a lawyer and founded the San Francisco Street Artists Guild. There were protests, press conferences, more arrests. Eventually, the street artists unearthed an obscure law enacted after half of San Francisco's merchants lost their places of business to the 1906 earthquake and fire. This statute entitled anyone the right to a peddler's permit provided they'd made their goods by hand.

The artisans had an effect on Fisherman's Wharf that neither the merchants nor the politicians nor even the street artists seem to have anticipated: tourists loved it. People visiting San Francisco in the decade following the Summer of Love media circus wanted to see, smell, and even touch real hippies. Now they could take home a souvenir crystal necklace or hand-crocheted shawl that still smelled of Nag Champa incense.

To avoid jockeying over coveted spaces, the vendors came up with a lottery system. From then on, names were drawn from a diaper pail — which, rumor has it, got tossed into the bay more than once by grumpy street artists. The lottery was a slow process and mornings could be miserably cold especially in summer when massive fogbanks clung to the bay. Mer's mobile bakery had a captive audience.

When the lottery wrapped up at nine in the morning, Mer would head home to take advantage of the morning light. She'd lose herself in drawing or painting; her style evolved, becoming looser and more colorful.

In the afternoon, she'd meet Barb to restock before heading back to the wharf for a second round of sales, now strolling with a basket of baked goods and a Guatemalan pouch of magic brownies. Mer favored jeans or harem pants tucked into shitkickers with heavy wooden heels that made a satisfying *whock* with every step. She wore a men's bomber jacket, soft and scuffed, with a sterling silver housefly pinned to the lapel. While traveling in Morocco, she'd learned to tie elaborate turbans and lined her eyes with Egyptian kohl. Mer had never been girly like the Rainbow Lady with her flowing dresses and sweet giggle; Mer's laugh was a guffaw.

The wharf crafts market had become enormous by 1976, now circling several blocks. Folks sold hand-painted silk scarves, buckskin moccasins, stained glass with flowers pressed between panes, perfumes, and carved wooden toys. Working alongside urban hippies were back-to-the-landers who drove in from the rugged parts of California Mer had yet to see, people whose eyes reflected the forest.

On street corners and stages set up in the outdoor malls, buskers gathered crowds. Among them were the up-and-coming comedians Penn & Teller, A. Whitney Brown, and Robin Williams. A classical pianist wearing a white tuxedo and tails played a white baby grand on a truck bed. A scraggly-haired hippie calling himself the Automatic Human Jukebox sang tunelessly and played a horn through a hole cut into a painted refrigerator box. Busking historian Patricia Campbell describes San Francisco as the "very best of the good places." Magician Harry Anderson tells me that his Fisherman's Wharf period was a "band of time when the street was really a spectacular place." There were ventriloquists and mimes and puppeteers and jugglers and magicians. "Not a square peg among them," Mer says of the performers. "All of those guys bought. All of them."

Occasionally, tourists might buy the breads and muffins that Mer carried in her basket, but she kept the magic brownies in a separate pouch and sold them only to the craftspeople and buskers who became her regulars.

While Shari Mueller had called herself the Rainbow Lady, Mer's handle seemed to find her organically. People started calling her the Brownie Lady and it stuck.

Busking has a deep history; it's nearly as old as money. It came to the New World with the colonists and found early expression in political ballads sung on street corners with printed broadsides for sale. Circuses roamed the country, and lightning-tongued illusionists hawked elixirs from traveling medicine shows. With the rise of radio and moving pictures in the early twentieth century, street performing fell out of vogue, becoming a pitiful last resort for the blind or maimed who might saw away at a violin

or saggy accordion — on a social par with begging. Hippies resus-
citated the art of busking in California. Fisherman's Wharf became the epicenter and cradle of a renaissance that spread to major cities throughout the country. It came to be known as New
Vaudeville.

The buskers were a closely knit, supportive community. They
worked on routines together, traded tricks and influences, shared
drugs and lovers, and bailed one another out of jail. Harry Lovecraft did a magic act in the guise of an Old West snake-oil sales-
man. He'd pull up in Francis Vancisco, a 1938 bread truck painted
with DR. H. P. LOVECRAFT AND HIS MAGICAL MEDICINE SHOW
in fanciful calligraphy, and step out wearing a top hat and vintage waistcoat. "Looky, looky, looky!" he'd bark. "I've got something here and I'm gonna show it to ya!" Lovecraft sold glass vials
that he claimed held "billions of dehydrated time-release voids;
just add water and, abracadabra, you have a universal solvent!"
He'd lure a trained dove into a paper bag, add a drop of liquid, and
the dove would turn into an egg — a product demonstration for his
"youth serum."

Patty Lovecraft, Harry's wife, performed as Sister San Andreas
the Tap-Dancing Nun and specialized in hot-tub christenings. A
Brownie Lady devotee, Patty would run giddily around the wharf
looking for Mer between acts. "Have you seen the Brownie Lady?"
she'd ask friends. "I have to find her *right now!*"

On the stages at the Cannery and Ghirardelli malls, busking
was not only tolerated, it was encouraged; free performances lured
shoppers and buskers enjoyed freedom from police interference.
Out on the streets, it was a different story. Business owners — worried that performers were literally and figuratively stealing the
show — filed complaints with the city.

"Whenever somebody who's paying for a business license and
paying taxes on his property sees a crowd of people facing away
from him, they immediately assume that business is being lost,"

says tap dancer Rosie Radiator. "Now, art being the glue of all of us, it was, of course, the street performers who were drawing the people to the location. They weren't coming for the trinkets in the shops as much as they were coming for the artisans on the sidewalks and the street performers who gave it ambiance and personality and the fun aspects of a destination."

Rosie had jump-started her career on Labor Day 1976 when she tap-danced across the 1.7-mile-long Golden Gate Bridge accompanied by her terrier, Lulu. In her backpack, she carried an American flag that had been presented to her grandmother when she was Miss Liberty of the 1915 Panama-Pacific International Exposition. The press swooned, so Rosie repeated the stunt the following year, adding distance — and more dancers. *The Guinness Book of World Records* created the "longest distance tap-danced" category for Rosie and her troupe in 1978, a surprisingly competitive title they would defend for decades.

Marijuana, according to Rosie, was crucial in developing her long-distance tap technique. "What we do is based on a THC-inspired release," she says. "You can't have tension in your feet, and you can't be fighting your natural movement." She credits the Brownie Lady with helping performers like her get through long Saturdays. "Working on the streets is not easy," she says. "It's physically demanding. It's hard on your voice, it's hard on your feet, it's hard on your psyche. It's the best theater training on the planet because no show is a problem after working the streets of San Francisco! Every stage is like Club Med in comparison. So, you know, your mom actually made it possible for us to weather those difficulties and continue moving forward as artists. She validated us because she was an element of the scene that represented the sweet, heartfelt relationship with marijuana that we had, and she also helped us continue to get through some of the tough times and rise to a higher level of consciousness while we were struggling."

As demand grew, the bakers had to find new sources for their bricks of Mexican gold. Quality varied. One week, Donald peeled open a brick of pot and noticed something amiss. Somewhere on its journey up from Mexico, it must have gotten wet. It smelled faintly of mildew. No way this damp pot would break down to the floury consistency they needed for baking. After picking out the seeds, Donald arrayed the damp weed on cookie sheets and heated it slowly to sap the moisture. The unmistakable dusky scent of marijuana bloomed through the flat. Donald closed the windows to trap it inside, worried about neighbors.

The improvisation worked, and Donald was able to grind it in the blender like usual. As he ran it through the hand sifter, pot powder billowed into the room, dusting the cooking utensils with green ash. Stevie Wonder's *Innervisions* was blasting from the living-room stereo loud enough to groove in the kitchen, and he cranked the sifter's handle to the beat with a satisfying *chk-ah, chk-ah*. He didn't hear Sharon, one of the other roommates, come in.

"My house is some kind of drug den now?" Sharon snapped. Of the five Bush Street residents, hers was the name on the lease. "This is what's going on?"

Donald glanced over his shoulder, gave a queenly roll of the eyes, and continued sifting.

Always high-strung, Sharon laid into Donald for a good twenty minutes before he slammed and locked his bedroom door. They reached a truce later, but the atmosphere remained tense.

Mer phoned Milwaukee to talk to Bill as she did every Sunday. She'd already told her dad about the cookies and muffins, though not about the illegal brownies. But the secret had been weighing on her, so she took the plunge. "You know what magic brownies are, right, Daddy?" she said. "We handle some of those."

Bill was quiet for a beat. "Be careful, honey," he said. "Make sure you're with good people."

"I'll be smart, I promise."

After hanging up, Mer got out her *I Ching* coins to think things over. Donald had told her about the fight with Sharon. Maybe it was time to relocate.

That week, she and Donald rolled around town, copying numbers from for rent signs taped in windows. They found a cheap upstairs apartment in an Edwardian building on Shrader and Waller streets in the Haight. It was small and had no living room, but one bedroom got southern light — good for painting — and the landlord was willing to rent for $300 per month and a handshake.

The Haight of 1976 was scummy and a little dangerous, crowded with droopy heroin burnouts, jittery speed burnouts, and goggle-eyed tourists. But it served their needs. In nearby Golden Gate Park, mist drifted between graceful stands of eucalyptus and the gnarled cypress groves where strangers sometimes met for outdoor sex. There were enough cheap restaurants within walking distance that Mer could avoid the kitchen. And the aroma of Donald's ghee could waft out the window into air already thick with marijuana smoke.

Barb sometimes pulled all-nighters to keep up with baking, and occasionally lubricated her gears with Jack Daniel's or a bottle of sweet wine. During the blue hours of one such night-come-morning, she omitted a crucial ingredient from a batch of magic brownie batter: flour.

After twenty-five minutes in the oven, her batter had transformed into chocolaty tar. Barb pulled out the pans with a sinking feeling. Eight ounces of pot gone to waste. Stacking the pans of ruined brownies on the counter, she rushed to prepare a new batch.

Barb's roommate, Annie, was leaving for Hawaii later that morning to join the Chinese Acrobats of Taiwan as a wardrobe tech on their world tour. She was hanging out in the kitchen with Barb while waiting for her ride to the airport. Though Annie rarely smoked weed, she absent-mindedly swiped the goop from a pan of ruined brownies and licked it off her finger. It was chocolate, after all. Barb joined in.

By the time Annie caught her flight, Barb was so high that vivid colors seemed to rain from the sky. When Mer came to pick up the goods for her afternoon run, Barb met her at the door.

"Get in here. You've got to try this."

Mer squinted at the pans on the counter. "That doesn't look right to me."

"Eat some. This stuff is like acid!" Barb waved her hand through the air and followed it with her eyes. "Want a spoon or something?"

"Who, me?" Mer ran her pointer finger through the goop and brought it to her lips. It tasted the same as a brownie, maybe a tad sweeter and more concentrated. The texture was like slightly gritty melted fudge.

Twenty minutes later, Mer had her bare feet kicked up on Barb's coffee table and was giggling like a little girl. Customers were going to have to wait because she was in no condition to sell.

Barb had stepped in something extraordinary. And its dark brown color and mushy texture brought one thing to mind.

"We'll call it Dynamic Diarrhea!"

"Funny Fairy Feces!"

"Cannabis Crap!"

That night, while Barb was scarfing everything in her fridge, her roommate phoned from Hawaii.

"Oh, my God, Barbara, I am so stoned I don't know what to do with myself. When I got here, the acrobats were all speaking Chinese — and I could understand them!"

Barb experimented over the next week, trying to figure out what made the goop so potent and how she might harness that strength. The high was giddy and electric, with sugar and caffeine complementing the marijuana. The absence of flour allowed the body to process it much faster. If a magic brownie was a cup of instant Folgers, this was a double espresso. Barb named the new product Fantasy Fudge.

Undercooking turned out to be key. She learned to heat the matter long enough to release the THC without beginning to kill it off. Once she figured that out, Barb not only applied it to Fantasy Fudge but also to her brownies. Leaving them slightly undercooked — a little gooey in the center — increased potency.

Today's cannabis chefs draw from decades of culinary refinement and horticultural advancement to create everything from peanut-butter cups and lollipops to sodas and potato chips. Modern edibles utilize extractions and infusions, so there's none of the grassy texture the old-school brownies had. Save for a slightly herbal taste, easily blended into many flavor profiles, weed food has become virtually indistinguishable from straight food. Netflix even launched a competitive reality show called *Cooking on High,* where chefs compete for glory with marijuana mole and ganja soufflés.

Dosages are now precise to the milligram, and most California pot products come labeled with the ratio of THC, known to eggheads as delta-9-tetrahydrocannabinol, and CBD, or cannabidiol. These are the two most famous of marijuana's one hundred or so chemical compounds called cannabinoids.

Beginning in the late eighties, scientists studying the chemistry of marijuana stumbled upon an amazing discovery: the largest signaling network found in the human body. This system of receptors, ligands, and enzymes has since been identified at work in the brain, organs, connective tissues, glands, and immune cells.

Because the receptors seem ideally shaped to interact with marijuana's chemicals, scientists named this network the endocannabinoid system.

Our understanding of how this system responds to THC and CBD — and what potential the other cannabinoids might hold — is young and rapidly evolving. We know that THC stimulates receptors in the peripheral organs, immune system, and central nervous system — including the brain's pleasure center, which releases dopamine; that's why you feel "high." CBD is different. Rather than binding to specific receptors, it enhances endocannabinoid responses overall. CBD has been shown to act as an antianxiety, antiepileptic, antispasmodic, and anti-inflammatory agent — but it doesn't tickle the pleasure center and has no psychoactive effects.

None of this was on the horizon in 1976. Until recently, the US cannabis food industry was all about experimentation. Or, to quote my mom, "For a while there, every batch was a crapshoot. You never knew what you were gonna get."

The first day the fudge hit the wharf, Mer and Barb split the afternoon run. They were both curious to gauge reactions to the new product. Mer started down by the longshoremen's lot and worked her way west; Barb began at Polk and Beach streets and moved east.

When Barb sold on the wharf, she liked to dress up as a milkmaid in a long calico skirt, high-collared blouse, and straw hat. She carried her goods in a picnic basket she'd named Harriet. Boogie, her shaggy companion, strolled by her side. Barb looked so wholesome and cute that tourists kept asking her to pose for pictures, which she found hilarious. To think that the woman in the picnic outfit was selling drugs.

The big picnic basket got heavy, so Barb decided to leave Harriet with a street artist she trusted and carry a more diminutive load in a smaller basket over her arm. If she ran out of anything, she could trek back to Harriet to restock.

Throughout the day, Barb warned customers, "This stuff is very, very strong. Just nibble a corner and wait half an hour before eating more. You do *not* want to eat too much."

Not everyone listened. Two of the craftspeople on Barb's side of the wharf had to close their booths early because they couldn't communicate with the public or keep track of cash. Barb felt guilty. She loaded their wares into the back of her pickup and drove the vendors to their respective homes.

Not until she got back to her apartment in the evening did Barb realize that she'd forgotten to collect Harriet from the street vendor. She drove back across town in a panic. Most of the artisans had gone home for the day, but tourists still clotted the wharf, rubbing goose pimples from their arms.

There, sitting innocently on the sidewalk, was the basket full of chocolaty dope.

Fantasy Fudge was difficult to package. You'd use the spatula to scoop it onto a square of cellophane, just like a regular brownie, but once wrapped, it dissolved into a formless packet of goop. It had to be kept in a cooler or the fudge would slowly liquify. Even handling wrapped fudge turned your hands greenish black with sticky residue.

One warm Saturday after a sales run, Barb stopped by the Shrader apartment, exhausted. Boogie drooped at her heels. Donald was in the kitchen reading a novel. Barb sank into a chair with a sigh. "Where's Mer?" she asked.

"I think she's still on the wharf."

Barb wiggled her tarred fingers. "It looks like I've been working on cars," she said. Then she broke into a dazzling grin. "I've got it! We'll call them Sticky Fingers brownies."

Donald rubbed his jeans as if he were wiping off goop. He trotted into his room, returning with the *Sticky Fingers* album, which he slid onto the turntable. With the Rolling Stones rocking on the record player and a fresh fog greasing the Haight like Crisco, Barb and Donald twisted up a celebratory joint.

sticky fingers brownies..

September's Song

4

September's Song

B oogie braced himself in the truck bed, absorbing the flaws of the road. He nipped at the wind, shaggy ears whipping inside out, tongue flapping like a flag. Inside the cab, Mer extracted a joint from her purse, elbowing Donald, who rode in the middle. Barb was steering and simultaneously rooting in her pockets for a lighter. Knee to knee, elbow to elbow, they chugged past the tollbooths, then mounted the span, heading north across the Golden Gate.

Approaching the first of the two towers, the perspective aligned such that the north tower was framed within the lower portal of the south tower like a Russian nesting doll. The first tower engulfed the truck in vermilion. Time froze. Click. As they emerged onto the bridge's central span, the world began again.

September 1976. A new variety of marijuana was hitting the streets of San Francisco and sending shock waves throughout the country: California-grown *sinsemilla* (Spanish for "seedless"). An executive editor at *High Times* dubbed it "superweed" and called its farmers "supergrowers." If this trip turned out the way Mer hoped, it could be a game changer for Sticky Fingers.

Glancing east beyond the blur of suspension cables, she caught sight of the Bay Bridge, the Golden Gate's homely older sister. There was Alcatraz floating in a dreamy haze, and a modest skyline punctuated by the garish Transamerica Pyramid. The City looked fragile and fantastical, like it might skid into the bay with the next twitch of the San Andreas Fault.

At the highest point of the span, the girthy main cable descended to eye level, then swooped to the top of the north tower. *Whoosh.* The second tower spat them out the other side into a rural landscape with immediately warmer weather. This happened so fast; on one side was urban civilization, and on the other, gnarled oaks and butterflies.

No moisture followed them from the bay. Inland, the sky was robin's-egg blue. Mer got that joint lit and Barb cracked the window. Donald tuned the radio to KSAN. "Ch-ch-ch-ch-changes!" They sang along with Bowie as the truck descended into Marin. Clumps of sycamores wearing slow-burn autumnal colors stood in toasted brown fields. Petaluma, Santa Rosa, Cloverdale: grazing cows, apple orchards, half-collapsed barns. KSAN fuzzed out, sticking them with two Christian stations and one playing country and western. Purpling grapevines blanketed the fields along the highway. Hopland, Ukiah, Willits. After four sun-smacked hours in the truck, they blew across the Humboldt County line.

Neither Barb nor Mer had been this far north, but Donald knew the area well. An old pal of his lived in the woods near Garberville. He'd met Mumser — who'd taken her moniker from a Yiddish word meaning "bastard" — in the UW-Milwaukee theater department, and they'd hitchhiked to California together in 1971. Now, five years later, Mumser was living on a rural parcel with a burly mountain woman whom I'll call Betsy. The collapse of the logging industry had flooded the market with large tracts of unwanted land, where rough, swooping hills discouraged people from living in close proximity. Donald had helped Mumser build her cabin using homesteading catalogs and how-to manuals. The result was rickety, full of chinks and corners that didn't quite meet. But Mumser moved in anyway.

Thereafter, Donald had a home away from home in the country. After a few months in San Francisco, he'd either (a) burn out on the pace, (b) get strung out on smack, (c) fall out of grace with friends/lovers/dealers, or (d) all of the above. Then it would be time to cool out in the woods before thumbing a ride back to the City to spin the wheel again.

At Garberville — a one-horse town with a population of around eight hundred, a seedy motel, and a redneck bar called the Branding Iron Saloon — Donald guided them off the highway onto an intricate maze of dirt roads. Trees ruled the region: towering Douglas firs, expansive oaks, slick madrones with blood-colored skin curling away from the lime-green flesh underneath. Despite the worsening drought, fragrant redwood groves still seemed cool and moist, with tree trunks as wide as Barb's truck. There were also ugly stretches of clear-cut land, scarred and eroded, barren but for stumps and weeds. They snaked over hills, around hairpin corners, and alongside sheer drops. Meridy stared out the truck window, awed by the majesty of this rough, unbridled wilderness.

A couple of weeks prior, Mer was kicked back on the barge watching TV and eating takeout from the Palace Chop Suey Café when she heard Donald jog up the stairs to their flat, back from visiting his friends in Garberville.

The crucial gestures of the 1976 presidential election were unfolding on TV, and as political races went, it was entertaining. "I wanna wish you a nice day and ask for your help," Jimmy Carter said, pumping the hand of a bemused passerby. "I'm from Georgia and I'm running for president, yes, president of the United States." He chuckled, as if to himself, then flashed a cheek-busting grin. The press followed him to bus stops and hotdog stands, where he'd natter amiably like he had nowhere else to be. Pundits doubted he could run a church picnic. But Carter's down-home earnestness had an appeal in the aftermath of Watergate; he didn't seem likely to steal a grape at the supermarket.

Gerald Ford wasn't cut out to compete with a nice guy. After inheriting a furious country, he'd turned around and pardoned

Tricky Dick, a move criticized from both sides of the aisle. He'd presided over a severe recession and the highest unemployment rates since the 1930s; vets returning from Vietnam couldn't find work. Ford was also preternaturally clumsy; he'd slid head-first down the steps of Air Force One, then popped up to shake the Austrian chancellor's hand as if nothing had happened — a clip that got funnier every time it aired. Mer almost felt sorry for him.

Donald poked his head into her room. "A rose is a rose is a rose," he said.

"Chow mein?" Mer offered, holding up a carton.

Donald perched on the bed next to her. "Listen to me. A rose is a rose is a rose."

He explained that Mumser and Betsy were preparing to harvest a spectacular crop with huge sticky sinsemilla buds the likes of which he'd never seen. Once the plants were dry, they would use tiny sewing scissors to snip stems and leaves away from the juicy buds. The detritus from trimming — known as "shake" — would get shoveled into garbage bags. That got Donald's wheels turning.

"Say Mumser and Betsy get busted, God forbid," Donald said. "The cops won't care if it's connoisseur bud or moldy old shake. A pound is a pound is a pound. Having this stuff lying around is a liability to them." He popped a wonton into his mouth.

"What do they do with it?" Mer asked.

"It's hard to get rid of," he said, chewing. "Mumser still has a couple trash bags full from last year's crop. She was about to burn it, but I stopped her."

Mer shook her head. "Won't the brownies be weak if we use shake instead of bud?"

"Not *this* shake."

Donald's Garberville friends were at the forefront of the California sinsemilla revolution. This new weed didn't come compacted into bricks with sugar water or bound onto sticks. It grew regal and tall on hidden sunbathed hillsides. The buds were large, pert, and garnished with tiny crystals. Like Christmas trees for psychedelic dollhouses. Sinsemilla bud was too expensive to waste on brownies. Furthermore, it was too strong; the idea was to get people high, not put them in a coma. But then Donald thought: *What about the shake?*

"You know," Mer said, dropping her chopsticks into the chow mein. "If this works, it could be big."

"Gigantic."

"Can you get us some to try?"

Donald hustled out to his room and came back with a large paper sack. "They *gave* me this to play with."

After a Saturday sales run, Mer and Donald brought pizza to Barb's and hung out while she experimented. Then they sampled the result and watched *Saturday Night Live* together. When Chevy Chase careened across the screen doing one of his Gerald Ford pratfalls, Mer laughed so hard she peed her jeans and had to borrow sweats from Barb.

The new brownies were stronger than what they'd been making with expensive Mexican bud and had the bright, fresh flavor of California's finest.

Mumser didn't have a telephone. So the crew had piled into Barb's pickup that September morning without a plan — unless you consider showing up unannounced on an illegal pot farm in the woods a plan.

The cabin stood at the end of a long private driveway bristling with ponderosa pines. It was a crooked structure with a misshapen deck slouching off the side. Donald knocked on the door and peered through the window.

"I'll find her," he said. "Don't wander around." He jogged off behind the cabin, curls bouncing down his back.

"Oh, for God's sake," Mer muttered. "Tell me she's here."

"If we drove all the way up here for nothing, I'll kill both of you," Barb said. "I *knew* we should've sent a letter first."

"It's pretty up here anyway." A fat white mare ambled up to the nearby deer fencing to check them out, chewing on a mouthful of dry grass. Barb smoked a cigarette while Boogie chased a squirrel and Mer made friends with the horse.

Fifteen minutes later, Donald trudged back up.

"Mumser's visiting her folks in Milwaukee."

Barb groaned.

Donald held his palms out soothingly. "It's cool. Betsy says she'll meet with us. The stuff is half hers anyway. We just have to wait for a couple of hours so she can finish her chores."

Shading her eyes, Barb looked around at the treetops and the clear blue sky. "I have some mescaline we could do."

Today, California pot growers can apply for licenses to operate legally. The associated cost and requirements vary by county and city, and can be discouraging to small farmers — but it's a vastly different world. Throughout the seventies and eighties, growing a single plant was a felony offense in California. Decades later, Betsy is still reluctant to discuss their farm, but Mumser agrees to a phone call after some consideration. She still lives in Garberville, though she has moved into town and no longer farms.

"It was all for fun," she says. "We didn't come up here to grow. We didn't! We just wanted to be in the country."

After hitchhiking from Milwaukee with Donald, Mumser had initially settled in San Francisco. One night, she attended a gay and lesbian rally, and a drag queen got onstage. Some women in the audience took offense to the drag — viewing it as a parody of womanhood — and made a fuss. The LGBTQ+ community would become more united in later decades, but separatist movements were on the rise back then. Mumser left the rally disgusted. She'd come to California seeking an environment where living out of the closet wasn't such a hassle only to get sucked into infighting. When Betsy invited her to build a cabin in the country, she went for it.

They were both urban women who knew nothing about homesteading, but they were enamored with the notion of living off the fat of the earth. The early 1970s was a rare moment in US history when the pace of urban migration slowed to a crawl as young people ditched cities in search of a simpler life. Land was cheap in Humboldt County then. The once-flourishing lumber industry — forty-seven sawmills within twenty-fives miles of Garberville in the 1950s — had dwindled as the hills were logged out; by 1976, two sawmills remained. Back-to-the-landers erected cabins and outhouses, planted sustenance gardens, raised goats and chickens, and set about living rustically. But while you're planting tomatoes — and buying weed from someone else — you might as well plant your own weed. Then, while you're planting your own weed, you might as well plant extra to sell. That money could buy a wood-stove or badly needed insulation. Someday you might upgrade from an outhouse to a flushing toilet. And how are you going to afford a septic tank with organic tomatoes and welfare checks?

"We saw that people were getting new trucks and all this stuff," Mumser says. "And we were like, *Whoa, where did they get the money for that?* And then we were like, *Ooh.*"

Cultivating high-quality pot was not a job for the lazy or unfocused as Mumser and Betsy soon discovered. They installed a water tank on a hilltop and ran lines to their patch, then lugged soil and fertilizer into the woods in fifty-pound sacks. Rabbits, deer, caterpillars, molds, fungi, and human thieves posed constant threats. In late summer, when the female plants produced psychoactive resin, every day of sunshine made the product stronger. But an early frost could ruin everything. Timing was essential. Once pulled, the plants were hung to dry on hooks in the cabins, where the growers could watch obsessively for signs of mildew.

It took about nine months of daily labor to usher an outdoor crop from soil prep to sale. At any stage, local police or federal drug enforcement could have seized everything — including their freedom.

"There were a lot of big people," Mumser says. "But we weren't big. We were just like a little small thing, just a little thing."

By all accounts, their farm was small but mighty, and their homegrown packed a punch.

The Sticky Fingers crew drank foul-tasting mescaline tea on Mumser's deck. Red-tailed hawks carved circles overhead. Barb sat on a rocking chair, Donald on the deck's edge, Mer on a stump.

While waiting for the drugs to kick in or the grower to show up and do the deal — whichever happened first — they discussed a spectacularly complicated romantic entanglement Barb had fallen into. Her on-again, off-again boyfriend was sneaking around with another woman, his best friend's girlfriend. So Barb started sleeping with the best friend, a burly carpenter named John Battle. John was supposed to be a fling, but Barb fell in love with him. It was mess worthy of a Jacqueline Susann novel and it was causing Barb a lot of heartache.

"So what's with you and these Viking types?" Mer asked. John Battle, like most of Barb's crushes, was tall, pale, and heavyset, with a bushy red beard. "Must be something from a past life."

Barb grinned. "Call me Helga."

"Not that I'm doing any better," Mer said. She'd been nursing a crush on a wiry Scorpio who called himself Spider. They'd met at a party and talked for hours about art, love, spirituality — everything Mer cared about. But after flirting with her all night, Spider left with his arm around a squeaky petite blonde who'd had too much to drink. Mer's love life was an endless series of almosts and nahs and whatevers punctuated by unbearable stretches of unrequited infatuation.

"We need to find you a magician," Barb said. "Someone magical."

Mer chuffed. "I won't hold my breath."

"Don't be so negative. You have to visualize what you want in life," Barb said. She tipped back in the rocking chair to gaze up at the sky. "Look," she said. "There's my Viking ship in the clouds. Come and get it, boys!"

A wave of laughter seemed to lift Mer off the deck then place her gently back down. "I just came on big time," she said. Vibrations twanged along her arms as if each hair were an antenna tuned to a different radio station.

"I think I'm gonna barf," Barb said.

Mer felt it, too: pangs in her gut like the beginning of food poisoning. The landscape suddenly exploded into intricate geometry. The firs and pines broke into interlocking triangles in varying shades of green. The clouds were layered circles of white and silver. Everything slowly rotated as if in a kaleidoscope. She vaguely heard Barb retching over the side of the deck. Donald began to sing, his rich tenor rising through the hush of the woods, and a flock of small brown birds burst from a nearby tree to perform spirals and loop the loops in time with his wordless song.

In a snapshot Donald took that day, Barb sits in a rocking chair on the dirt in Mumser's yard, smiling. A jean jacket covers her knees, and she wears a white engineer's cap over her blonde hair. Mer stands with one foot cocked on the chair and Barb's arm slung over her knee. She wears an embroidered purple blouse, harem pants tucked into red knee socks, and no shoes, grass and twigs clinging to her feet. Her hair is in tight, uneven curls, and she's grinning at the camera over dark sunglasses. Under her left arm, she clutches a copy of the *I Ching*. Behind them, there's Barb's white truck and tangled woods stretching toward golden-brown hills.

They spent the afternoon there, taking blurry pictures of one another's dilated eyes and Boogie's snout, and acquiring sunburns. Meridy tried to ride Betsy's horse around the pasture and toppled off.

Betsy stopped by to greet them wearing nothing but jeans and muck boots, belly hanging over the waistband, breasts loose. She had curly blonde hair, and freckles across her chest and shoulders. She squatted on the porch. "What are you guys tripping on?"

"Oh, a little mescaline."

Betsy's smile was beautiful. "Well, come down to my house in an hour or so. No rush. I'll be there."

And she was gone.

Mer was amazed. She'd never met a woman who so obviously didn't care what anyone thought of her — completely owning her boobs and belly. Betsy seemed to have discovered the secret to un-selfconsciousness.

"I wish I could be natural like that," Mer said. "I mean, how much time do we spend worrying about how we look? Worrying about those last five pounds."

Barb snorted. "Or ten."

Donald rolled a joint from sinsemilla raised on that very farm. Being there — where the marijuana consumed sunlight through its leaves and minerals through its roots, where it grew from tender sprouts to towering goddesses — changed the experience. From then on, when Mer smoked California sinsemilla, she would think of this place. The smell of the trees, the harmony of the colors.

Decades later, seedy weed has gone the way of VHS tapes; only people of a certain age will remember what a pain in the neck it was to deal with — and how mediocre the buzz could be.

The key to growing sinsemilla is murdering the men; one must kill every male marijuana plant before it can pollinate the females. Then, instead of producing seeds, the unfertilized females ooze gooey psychoactive resin. Stickier means stonier. But the differences between male and female plants are subtle and apparent only at certain stages in the plant's growth. Sinsemilla farming

is a delicate art, requiring horticultural knowledge and expert timing.

These techniques were new to the United States back then. The
1976 publication of *Sinsemilla: Marijuana Flowers* by Jim Richardson was a turning point. It's a handsome coffee-table book
with more space dedicated to photographs than words. The sparse
writing makes an impact. Part practical manual, part pot porn, it
gives step-by-step instructions that one doesn't have to be a horti-
culturist to understand. And the language is so suggestive that it's
tempting to read it aloud in a phone-sex voice.

> The virgin blossoms swell with sexual energy eager for consumma-
> tion. But the breeze brings no pollen and the rhythm continues to
> intensify . . . As the last pistils come into the tips, the clusters turn
> pure white. The pods swell and the resinous coating thickens. The
> true sweetness of the flowers comes forth and becomes so strong it
> is almost too much to bear.

Macrophotography shot with the same erotic sensibility ac-
companies the writing. Seed pods shaped like vulvas, pistils that
look like erect penises. It's over the top but also useful. The photos teach you to identify the plant's sex organs at various stages so
you'll know when to kill males, when to wait, and when to harvest
mature females.

This book passed from hippie to hippie in the California backwoods. Growing good sinsemilla is difficult — so much can go
wrong — but the guide made the subtle art appear accessible, even
fun.

The three friends lay side by side on a blanket on Mumser's deck
looking up at the clouds. Mer was in the middle, holding hands on
one side with Barb and with Donald on the other side, enjoying the
energy flowing between them. The mescaline trip had mellowed,
but she still felt quietly ecstatic, glad to be with close friends.

"You know, Donald, I always wanted you to be straight," Mer said. "You're *so* my type. Why can't you be straight?"

Donald stuck out his tongue. "Ew."

"Seriously? Go to hell."

"Did you always know you liked guys?" Barb asked, breaking the chain to prop herself on one elbow.

"I was never really in the closet," Donald said. "I don't think I could *find* the closet."

They fell quiet for a time. Then Donald sat up, clasping his hands around his knees. "I actually remember the exact moment. I think I was maybe thirteen, and I ran across the word 'homosexual' in my father's dictionary. I remember turning beet red and realizing, *Oh, my God, that's me. There's a word for what I am.*"

"What about your parents?" Barb asked. "Were they, you know, cool?"

"Oh, no. I came home one day from school, and my father had intercepted a letter from my boyfriend, this was like in high school. He called me into his office, and he was shaking this letter at me, and he said, *Is your girlfriend's name Gary?*"

The women laughed.

"He was furious. He chased me out into the car, then he and my mother took me down to the police station in Green Bay, where they locked me in an interrogation room. This police psychiatrist came in and told me all the horrible things that were going to happen to me if I stayed a faggot. He said I was going to die in a gutter, shot by a jealous lover."

A smile swept across his face. "I'll never forget that phrase. It's got a certain poetry, don't you think? It sounded ... wonderful to me."

Late in the afternoon, the group gathered in Betsy's kitchen to talk business. Her place was nicer and larger than Mumser's. Betsy had thrown on a plaid flannel shirt and put her hair in a low ponytail.

She dragged in a giant garbage bag, opened it, and ran her fingers through the leaves and stems inside.

"We haven't harvested the new crop yet, so this is what's left over from last year. We were trying to figure out whether to burn it or compost it or what, so if you guys can use it for your cooking, more power to you."

Mer felt giddy. Here was a part of the ganja plant that usually went to waste; in the brownies, it would find new life. She tried to sound casual. "How much are you asking?"

Betsy shrugged. "Eh, I don't know . . . How about fifty a pound?"

They were paying six times that amount for lousy Mexican bud. Riding the end of her trip, Mer envisioned their profit margin as a glowing green line shooting to the ceiling where it burst into greenish-golden light that bathed the room.

"We'll take everything you've got."

Barb gave her bug eyes, but Mer just smiled.

Betsy weighed the shake in batches on a triple beam. There were ten pounds total.

If only Patrolman Buxbaum could see Meridy now.

At sunset, when the light poured soupy and orange through the treetops, Barb crammed the garbage bag of shake into an antique icebox she kept in her truck bed. Boogie hopped in back to stand guard. "We should put a blessing on the drive," Barb said. She closed her eyes. Mer and Donald followed suit. "I'm envisioning a golden bubble around this truck that will carry us home safely, no funny business."

Thus guarded against calamity, they began the bumpy trek down from the hills. They'd gotten a late start, and by the time they'd stopped for dinner at a greasy spoon, the sky was a velvety black. The afternoon of drug-fueled frolicking was catching up to Barb, making the two hundred or so miles feel like eight hundred. "Guys, I've got to pull over," she said. "I have to get some sleep or I won't make it."

Barb exited the 101 at a small state park and followed a fire road to a grassy clearing. A half-moon crept above jagged silhouettes of pine trees. Barb cuddled up with Boogie. Mer and Donald laid out blankets in the dry grass. Cricket song lulled them to sleep.

Mer awoke in the crisp blue of early morning to find a park ranger in a broad-brimmed hat standing over her. "Ma'am, do you have a camping permit?"

She blinked up at him.

Barb sat up in the truck bed, blonde hair awry, mascara smeared. "I got tired so I pulled over," she said. "What's the big deal?"

The ranger looked nonplussed. "You can't be here without a permit. I need you to leave."

"For God's sake," Barb snapped. "Do you have to be all bossy and uptight just because you're wearing a big stupid hat?"

"Um, Barb," Mer said, getting to her feet. "Calm down."

"Oh, please," Barb said. "Smokey Bear over here would rather we had an accident than sleep in his precious park."

Boogie growled, baring his teeth.

The ranger placed a hand on his gun holster. "Ma'am, you need to call off your dog!"

Out of the corner of her eye, Mer saw Donald taking small steps backward, eyes darting, ready to break and run for the woods.

"Look, we're really sorry," Mer told the ranger. "We'll get going right now. Come on, Barb, let's go home. Now."

"All right. *Sorry,*" Barb said. "Give us a minute to pack up, would you?"

Luckily, the ranger only wanted them to leave, which they managed to do despite Barb's tongue.

The incident wouldn't seem funny until years later. "Never fuck with Barb early in the morning." My mom laughs a little ruefully. "You know how she can get. She has that Scorpio rising, so there's a nasty streak, especially if she hasn't had her coffee and her first cigarette. We're carrying ten pounds of pot, and she's laying into this ranger like he's some schmuck fighting over a parking space."

It was with a profound sense of relief that they crossed the Golden Gate later that morning. Pores opened to the damp bay air. Nature had its charms, but there was nothing like coming home to the City.

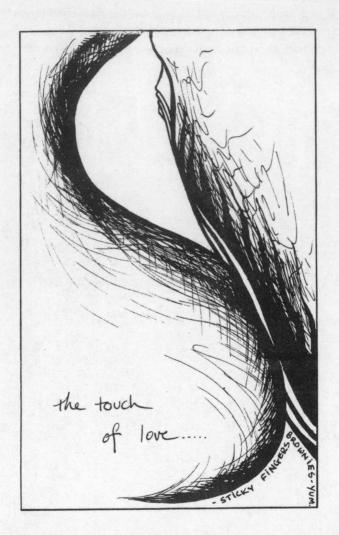

the touch
of love......

5

The Touch

Meridy liked this new side of herself: the outlaw entrepreneur. Stepping out to work the wharf each weekend, looking sharp, she felt her energy crackling dangerously — a stripped wire. Her circle of acquaintances grew exponentially, and her reputation began to precede her. "Oh, *you're* the Brownie Lady!" Among the wharf characters were several fine men to flirt with. She had fair-weather boyfriends here and there, hey baby-free-love romps, and the occasional awkward orgy — but nothing she could hold, nothing to return to. Most nights, she spent sprawled between cold sheets.

Granted, she was choosy. She wanted a knock-down, drag-out, transcendental romance. She didn't go for the bucket jaw, toothpaste teeth, harmonica mustache look that was mainstream. Forget Burt Reynolds; bring on David Bowie! Creative, slightly broken, effeminate types gave her butterflies. She considered herself an artistic genius and was, at the very least, an artist of significant promise, therefore she wanted a lover of the same ilk. A Diego to her Frida, a Rodin to her Claudel. A man who dealt from a full deck of cards.

Preferably tarot cards.

But whenever Mer felt a genuine zap, the guy backed off. She had a knack for both dazzling and scaring the shit out of the opposite sex. As the Butterfly Man, one of her wharf customers, would recall decades later, "She was a striking lady. Kind of terrifying, to tell you the truth." So despite possessing intelligence, good looks, and *cojones* — or maybe because of these traits — Mer drummed her fingers in fern bars on Clement Street and cafés in North Beach, waiting.

Barb kept saying they needed to find her a magician.

He's here somewhere, Mer thought. *Somewhere in this seven-mile town.*

He was about three miles away.

My future father walked the Mission toward what he didn't know. He liked to be on the street, checking people out, getting checked out. He stood an even six feet, with good posture beaten into him at boarding school, and moved with an easy long-legged swing. Music in the wooden heels of his cowboy boots striking the sidewalk, rhythm in his hips. On a clear day, he was the kind of guy who would try to stare directly at the sun and meditate — once burning his corneas so badly that he had to wear gauze patches.

He walked, destination wherever, soaking in the scene. Passing the Sixteenth Street BART station, he checked out the Chicanos in high-waisted slacks and bandannas. Round brown-skinned women selling tamales. The crowd surged and ebbed. Occasionally, he'd see another freak coming the other way. They'd lock eyes and nod, a current passing between them. He could get overloaded with energy, like a circuit breaker receiving too much juice. He'd been trained to read auras, and sometimes he couldn't turn off the colors enveloping strangers. He liked the smell of grilling meat, the sound of *ranchera* music a little circusy to his ears. The funk of junkies, the occasional rainbow of a kindred spirit. He walked, feeling alive inside his skin. *We are all one light*, he thought. *All the world's children . . .*

It was Barb who found him.

John Battle, the Viking carpenter she was dating, had recently moved into an enormous warehouse on Twentieth and Alabama streets in the Mission. "I'm living with all these kooky psychic hippies," he told her. "You won't believe my housemates."

Barb liked kooky psychic hippies. She visited John at his new space, and that's where she met Doug Volz.

Doug told her that he'd graduated from the Berkeley Psychic Institute the prior autumn, earning the grandiose title of ordained reverend of the Church of Divine Man. Barb had never heard of it. Doug explained that they trained students in clairvoyance, aura readings, chakra readings, telepathy, and telekinesis. When he mentioned that he'd painted a mural of all the graduates who'd preceded him in exchange for his tuition, Barb's ears perked.

"Oh, you're an artist?" she said.

"Come right this way."

He directed her to sit in a straight-backed wooden chair facing an enormous triptych of canvases about seven feet tall and three feet wide. The central panel featured a life-size woman with long blonde hair sitting on a wooden chair and staring frankly out at the viewer, palms resting on her knees, as if about to give a psychic reading.

"I call this piece *My Old Lady Is a Dancer*," Doug said. "It might not look like she's dancing, but sit with her for a little while. See what happens."

Barb could feel Doug eyeing her for a response as she tried to relax and focus on the painting. A green field stretched toward barren trees behind the seated figure and filled the other two panels. Puffy clouds drifted across an intensely blue sky. Doug's style was photo-realistic; the detail was so fine that she thought he must have painted with the tiniest brush imaginable. But there was something otherworldly about the image, too. She looked at the woman's calm brown eyes, and the painting began to move: the grass swayed, the blonde hair twisted in the wind.

Oh, my God, Barb thought. *Doug and Meridy are going to be together.*

————

By early November, the bakery was running low on magic ingredient. Mer sent a letter to Betsy and Mumser saying that she was coming back up for another visit. She didn't hear back right away, so she and Barb decided to drive up on a Sunday and take their chances. The season had been dry, the drought deepening, but a soft, welcome rain fell that afternoon.

On the way up, Barb told Mer about the handsome psychic she'd met. "I got his number for you."

"I can't call this guy out of the blue," Mer said. "I've never met him."

"Oh, come on," Barb said. "What do you have to lose?" She cajoled, but Mer dug her heels in and changed subjects.

They drove all the way to Garberville only to find out that Betsy and Mumser had harvested late and were still drying their plants; they didn't have any shake ready.

"It'll be all right," Mumser said. "Plenty of us up here." She put a call out on her CB — which people in the community used to track storms and wildfires and notify one another when law enforcement was prowling. "This is Merry Widow," she said, winking at Barb and Mer. "Anybody got eggs for sale out there? Got friends up here looking for eggs. Over."

Eggs. A codeword, apparently.

The radio was quiet. Then a voice broke through. "Affirmative, Merry Widow, I got some eggs."

Mumser drew a complicated map, which Mer and Barb followed down unmarked dirt roads into the deep woods. The rain swelled from a sloppy drizzle into a downpour, and liquified clay streamed from the roads, exposing hunks of rock and giant potholes. They ground up a precipitous hill, then sharply down. At the nadir, a roiling brown creek cut across the road. Someone had laid two planks across the surging water.

Barb hit the brakes. "I don't know about this. If we go in that creek, we're screwed." Barb's 1966 Datsun pickup didn't have four-wheel drive. If they got stuck, they'd be marooned in the deep boonies. Miles from any phone booth, they'd have no way to call for a tow truck. It was a narrow road. On one side, snaky black roots laced a tall clay bank. On the other was a sheer drop into the woods, an ocean of pines and redwoods rolling into the gray distance.

There was no room to turn around, no chance of backing up the steep hill.

Nowhere to go but forward.

Barb exhaled slowly. "Promise me you'll call this guy and I promise you we'll make it."

Mer gave her a sidelong look. "Fine. It's a deal."

Barb patted the dash, and Mer white-knuckled the door handle, as they eased toward the creek. Milkshake-brown water licked the boards. Barb kept her foot steady on the gas and gripped the steering wheel at ten and two. The boards shuddered under the truck's weight but did not give.

"Yahoo!" Barb screamed on the way up the next hill. "I feel like we're in a movie!"

Mer and Barb bought everything the guy had, three fat black garbage bags full of shake — thirty pounds total — crammed it into the cooler in the back of the truck, and covered it with a tarp.

The drive home was nervous, slow, careful.

That much weed, they knew, could send them to prison for years.

The first phone call between Mer and Doug was awkward, but Barb had prepared them both.

"I hear you're good with the tarot," Doug said. "Well, you know, I'm trained to read auras. Since we're both into psychic work, why don't we exchange readings? Let's skip all the bullshit and pretension, and find out who we *really* are." He laughed in a way that made it sound like an adventure.

Mer always liked to put her skills forward first, and she was confidant with the tarot. No matter what else happened, she figured she could give a decent reading. They agreed that Doug would come to her house first. Then, the following day, he'd read her aura at his warehouse. Tit for tat.

No coffee, no concert in the park, no wine to break the ice. Just a hard-core display of psychic chops: the hippie blind date par excellence.

Four decades later, two loose pages of my dad's 1976 day planner surface in a box of old letters, offering a snapshot of his life. On November 8, there's a dental appointment and the name Barbara Hartman circled, the day they first met. Later that week, my dad has scheduled three psychic readings, including one with someone named Estania and the parenthetical note SPIRITUAL-SEXUAL UNION.

I don't know what that entails, and maybe that's for the best. But it's clear that my dad was making a go at becoming a professional. It might seem outlandish in any other time or place, but psychic work was serious business in the Bay Area in 1976. Multiple cities were currently embroiled in debates over the legalities of psychic services. The ACLU was suing the city of San Francisco over the right of palmists and other occult practitioners to advertise their services. And the California state senate was holding hearings on a bill to set up a statewide licensing system for astrologers.

On Sunday, November 14, Doug planned to fast, take mushrooms, and see a double feature of *The Exorcist* and *The Other*. Then, on Tuesday, November 16, there's Meridy Domnitz's name along with her address and phone number and the note 8:00 P.M. READING WITH.

"I have this clear image of the first moment I saw your mother," my dad says, looking back. "Her apartment was up these long narrow Victorian stairs, and she was standing at the top with the light from the door shining behind her. I had to climb all the way up there to reach her. She didn't budge, like, to meet me halfway or anything. It seemed to take a really long time. She was like no one I'd ever met before, that's for sure."

Meridy eyeballed her date as he climbed the stairs, thinking that Barb certainly had fixed her up with a good-looking guy. Doug had a full reddish beard; a strong, straight nose; high cheekbones; freckles; and light-blue eyes. He was tall, lean, and loose-limbed. He wore shitkickers and a leather cowboy hat — which made Mer smile. (She and Barb were both reading *Even Cowgirls Get the Blues* by Tom Robbins that fall.) Doug removed his hat at the top of the stairs, revealing a shiny bald crown like that of a much older man, though his skin was smooth and youthful.

She led him into her bedroom, which Mer had obsessively cleaned and arranged to perfect the gypsy boudoir vibe, replete with incense and flickering candles. She'd dressed simply in jeans and a slimming black turtleneck with an oversize ankh necklace. Her eyes were elaborately kohled and shadowed.

Mer chattered to fill the silence while showing Doug her latest artwork, mostly watercolors. The conversation began haltingly, but art loosened both of their tongues. They fell into a natural one-upmanship, each waxing about their own creative obsessions.

For the reading, they sat facing each other on Meridy's queen-size bed. She felt a little intimidated — Doug was so cute and seemed to fit her parameters — so she took deep breaths to clear her mind. Once she hit her stride in the reading, she relaxed and let the cards guide her.

I wish I knew what my mom saw in the cards that night, but all she remembers is congratulating herself on giving him a good reading. My dad isn't any more helpful, his memory coming up blank.

Did she draw the *Lovers* and get distracted by a fluttering in her stomach, wondering if the lover in question might be her?

Did she see opportunity on his horizon, maybe the *Ten of Pentacles*, a hint that he was about to go from chronically broke to joining an increasingly lucrative illegal enterprise that would sustain him for years?

Did she glean from the *Empress* card that he would soon create a child?

It's also possible that she saw none of this, her reading totally off the mark, blinded by attraction.

Doug had an aloof air, traces of a British accent, and a goofy sense of humor that helped offset his arrogance. The reading opened lines of communication between them, and Meridy was struck by a sense of being on the same level, playing by similar rules.

"I have a little side gig," she said, with a half smile she hoped was sexy. "I sell magic brownies on the wharf."

"Well! I might have to try one."

Perfect response. They shared a small dose, and Mer made herself more comfortable, propped on pillows. When she asked Doug about his family, his answer took her by surprise. His grandmother, Paula, who at that time was seventy-four years old, was married to a ghost.

He explained: Lieutenant Commander Edward P. Clayton had been a decorated frogman in World War II and Korea. He and Paula had had a tumultuous on-again, off-again affair for years, but circumstances kept them apart. Ed died of lung cancer in 1969. One year later, his ghost showed up in Paula's bed and made love to her. She could neither hear nor see him, but she felt his touch. When the ghost proposed marriage through a Ouija board, Paula accepted and assumed his last name.

"She talks to him all day long," Doug said. "In some ways, they're like any married couple except that you can't hear his side of the conversation."

"Like *The Ghost and Mrs. Muir*," Mer said.

"Every afternoon she has what she calls her 'quiet time' with Ed when she disappears into her back bedroom and he takes her all around the universe."

"And is she otherwise . . . ?"

"Sharp as a tack. Totally conscious and present to this day. She just has an invisible husband." He grinned at Mer's astonished expression. "Gramsy's not ashamed either, let me tell you. She is absolutely in love with her own story and trusts herself with complete conviction. Growing up, we were kind of like *The Addams Family*, you know? Anything was possible."

An extraordinary response to an ordinary question. An answer a magician would give.

Doug drove away at midnight in a white VW notchback. From her window, Mer watched the taillights shrink, then flare, before vanishing around a corner. They had agreed that she would visit him at his warehouse the next day for her Berkeley Psychic Institute–style aura reading. She lay awake for hours after he was gone, replaying the evening.

Meridy's footsteps boomed through the barnlike warehouse at 3117 Twentieth Street. Its floors were of rough, unvarnished wood and its ceiling soared high overhead. Skylights flooded the space with natural light. Freestanding walls, half-built rooms, and makeshift partitions, art everywhere. Doug showed her his visionary artwork — the large triptych Barb had described and a series of mandalas. His use of vivid color turned her on more than anything else.

In an open central space, Doug set up two chairs facing each other and directed her to sit, legs uncrossed, hands on knees. He closed his pale-blue eyes. "I want you to ground yourself," he said. "Envision a blue cord running the length of your spine down through the floor and the building's foundation into the earth itself. Plug yourself into the source." He took long breaths through his nose, his features slackening.

Doug in trance.

Moments passed. A truck backfired outside. Then Doug extended the fingers of one hand toward Meridy's lap. "This is the
root chakra that connects you to Mother Earth. If anyone has
hooked a cord into your root chakra, we're going to detach it right
now and send them on their way." He flicked his wrist to the right,
and Mer felt a lightness through her lower torso and groin. He
moved up through the seven chakras, cleaning each one in turn.
As he went, he mentioned images and feelings he found there. At
one point, he smiled slightly. "I'm getting a clear picture of Shirley
Temple," he said. "A pudgy little girl in tap shoes trying to win the
world over with a giggle."

Mer had indeed looked like a brunette version of Shirley Temple as a kid. She'd taken tap lessons throughout her childhood, and
she still saw herself that way—as a beaming, curly-haired stage
hog dancing up a storm to make the City smile. He couldn't have
known her that well, and yet he did.

Doug had seen through the adult mask to the child she still was inside. The reading left Mer's brain buzzing, a vibration around her third eye so intense it was slightly painful. Like coming down from an acid trip. She felt spacey and exhausted, but wide open.

She expected Doug to ask her on a real date. Now that they'd plumbed the depths, they could take a step back and have a little fun along with the intensity. She was ready to enjoy this guy.

But if Doug's finest characteristics were on display in those first interactions, his worst were not far behind. Apropos of nothing, he said, "You know, Meridy, I was going to ask you on a date. But I'm going to have to reconsider. You're holding on to too much, and it shows. You need to lose the weight."

"You know your father," my mom says, decades later. "Mr. Tactful."

It's true: my dad is infamous among our family and friends for making biting, off-the-cuff observations.

"How did you respond?" I ask.

"I was stunned. Hurt. After someone reads your aura, you're very vulnerable. I left quickly."

Doug doesn't remember making this comment at all. Nor does he remember *not* making it. This isn't unusual for him. My dad's memory has gaps, some quite large. My family's version of *he said, she said* arguments would be *she said; he doesn't remember.*

My mom's version prevails, though it bears mentioning that it's not the only possibility.

At five feet five and around 150 pounds, Mer was a little plump, as she'd been since childhood. She dieted, did cleanses, took dance classes, overate, dieted again. Even her skinniest wasn't *skinny*. She'd never have a Julie Christie figure. *If that's what Doug wants*, she thought, *we have no business dating*. Another rejection for the compost heap. But this one stung more than usual because everything else had felt so right.

No time to mope. With Thanksgiving coming up, advance orders for brownies were rolling in. Sticky Fingers kept Mer busy, but it didn't stop her from obsessing. She vented her outrage to Barb and Donald — sucking up all the air while the three of them wrapped brownies together. At night, she lay awake in bed, thinking up comebacks. Mentally, she gave him a whole different type of reading. She told herself she didn't want to see him again. But she couldn't leave well enough alone.

After days of stewing, she settled on a comeback she liked and wrote it on a scrap of paper: *Shirley Temple didn't become Shirley Temple Black for nothing. 'Twasn't necessary to shoot.*

Cryptic. Give him something to chew on since he was such a smart-ass. She found his car parked near his warehouse in the Mission and tucked the note under his windshield wiper.

She had meant this to be the last word between them, but a few days later, Doug called. With no mention of the note or the rude comment he'd made, he asked her out to dinner. In spite of herself, Mer didn't turn him down.

They sat in the window seat of an inexpensive Chinese restaurant. Mer felt fidgety under Doug's iceberg eyes. Beautiful, ethereal eyes, somehow distant. Mer ate what was on her plate — *Slowly, don't be a piggy* — but didn't take the second serving she wanted and toyed with the soy sauce and chili bottles instead as he gobbled the rest of the chicken lo mein.

They'd shared a brownie and a little coke before dinner, which made them both talkative. Mer told Doug about her travels in Europe and Morocco, how she'd nearly married a Berber. She talked about her father, the teddy-bear tough guy, her idol. She spun a yarn about narrowly escaping a gang bang in Florida, turning it into an adventure story, a laugh riot.

Doug deepened his own history in response. He came from a long line of intense female artists — his mother, grandmother, aunt, and great-aunt. His father, a brilliant navy engineer who'd taught at MIT, had died in a freak drowning accident on a salvage dive at Pearl Harbor. Doug was only five.

"I grew up fatherless," he said, "surrounded by strong women, with no men anywhere around. Sometimes I don't know how a man is supposed to act. I don't always say the right thing. You might have noticed that."

Not an apology, exactly, but Mer decided it was an attempt at one.

After his father's death, Doug's mother took her sons to England, where she suffered a nervous breakdown that kept her bedridden for most of a year. Unable to care for Doug and his older brother, she sent them to boarding school. "Let me tell you," Doug said. "That place was cold on every level." Holmewood House was a hulking, castlelike stone structure originally occupied by Queen Victoria's gynecologist. Since Doug and his brother were in different grades, they rarely interacted. Between his father's death, his mother's collapse, and this final separation from his older brother, Doug's childhood had been overwhelmingly lonesome.

Mer felt herself softening. Wasn't everyone a little broken? Weren't they all doing the best they could?

Art had been Doug's refuge. "All the other boys would be out playing sports, which I never, ever did, and I'd be in the art department on my lunch break."

Mer wasn't a loner like Doug, but art had been her way of escaping her mother's meanness. She'd lock herself in her bedroom and draw for hours.

Eventually, Doug had entered a fine arts program at UC Berkeley with a full scholarship. But he dropped out in 1975, months before he would've graduated. "I had this painting teacher who was all about modernism and understatement," he said. "He didn't get my work. And you know what? Fuck that. I went to the Berkeley Psychic Institute instead."

An uncompromising artist. Finally.

———

"The first week I spent with your mother," my dad says, looking back, "I did greater quantities of more kinds of drugs than I had done in my entire life up to that point. I remember coming to a point — maybe we were experimenting with brownies or something — of lying on the kitchen floor. I was totally wiped out, totally unable to stand. All I could do was lie there on the linoleum. And I was laughing, rolling on the ground and laughing with total abandon."

They had gotten off to a rocky start, but my parents found a lot of common ground. They were both bright, sensitive, and creative, rollicking full throttle through their lives. Maybe they were too similar. As artists, they would become natural rivals, mutually inspiring but also resentful of each other's accomplishments.

The seeds of destruction nestled inside love's first bloom.

After dinner at the Chinese restaurant, they went back to Meridy's flat in the Haight and had sex for the first time. It was awkward, eager, intense. They fell asleep lying side by side in guttering candlelight, the room wreathed in incense.

Mer awoke in the lightless early morning with her bed violently shaking.

"Earthquake!" she gasped, sitting bolt upright.

But the room was still. Nothing rattled; nothing toppled. Doug thrashed beside her under the blankets.

"Hey — hey, Doug!" She nudged his shoulder and found it slick with sweat. Grabbing his bicep, she tried to squeeze him awake. He made gurgling sounds, then stilled.

Was he having some kind of overdose? She flicked on her light, ready to call an ambulance, and there was Doug, expression placid, his breathing regular. She watched him swallow, his Adam's apple sliding up his throat and back down. Sleeping like an angel.

"Hey, Doug, you okay?"

He murmured and rolled away toward the wall. She watched

him for a while, then clicked the light back off and pulled the covers up to her chin. The sheets were soaked with cooling sweat. She didn't sleep again until sunrise.

Over coffee that morning, Meridy waited for Doug to mention something — anything — about the night before, but he seemed mysteriously detached. He sat at the kitchen table flipping through a book of Aubrey Beardsley prints. Mer's attempts at conversation fell flat. *Typical,* she thought. *Wham, bam, freak out in your bed, thank you, ma'am.*

Donald padded into the kitchen for his morning coffee. Seeing Doug there, he smiled knowingly. "Good morning, you two. Nice night?"

Mer narrowed her eyes at Donald. He pursed his lips and took his mug to his room.

"So . . ." Mer ventured. "You slept really rough. You were kind of kicking in your sleep. Did you have a bad dream?"

Doug didn't respond at all, apparently too absorbed in the book.

"Hey, hello there, Doug." His eyes snapped into focus. "You were kicking in your sleep. Seemed like you had a bad dream. Is everything okay?"

"I'm fine," he said with complete nonchalance. "No dreams I remember."

Men could be so damned cold. The night suddenly seemed like a mistake.

But Doug warmed up after coffee and a joint. As he prepared to leave midmorning, he planted a sweet-enough kiss on Mer's lips to make her feel floaty throughout the day.

Not until late afternoon, when the smell set in, did she realize that he had urinated in her bed.

A zillion
and one
raindrops

-Sticky Fingers Brownies-

A Zillion and One Raindrops

The holiday season of 1976 looms large in Sticky Fingers lore. The story revolves around a defunct department store called Ransohoff's near Union Square. Since opening in 1929, Ransohoff's had been a source for upscale women's fashion in the tradition of I. Magnin. Models walked the showroom floor in outfits clients could purchase with a flick of the wrist. In Alfred Hitchcock's *Vertigo,* this is where Jimmy Stewart drags Kim Novak to clothe her in the image of his presumed-dead love. The grand old store failed in 1976 after "losing piles of money" to the recession, the owner told reporters.

Soon after Thanksgiving, the Street Artists Guild pooled resources to lease the empty space for an indoor artisan fair. The elegant gilded fixtures were still in place. An open showroom floor led to a dramatic staircase that circulated through multiple balcony levels. The ceiling soared high overhead.

Through the month of December, showcases that had held perfume and opera gloves now carried handmade moccasins and mosaic boxes. Shoppers who'd likely come to Union Square for its department stores and designer boutiques were lured inside for something completely different.

The economy was improving by 1976, but shoppers still felt the pinch, and it was a drought year. Tight and dry. Whether because money went further on handmade trinkets than on pricier consumer goods, or because the hippie ethos held sway, or because the environmental movement was steering people away from mass-produced goods — the street artists had a boom season in the old department store.

Sticky Fingers did, too.

On the wharf, the street artists were always glad to see the Brownie Lady, but at Ransohoff's, they seemed downright jubilant. There was nowhere to smoke a joint on Union Square — security guards and cops everywhere — and Mer offered an alternative.

The mobile bakery had been going since July. Mer, Barb, and Donald were each earning several hundred bucks per week. It was enough to pay rent, buy pot for smoking and cooking, and other drugs for snorting and swallowing. It kept the telephone on. But Mer thought there was untapped potential.

In the parched days of early December, something began to gnaw at her. A dry ache, almost a thirst. It built slowly through the month.

Barb's dad picked up on the potential from all the way in Milwaukee. "Your mom and I have been talking," he told her on the phone. "We want to invest in your bakery. Help you get this off the ground."

"Invest?"

"Yeah," he said. "Find yourself a storefront with a nice kitchen, and we'll loan you enough to get in the door. Look, Barbara, I know you're working hard out there. It's tough to launch a business without seed money."

Barb planted her forehead in her palm. She'd always been close to her dad. Henry Harry Hartman — most people called him Hank — was a well digger who'd started his own company and worked two jobs throughout much of Barb's childhood. Of the nine kids, Barb had always suspected she was his favorite, the first of the Hartman girls to break the Milwaukee-housewife mold and strike out on her own.

Naturally, Barb hadn't told him that the bakery's most popular product couldn't be sold in a storefront.

She offered various reasons for turning the loan down, but Hank kept bringing it up.

In truth, Barb liked the idea of a charming neighborhood bakeshop. Mer dismissed it without a moment's thought. Though Barb hadn't expected her to go for something so traditional, the response still stung.

Why couldn't they have a sweet little bakery? Why did it have to be weed?

Doug squinted at Mer through the bottom of his water glass, an imitation of Inspector Clouseau.

Mer smiled. They'd seen *The Pink Panther Strikes Again* at the Roxie, then stopped for a coffee at a corner café.

"I had a great time with you the other night," he said with an easy smile.

Mer noticed his slight overbite for the first time. Long dimples puckered the edges of his beard and mustache. Handsome, unusual.

Mer had been a little surprised to hear from him again, thinking he might be embarrassed. She kept expecting him to allude to it, but he acted as if nothing had happened — like he hadn't wet her bed. Was it possible that he hadn't noticed? Was he hoping that maybe she hadn't?

Their conversation meandered. Then Doug mentioned, as if it was an afterthought, that he was epileptic. "You should know in case it happens when you're around," he said. "It's no big deal, but if you see me fall down or if I start seizing in bed, roll me onto my side so I don't choke on my tongue. It'll pass on its own."

The mystery unraveled. "I think you maybe had a seizure when you slept over. You were thrashing, and you . . ."

"What?"

"Well, you kind of had an . . . accident."

Doug blushed deeply. "That happens very occasionally. I'm not always aware of it."

"Actually," Mer said, pitching her voice low for comic effect. "I thought it was kinda sexy."

They laughed and moved on.

And it was attractive in an odd way; it made him vulnerable. Meridy let her guard down and Doug eased into her life.

In those first weeks, she learned several intriguing things. That he was a soulful, groovy dancer. That he was usually broke. That he'd let her pay for their dates but might sulk about it afterward. That he sometimes put random objects on his head to be silly. That he trusted his spiritual wisdom above all else. That he believed an environmental apocalypse was coming and that hundreds of thousands of people were going to die in floods, fires, and earthquakes. That he could make her feel beautiful and ugly in the same breath. And that once she'd invited him into her mind she didn't want to let him out.

Finally, she learned about the spirit-child.

They were eating at a cheap Italian place, the kind where "That's Amore" plays on an infinite loop. Doug had been pensive for several minutes when he put his fork down midbite and said, "Meridy, I have to tell you something."

Mer braced herself for the big bummer: he would feed her a line and bail out just when things were getting good.

"I'm carrying a child."

Mer chuckled, relieved. It was just his quirky sense of humor. But Doug's pale eyes were unwavering. "I had a reading with a friend from the psychic institute the other day," he said. "Though I really didn't need her to tell me. This is something I've been aware of for a while. There's a being traveling with me, a little boy who kind of floats along wherever I go. And he's eager to be born into the here and now."

Releasing his gaze, Mer extracted a cigarette from her purse and fished for a lighter.

"Now I don't know when it's going to happen, or who is supposed to bring this child into the world with me," Doug continued. "I'm not saying it's you. I only know that this spirit is waiting for me to get my act together so he can come through."

Mer exhaled a stream of smoke and waited for the calm to descend. What could she say to that?

Doug frowned; he clearly didn't like tobacco. "Anyway," he said. "I thought you should know."

Mer spent the night at his warehouse, but she couldn't focus on sex and couldn't relax afterward. She lay fretting in the dark, staring into the void between Doug's bed and the skylights high overhead. She could hear his roommates breathing at the other end of the warehouse, their nighttime noises unobstructed by walls or ceilings.

So Doug's seed needed soil. Fine. But Mer didn't see herself as mother material. A woman's maternal clock was supposed to be loud at twenty-nine; she hadn't heard it tick yet. Crying babies grated on her nerves. She couldn't picture bending her lifestyle around a child. She had paintings to paint, a business to run. Yet here was a guy, finally, who matched her intensity. She wasn't ready to give him up. It hadn't been an easy beginning, but now they seemed to be rolling on twin tracks.

Doug was dangerous and mystical. Capable of surprise.

Magician indeed.

At Ransohoff's, the magic was getting out of hand.

Demand climbed through the holidays, sending the Sticky Fingers crew into overdrive. Barb spent long nights in the kitchen. Donald wrapped the products, made shopping trips on his skateboard, and sometimes traveled downtown to refresh Mer's supply. And Mer was selling, selling, selling. Every load they brought to

Ransohoff's sold out. The only limitations seemed to be the speed with which Barb could bake and the amount of product Mer could schlep.

Serving brownies as refreshment at parties had come into vogue that season. Some customers wanted five dozen, ten dozen, twenty dozen. Mer had to haul those big orders in grocery bags — separate from her basket of breads and such, her cooler of Fantasy Fudge, and the Guatemalan pouch of single brownies over her shoulder.

Barb joked that she should load Boogie with product and use him for a pack mule. Which didn't seem like a half-bad idea except that Boogie would probably disappear with the drugs.

All of Barb's baked treats were popular, but nothing sold like the brownies. People clamored for them. The other products started to feel like a burden to Mer. Fantasy Fudge was a pain in the ass. It had to be kept cold or it turned into goop — hence the cooler she was lugging to Ransohoff's. The "straight" goods in Mer's basket provided good cover because they looked so innocent — but one could only charge so much for products that didn't have the magic ingredient. And Barb spent a lot of her time trying new recipes every week.

Barb's oven had capacity for four nine-by-thirteen-inch pans, each of which held two dozen brownies. Each batch had to cool for about forty-five minutes before the brownies could be wrapped. *If we streamlined*, Mer thought, *we could keep the brownies going all day*. Why drag those extra products around? Why squander valuable time on cinnamon buns?

One night in mid-December, Mer opened her *I Ching* to weigh some ideas. The results were unequivocal. The dead weight had to go.

"I can't believe you're even considering this, Mer." Barb's voice crackled through a bad line. Her Wisconsin accent grew sharper when she was annoyed, clipped and nasal.

"All I'm saying is we should give customers what they want. People are into having a good time."

"Well, some people really appreciate my breads and stuff, you know, so I don't think that's correct. I'm the one baking. I should have some say."

Crackle, hiss.

"We could double our cash if you'd go with the flow."

"Mer, if we stop doing breads and stuff — and you know that's what I really enjoy making —"

"I know, but —"

"Then we're just dealers. We might as well stand out on the corner, like, *Hey, man, wanna buy some weed?*"

"The hexagrams were so clear, Barb. It was Abundance changing to Possession in Great Measure. I mean, how great is that?"

"You know what, Meridy? If you're coming from a selfish place in your heart, a place of greed, your hexagrams are going to reflect that. Just because the *I Ching* says it's favorable doesn't mean it's karmically okay."

"That's not fair."

"I believe you get back what you put into the universe. You know, a few pot brownies mixed in with a bunch of regular-type stuff in the basket is no big whoop. No one's going to get in trouble for that. But you're talking about a big fat dope show."

"Wait, is this about your dad wanting to invest?"

There was a long staticky silence. When Barb spoke again, her voice was low. "I think I'd better throw some hexagrams of my own."

"Barb, come on —"

Click.

Mer slammed the receiver into the cradle, picked it up, slammed it again. She knew she went overboard sometimes. That was her Sagittarius rising, always aiming for the stars. Barb thought she was after money — but that wasn't it, not really. It was more about feeling alive, tasting the fullness of experience. If Barb wanted to open a little bakery with frilly curtains, fine. It just seemed . . . dull. Here they had a product that was so hot that they couldn't crank the brownies out fast enough. And Barb was digging her heels in over cranberry bread?

When Barb was truly furious, she didn't debate, return phone calls, or answer letters. She disappeared, as if swallowed by a massive fogbank. *She'll come around*, Mer thought, but days passed without a word.

Fog moves in peculiar patterns in San Francisco. The Golden Gate forms the only sea-level break in the spine of hills running the length of the California coast. Winds from three directions can't resist ducking into that gap and dragging fog in with them. As much as a million gallons of airborne water *per hour* might cross the Golden Gate to linger over the City. In a lengthy friendship like Mer and Barb's, an occasional rupture was fog over the bridge; it would eventually pass. Mer had known Barb long enough to expect the silent treatment, but that didn't make it easier.

Christmas weekend approached. With the holiday falling on Saturday, Mer had planned to do her run on Friday. They had advance orders — and no baker.

Wednesday morning, Donald leaned in the doorway of Mer's bedroom. "Still no Barb?"

Mer shook her head. She'd been awake half the night.

"Make some calls," Donald said. "Get us a gram of blow. We'll stay up and bake."

"Do you know Barb's recipe? It's all different."

He shrugged. "More or less." He started down the hall, then popped his head back in. "But I'm not doing *all* the baking. You're going to have to get your hands dirty, darling."

Words of doom.

An hour later, coked to the gills, Mer stood in the kitchen with Donald, sweating through her T-shirt. She had unearthed the

Rainbow Lady's old recipe for ganja brownies and read and reread it until the handwriting looked like a foreign language.

She stared blankly at a set of measuring spoons. "I'm supposed to use the t-s-p. Which one is that?"

"You mean the teaspoon?" Donald said.

"I guess."

"It's engraved on the handles."

"Oh."

Mer agonized through every step — cracking eggs (fishing the shells out), measuring sugar (spilling it everywhere), melting bitter chocolate (burning the first round), mixing ingredients (splattering the wall). She and Donald alternately bickered and cracked each other up. They ended up with several batches of mostly edible brownies — but there weren't nearly enough and they weren't very good.

Thursday morning, Barb finally phoned

In a "you're still in trouble with me" tone of voice, she said she'd already started baking that morning — just brownies, like Mer wanted — though she made it clear that she wasn't thrilled about it.

"Oh, thank God," Mer said. "I was so desperate I started baking."

"You did *what?*"

Christmas Eve day dawned sunny and cool. To get in the holiday spirit, Meridy — who was raised Jewish and had never celebrated Christmas — wore a red velvet jacket from the 1940s, her sterling-silver housefly pinned to the lapel, and her mother's ocelot dress hat cocked at an angle. She carried a grocery bag stocked with 384 brownies, each swaddled tightly in cellophane, and two Guatemalan bags of brownies, one over each shoulder. She had a cocaine buzz spinning behind her eyes and her own brownie trip was going full bore. The season was climaxing, and Mer cradled in her arms something everyone seemed to want: a good time.

She propped the grocery bag on one hip and pulled open the golden door of the old Ransohoff's. The place was packed, the holiday crowd stewing in its own stress, shoppers looking for last-ditch purchases. For the street artists, this was the big day, their chance to save for the postseason slump. Most were putting in twelve to fourteen hours at a stretch — a captive audience. Their relief came in brownie form.

A mighty Christmas tree stood in the center of the main floor, its arms bristling past two levels. Mer maneuvered through the throng to a display case housing stained glass window ornaments. The guy who made them, Tom, was usually easygoing, but today he looked as stiff as a holiday nutcracker.

"Hey, what's the word?" Mer said.

Breaking into a gap-toothed smile, Tom extended his arms as if to hug Mer over the display case, then he turned toward the balconies. "She's here!" he hollered. "Merry Christmas, folks — the Brownie Lady's here!"

"All right!" someone called back from the second floor.

"She's heeere!" sang a sonorous voice upstairs.

The clapping began somewhere nearby and spread, clattering up and down the levels — unwelcome attention for someone carrying hundreds of illegal brownies. Even shoppers joined in, looking bewildered. Suddenly claustrophobic, Mer wished for the anonymity of the open sidewalk. The room seemed to tilt. She set her bags on the glass counter and tried to breathe.

"You okay?" Tom said. "Need to sit down?"

Relax, she told herself. *They're just a little enthusiastic.*

She offered a smile. "I guess this is how it feels to play Carnegie Hall."

That big load of brownies sold out before Mer could get off the first floor. She dodged traffic to a pay phone across the street from Ransohoff's and called home to arrange a rendezvous as soon as Barb and Donald could get the next round baked and wrapped.

While waiting to restock, Mer milled around, browsing the booths. She arranged a trade for a pair of earrings to give Barb and wrote down another large order of brownies for an upcoming New Year's Eve party. Crashing from the coke and a string of sleepless nights, Mer rested on a bench that faced the giant Christmas tree casting its heady fragrance throughout the room. Its shape called to mind a mastodon green bud, like the fine sinsemilla the Humboldt women were producing with their powerhouse female plants.

The inspiration that had been tugging at her all month gave a yank she couldn't ignore. Sticky Fingers Brownies was going to unfurl, plantlike, beyond this community of craftspeople into the city at large. She would sell to waiters and clothiers and hairdressers and dentists and bartenders and go-go dancers and goddamn real estate agents! The business was a mere seedling now. It *had* to grow — to vegetate, to flower; that was its nature. What they needed wasn't a little storefront where they could set down roots but the opposite of that: a bigger garden. They had to become *more* mobile.

The key, Mer saw clearly, was to meet clients in their places of business. When did people most want to get high? When they were looking at eight hours on the clock! She'd cater to working stiffs and slide invisibly into the City's machinery to grease its cogs.

Sticky Fingers Brownies would stone the labor market.

Mer slipped into the bathroom and entered a stall. She rested her purse on the back of the toilet, fished around in its pockets, extracted a miniature origami envelope, and unfolded it: the last of the blow from their baking frenzy. She heard the bathroom door creak open and a pair of high heels clack into the next stall. With her house key, Mer scooped up a tiny mound of finely chopped powder. When her neighbor flushed, Mer sniffed the snowcap up her nose. As the lady washed her hands, Mer fed the other nostril.

Mer exited the bathroom ebullient, gratitude surging. With no one to express it to, she edged over to the big tree. "Thanks," she whispered. "And a very merry Christmas to you." She grasped a branch and shook it, sending jitters through the ornaments.

Hank Hartman kept pushing his daughter to accept his loan. He was so earnest about helping that Barb felt guilty. She booked a flight home right after Christmas. It was time to come clean. Her dad had known for years that she smoked marijuana, but what would he think of her cooking with it for profit?

As it turned out, Hank thought it was hilarious.

He dropped the investment idea and warned Barb to be cautious, but he didn't seem angry. Barb suspected that he admired her moxie.

On December 29, 1976, clouds gathered over the City. Throughout the Bay Area, eyes turned upward toward the sky's gray underbelly. Prayers were said, fingers crossed. Forty-six dry winter days had passed since the area's last rainfall. By year's end, according to the *San Francisco Chronicle*, the drought had cost California farmers an estimated $510 million. The governor had declared twenty-nine counties disaster areas. The cloud mass shifted throughout the day. Early evening, with a gallop of thunder, the first drops appeared on windshields, pale sidewalks, dusty fire roads, and desiccated fields. The deluge that followed flooded gutters.

Mer unearthed an umbrella from deep in her closet and headed outside to gulp lungfuls of petrichor — the smell of fresh rain after a dry spell, her favorite scent. Droplets feathered off the edges of her umbrella. She strolled the Haight throughout the evening, finding excuses to stay out and enjoy the streets washed clean.

Though no one knew it, the drought was far from over; 1977 would be the driest year recorded in California up to that point. But on December 29, and throughout the coming weeks, the sky released a long, wet sigh.

It had been a momentous year. Mer had glimpsed herself as a

celebrity outlaw with a magician by her side. She imagined the two of them painting and healing people with their hippie witchcraft during the week. On weekends, Mer would play the good criminal, the beloved scofflaw. Getting one over on the squares, the rule makers, the money hoarders, the warmongers — the Patrolman Buxbaums of the world.

At the end of 1976, my mom imagined herself rising on a gleaming ocean swell.

The problem with waves, of course, is that they crash.

In the movies, drug dealers — and women who snort coke in bathrooms — end up either in prison or rehab or dead. That's Hollywood.

But this is San Francisco, and real life is much more complicated. The wave my mom was riding wouldn't crash for a while. Maybe the whole city was on that wave. It was still amassing power in late 1976. No reason to worry about inevitable crashes. Not yet.

THE AMOUNT OF PERSONAL POWER THAT ONE HAS AT HAND IS DEFINED BY THE LIMITATIONS THAT ONE PLACES ON ONE'S SELF

The Power at Hand

After the big season at Ransohoff's, Meridy was ready to cut loose. She wanted to ring in 1977 with romance, so she invited Doug on an escapade. They wound down Highway 1 to Big Sur, where majestic redwood forests met the Pacific and waves hurled themselves against rugged cliffs. Mer rented a rustic cabin near the coast. Barb was still visiting family in Milwaukee, so Boogie came along for the ride.

On New Year's Eve, a powerful storm blew in off the ocean. Rain pummeled the roof. There was the loamy aroma of redwood mulch and mud. A fire crackled in the woodstove. The elements converged.

It was here that Doug and Mer first professed their love.

They sat facing each other in straight-backed chairs. Knees touching. Eyes closed. Holding hands. Doug guided them through a visualization to remove the psychic hooks sunk into their chakras by ex-lovers, needy friends, parental trips, and societal expectations. Cleansed, impurities shed, they aligned their intentions.

To love each other. To learn from each other. To be king and queen of their shared space. To promote peace and healing and enlightenment with their words and their work.

"Now picture a perfect red rose," Doug said. "Spread the petals of this rose open and place all of your desires and intentions inside. Allow the petals to close so the rose holds everything you want from the new year. Ready?"

"Ready."

"You sure?" Mer could hear him smile around the words.

"Absolutely."

"Then blast that rose into smithereens!"

"Give it up and you get it all," Mer said.

The next day, they ate mushrooms and tripped out on each other, on their melding minds and melting skin, on roaring oceans of love and the infinite white sky.

They shot their first roll of film together that weekend. My mom wears a blue flannel shirt, jeans tucked into leather boots laced up to the knee, and a come-hither look on her face. Her curls are springy in the Pacific wind. In one photo, she's draped kelp around her neck like a feather boa and appears to be doing a shroomy dance routine. My dad, wearing his leather cowboy hat and tight jeans, hunches in front of a massive redwood with his fingers drawn like pistols. Their eyes are like pinwheels. Boogie wanders through the pictures, drenched, a long-legged mop, looking happy and a little mystified by the humans.

In a series snapped during a downpour, Mer, wearing a floppy fisherman's hat and a plastic poncho, poses beside a road sign that reads IMPASSABLE IN WET WEATHER. She's pink with laughter.

I can just hear my dad saying, "Dahling, you're impahssible in wet weather!" in an exaggerated English accent.

And how my mom would give it a raunchy spin: "Baby, I'm just impossibly wet."

Sometime during this adventure, my dad had a vision. Neither he nor Mer remembers the circumstances — whether he walked off alone to meditate while my mom drew, if it zapped into his mind out of nowhere or bloomed into a dream. He saw a man standing with his arms wrapped around a woman who cradled a blond baby boy. The infant clasped the world in his pudgy little hands. Glorious light beamed from the baby into the surrounding darkness: the spirit-child.

———

Doug was the kind of guy who'd trap a near stranger in his gaze and ask, dead serious, "So what is your purpose on this planet?" He was a seeker — the subcategory of hippie obsessed with spirituality. This would not turn out to be a phase for Doug but an enduring and defining characteristic of his personality.

Summer of 1971, when Doug was seventeen, he hitchhiked to Quebec — a last hurrah before beginning classes at UC Berkeley that fall. Having spent time in France as a preteen, he enjoyed this chance to use the language again. Somewhere on the Trans-Canada Highway, he climbed into a VW bus with a half-dozen longhairs. They smoked rubbery joints and gnawed magic mushrooms, while magnificent woods scrolled by outside the dingy bus windows.

The group stopped at a cool bottle-green river surrounded by high canyon walls. A girl from the van shed her skirts and stretched out naked on a rock slab, basking like a snake. She and Doug had stared into each other's eyes on the ride up. He wanted to impress her.

Doug climbed to a jutting ledge twenty-five feet above the river. Nearby rapids drowned his companions' voices and shushed the birds and insects. The sky was a devastation of blue. Gripping the edge with his toes, Doug squinted through the water's surface for submerged boulders. It was a long way down. His blood sang in his skull and his gut ached from the psilocybin. A droplet of sweat tickled a path down his back.

A voice inside whispered. He didn't listen.

Doug sprang into a sleek dive. Not even an illusion of flying, only plummeting. The surface broke with the sound of shattering glass, and there was a blast of wonder, a million cool tongues on his skin.

Then his head smacked the shallow riverbed, and he was lost.

When he crawled out of the water, his head was cocked at a forty-five-degree angle. He couldn't straighten it. The pain wasn't terrible once the dizziness passed, but his companions panicked and left him outside a doctor's office in the nearest mountain village. Doug thought the country doctor seemed at a loss; after a cursory examination, Doug was sent on his way with a fistful of anti-inflammatories. He began hitchhiking toward his aunt's home in Chicago for help. Then he met a guy who was heading to an ashram near the border. Doug had never seen one before; Chicago, he decided, could wait.

The ashram consisted of a large Victorian farmhouse and various outbuildings on a stretch of wild land. No heat or flushing toilets, but there was a fresh spring nearby. The communards raised animals and grew their own food in a vast garden. Everyone was expected to contribute. Doug, whose neck was still crooked, couldn't do heavy labor with the other men, so they asked him to stay behind and paint a dingy outhouse white. It was an unpleasant job, but Doug saw it as an opportunity to work out some karma.

He would've liked to stay, but he got caught fooling around with a girl — verboten at this ashram. Four guys surrounded him and strongly suggested that he leave to get medical attention. As one man put it, "Go get your head on straight."

Doug returned to the road, made his way to Chicago, then took a bus to Berkeley to begin school. His neck eventually healed.

Months later, he was working on a drawing assignment at his drafting table when he felt intense pressure from above that knocked him off his stool. The floor and ceiling seemed to squeeze him like a vise. Carpet fibers burrowed into his cheek. Doug saw his futon mattress nearby, though it looked to him like negative space, an empty grave. He dragged himself toward it, then tumbled into bottomless darkness.

It was his first epileptic seizure.

The attacks that followed were different. They began with multicolored lights floating into his peripheral vision, kaleidoscopic orbs of gold and violet and luscious green that looked like mandalas. Doug felt an overpowering attraction to the lights, but the moment he tried to look at them directly, he seized, and everything went black until he regained consciousness. The attacks varied in intensity. His petit mal seizures were brief lapses that could go unnoticed in company, like a stylus skipping over a scratch on a record. Grand mal whoppers laid him flat about once a month. Recovery could be intense: headaches, nausea, vomiting, confusion, and the looming danger of permanent damage.

But these experiences weren't entirely bad. Waves of ecstasy sometimes accompanied his preseizure auras. These many-hued mandalas manifesting in his peripheral vision before each attack could be incredibly beautiful. Like looking at God.

Doug's doctor prescribed Dilantin, which controlled the attacks but made his gums bleed, and he resented having to take pills all the time. He'd taper off for days or weeks at a stretch, then start up again when the seizures got scary.

Doug's mother, Jan, says he's got his story all mixed up. According to her, the seizures started after a body-surfing accident in the South of France a year or two earlier — another incident in which his head met the ground beneath a body of water at high velocity. Jan's memory is generally sharp; she may be right, though my dad is adamant about his version. Either way, my dad got his bell rung in his late teens, and his brain has periodically shorted out ever since.

The beginning of his epilepsy became one of my dad's origin stories. He doesn't have a ton of them. Decades of seizures and anticonvulsive medications have Swiss-cheesed his memory; entire swaths of history are simply gone. The stories he retains are often those he's told many times, cemented by repetition. His own mythology.

Like my mom's tale about Patrolman Buxbaum, the story might not be 100 percent accurate, but it does reveal some things he believes about himself: That he is damaged. That his life lessons must be painful. That he is touched by God.

A few years after the accident, a friend told Doug about the Berkeley Psychic Institute near the university. The founder and guru of BPI, Reverend Lewis Bostwick, was a robust man in his late fifties with sparkling eyes, a mischievous sense of humor, and a warm, paternal affect. "A psychic," Bostwick said in a 1974 interview with *Psychic Times,* "is a person whose spiritual abilities are out of control and the minute he gets them under control he is no longer psychic; he's a spiritual being." He believed that the surge of energy from an epileptic attack could be harnessed and controlled without medication. "[O]ut of every ten people we get," Bostwick said, "seven of our students are epileptics, or have a history of epilepsy and all of the sudden when we teach them to run the energy correctly, the epilepsy goes away."

Doug's grandmother Paula claimed to be married to a ghost. And his mother Jan had been the research director of a small paranormal society while Doug was in high school. An affinity for the occult ran in the family. Add to that Doug's perennial yearning for a father figure and his frustration with epileptic meds, and you can see how he slipped into Bostwick's orbit. The BPI guru once boasted to the *San Francisco Chronicle* that he could "make a phone call and have 200 psychics here in an hour." In 1975, Doug dropped out of UC Berkeley to become one of them.

As a reverend of the Church of Divine Man, Doug was charged with "spreading the word." In addition to private aura readings and cleanses, he teamed up with two other guys from BPI to offer trio readings for men only. The three male psychics would sit in a row facing their client, go into trance, and telepathically send one another impressions and images. The psychic sitting in the middle would speak, translating the images into words. They called themselves the Triangle, and printed business cards and flyers featuring a logo of triangles within triangles, black on white on black. Doug also taught BPI classes at his warehouse in the Mission.

Bostwick regarded drugs — including marijuana — as a distraction for the evolving psychic, a perceived shortcut that didn't lead to genuine enlightenment.

After meeting Mer, Doug found himself pulled in two directions. His training would suggest disengaging from someone so enamored of indulgence. Doug had always cheated a little on the antidrug policy, but Mer tempted him into daily use. They'd split a magic brownie in the afternoon, then hit the town at night, spending her drug money on dinners and disco dancing — lights swimming across skin gleaming with sweat, the metallic tang of poppers in the air, a cocaine jitter channeled into his pumping hips and shimmying shoulders. Meridy's eyes reflecting strobes of red and indigo. It was not what he had trained for, but it set him free.

Doug didn't have an easy personality, as Mer quickly learned.

He could be giddy and playful, suddenly twirling her into a dip or prancing around with a bell pepper hanging from his ear. He giggled like a child. But he didn't like being bested at anything and sometimes sank into black moods without warning. He seemed to enjoy throwing people off their game. His attention was heavy, his questions exacting to the point of interrogation.

But if you were sick of frivolity, if you sought life's extremes, if you were looking for a magician, Doug hit all the marks. To Meridy, his self-seriousness was alluring, his intensity enchanting, his artistic eye impressive, his spiritual convictions captivating.

She was smitten.

She and Barb both started taking Doug's psychic classes. Mer was learning to see auras — something she'd never been able to do. She loved color more than anything, and when she concentrated and trusted herself, she could now see colors swirling around people as they moved through the world. In figure-drawing sessions at the Art Institute, she replaced her charcoal with bright Conté crayons to capture the hues she'd begun to recognize. This one with cleansing purple, that one with the green of imminent change . . .

Of course, Mer had tricks up her sleeve, too. While Doug schooled her about auras and chakras, she taught him to use the tarot, astrology, and the *I Ching*. They rented side-by-side booths at a psychic fair; Doug read auras and Mer did tarot.

Their skills were complementary in a way that enthralled them both.

In the wet, early weeks of January, Mer implemented her new strategy of selling to people in their workplaces. She started on the wharf, going into touristy shops and galleries along Beach and Francisco streets. Next, she tackled the boutiques of Ghirardelli Square. She thought of it as "breaking in" new businesses, like walking in a stiff pair of shoes until the leather softened. She developed a five-step technique.

Step 1: Case the joint. Mosey in casually, as if by happenstance. Peruse the merchandise while getting a feel for the place. Do they have security? How many people are on staff and which one is in charge? Make small talk with the salesperson. "Wow, you've got fabulous stuff in here! Love the whole wall of scarves. Great colors." Ignore your pounding heart but trust your gut. Don't glance around wide-eyed like a prepubescent shoplifter.

Step 2: Pop the question. "Do you like brownies?" Waggle an eyebrow so they know you're not talking about Sara Lee. If it's a 'no,' exit calmly, making a mental note to steer clear.

Step 3: Drop a sample. "Try one, my treat." Hand it over casually, as if it were a breath mint. Warn them to start with a quarter of a brownie. Then go on your way, all smiles.

Step 4: Make the sale. Stop by again a week later. You'll know immediately if it's a go. Some customers will invite you into a private room. Others will do the deal right at the cash register as you pretend to buy one of those colorful scarves. While you're at it, buy a scarf. You can afford it.

Step 5: Watch it grow. The new client may buy a single brownie, a dozen, or several dozen. They'll come to expect you every Saturday and will have the money ready. They may say, "Pop into the ice cream parlor on the corner. Peter is dying to meet you."

The business spread organically — from Ghirardelli Square to the Cannery and the upper-floor office spaces where desk drones and telephone salespeople were trapped in a workday frame of reference; Meridy could snap them out of that. The ticket taker at the Wax Museum at Fisherman's Wharf always bought a dozen. To do the transaction, he led Mer through a hidden door into a room cluttered with celebrity body parts: Judy Garland's head waiting for repainting, Dolly Parton's chipped little finger.

She learned the landscapes of kitchens and supply closets, and got to know people working behind the scenes — the cooks and dishwashers, the back-of-house managers, the seamstresses and warehousemen. There was something delicious about peering behind the facade of the City, like opening a mechanical clock to see the cogs dance.

Expansion was easy, so she kept going. Mer hired an underemployed musician named Cam Bruce to circle the block with extra brownies in his beater car while she ducked into the cafés, bookstores, and strip clubs of North Beach humming southeast of the wharf: City Lights bookstore, Vesuvio Café, the Savoy Tivoli, and North Beach Leather.

One January afternoon in North Beach, Mer found herself walking past Club Fugazi on Green Street, home to a cabaret called *Beach Blanket Babylon Goes Bananas,* a hot ticket for the past three years. Fugazi was closed, but the door stood ajar, and she heard a singer rehearsing inside. On a whim, she slipped into the dim theater, where a busty brunette was working through a song at the piano. A man sat alone near the entrance. "Can I help you?"

Mer offered him a free brownie in a stage whisper.

"You must be the Brownie Lady!" he cried, not so quietly. "I've heard about you. Sure, I'll try one of your treats."

The following Saturday, he bought two dozen, and introduced her to more cast members, who seemed delighted. It made sense: smoking marijuana could leave singers hoarse, but brownies did no harm. The show was on hiatus, rehearsing acts for the coming season. They gave Mer comp tickets for opening night later that month.

Mer soon turned her attention to the neighborhood surrounding the flat she and Donald shared. She faced unique challenges there. Cops might not expect dealers on Fisherman's Wharf, but the Haight was already an outdoor mall for drugs. Cruising down the sidewalk with a purse full of brownies slung over her shoulder, Mer would hear, "Lids . . . lids . . . lids." People tried to sell her LSD, quaaludes, angel dust, speed, and smack. Rumors abounded of narcs ensconced among the street dealers.

Mer made it her rule not to do business on the street. She focused on people working in boutiques and eateries who might not want to slink to the corner to buy pot. They could get brownies from a clean, good-looking girl who came to them. She'd stop by every Saturday, requiring neither a phone call nor a commitment. Discretion — probably the one angle that hadn't been worked in the Haight — became her calling card.

Among her first Haight-Ashbury customers was Bette Herscowitz at a fabric and art supply store called Mendel's. Mer traded brownies for paint, canvases, and all sorts of fun stuff. Bette liked to keep brownies behind the register to share with friends. As it turned out, she had deep roots in the neighborhood and seemed to know everyone for blocks around.

Mendel Herscowitz, Bette's father, had founded U-Save Paint and Linoleum with his best friend Vic in the 1950s. Mendel was white and Jewish; Vic was black. Interracial partnerships were rare in those days, but Haight-Ashbury had a surging black population (it grew from 4 percent to 30 percent during the 1950s, then to more than 50 percent over the next decade), and U-Save did well catering to local families. In the late 1960s, young white people arrived in droves, displacing some black families that had put down roots. Absentee landlords didn't seem to care how many kids crammed themselves into a commune so long as rent got paid.

The Summer of Love media coverage triggered one of the largest, fastest migrations in American history. Some 100,000 people, many of them teenagers, traveled from all over the world to join the party at Haight-Ashbury. Bette, who was then in her mid-twenties, was struck by how young and ill-prepared the flower children seemed. "A lot of people, I think, assume the hippies were more enlightened than they were," she says, thinking back. "But they were just kids!" Bette was mystified by the tour buses that clogged Haight Street, people leaning out of windows to snap photos of longhairs sitting on the sidewalk. "I'm not sure why it was such a tourist attraction for people to come and see runaway kids," she says.

Traffic got so congested that U-Save's customers could no longer load in front of the store, and the business suffered. Vic and his family moved out of town. But Mendel Herscowitz adapted. He began carrying fluorescent paint that glowed under black light, which Bette describes as "the biggest thing since white bread." When the landlord jacked his rent, Mendel bought a building up the block, added a range of art supplies and fabrics, and renamed it Mendel's. As the only place in that district selling feathers and beading supplies, the store thrived.

By the turn of the decade, the party had crashed. Amphetamines and heroin flooded the neighborhood, bringing hard-core dealers, pimps, and violence. "I would see these sweet little girls come and then transform, and it was a little bit more than they could handle," Bette says. "That always used to make my heart cry." There were gruesome, drug-fueled murders. Historian David Talbot points out that, in 1969, the SFPD reported confiscating more deadly weapons in the Haight than in any other district.

By 1977, when Sticky Fingers rolled in, a new cycle was beginning. People trickled over the hill from the burgeoning gay community in Eureka Valley, inspiring the *Bay Area Reporter* to proclaim Haight-Ashbury "the newest location of the gay population explosion." Neglected Victorians could be bought cheap, beautified, and resold. New businesses catered not only to tourists and broke hippies but also to locals with more money.

Many of Mer's new customers worked at gay-owned bars and restaurants like the Anxious Asp and Mommy Fortuna's. Even the army surplus store was staffed by gay guys — including a soft-spoken Virginia transplant named Bill Pandolf. On his off-hours, Bill liked to hang out at Febe's, a leather bar South of Market famous for being among the first of its ilk. Bill's routine was to buy a few dozen brownies to sell to the bartender, who in turn sold them to patrons. The brownies were becoming a kind of currency.

Another Haight Street stop was Verdi's Pizza, a sit-down restaurant with a walk-up counter for slices to go. Most of the waitstaff bought. The young man who served slices to go at the counter started out buying two or three brownies at a time, but his purchases soon ballooned. Mer rarely asked what customers did with their brownies, but one day, the pizza guy volunteered a surprising tidbit.

"You know who these are for?" he said with a sly smile. "Hongisto."

"*Sheriff* Hongisto?"

The kid shrugged. "He's a friend of the family."

Granted, Richard Hongisto was not your typical sheriff. He was a rabble-rouser. For a week during his first term, he'd shown up to work at city hall wearing tattered inmate clothing to dramatize the poor conditions in county jails. He had appointed San Francisco's first African American undersheriff and was actively trying to recruit gay and lesbian deputies. Hongisto was currently embroiled — alongside Jim Jones and the Peoples Temple — in a fight to halt the eviction of some two hundred people, mostly elderly Filipinos, from the decrepit International Hotel, which a foreign corporation had bought as a tear-down. The sheriff had been charged with contempt of court for refusing to enforce the eviction — for which he would serve five days in his own county jail.

Hongisto was an advocate of drug policy reform, especially with respect to marijuana. He'd even had his badge modified to replace the city seal with a peace symbol. "I'm a liberal," he once said while dining with inmates in jail. "Maybe even a radical."

It wasn't such a stretch to imagine Hongisto's catlike mouth closing around a brownie. But tasking the pizza guy with buying them?

Mer never found out for sure if the Sheriff of San Francisco really was buying her brownies or if it was just a story the kid told. But she let herself savor the notion. Strutting down Haight Street, digging the rhythm of her boot heels on the sidewalk, she put extra swing into her walk.

As the business flourished, tensions mounted between the Sticky Fingers partners.

Donald had expected the workload to lighten after the holiday season. It dipped slightly after New Year's but climbed again with the expanded routes. Donald enjoyed wrapping, which meant shooting the shit with the girls. But preparing the pot — his main responsibility — was dirty, sweaty labor. At this inflated volume, it was just *work*, and it was chafing his nerves.

Then there was the Mer and Doug show.

Donald looked on in dismay while his roommate mooned and sunned and preened and schemed about her new boyfriend. Meridy in love was insufferable. She spent all her time wrapped up in Doug — if not in his company, then obsessing over him. If Doug neglected to phone, she agonized, tossing hexagram after hexagram; when he did call, she recounted the conversation to Donald in exhaustive detail, weighing each word, asking his advice, then arguing if she didn't like what he said. When Donald suggested she slow down, she got defensive.

"You can't stand to see me happy, can you?"

"This is you happy?" he drawled. "Okay, Liz Taylor."

Doors were slammed.

Donald didn't dislike Mer's boyfriend, but an awkwardness hung between them. Doug seemed to get tense whenever Donald walked into the room. And since he was coming over all the time lately, this left Donald feeling uncomfortable in his own home. He'd retire to his bedroom and wait for the lovebirds to go out.

Something was amiss, and Donald had a hunch as to what it might be. His gay antenna tingled whenever that tall cagey hippie came around.

It was merely a suspicion until a friend told Donald about a smutty adventure he'd had at Finnila's Finnish Baths. Finnila's wasn't a hard-core bathhouse like the Slot or the Folsom Street Barracks. It attracted a mixed crowd of mainly three types that Donald had noticed: (1) old Europeans who self-flagellated in the sauna with birch switches, (2) bisexual boys or closet cases cruising while pretending not to cruise, and (3) oblivious breeders. Sex wasn't a given at Finnila's, but when the vibe was right in the men's sauna, something usually happened. The lights would be low, and you'd see vague shapes of people through the volcanic steam. Sweaty. Slippery. Anonymous. Then you'd shower the strangers off and hit the streets refreshed, relaxed, and smelling of organic lemongrass soap.

Donald's friend was going on about a hot guy he'd hooked up with in the sauna. "I kept thinking, *Haven't I met you before?* Didn't hit me until later that he's the dude who always hangs out at your place."

"Doug?"

"Mm-hmm."

Donald shook his head. "Meridy is probably the one taking him there. I guess she doesn't know what it's like on the men's side."

"Are they serious?"

"Deathly."

Far be it from Donald to judge, but he didn't want to see Mer get her heart broken. She acted tough, but she was an old-fashioned romantic whose dreamy notion of forever-after monogamy had gone out of style in the sixties. Donald felt squirmy keeping secrets. But he feared that saying anything would damage their friendship.

Either way, he was screwed.

Donald wasn't going to wait for this to blow up in his face. With cash socked away from the brownies, it was time for a vacation. Mazatlán, maybe. Someplace to wiggle his toes in the sand. Zihuantanejo. Puerto Vallarta. One of those.

Mid-January, Donald announced he was leaving "for a while." He would eventually return to San Francisco but not to Sticky Fingers.

Donald was right about Doug, though my dad wouldn't come out as bisexual for a long time. He'd never gone to a bathhouse until Mer brought him to Finnila's. When he saw guys fooling around in the steam, he felt unable to resist. But Doug's bathhouse jaunts were rare. Deep in the closet and profoundly confused, he sought ways to sublimate his desire.

Consider the Triangle, for example — the trio of male BPI graduates specializing in readings for men that disbanded shortly after Mer came into the picture. One of my dad's partners, Gunter Benz, would later describe it this way: "We did readings at night for men only — in San Francisco. So, you know, we had all kinds of gay guys coming in. There's the three of us, all with the same intensity, reading people who are mostly gay, and it was hilarious! We really got a kick out of it."

I'm not sure what was hilarious about reading gay men. But I don't think my dad knew how to have a male relationship without an orchestrated production. Looking back, he insists that he was only trying to help his clients. Still, prying into their minds probably gave him a glimpse of a lifestyle he lacked the courage to explore. From this distance of years, I feel sorry for my dad — and for the men who looked to the Triangle for guidance and got used in the process.

Late January, when *Beach Blanket Babylon Goes Bananas* opened its new season, Mer took Doug as her date. The loose plot followed a squeaky-voiced Snow White on her search for her Prince Charming. Along the way, she met James Brown (two-foot pompadour), Louis XIV (baby-pink wig whipped into twin beehives that looked like cartoon boobs), an Italian waitress (three-foot-tall pile of spaghetti and meatballs on her head), Carmen Miranda (wearing the whole produce aisle), and Jimmy Carter (dwarfed by his billboard-size grin). In the finale, singer Val Diamond belted out the song "San Francisco," wearing a model of the City's top tourist attractions on a hat two yards wide.

After the show, Mer and Doug strolled along Columbus, past Italian eateries and neon strip clubs with barkers offering two-for-one admission to the girlie shows.

"Walking is free and so are we," said Doug.

They held hands, arms swinging lightly. Mer looked down at Doug's long wizardlike fingers, her long witchy nails. She lifted their interlaced hands. "Lots of potential right here."

She was talking about the art they could make, but Doug seemed to take it differently.

He stopped, faced her. "You know the woman I saw in my vision of the family on New Year's Day? I didn't tell you this part, but she looked like you. She had your hair and your big blue eyes." He smiled. "But like a version of you if you were to slim down."

She slipped her hand out of his, stung. He seemed unaware.

"And that little boy you were holding," he continued. "The most amazingly beautiful pure white light was shooting out of him in all directions. I mean, that child is going to be a healer!"

They paused near the entrance to the Condor strip club. Carol Doda's neon nipples blinked on and off overhead. Mer didn't know what to say. How could he build her up and tear her down at the same time? She was perfect for him, yet not perfect enough.

And a baby right now? She was dealing dope and liking it. Was she supposed to do this with a child strapped to her back in a papoose? She hadn't made her mark as an artist yet. Mer refused to be the woman who forever resented giving up her freedom in order to have kids. Like Florence, her own mother: over-educated, bored, bitter, cruel. Mer was more like her daddy Bill, a wheeler and dealer, a man about town.

She looked down Broadway, past neon signs and hazy street-lamps to the black glass of the bay.

Doug took her hand again, pulling her attention back. "I believe you and I are meant to bring this child into the world."

Mer exhaled slowly. They had been dating less than two months. "I don't know if I'm ready. I want to enjoy *us* for a while."

He kissed her then. Her mind was loud at first but quieted in the moment's flow. She could feel energy sparking where their skin touched.

After Donald left Sticky Fingers, Barb found herself teetering, too.

She had enjoyed paging through her cookbooks for new muffins to try out on the wharf. And early on, when the brownie recipe was still under construction, that had felt creative, too. Her interest in Sticky Fingers had been waning ever since they'd stopped carrying her "straight" baked goods. Every new block Mer broke in meant more identical pans of brownies for Barb.

Melt, measure, mix, bake, repeat.

She was fed up with picking pot leaves out of the dryer filter when she did her laundry. Barb had dope coming out of her ears, literally; cleaning them turned Q-tips green.

When Barb threw a winter party, a bunch of her old theater pals showed up. She hustled between the kitchen and living room, serving trays of homemade hors d'oeuvres and catching up with friends she hadn't seen since quitting *The Wiz*. She'd fallen behind on all the gossip.

"Lucky you're the Brownie Lady now," a makeup-artist friend remarked. "You don't have to deal with actors anymore."

"Oh," Barb said, embarrassed. "I came up with the recipe, but it's not like my main thing."

"False modesty. Your brownies are all the rage."

Meridy and Gunter on a Humboldt buying trip.

Barb wanted to be respected for her professionalism and skill as a costumer — not as everyone's favorite dealer. What if this harmed her career?

She had made marijuana-laced peanut brittle for the party. Everyone got wasted. People passed out on the sofa, even on the floor. Barb awoke the next day in a bleary, hungover panic. The theater community would be abuzz over how fucked-up everyone got at the Brownie Lady's house.

"I want out," she told Mer. "All you do is yak about how we can make this bigger, more customers, more dope —"

"Cha-ching."

"Well, I'm tired of blowing green snot out of my nose. My life has to have more meaning than pot brownies."

"Barb, you know I can't bake!"

"You'll figure something out."

Barb put out feelers. The Local 16 stagehands' union soon came through with a job costuming *The Wonderful World of Burlesque,* a Barry Ashton review on tour from Las Vegas that featured topless showgirls in feather headdresses and beaded corsets. The brownies had been a lark; returning to the theater felt like coming home.

Mer, on the other hand, was just getting started.

PART II

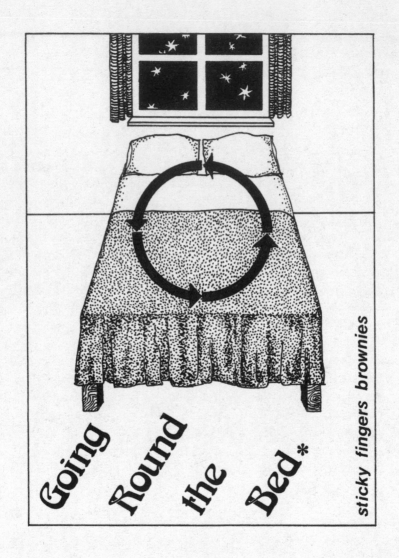

Going Round the Bed*

sticky fingers brownies

8

Going Round the Bed

My mom and I are stretched out on the barge at her current home in Desert Hot Springs, California — a sand-choked suburb beyond the artificial green of the Palm Springs golf courses. She's a full-time artist now, living on the sales of her paintings and commissioned portraits, and teaching art to at-risk youth and wealthy retirees. I've flown down from San Francisco for an art opening at a gallery in the posh part of Palm Springs. At sixty-nine, my mom is still strong, though her lifestyle has taken a toll: diabetes, hepatitis C, high cholesterol. She's waiting for surgery to repair a torn rotator cuff and props herself uncomfortably on pillows piled on the barge.

It's 118 degrees and gusty, so we're hiding indoors. I've dragged a box of memorabilia in from the garage. It holds photos, clippings, and old drawings, a hodgepodge of stuff from various decades. Nothing's labeled, no logic. My mom has always pooh-poohed organization as bourgeois.

I find an envelope postmarked February 1977. It's addressed to Meridy Domnitz c/o her brother in New Jersey, from Douglas Volz in San Francisco.

"What's this?" I ask.

She scrunches her face. "Maybe a love letter."

"You're kidding." I can't bend my father's voice into the shape of a love letter.

"Open it and see."

This is how we are, how we've always been. No secrets from each other.

As I extract the single typed sheet from the envelope, a Polaroid photograph falls onto my lap. A selfie of sorts. My dad stands reflected in a full-length mirror, bulky camera obscuring his face. Stark nude. Enormous pink erection.

I scream, brush the Polaroid off my lap like it's a spider, scream again.

"What is it?" my mom demands.

I hand her the photo. She screams.

My dad sent my mom a dick pic.

I'm simultaneously laughing and crying—in actual hysterics. The letter, single-spaced in a tiny font, covers one full page with scribbles in the margins.

"Read it," she wheezes. "Read it out loud!"

"I need a drink for this." I stagger to the kitchen to pour myself a mostly vodka greyhound. Tumbler in hand, I return to my mom's bedroom, stand at the foot of the barge, and begin.

It's raunchy: seventies porn starring my parents. Choice phrases include "throbbing aching cock," "rod of power," and "drink your love juices." I read the letter in a mechanical monotone while my mom giggles so hard her breath shrinks to a squeak.

"I want to fuck you on the floor of the men's bathroom on the top floor of the Hyatt Regency," I intone. "I want to rape you in the fields of Southern France between the shafts of wheat. Raped by my shaft of heat."

The phrase "I love you" appears fifty-three times.

There are three more letters in the box, all postmarked between January 27 and February 11, 1977. Only the first one is pure smut.

Mostly, they're terribly romantic: "I don't really want to say anything besides the fact that I am beside myself with love for you (interesting picture). I mean, what else matters? You are there (or here), and I am here (or there). There is no space or time."

The letters are also rich with anecdotes from the aura readings my dad was doing, his armchair psychoanalysis of their mutual friends, and highlights from his first week of baking and selling Sticky Fingers brownies.

When Meridy's dad asked her to visit her brother in New Jersey at the end of January 1977, she wanted to say no. The brownie business was in flux and her romance was hitting a new high. Winter would be miserable there.

Mer had never gotten along with her brother, Jeff. Growing up, the more exuberant she became, the more he seemed to withdraw. Jeff excelled in science and math. He married his hometown sweetheart, attended medical school, became a respected dermatologist, and settled in an affluent suburb. Meanwhile, Mer galivanted around Europe, moved to San Francisco, and dealt weed brownies. Mer and Jeff didn't bother with frequent telephone calls or letters. Just fine on separate coasts, thank you.

But with Jeff's wife due to have their third baby, Bill asked Mer to fly out to help look after their other two toddlers during the birth. And she could never refuse her dad.

She set out to talk her boyfriend into handling the brownies while she was away.

Doug hesitated. He didn't mind the idea of baking, and Mer made the sales process sound fun. But he doubted that Reverend Lewis Bostwick would approve of his getting involved. Doug already felt a little lost in Meridy, too easily swept up in her lush pleasures and giddy schemes. On the other hand, he was broke and tired of feeling sheepish when she paid his way.

Mer wheedled. "You're such a *wonderful* cook. I know you'll be great at baking. And selling brownies could be very positive for you as a psychic. You'll meet all kinds of people who need healing."

The weed, she suggested, could carry the word.

Doug felt dubious about it, but he gave in.

In advance of Mer's trip, Barb walked Doug and Cam (the driver who would now help with baking and sales) through the recipe.

Doug was a natural in the kitchen. His mother and grandmother were both superb, butter-heavy cooks, and he'd picked up a knack from them. He liked getting his hands dirty and found satisfaction in ushering raw ingredients into a new form, the end that was greater than the sum of its parts.

The Saturday before Mer left for New Jersey, she brought Doug and Cam along on her runs and introduced them to her regulars. Later, she drew a map of the businesses she'd broken in and made notes for each stop.

- Army-Navy Surplus. Bill, Southern accent. Buys 3–4 doz.
- Mendel's art supply store. Bette, curly blonde hair. Buys 2–3 doz. See if she wants a reading!

She warned the men to be subtle and speak in code — never say outright that they were selling pot brownies. The *I Ching* hexagrams she'd tossed about Doug and Cam doing the runs indicated that doors would open for them. She handed over her notes and left for the East Coast.

Once Doug gave himself permission, his adventurous nature took the reins.

Early in the week, he and Cam each reached out to acquaintances to drum up advance orders. "It's only Thursday and we've already sold 8 dozen plus brownies," he wrote in a letter to Meridy on January 27. "Not bad for a first day of business. Now all we have to do is bake them. Sorry," he added, "that's the last time I'll say 'brownies.' It's just such a strong reality for me right now."

Doug found walking around with a satchel full of contraband surprisingly thrilling. He looked passersby squarely in the eye and thought, *If only you knew what's in my little bag . . .* Approaching people in stores was more awkward; he lacked Meridy's natural social ease and found it hard to talk around things. Most customers were ready for him, so he didn't have to say much, but one clerk in a music store balked. "I don't know what you're talking about."

"Brownies. You know . . . um, Sticky Fingers? The kind that make you feel good?"

"I don't think you should be here."

Doug made an about-face and hit the street again, heart thudding. But most exchanges were pleasant. After walking back to Cam's car twice to restock, Doug decided it was inefficient to carry such small quantities. He could handle more weight if it were well balanced. In the army surplus store, he spotted a rack of olive-green canvas duffel bags. Military grade, durable, voluminous but easy to carry. Mer had encouraged him to do trades with proprietors if he saw things he wanted — "That's part of the fun," she'd said — so he picked up four duffels. At the warehouse later that night, he made a large stencil of the letters *S* and *F* inside a circle and painted them on the army duffels as a gift.

Most nights, he dreamed of Mer. Strange, sexually charged, portentous dreams. Having exposed his heart to this woman, he felt vulnerable now that she was gone. He imagined himself leaking pink light into the atmosphere. Despite physical distance, Doug felt more connected to Meridy than ever, their melded minds seeming to stretch like taffy over the land between them.

He wanted to keep her closer. The roommate situation at the warehouse had been unstable in recent months. Now, when he looked around the open space and the naked walls, he pictured Mer moving in with him.

Doug poured all of this into letters.

"I'm just not going to let you live anywhere else, Dear Lady," he wrote. "I think things could be very positive for us here. For our Great, Infinite Love."

I grew up in the aftermath of this bliss. My childhood memories center around the fights: epic yelling matches, shattered dishes, a kitchen chair broken against the wall. My parents split up when I was nine, though their relationship had soured years before that. Then came the long cold war of divorced parenting.

These letters expose facets of their relationship I've never seen before — romantic, lighthearted, optimistic. They also contain previews of their later issues.

In a letter dated February 7, 1977, my dad describes a dream in which my mom was as thin as a fashion model but wearing clothes that were obviously too big, which, he says, "would've shocked Yves Saint Laurent." Her pants were falling off, and she kept bending over to pull them back up. "Some great beaver shots, by the way," he writes. Then, "I suddenly noticed how weak you were from the fasting. Your energy was very very low, and I became concerned." At the end, he warns her to "look after that fine looking body," both for him and the child he wants her to carry.

He manages to sexualize a thinner version of her body, shame a fatter version, admonish her not to try too hard to lose weight, and remind her of her destiny to bear his child — all in one paragraph.

Switching topics, he catches her up on the psychic entanglements of their mutual acquaintances and the minutia of his day. He ends with a return to the sugary language of love: "Rather than write out that damn fool word 54 times, I'm going to use this word just once, and the ripples and emanations will circle the world three times, before jetting off to space. My fine and fancy Lady Meridy, I Love You."

Now I want to see the other half: Mer's love letters to Doug.

This is trickier territory. It's natural for me to rummage through my mom's belongings. But the story is different with my dad. He drifted out of my life after the divorce, our visits gradually becoming infrequent and strained. At sixteen, I cut our communication off completely for a few years. Though we've patched things up, we are both still guarded. I can't predict how he'll react.

I tell him about the love letters over the phone. When I mention that one of them was particularly racy and came with a nude Polaroid, he surprises me by cackling.

"Well, kiddo," he says. "That's how you were made."

Score one for Doug.

Then he says, "So . . . do you still have that photo? I'd kind of like to see what I used to look like naked."

He lives in Redwood Valley, a rural town two hours' drive from where I live in San Francisco. His home is a one-room structure with an adjacent bathroom—a sort of hybrid between a trailer and a warehouse—and he's sharing it with his ninety-two-year-old mother. They each have a twin bed squeezed against the wall opposite an open-plan kitchen, and there's a pool table in the center of the room. Apart from the bathroom, there's no privacy. The space feels simultaneously airy and claustrophobic.

My dad has aged well. He sports a trim gray mustache and shaves his head. Tattoos cover his forearms: a Chinese dragon, a lotus blossom. At sixty-three, he's thickened through the middle but has retained his good posture and easy movement.

Over dinner, he asks to see the letters. I hand him one of the tamer ones, which he skims between bites of macaroni and cheese. He reads one passage aloud. "We were sitting and listening to some music," he says. "I heard the diddle-time theme come floating in on my airwaves, so I looked over at Jerry and noticed his Seventh was closed. So I shot some gold up his spine, blew up the game in his head, and he immediately jumped up, quick as a fox, and ran into the kitchen. Fast reflexes, that man! Then he came back and sat down, but he was looking rather befuddled. I call it Clarity."

He shakes his head. "I can't believe I wrote that."

I assume he must be embarrassed at the ideas that used to preoccupy him—at believing he could psychically change someone else's thought patterns—but I'm mistaken.

"I mean, I would *never* mess with someone's seventh chakra now," he says. "Like where I say I'm blowing gold up his spine? The seventh chakra is your connection to the godhead. You don't go in there without permission. That is really messed up."

He still perceives the world in essentially the same way, I realize

— ruled by numerology, astrology, chakras, auras. The difference is how he understands his role. Back in 1977, he got a rush out of tinkering with people's heads. Graduating from the Berkeley Psychic Institute inflamed his arrogance. Not only did Doug believe himself capable of entering someone's mind and rearranging it psychically, he thought they'd be better for it.

Today, my dad works as a home-care nurse, though he still gives occasional aura readings. He takes pride in his psychic abilities. But he's become more aware of boundaries and cautious about doing harm.

After dinner, my dad slides a box from under the pool table. He doesn't invite me to look through it myself, but we squat together on the floor, and he hands me what he wants to share. His keepsakes are well organized and neatly labeled. His home is crammed with artwork, like my mom's, but with an eighth of her clutter. He finds six letters from Meridy in the box.

"Uh-oh," I say, grinning.

He reads each missive to himself, voicing some lines aloud and wincing silently at others. He shies from the steamier passages.

We're still getting to know each other as adults, and this is a new kind of sharing. Our conversations will end up becoming easier after this, more natural. I'll feel grateful for his willingness to speak honestly about the old days, and he'll be grateful for my interest. Later, I'll reflect on this night as the beginning of a new phase in our relationship.

At one point in the evening, my dad is reading one of the letters when his face and bald pate turn bright crimson. He grows serious.

"What is it?" I ask.

He doesn't look at me. "I can't believe Meridy and I lost each other," he says quietly. "How could we throw this away?"

Mer had barely left the ground when she started her first letter to Doug on complimentary American Airlines stationery. "Altitude:

37,000 feet," she began. "Location: In the Heavens." She wrote in a style cluttered with ellipses that the plane was crawling with businessmen: "briefcases filled with lies . . . starched collars pushing up fleshy jowls . . . alcoholic bellies housing ulcers, resistance to the truth." A young man dressed in a Brooks Brothers suit sat next to her to smoke a cigarette. After a month of aura classes with Doug, she felt she could read him and sensed he had an open fifth chakra — meaning that he was a natural communicator. "The young Gemini, a novice in the game, came to me for the truth," she wrote. "I told him the truth about himself, grounded him when he lit my smoke . . . Oh darling, you are wonderful, and I am learning!"

Mailed on the same day as Doug's letter about "diddling" his friend's seventh chakra, these missives crossed the country in opposite directions at the same time. Cosmic lovers, heading out into the world and fixing people's auras.

Mer saw her trip to New Jersey as a chance to practice healing work on Jeff and her sister-in-law, Sue. They lived in a cookie-cutter ranch house decorated in beige and brown. Jeff was a model of American upward mobility. Mer thought him an insufferable square. For days, she tried to pry open his chakras without his knowing it.

With nothing to do besides entertain the toddlers and play psychic games with her brother and sister in-law, Mer spent inordinate energy rhapsodizing about Doug. "Our love together seems to define an entire universe," she wrote, "so vast, so infinite and so damned beautiful. It's like, as the world begins to fall catastrophically apart around us, we can always climb into the beautiful world which our love has created, our own powerful empire."

She tossed hexagrams and did grounding exercises, but the waiting was killing her. She wanted magic, art, and romance.

She wanted to get stoned.

On day six, she wrote Doug to ask him to mail her some brownies.

The irony escaped her. Back in 1969 — when Patrolman Buxbaum busted Mer for picking up a kilo of weed addressed to her cousin's baby in Milwaukee — Sue had gotten arrested with the other women. Now, eight years later, good old Meridy wanted to smuggle pot through the mail again — this time directly to Jeff and Sue's house. But Doug balked at trafficking across state lines, and Mer dropped the subject.

One week dragged into two. Stir-crazy, Mer took a train to Levittown, Long Island, to meet Doug's grandmother, Paula Long-Clayton.

Paula lived in America's first suburb, founded in 1947. Her house, which stood on the corner of a quiet street lined with elms and maples, had been a simple Cape Cod model home when Paula bought it in 1952. She added a second floor, an extended garage, and bay windows, and sheathed the whole thing in dark cedar shingles. Fringed by a lush English garden, the result was rambling and asymmetrical. Dozens of stained glass angels clinked against the windowpanes. Even from the outside it looked haunted.

Paula answered the door dressed in an ankle-length velour caftan and oversize ethnic jewelry, a sweet-faced woman in her late seventies with a curly gray bob and mirthful brown eyes. "Come in, darling!" she said, folding Mer into a hug.

Paula's artwork cluttered her home: Egyptian motifs from the *Book of the Dead* carved into leather and painted in gold leaf and vivid pigments; a detailed mural of ice-skaters on a frozen Pennsylvania river; handmade mosaics and pounded-copper bas-reliefs. Mer marveled at the rich, creative environment that had nurtured her lover.

"I'd like you to meet Ed," Paula said, gesturing to an oil portrait of a handsome blond man in military dress. The painting hung suspended by wires from the ceiling, so it appeared to float in mid-air. Mer's skin tingled. *The ghost she married!* The house did seem inhabited by some unusual presence that became more intense once Mer intentionally tuned in. The air felt alive.

"Pleased to meet you, Ed," Mer said to the ghost in the painting.

Over the next two days, Mer and Paula indulged in long conversations about psychic phenomena and everlasting love, though the older woman did most of the talking. Mer felt like a student; she could sit at Paula's feet and listen to her talk forever. Paula explained that she and Ed had been star-crossed lovers, kept apart by misfortune and their own mistakes. Then Ed died young of lung cancer. Soon thereafter, his ghost manifested in her bed. Invisible yet warm and corporeal to the touch. He made passionate love to her. Paula had now been married to her spectral husband for five years. They communicated through a Ouija board and, Paula said laughingly, had their share of arguments that way. At one o'clock each afternoon, Paula shuffled into a tomblike bedroom built into the garage for her "quiet time" with Ed — which Doug had already explained meant sex with the ghost. Whenever she talked about Ed, Paula's skin seemed to glow faintly.

Outrageous, all of it, and yet Meridy *wanted* to believe in a love that could transcend death. Paula didn't say much about Doug — she mostly talked about Ed — but it wasn't necessary. Mer absorbed what she needed to know about him just by being in that charmed house and in Paula's presence.

Mer would have liked to stay longer, but Sue expected to go into labor at any moment, so she reluctantly returned to the prosaic drama unfolding at her brother's house.

"The lady is a supreme and divine soul," Mer gushed in a letter to Doug the night she got back to New Jersey. "She is your heritage smiling at me."

In Paula's world, romance was the fabric of the universe — vital as art, vital as air. Mer wanted to live in that world! And if Doug, the descendent of this powerful medium, felt certain that they were meant to create a child together, she wouldn't resist him.

"Your love fills me with a quiet joy this evening," she wrote. "You fill me with more ecstasy than I ever dreamed of. The magnitude of your wit, and your brilliance . . . yes, your brilliance, is making me so proud to be your lady, and have your child . . . accept your seed . . . your beautiful and perfect seed . . . a divine child . . . one manifested out of divine love."

Mer thrilled at the momentousness of her decision — promised in writing. The fact that she hadn't imagined herself as a mother made the move seem even more daring. As if having a baby was the most rebellious thing she could do. And in a way, it was. Not rebellious against her parents or society — but against her own expectations.

She could still surprise herself.

Doug's response was ecstatic: "Really supreme to hear some new words coming from you that I have never heard before," he wrote, "especially since they emanate from the heart chakra . . . And now, with no concept of time and space, back to the limitless love we have for each other. Thoughts have come and gone, and my first, second, third, fourth, and fifth shout in unison, 'We're going to have a baby!'"

"Percy's a good name," he joked in a postscript. "Percival Volz."

On February 6, Sue gave birth to a brown-eyed girl with a fuzz of dark hair.

Holding her squirmy little niece, Mer imagined the baby surrounded by golden light. As she described in a letter to Doug later that night, she had a "vision" of holding their own blond baby — the spirit-child — in her arms as she breastfed. She pictured Doug at her side, "smiling with love and paternal pride."

By the time she'd returned to San Francisco, the image of a family of three had replaced Mer's perception of herself as a solitary, independent woman.

These letters send me spinning. It's obvious that my parents were in the flip-out stage of falling in love, and that this level of intensity couldn't last forever. But I consume their words greedily, with an unexpected thirst.

True, their marriage didn't make it through the eighties, much less transcend death. I was raised in a broken home by a single mother and a mostly absent father. The magic turned out to be fleeting, while the bitterness lasted decades. That's all true.

So were these letters, this perfect love.

"I know that with this trust we won't fail each other," my mom wrote. She was wrong; they would fail each other again and again.

But I know now that I was born of delirious, audacious love.

Kings
and
Queens.

:∽ STICKY FINGERS BROWNIES ∽:

9

Kings and Queens

bike to the Mission on a brilliant day in 2018. The temperature hovers at around eighty-five — warm enough for shorts, but not so hot that I'll sweat standing still. Situated between Twin Peaks, Mint Hill, Potrero Hill, and Bernal Heights, the Mission simmers close to sea level. The hills shoulder off wind and moisture, so this area often cooks when other parts of town are swaddled in fog.

I pause for a red light beside Dolores Park, birthplace of my hometown. It used to be a lagoon. The Ohlone peoples (as the tribal communities from this region are collectively known today) had hunted and fished by its fertile banks for several thousand years before the Spaniards showed up. Friar Francisco Palóu said mass by the lagoon in 1776, and with that, the Mission Dolores introduced the heathen public to "civilization." They served a typical colonial cocktail: European disease, enslavement, cultural erasure, and outright slaughter. Within a century, some 90 percent of the Ohlone population had been wiped out.

Today, the only evidence of the lagoon are the puddles that gather beneath the swing sets when it rains and linger there for days. Kids swarm the play structures, Crayola-bright blurs. A *paletero* pushes his popsicle cart through the crowded park. The tennis courts are in use, and there's a herd of tech bros playing Frisbee. On picnic blankets, people vape now-legal cannabis oil and gaze at their tablets. Couples grin into phones for that us-on-a-picnic selfie.

With the Bay Area serving as headquarters for today's most

powerful tech companies — Google, Facebook, Twitter, Airbnb, Salesforce — we've been walloped by gentrification. The Mission is a hotbed of dastardly evictions and suspicious building fires. Condos rise from the ashes of community institutions and rent-controlled housing. Fancy mixology bars replace rock 'n' roll dives and LGBTQ+ hangouts. The Mission of today is mostly white, mostly moneyed. No longer a haven for recent immigrants, artists, and freaks.

My parents belonged to the classic first wave of gentrifiers: white bohemians who moved into an inexpensive ethnic neighborhood and made it appear trendy. I took my first breaths walking distance from here. This is the point from which my universe expanded.

Heart of this city, heart of memory.

I pedal east, passing two Teslas and a Maserati. An Uber driver brakes in the middle of a narrow street, clogging traffic in both directions, while three white women pile out squawking on cell phones. Squeezed onto the tip of a peninsula and hemmed by water on three sides, San Francisco will never extend beyond its forty-seven square miles. When new people arrive, others must leave. Most of my friends are already gone — evicted, priced out, or simply disgusted.

I know better than to come to the Mission, but I was thinking about beginnings and wanted to visit mine. Eight blocks later, I lean my bike on a lamppost at Twentieth and Alabama streets. The warehouse. Its facade of eggnog-yellow boards with powder-blue trim looks the same except for a new row of windows at second-floor height. A brownie customer named Sian used to tell me, "Look up when you walk down the street, punkin; you see the most *innnterrresting* things in upstairs windows." And he was right: a shadow is moving behind one of the new windows. I've come here before and left notes for the current resident but never heard back, so now I'm yelling and waving. "Excuse me! Hello!"

The window slides open. A handsome man with salt-and-pepper hair pokes his head out. "Can I help you?"

"Do you live here?"

"This isn't a residence," he says.

"It used to be."

"No, there was a start-up here before us. I know that for a fact."

"I lived here when I was little," I say. "I'm curious to know what's become of it."

He comes downstairs and we introduce ourselves on the sidewalk. The warehouse, he tells me, is headquarters for the Gurdjieff Foundation of California.

It seems too esoteric for today's Mission. George Gurdjieff was an Armenian guru whose ideas were popularized in the United States during the fifties and sixties after his death. Gurdjieff believed that humans moved through life in a daydream. He devised methods for awakening the sleepers, including ritualistic dance, music composition, and marathon meetings. There are currently forty-three Gurdjieff study centers worldwide. Some people consider it a cult.

I tell him about the magic-brownie business and the parties that used to shake the rafters.

"We can feel those vibrations. It's a very energy-rich place." He pauses, smiles. "You know, when we moved in, we had to replace the floors. We jackhammered through the concrete foundation, and in the dirt underneath, we found a bunch of broken china and rubble from the 1906 quake."

Could the warehouse truly carry our imprint — and of those who came before? As my hometown becomes unrecognizable to me, is there some essence that remains forever local? A current running all the way back to the Ohlone?

I ask if there's any chance I could peek inside the building just to see if I recognize it after all these years.

"Absolutely not." His tone is stern. "People are meditating."

He shakes my hand to let me know our conversation is over and slips back inside. I hear a dead bolt slide shut.

Soon after Mer returned from New Jersey, she moved into the warehouse. A narrow facade made the structure look deceptively small. You entered through a tight hallway, rounded a corner, and the space exploded into four thousand square feet. Skylights ran the length of thirty-foot ceilings. Heavy beams crossed overhead. Its barnlike quality fascinated her. It had, in fact, been a livery stable in the 1920s; the grayish wood floors bore faint horseshoe tattoos.

Near the entrance, a rustic bathroom stood on a low platform: claw-foot bathtub, mismatched toilet and sink, ten-foot walls, and no ceiling. Next, primitive stairs led up to the empty loft where Doug's roommates had lived before moving out. The kitchen had a leaky Frigidaire, a utilitarian steel sink, rough-hewn shelving draped with Indian saris, and a Wedgewood oven from the 1950s. Cooking utensils hung from nails on a freestanding wall. This was where the brownies would be baked from now on. Beyond the kitchen was an open area where Mer piled her belongings and set up her armoire and chest of drawers. She'd never had so much room.

The back third of the warehouse was Doug's territory, his space delineated by plywood walls and a pair of copper bank doors he'd scored dumpster diving. Passing through these, you reached his art studio and, farther back still, in the deepest recess, his bedroom.

On the wall above his bed, Doug had built a large three-dimensional wooden sculpture using driftwood from Ocean Beach, ornate table legs found on the street, wainscoting from a demolished Victorian, fence posts, and other scraps. He called it *The Eye of God*.

The raw nakedness of the warehouse invited transformation. Walls went up and came down. Stretches of spackled drywall alternated with murals. There were drawings, collages, mirrors, mannequins, piñatas, musical instruments, and a real taxidermied chicken.

The Mission was funky and vital, largely populated by Chicano families. Weekend nights, lowriders bumped down the main artery in gleaming American cars tricked out with hydraulics, their mufflers chugging alternative base lines to mellow Latin soul tunes. Crowds clustered along Mission Street to cheer and catcall the slow-going cars. When the cops didn't swarm in to break up the party, it went all night.

Art collectives and communes dotted the area east of Mission Street. Three blocks from the warehouse was a multidisciplinary live-work art space and theater called Project Artaud. Last Gasp, a publisher of underground comix like *Slow Death* and *Young Lust,* was nearby. A vibrant lesbian community had taken root on nearby Valencia Street, with women's cafés and bars and a broad range of businesses run by women for women — including typically male-dominated services like auto repair and construction. There was even a new woman-owned sex-toy shop called Good Vibrations, thought to be the first sex shop in the world tuned specifically to female pleasure.

Two of the City's largest housing projects were also within walking distance. Muggings and street violence populated news reports. Drunks, junkies, and acid casualties camped in doorways and loading docks. Still, Doug and Mer felt safe enough to keep the front door unlocked. The real neighborhood menace was a mayonnaise plant that on windless days made the whole district stink like rotten eggs.

Soon after Mer moved in, the Sticky Fingers driver-*cum*-baker took a job offer in Hawaii. Before leaving, Cam introduced Doug and Mer to Carmen Vigil. Carmen looked like a jolly, disarming cross between Santa Claus and Tommy Chong. He made his own wine and worked part-time at an avant-garde film collective known as the Cinematheque.

Carmen became the official Sticky Fingers baker at twenty dollars per pan. His wife didn't want the risk of him baking at home, so the whole operation unfolded in the warehouse. An early riser, Carmen would arrive on Friday mornings while the household was sleeping, let himself in, and begin (Doug would have already ground the pot and left it waiting). The creaky Wedgewood was a workhorse, though it only fit four pans at a time. Carmen usually churned out three batches before anyone else got up. Along the way, he'd lick spoons and nibble crumbs until he felt like a helium balloon floating in the rafters. "Never come down 'til Monday," he'd say. He whistled while he baked.

Carmen's wife, Susan, came on board to wrap brownies. She'd bring her toddler son and usually a girlfriend to help. The wrapping crew — nicknamed the Wrapettes — would spend the afternoon at the large kitchen table in a haze of pot smoke, snacking and drinking wine as they worked.

Saturday afternoons, Mer and Doug went out to sell.

The "green routine" became the heartbeat of warehouse life. It gave rhythm to a week that otherwise lacked structure.

Doug had abandoned his reservations about working with pot now that he and Meridy were partners. Every week, he tied a bandanna over his nose and mouth, and pulverized dry Humboldt shake in a food processor before running the powder through a flour sifter until it was fine. Fragrant green dust billowed around him, clinging to his arm hair and eyebrows.

He kept the Haight route and decided to try breaking in another area of his own. Noe Valley, to the immediate west of the Mission, caught his eye.

Today, Noe Valley is stroller central. It's a posh neighborhood of high-end boutiques and the subset of jewelry store that displays diamond rings on mossy tree branches.

Back in 1977, it was a small enclave of arty types. Hip cafés and restaurants lined the main drag along Twenty-fourth Street. On his first day, Doug walked into a little coffeehouse called Acme Café and was assaulted by the most abrasive music he'd ever heard. Jarring atonal guitar noodled over a frenetic drumbeat. A guy snarled repeatedly about how repulsive his lover was. Flyers plastered the walls with images that seemed intentionally disturbing: screaming faces, rabid dogs, men wearing hazmat suits. Customers were scattered around the café. Doug tried not to stare at a woman with a shaved head and safety pins holding her tattered shirt together.

Unbeknownst to Doug, the San Francisco punk scene had recently barreled into existence. The Ramones had blown some thirty people away at the Savoy Tivoli in August 1976. A couple of months later, a local guitarist cajoled the owner of a Filipino dinner club into letting his band, the Nuns, play on a dead Monday. So many people showed up that the club soon gave itself entirely over to punk. The Mabuhay Gardens, known to denizens as the Mab, became the grimy, graffitied heart of an intense demimonde. The Acme, which had always been a little freaky, was tipping that way, too.

Doug felt like turning tail, but the discomfort intrigued him. Whatever was happening here, it was new . . . And these people certainly looked like they got high.

The guy behind the counter wore a scuffed leather motorcycle jacket covered in cryptic pinbacks. His hair was dyed an unnatural blue-black. Doug had only dealt with established customers before. Mer, he knew, would suggest making small talk before sliding into the subject of brownies almost as if it were an afterthought. But Doug hated small talk. And what were you supposed to say to a guy like this?

Doug cleared his throat. "What's this music you're playing?"

"Crime. It's the B side of 'Hot Wire My Heart.'"

"Doesn't the negativity get you down?"

The counterman smiled with half his mouth.

"Okay." Doug faltered. "Well, what I wanted to ask was . . . What would you say to a magic brownie?"

"I'd say, 'Hello, beautiful.'"

"Then here's one for you to try." Doug pushed a cellophane-wrapped brownie across the counter. "It's on me."

Decades later, Kevin Kearney aka Stannous Flouride still remembers the day the lanky hippie with the leather hat came in and gave him a free pot brownie. Stannous considered himself an experienced pothead, so when my dad cautioned him to eat a quarter of the brownie, then wait at least forty-five minutes before trying more, he smirked. *Yeah, whatever you say, space cowboy.* He ignored the advice and regretted it. "I ate it at work," he says, "which I shouldn't have done. And I got really, really blitzed. Oh, these were gooood."

Stannous fumbled through his shift, seeing tracers, his body vibrating. Too stoned to converse cogently or assemble a decent sandwich. The following Saturday, when Doug came back in, he bought a dozen.

Stannous picked up on the concept right away. If you sold to people working in businesses and left the after-market sales up to them, you'd be less likely to get busted. The cops wouldn't be able to pinpoint the origin of your product. You're not approaching strangers on the street or dealing out of your home. It had none of the usual trappings. It struck him as subversive and smart. Stannous began buying for the café. He saved the greasiest brownies — the ones visibly oozing green oil — for himself and kept the rest near the register. Once word got around, people knew they could talk to a certain punk at the Acme if they wanted Sticky Fingers brownies.

Doug had never run a business before and the prospect excited him. He wanted to approach it properly. Mer, he thought, was used to running things with a feminine flow, but disorganization irked him. One thing Doug knew for sure: businessmen kept ledgers. So he bought an account book, the kind with columns labeled for gross income, wages paid, expenses, etc. It would help them stay focused and organized.

Mer didn't seem to understand. "You can't write this stuff down. Are you crazy?"

"How else are we supposed to track our progress?"

"Why on earth would we do that?"

"This is what businessmen do!" Doug snapped, feeling dismissed.

"If we get busted, this is evidence against us."

It escalated into a screaming fight, their first real battle. When the next weekend came around, Doug didn't ask Mer's opinion. He recorded his figures and stashed the ledger among his things.

Four thousand square feet was a lot of room for two people. At $400 per month, the rent was more than either of them was used to scraping together without roommates. Since the loft up front sat empty, they decided to look for a housemate. Doug posted flyers on community boards along his new route to see who might turn up.

They got Jeep.

Eugene "Jeep" Phillips was an artist, photographer, carpenter, and jeweler. He was tall and wiry, with keen blue eyes, an avian profile, and curly brown hair that frizzed around his temples and floated down his back. An Aquarius with a quick, creative mind, Jeep had a funny habit of adding "blah, blah" or "da, da, da" to most sentences, as if his brain moved too quickly for his mouth. He had been a biology major in his hometown of San Luis Obispo but got sidetracked into doing psychedelic light shows. He developed a technique for preprogramming multiple projectors with punch tape—cutting-edge back then. With that segue into the party scene, he moved to the City and enrolled in the San Francisco Art Institute.

"I have to ask you something," Doug said, when Jeep came to see the warehouse. "Do you smoke marijuana?"

"Occaaaaaasionally."

"Have you tried magic brownies? We, uh, make them here sometimes."

"Sure," he said. "I kind of make brownies, too, sometimes."

That was the magic answer.

A week later, Jeep was using a spray gun to paint a seascape mural in his new loft in the warehouse when he heard a ruckus in the kitchen below. Peering over the railing, he was surprised to see Doug grinding what looked like an entire plant's worth of marijuana leaves in a food processor, enveloped in a dust storm of pot like some desert traveler on a green Sahara. Then Carmen and the Wrapettes showed up. Jeep hadn't realized it was a major operation.

Jeep was a birdman. He liked being up in the rafters where errant pigeons occasionally roosted. He'd watch the goings-on from his aerial vantage, feeling that if he was quiet enough people forgot he was there. He came to love the slow process of waking up on weekend mornings to the sound of banter in the kitchen below. He'd descend, half-dressed; make an espresso; and eat a brownie fresh from the oven and topped with milk or ice cream. He'd fall into lively conversation or drift into his studio to make art. Through the life of Sticky Fingers, Jeep would be the sole person to experience the full process intimately without getting sucked into the business — an inside outsider.

The most outlandish part to Jeep was how many decisions were made using the *I Ching,* from the life-changing to the trivial. Once, when Jeep accompanied Mer to Cala Foods for baking supplies, she amazed him by whipping out her brass coins — right in the grocery store — to determine whether to buy organic flour or the usual cheap stuff. In this big illegal business, hippie magic was calling the shots.

Doug and Meridy were not quiet roommates. They fought often and loudly. Thinking back on it, Jeep says, "There was a kind of volatility. You know, they both have strong personalities, very dramatic, and so I think it would play out in anger and a certain amount of yelling or loud interaction, etcetera, etcetera."

Perched up in his loft, Jeep would shake his head. *What month is it? Where is the moon? Them people at the other end of the building sure are making a lot of noise . . .*

All three roommates had active, messy studios. The warehouse was organic, alive, ever changing. It became a fertile scene, a place for throwing parties, holding court, and spreading your wings as wide as you pleased.

Doug sought ways to make Sticky Fingers more spiritually and artistically satisfying. He realized that the lunch sacks they used to package each dozen could become a medium for communicating with the City. He started coming up with an original design each week and spent hours copying it onto hundreds of pastel-colored lunch bags. The designs were necessarily simple at first: a series of squares within squares within squares and the phrase *The Space Within;* a female figure and the words *Green Goddess.*

He also began a large painting of the warehouse crew, entitled *We Are All One. We Are None the Same,* featuring photo-realistic portraits of Barb, Carmen, Jeep, Mer, himself, a friend from the Berkeley Psychic Institute, and a homeless alcoholic from up the block. The symbol for each person's astrological sign floated beside them. Behind the homeless man, the door to enlightenment stood slightly ajar.

Mer had been hearing about Doug's spirit-child for months. One night in March 1977, Doug lay back on the bed after lovemaking, sweat shining on his nose in the dim light drifting down from the skylights. "There," he said. "Now you're pregnant."

Then he draped his forearm over his eyes and slept.

Mer lay awake as Doug's breath elongated. She felt uneasy. He was startlingly psychic, but how could he possibly know? In four months of dating Doug, she'd gone from not wanting a child to letting him talk her into it. Was she midcycle? She was. A baby would change everything. Maybe she should have stayed on the pill a little longer.

As she listened to her lover sleep that night, Meridy imagined a small flash of lightning — the beginning of new life inside her body. And as she visualized this happening, she felt it happen.

She didn't bother with a pregnancy test.

"None of us could imagine your mom with kids," Donald says now. He'd returned to San Francisco by April 1977 — though not to the business. Having known Mer since the Milwaukee days, he was skeptical of her conversion. "She was never into children, just not a kid person. And she was this total party girl, you know. So when she announced that she was pregnant, it was like, *Oh, my God, that poor kid!* It was impossible to imagine."

Mer enjoyed a variety of drugs. Alphabet-soup drugs like LSD and PCP. The naturals: weed, shrooms, mescaline, opiated hash, peyote. She'd tried heroin a couple of times and didn't like the nausea. But quaaludes, poppers, cocaine? Sure.

When I ask her if it was difficult to sober up during her pregnancy, I'm a little nervous that she might tell me she didn't.

"Nah, it was easy," she says. "Hormones pretty much took care of that. Everything made me want to puke."

Morning sickness usually hit her at two or three in the afternoon, woozy waves rising through her guts. Sometimes she'd have to stagger to the nearest bathroom right in the middle of her sales run.

She quit cigarettes, alcohol, and coke right away. And who needed psychedelics? She could feel another consciousness awakening inside of her own. Part of her yet separate. The loneliness that had often tugged her sleeve dissipated; wherever she went, she had company. This was trippier than any drug.

She'd been fasting off and on since meeting Doug. Now he encouraged her to eat, eat, eat — which would've been fun had the queasiness not stripped the pleasure out of it. She went from fasting to force-feeding herself. Doug made stir-fries with brown rice, great heaps of scrambled eggs, salads, and all the tofu she could stand.

Sometime during the early days of this pregnancy, my parents agreed to marry. Neither of them remembers a proposal. "I don't know," my mom says. "I was pregnant with you. It was the thing to do."

So pragmatic, so conventional, so uncharacteristically dull. A love letter from her time in New Jersey gives a more colorful answer. On February 10, she wrote, "To me, first of all, [marriage] is merely another contract. One which I feel that we have already made to each other, perhaps New Year's Eve in the cabin . . . In terms of myself alone, I love you so deeply that with or without it, I would love you the same." Then this: "In terms of our child, it is of great importance . . . that he have his father's name, to carry out the word, to carry on the great Volz empire."

Somewhere under the overblown language, Mer was hiding a dreamy midwestern heart. As much as she might've wished herself immune, she yearned for a storybook romance. Take the matter of the wedding ring. She wanted one while Doug couldn't fathom spending hundreds of dollars on a bourgeois tradition.

"You care about that stuff?" he said, squinting at her appraisingly. "We don't need some status symbol to prove that we're united on a deeper level. Anyway, I don't have the money for fancy rings. Maybe down the road or something."

"Forget about it," Mer said. "Sorry I brought it up."

Doug left the room, his boots echoing off the wood floors. She heard him pause and draw a deep nasal breath and slowly release it through his mouth, grounding himself. Then his footsteps returned. He stood in the doorway with one hip cocked in that loose way of his.

"I've got two hands," he said. "I'll make them myself."

Doug stayed up late that night hunched over his drafting table, the white cone of light from his metal desk lamp illuminating his busy hands. When Mer edged over to see what he was doing, he shooed her away.

The next morning, he sat beside her on the bed and opened his hand to reveal two strips of bright rainbow plastic.

"Electrical wire," he said. "From a carpentry job before we met. I knew I was saving it for something special." He'd taken cuts of flat two-millimeter electrical cord in bright colors, aligned the strands into a rainbow, and meticulously glued them in place.

"Isn't it neat?" he said. "You and me, baby. We got electricity."

With a small smile, a one-sided dimple, he wrapped the rainbow around her finger.

Doug had always gotten a small thrill from shocking his mother. It wasn't easy to do; Jan was an independent widow, an artist herself, a traveler — usually unflappable. She had bought a house in Mijas, Spain, and was in the middle of elaborate renovations. Doug phoned long distance and caught her coming in from the garden. She launched into grievances about a worker who hadn't shown up and how difficult it was to find good help in Spain.

Doug cut her off. "I'm getting married."

"Well, you'll have to wait until I get a roof on the house."

"It's no big deal, Mom. Just a small ceremony."

"What does Judith think about that?"

"I'm not marrying Judith."

That got a stammer. "Wh-wh — *what* are you talking about?"

When his mother left California months before, Doug had been dating a different woman — Judith, one of his fellow psychics from the institute. Jan knew Judith and liked her. Doug hadn't mentioned the break up — or his new girlfriend.

"Please tell me what you mean," Jan said, with forced calm. "You're not making sense."

"I'm engaged to Meridy."

"Mary what?"

"Meri-dee."

"Mary B?"

And so on.

"Doug, you don't even *know* this person!"

"I know she is the woman I'm supposed to be with."

Jan tried to talk him out of it. If nothing else, she wanted him to wait until she could come to the wedding.

"There's something else," Doug said, going for the big kaboom. "We're having a son."

By then, Jan was too upset to consider planning a trip. She wouldn't meet Mer for another year. This awkward beginning placed the two women in positions of guarded suspicion, a mutual stiffness that would take years to soften.

Mer knew her parents wouldn't be able to come to California. Bill had lost his leg below the knee to diabetes years before. He suffered constant back pain, the result of slipping two disks while lifting a keg of beer. Her mother was deep in Alzheimer's dementia. Bill gave his blessing over the phone. "If you're happy, I'm happy," he said. Mer promised that she and Doug would visit at the first opportunity. She didn't mention the baby then, not wanting them to think she was marrying because she'd gotten knocked up.

No parents would witness the union, but there would be friends, lots of friends, and a hell of a party. They settled on Sunday, May

15, choosing the date because Mer's favorite hexagram was "15. *Ch'ien*/Modesty" and because the moon would be entering Taurus, a good phase for staying grounded in a large group of people.

Doug was twenty-three, Mer was twenty-nine. Both were adults; and yet this was in some ways a marriage between children living in the make-it-up-as-you-go-along fantasy world of 1977 San Francisco.

"See?" Doug said, as they exited the 101. "It looks like a woman sleeping."

Mer squinted at Mount Tamalpais, the triangular hill rising some 2,600 feet above Marin County. "Maybe it's my angle . . ."

"She's lying on her back, staring up at the clouds, waiting for her lover."

Mer could kind of see it. The highest green peak formed the Miwok maiden's face, her hair flowing in waves down the mountainside. A lower peak shaped her breasts. There was the small rise of her hip bones and the smooth declination of her legs stretching into the green-gold foothills.

They drove through tree-lined Fairfax and up the swooping curves of Mount Tamalpais. Doug parked the VW at a widening of the road. Taking Mer's hand, he guided her between oak trees and through knee-high grass to an elevated clearing.

"This feels like the spot. What do you think?"

"Is this one of her boobs?"

"I don't think so. The boobs are that way. We might be on her shoulder."

"As long as it's not her armpit," Mer said.

"Or her beaver."

They giggled. Mer turned a slow circle. Insects hummed in the grass. The wind picked up, smelling of ocean and dust. To the south, the towers of the Golden Gate Bridge blazed between rolling hills. She could see stretches of Ocean Beach, its ragged lines of surf, and the downtown skyline with its construction cranes and money vibes. To the east, the silver gleam of the bay, and beyond that, smoggy Richmond. To the west, the Pacific sprawled under a sky crosshatched with clouds and contrails. A meeting of earth, sun, wind, and water.

Through a dry spring of exceptionally blue skies, Mer's breasts swelled and ached. She felt voluptuous. Sometimes she thought her pregnancy must be obvious to everyone, not because of her body, not yet, but because of how she moved and the energy she exuded.

Doug's handmade rings had been charming at first. But in the depths of an insomniac night, emotions churning, Mer decided she needed metal. Solid, unbreakable, permanent. It didn't have to be lavish, but rainbow electrical wire? Too weightless and silly, too easy to unravel. She'd get her own ring if necessary.

Jeep was taking jewelry design classes at the Art Institute, so Mer nosed around his workspace.

"I'm learning this really neat Japanese wood-grain technique," Jeep said. "You solder different colors of metal together, like silver and gold, and blah, blah, blah. Then you fuse them in a furnace and the colors kind of whorl." He wiggled his fingers. "Then, while the metal is still hot and soft, you can carve it so it looks like wood grain. The technique goes back to ancient Japan. It was used in crafting swords for samurai warriors, and etcetera, etcetera."

A samurai ring. Mer liked the sound of that. Tough.

Later, she and Barb sat at the kitchen table picking at chips and guac from El Faro. A joint smoldered in the ashtray, and light streamed through the skylights, illuminating rising swirls of smoke.

Barb tapped her pencil on a blank page of her sketch pad. "Are you thinking white?"

Mer snorted. "White is a mixer I use to lighten other colors of paint."

"Give me something to start with."

"All I know is I want to wear my shitkickers."

Barb came back with sketches of a Renaissance-inspired coat with dramatic bell sleeves, a gored skirt, a décolleté neckline, and leather lacing up the bodice. Boots peeked below the hem of a flowy underdress. The women chose a Japanese floral batik in royal blue and burnt sienna for the jacket and soft white muslin for the underdress.

In my mom's box of assorted papers, I find an itemized list of wedding expenses scribbled on the back of an envelope. My parents didn't pay for the patch of grass on Mount Tamalpais or rent a tent, tables, or chairs. Doug's BPI guru, Lewis Bostwick, and his wife, Susan, officiated the wedding free of charge. Guests brought drinks and potluck dishes. The list consisted of the fabric for Mer's dress, a few food items, wine and beer, a cake from Tassajara Bakery, and incidentals. The grand total came to $187.

A turkey was listed among the food items. Of the things that perplex me about the wedding — and there are a few — this is the detail that boggles my mind: on the morning of her wedding, a woman who to this day cannot reliably boil water roasted a twenty-pound turkey.

"I don't know what got into me," she admits. "Hormones, I guess." She doesn't know where the recipe came from, though she says she still remembers what it was. "You just get a big turkey, slather it all over with mayonnaise, throw it in the oven at like four hundred or whatever, and bake the hell out of it."

May 15 dawned chilly and gray, with heavy rainclouds that defied both the drought and predictions of fair weather.

"It'll clear up," Doug kept saying.

Fretful, Mer tossed hexagram after hexagram, repeating the same questions until the answers contradicted themselves. "It will be fine," she agreed, even as the first raindrops splattered the skylights.

They were halfway to Mount Tamalpais when the drizzle became a deluge. Doug gritted his teeth all the way up the mountain while Mer puffed on a joint to calm her nerves. Barb, in the back seat beside the turkey, was sewing finishing touches into Mer's coatdress. Guests were already waiting in their cars beside the road. Faces blurred through sheets of water cascading down the windows.

"This is positively biblical," Mer said.

"We need an ark," Barb added.

Doug twisted in his seat. "Would you two stop with the negativity pictures?"

Mer wiped mascara from her cheeks. Why were the omens turning heavy? How could the *I Ching* have misled them?

"Fuck a duck," she said, putting a plastic poncho on over her muslin underdress. She charged through the rain to the nearest car. Mer scrambled from back seat to back seat, asking if anyone knew where they could go. A restaurant? A sheltered patio? A freaking cave?

Finally, a couple who owned a crystal shop near Fisherman's Wharf offered their nearby home among the redwoods. The woman's parents happened to be quietly celebrating their fortieth wedding anniversary at the house that day, and there was no way to warn them of the impending arrival of seventy-five longhairs. But what better way to celebrate a wedding anniversary than with a wedding?

The ceremony was about to commence in the living room when sunbeams pierced the cloud cover outside. The rain let up. Everyone moved out into the backyard. Drops plinked from the redwood branches, catching sunlight so that everything sparkled.

"We are here today to witness the union of two spirits that have known each other through many lifetimes and have connected on this plane as lovers," Lewis Bostwick began. He led the guests through a group meditation. "Grounding in matter, grounding in the body, grounding in this moment in time." Then Susan Bostwick spoke of the importance of honoring each other through spiritual and sexual union.

They exchanged vows. Mer: "I vow to you my affinity and devotion, my queendom to complete your kingdom." Doug: "I vow to maintain a constant space within our relationship, as yin to your yang, as yang to your yin, as man to your woman."

The rings came out: rainbow wire for Doug, wood-grain metal for Meridy. Jeep had fashioned the ring from copper and brass with a core of nickel; the metals swirled up the band to form a yin-yang symbol at the center. No one had seen it before the ceremony.

Doug held the wood-grain ring up in a shaft of sunlight. "This ring! It's so beautiful!"

He passed it around to guests, drawing oohs and wows, until Mer grew impatient. "All right already, give me the damn ring!"

The older couple celebrating their anniversary stood with fingers entwined throughout the service. And that seemed to Mer like the best omen of all. There would be obstacles, but love would prevail. Perhaps the *I Ching* had steered them right after all.

I pore over a contact sheet of photos from the wedding. It begins with the two of them clowning before leaving the warehouse. In one shot, my dad dips my mom into a movie kiss. They look fresh-faced and happy. No war between them yet. Next comes the stormy hillside, a cluster of cars, and people huddled in trench coats and blankets, shoulders hunched. The atmosphere is so dismal, you can barely see the trees. Then the rustic Marin home, the relaxed smiles, the doumbek drums and flutes. The ceremony among the glittering redwoods. My mom beams, holding court with her friends, her curls fluffy from the rain. My dad stands tall; how proud he looks before his community.

In one of his love letters, my dad wrote, "You have the bearing of a Queen, and I am proud and animated to be standing at your side. You give my Kingly game the softness it so desperately

Meridy and Doug on their wedding day.

needs, at the same time that you are enlightening my softness with your strength." I can see that in the wedding photos: they elevate each other; they feel powerful together; they believe themselves in charge of their own world — what my mom dubbed the "great Volz empire."

Ride That Brownie

A kiss could be an act of rebellion, and in Eureka Valley 1977, boys kissed wherever they wanted: in bars and cafés, in doorways, or right out on the sidewalk. Castro Street buzzed with a heady mixture of celebration, sex, and defiance.

Freshly married and entering her second trimester of pregnancy, Mer had looked for a new route to open; a baby would cost money. Her nausea was abating and she felt glowy. In addition to her Saturdays on Fisherman's Wharf and North Beach, she added Fridays in Eureka Valley. Within weeks, it became her largest run.

The street had disco fever and Mer dressed for it. On the second Friday in June, she wore a cobalt-blue turban, sparkling turquoise top, flowy blue harem pants, and Candie's mules.

Among her first stops was Hot Flash of America, an eccentric shop on Market Street operated by an erudite, bespectacled pornographer named Wakefield Poole and his friends. The store's motto was "Everything you want but nothing you need!" You could buy a nineteenth-century French chifforobe, a 1940s gas pump repurposed as a tropical fish tank, or a rubber chicken. And you could get your hair cut in a salon overlooking the sales floor. A wildly creative party scene bubbled out of Hot Flash. The guys bought dozens of brownies every week and often sent Mer to new customers, including Michael Maletta, a hairstylist across the street who was becoming famous for throwing disco bashes of unprecedented opulence — early forerunners to modern raves.

After that, Mer stopped at Café Flore, Finnila's Finnish Baths, and other key spots before turning onto Castro Street. A couple of doors down from the art deco splendor of the Castro Theatre, she ducked into the Village Deli, a small café with rotating art exhibitions and floor-to-ceiling windows opening onto the street.

"Heya, Mer!" Kissie called, balancing plates on her forearms. "Be right there."

Mer took a table near a window to people watch. Outside, men stood in clusters and rows, hips cocked, bodies draped over cars and newspaper stands, draped around each other. Levi 501s and engineer boots were de rigueur. They were mostly white, mostly twentysomething, mostly mustachioed. ABBA's "Dancing Queen" was blaring in the café, a little saccharin for Mer's taste, but the boys liked it; hips pumped in their jeans.

Kissie was a tough, buxom New Yorker with a wild mop of blonde hair. Mer thought she looked like a Roller Derby Queen, like she could throw a hell of a punch. After dropping off the plates, Kissie pecked Mer on the cheek, smelling of cigarettes and April Rain essential oil.

Mer ordered a latte and Kissie ordered eight dozen brownies — which Mer dropped off in the café's tiny kitchen on her way to the funky bathroom in back before returning to her seat by the window. When Kissie brought the latte — no charge — she slipped Mer $120 for the eight dozen brownies. "You know Falcon Studios?" she said. "The porno place on Eighteenth?"

"I've walked past it."

"Ask for Steve. He's bugging me to get you over there. Oh, and Robert; he's a cook at the Neon Chicken."

Charging past with a sandwich exploding with sprouts, another waiter chimed in, "Don't forget Robbie!"

"I told her about Robert," Kissie said.

"No, the other one," he called over his shoulder. "The twinkie ice cream scooper at Double Rainbow."

"Oooh, *that* Robbie. Yeah, go see him, too."

Three new customers. And if the first weeks were an indication, those three would turn into ten. Word of mouth had carried her since the earliest days on the wharf, but in this neighborhood, it was more like a scream.

"Dancing Queen" faded into the driving bass line of "Over and Over" by a local diva named Sylvester who sang in a soulful falsetto and could whip any crowd into a sweat-soaked frenzy. This was the song of the moment on Castro Street, bumping from cars and bars, and bounding down from second-story windows, Sylvester's voice riding high over the horn breaks. The song was about being friends and lovers at the same time. It seemed to speak directly about this community — an elaborate Celtic knot of lovers and friends and acquaintances that was impossible to disentangle.

"They are part of what they call 'the gay world,'" wrote a journalist for *Life* magazine in 1964, "which is actually a sad and often sordid world." The sensationalized fourteen-page spread called "Homosexuality in America" included statements like "Often the only signs are a very subtle tendency to over-meticulous grooming, plus the failure to cast the ordinary man's customary admiring glance at every pretty girl who walks by." The authors supposed that gays were lured to urban centers by anonymity, established community, and careers in "interior decorating, fashion design, hairstyling, dance and theater." Out of four cities named as hotbeds, *Life* — with its average monthly readership of 8.5 million — proclaimed San Francisco America's "gay capital."

This hadn't happened overnight. Covert gay and lesbian establishments had flourished off and on since the Barbary Coast days. During World War II, the armed services set out to purge "sexual psychopaths" from its ranks, issuing thousands of undesirable discharges, known as "blue tickets" for the color of the paper. As a major administrative center of the Pacific theater, San Francisco became what historian Susan Stryker calls "something of a dumping ground for homosexuals dishonorably discharged from military service." Rather than face their families in disgrace, many opted to start fresh in the winsome city.

Blowback was intense. A series of sensational headlines — SEX DEVIATES ESTABLISH NATIONAL HEADQUARTERS IN SAN FRANCISCO and HOMOS INVADE S.F. — prompted bloody crackdowns in underground bars and city parks. Even when charges got dropped, police habitually reported names and workplaces to newspapers for public shaming. When cops enforced the 1863 ordinance forbidding anyone from wearing "dress not belonging to his or her sex," a Mexican American drag performer and activist named José Sarria encouraged queens to pin signs to their frocks reading, I AM A BOY! Arrests were made anyway, but the officers looked ridiculous in court. Sarria ran for the board of supervisors in 1961, becoming the first overtly gay political candidate in US history. Later that decade, the hippie phenomenon further telegraphed San Francisco as a haven for those who didn't fit the mold in their hometowns. Under the banner of free love, one could sometimes experiment with same-sex romance and simply be seen as a flower child.

Law enforcement tried to stem the tide. In the early seventies, according to journalist Randy Shilts, the SFPD busted an average of 2,800 gay men per year on public-sex charges — as compared with about 60 per year in New York City. In 1971 alone, 110 San Franciscans were sentenced to 15 years to life for "sodomy and oral copulation."

That same year, the words GAY LIBERATION blazed across the cover of *Life* magazine's annual *Year in Pictures* issue. The piece, titled "Homosexuals in Revolt," featured images of men and women in confrontations with police. At seventeen, future activist (and occasional brownie customer) Cleve Jones stole that issue of *Life* from his high school library while living in Scottsdale, Arizona, and hid it under his mattress to read and reread. For Cleve, the article was a clarion call.

He wasn't alone. By 1976, police estimated that out of San Francisco's 700,000 or so residents, 140,000 of them were homosexual (about one in five). Less hysterical estimates had it closer to 100,000, but as Shilts writes, "The guesswork left the estimators looking like medieval monks trying to figure how many gays could disco on the head of a peninsula."

San Francisco had become *the* place to come out of the closet.

"It was a visual thing," Cleve tells me. "Every week there were like a *thousand* more gay boys coming in — and gay girls, who were mostly up Valencia Street. It was electric! You didn't have to be political, or even all that bright, to know that you were being allowed to participate in something the likes of which really had never been seen before."

Meridy had blazed through one duffel bag of brownies and was almost sold out of the second. At the corner of Eighteenth and Castro streets, she maneuvered through a forest of bare shoulders in front of the Hibernia Bank — a stretch of sidewalk that on sunny days got so crowded with shirtless boys that it earned the nickname Hibernia Beach. Halfway up the block, she ducked into a small, cluttered photo lab called Castro Camera.

Mer's customer there, Scott Smith, was a handsome dishwater blond. Scott co-owned the shop with a lanky, opinionated Long Islander named Harvey Milk, who was making his fourth bid for political office, his third try for a seat on the board of supervisors.

In previous lives, Harvey had been a high school jock, a lieutenant junior grade in the navy, a numbers cruncher on Wall Street, a Goldwater Republican, and a stage actor and associate producer. By all accounts, he was a terrible businessman. He'd taken up politics impulsively in 1973 after becoming outraged at the bureaucratic obstacles confronting small businesses and the financial shortages public schools were facing. These weren't specifically gay issues. Harvey championed labor unions and housing rights, and stood against all forms of discrimination — not only homophobia. He even circulated a petition to save the last "straight" bar left in

Eureka Valley from greedy landlords. Though gay liberation was central to his platform, Milk was civic-minded in an earnest, big-picture way that won voters of all persuasions. His first campaign slogan had said it all: Milk Has Something for Everybody!

Mer rarely encountered Harvey at the camera shop during her Friday runs, though she often saw him out in the neighborhood, registering voters, passing out literature, chatting with constituents, cruising. The 1977 election would be Harvey's best shot — the first year that supervisors could be elected by district instead of by an at-large vote. This was crucial for Harvey, who might win on his own turf but didn't stand a chance in a citywide popularity contest. But Supervisor John Barbagelata, who'd narrowly lost the mayoral race to Moscone, was challenging the switch to district elections and had gathered enough signatures to require a special referendum set for August. The referendum would either make or break Harvey's chances of becoming a supervisor. His "human billboards" — handsome young men holding campaign signs — lined Market Street. As part of an image revamp after his first defeat, Harvey had sworn off drugs and bathhouses, and traded his hippie ponytail for an above-the-ears haircut.

But just because Harvey had gone clean didn't mean the rest of his crowd had. Scott always bought a couple of dozen brownies, as did Harvey's boyfriend, Jack Lira. Between the young photographers who hung around the photo lab, the comings and goings of the campaign being run in the back room, neighborhood guys lounging on the tattered maroon couch, and the floppy-eared mutt who greeted visitors from a 1950s barber chair near the window, the little camera shop was always buzzing.

Even as the gay liberation crowd staked out territory in San Francisco, an antigay movement was gaining steam in Florida, led by an orange juice spokeswoman, pop singer, and former beauty queen named Anita Bryant. With her voluminous coiffure and Miss Oklahoma smile, Bryant had become the face of homophobic bigotry. "As a mother," she often said in interviews, "I know that homosexuals cannot biologically reproduce children. Therefore, they must recruit *our* children."

Her organization, Save Our Children, had run television ads juxtaposing baton-twirling majorettes from the Orange Bowl parade with racy clips from Gay Freedom Day. "But in San Francisco," the voice-over intoned, "when they take to the streets, it's a parade of homosexuals. Men hugging other men. Cavorting with little boys."

Lesbian and gay communities responded with a national boycott — or "gaycott," as it was called at the time — against Florida citrus. In San Francisco, some bars stopped serving screwdrivers and tequila sunrises altogether; others offered half-price drinks to customers who squeezed their own juice from California-grown oranges.

Equating homosexuality with child molestation seemed outrageous to Mer, but it worked in Florida. In a special referendum on Tuesday, June 7, 1977, the people of Miami-Dade voted to overturn recent legislation meant to protect gays and lesbians from discrimination in housing and employment. After dancing a jig for the press, Anita Bryant intimated that she planned to take her antigay campaign on the road — all the way to California.

On the night of what became known as Orange Tuesday, an impromptu protest erupted on Castro Street. It moved through the City, building to an estimated five thousand people, with Harvey exhorting the crowd through a bullhorn. The rally continued well past midnight.

Secretly, Harvey saw Bryant as the best thing that could happen to the gay liberation movement — and as grist for his own political mill. As he said in a speech a few months later, "In the two weeks before and after Dade County, more was written about homosexuality than in the entire history of mankind. In every household they talked about it; they may have said, 'You fucking queens,' but they talked about it. And that was the opening of dialogue." It gave the movement a focal point, drew people out of closets, and politi-cized the apolitical.

Brownie customer Bruce York happened to be visiting his par-ents in Florida when the referendum happened. "I came out to my father at that time," he recalls. "I was so horrified and taken aback by that whole thing. I just firmly expressed my displeasure and said, 'This is who I am.'" Upon returning to San Francisco, Bruce, who'd avoided politics until then, started going to protests.

Harvey would soon tack a new introduction onto his stump speech, a play on Bryant's claim that gays were out to recruit chil-dren. "My name is Harvey Milk," he'd say. "And I'm here to recruit you."

Meridy was wrapping up her Friday run when she noticed clumps of people drifting toward the intersection of Market and Cas-tro streets. Some carried protest signs: ANITA BRYANT SUCKS ORANGES! SAVE OUR HUMAN RIGHTS! BOYCOTT FLORIDA ORANGE JUICE; SQUEEZE A CALIFORNIA FRUIT! Mer heard whistles and the first bursts of chanting.

She knew she shouldn't risk getting arrested while holding cash from her sales. But she had missed the big protests earlier in the week and wanted a piece of the action. She joined the crowd, promising herself she'd leave at the first sign of cops. "Two, four, six, eight, gay is just as good as straight!" she chanted, staying with the group down Market Street as it grew to about eight hundred. At Civic Center, where police presence thickened, she caught a BART train back to the Mission.

At the warehouse, Mer flopped onto the bed, exhausted. Music drifted up from Doug's studio: Earth, Wind & Fire. Blood pounded in Mer's feet. Then Doug appeared in the doorway. "What hap-pened? It's late."

"Oh, I was at a protest. That cow Anita Bryant."

"Everything go all right with the brownies?"

Mer rolled onto her side, unbuckled the army satchel, and pulled out a fistful of twenties and tens. "I could've sold twice as much," she laughed. "They *love* us!"

"It was an energy thing," Sian Van Cortlandt tells me. "It was something living and breathing, something really powerful." Sian worked at a men's clothing store on Castro called City Island Dry Goods. "It would be, literally, a buzz. Late Friday afternoon, what I call the 'coconut wireless' would start up, like jungle drums beating: *Today's the day for the Brownie Lady, the Brownie Lady, the Brownie Lady!* And then it was like, *She's up the street! She's up the street!* You'd be running around the store and going to friends, '*How many do you want? How many are we going to buy?*' Then she would come in wearing a big purple poncho with the bags strapped across her chest like Pancho Villa. We'd chat, and then she'd go off to make someone else happy."

I ask my mom to reconstruct her Eureka Valley sales run and get a forty-five-minute answer. She sold at coffeehouses, hair salons, sex clubs, novelty shops, florists, delis, bookstores, hardware stores, luggage stores, pet supply shops, chiropractors, bakeries, real estate offices, travel agencies, bathhouses, and myriad restaurants, bars, and discos. As editor in chief of *Drummer* magazine Jack Fritscher recalls, she was "like a milkman making a delivery."

By 1977, gay men had so thoroughly claimed the twelve blocks around Castro Street that you could almost forget that it had ever been otherwise. But this was new. For generations, Eureka Valley had been a quiet, working-class district of Irish, German, and Scandinavian families. A couple of low-key gay bars settled in during the 1960s. Then four appeared all at once in the summer of 1971. Two lesbians bought the Twin Peaks Tavern on the corner of Castro and Seventeenth streets and quietly made history — likely the first gay bar in the nation with plate-glass windows, the goings-on visible from the sidewalk. Eureka Valley had been gradually emptying since the mid-1960s as blue-collar jobs shifted from the waterfront and city center to the suburbs. There were vacancies. Gay businesses cropped up like wildflowers in spring.

Eureka Valley was neither the only gay neighborhood in San Francisco nor the first. North Beach came earlier, as did Polk Gulch — which still had more gay bars than Eureka Valley in 1977. The leather scene, along with many bathhouses and sex clubs, rollicked South of Market. Transgender women and other gender nonconformists carved out space in the Tenderloin and on Polk. The heart of the lesbian community beat in the Mission.

Factions that would later unite under the LGBTQ+ banner didn't all get along in the 1970s, as historian Josh Sides points out. Several women's spaces kept strict policies against allowing men through the door; a few also banished transgender women as infiltrators. Some gay establishments projected misogynistic attitudes and "boys only" policies, especially in the macho environs South of Market. "Leave your fag hag girlfriend behind," advised a writer for *Drummer*, adding that the action on Folsom Street "gets too heavy for female company." Bisexuals were widely dismissed as dabblers.

Eureka Valley became a world unto itself. It was unique in that it mimicked an all-American small town — but with a disproportionate population of young men in tight jeans. Mainstream dailies ran articles on the area's growing economic and political clout. A trend emerged of same-sex couples buying Victorians in disrepair and refurbishing them with fresh paint jobs and refinished floors. By 1977, the area looked less blue-collar and more like the Castro of today: clean and well kept, cheerfully painted, and expensive. Poet Aaron Shurin described it as the place "where gay men came to live out their bourgeois fantasies."

Which didn't mean they hadn't come to party. "The men of our dreams are on the streets every single day," a twentysomething-year-old Minnesota transplant named Mark Abramson wrote in his diary, "just waiting to be unwrapped and experienced on the spot . . . I'll never get through them all." At two a.m., when the

Moridy ready for a brownie run.

bars closed (by California law), crowds surged into the street, dispersing between discos, sex clubs and bathhouses, all-night diners, or cruisy parks. Music pounded through the hours like a ticking clock. When liquor sales resumed at six a.m., bars filled again even on weekdays. This was a far cry from the sleepy residential neighborhood of a few years before. Eureka Valley had changed so drastically that the name no longer fit. Newspapers, both gay and straight, waffled over what to call it: the Castro Corridor, Eureka Village, sometimes just the Village. Harvey leaned toward Castro Village. The name pinballed for months before coming to rest as the Castro. Residents could stay right there and have everything they needed without ever spending time or money in the straight world. "A whole neighborhood," Randy Shilts writes, "where it was safe to swish down the street."

Now Sticky Fingers Brownies was there, too. "That run was huge," my mom tells me. "It was the hugest! And I was *really* good at it, and I did it in high heels half the time. And pregnant!"

———————

Mer rang the doorbell to Sylvester's flat. She clutched his address scrawled on a scrap of paper. The singer had put the word out on Castro that he wanted the Brownie Lady to visit.

Mer had danced to Sylvester and Two Tons O'Fun countless times at City Disco, the Palms, and at home on the turntable. Sunday afternoons at the Elephant Walk, people flowed out of the bar to dance right in the street, traffic be damned. He seemed, somehow, to appeal to many factions at once — equally beloved by drag queens, leathermen, lesbians, clones, blacks, and whites, even straights. With his new single, Sylvester was becoming a national star. Local queen makes good.

A young man with long wavy blond hair came down to let Mer in, and she followed him upstairs. Battered antiques, lush fabrics, and erotic art were strewn about the flat amid half-unpacked moving boxes. She rounded a corner, and there was Sylvester: black, bold, and beautiful, stretched out on a tasseled velvet divan and wearing a glittery gold turban, purple blouse, wide-legged pants, and rings on every finger.

"Girl, don't mind the mess," Sylvester said. "I'm just getting started here." He spoke in a smooth, lilting voice that belied his powerful pipes. "Make yourself comfortable and tell me all about *you.*"

Mer eased herself into a frayed, ornate chair. Her feet throbbed. Someone passed her a fresh joint, and she slipped into easy rapport with the singer, the beginning of a camaraderie that would last for years. Sylvester bucked every stereotype and didn't seem to give a shit about trends.

He'd risen through the hippie era with the Cockettes, a radical genderfuck theater troupe that performed with beards, genitalia doused in glitter, clothing from every decade, and outsize headdresses — creating what John Waters called "complete sexual anarchy." That was ancient history. But Sylvester was still light-years from the hypermasculine Castro clone look that dominated the scene then. He wasn't trying to pass as female either. Sylvester, Mer would learn, didn't tolerate labels. "I'm not a drag queen," he'd say with a flourish of fingers. "I'm Sylvester."

Thereafter, she stopped by every Friday to do a deal and hang out for a while — a welcome break from the long walk around the neighborhood. It was always easy to land in that sumptuous environment and hard to take off again.

Sticky Fingers wasn't the only game in the Castro, as Mer soon found out. Since her first run, customers had been telling her, "Go see Dennis at the Island. He'll get your angle." And the way it was said — something in the inflection — gave Mer the impression that Dennis had a "biz" of his own.

One June afternoon, she walked into the Island restaurant on Sixteenth and Sanchez streets loaded with her duffels of brownies. It was cluttered and casual, with mismatched furniture, reclaimed wood, and abundant plants. She asked at the counter for Dennis, and a hippie popped up from one of the couches nearby.

"What can I do you for?" Dennis was petite and impish, with long shaggy hair and messy bangs. He spoke in a reedy Bronx accent and wore a ratty T-shirt, cutoffs, and flip-flops, eschewing fashion altogether.

Mer offered him a sample.

Dennis cheerfully unwrapped the brownie right there, sniffed it appraisingly, and took a bite. "*Mmm*," he said, admiring the green-tinted grease the brownie left on his fingertips. "Gooey!"

He bought two dozen right off the bat.

Little did Mer know that their futures were entwined.

"When Sticky Fingers started coming around," Dennis Peron says, "the Island café was my place. It was a great restaurant. Anything went. *Anything*. You could smoke pot. You could fuck there if you wanted . . . . The only thing we didn't have was really good food."

In later years, Dennis would be known as the single person

most responsible for reforming marijuana laws in California. He
says he's been busted for cannabis twenty-two times. The first arrest was right after returning from Vietnam, where he'd been assigned to the army morgue during the bloody Tet Offensive. While
bagging corpses, Dennis resolved that if he survived, he was coming out of the closet; life was too short. Upon being processed out
through San Francisco in 1969, he headed straight for Golden
Gate Park to start his new life as a gay hippie. Days later, he got arrested for possession of a joint. Dennis was tripping on LSD at the
time of arrest and couldn't stop giggling. "Hey, you, shut up," an
officer said, which made him crack up harder. The cop had Dennis stripped buck naked and locked in a cell alone. Dennis suffered
flashbacks, hallucinating that he'd been captured by the Vietcong.
It was a frightening night. By morning, his fear had morphed into
anger. He vowed to dedicate his life to legalizing weed.

Dennis opened the Big Top Marijuana Supermarket in his home
on Castro Street. Clients could choose from an array of products:
marijuana from around the world, hashish, kief, and brownies.
The vice squad mounted a massive sting in 1974 and arrested Dennis and forty-three of his employees and customers.

While serving part of his sentence through a work-furlough
program, Dennis opened the Island in a long-vacant storefront.
"I lovingly restored it," he says. "No two spoons matched, no forks
matched, no plates matched, no chairs matched, nothing matched!
I found it all in the garbage. I decorated that whole place with garbage, but 250 people could sit down in 250 chairs."

Like my mom, Dennis was better at finagling than cooking; he
hired friends to create one of the first entirely organic vegetarian
menus in town, serving macrobiotic stir-fries and stoner classics
like peanut butter and banana sandwiches.

Undaunted by his bust, he also reopened the Big Top. When
smugglers knocked on his door and offered him three hundred
pounds of high-grade bud at a blowout price, Dennis became the
self-proclaimed King of Colombian.

Dennis's ganja empire ran on sincere idealism. He never took money seriously and would hide cash in random places, like dirty laundry baskets, then forget about it for months. He didn't want to be rich, so he looked for ways to invest in his community. "That marijuana formed a lot of businesses around the Castro," he says. "Marcello's Pizza. Brad was my man there. I said, 'Hey, Brad, I got three hundred pounds of pot. Take ten and start selling it.' Falcon Studios, the porno place: 'Steve, I got tons of pot. Please take ten pounds!' Also, I helped Harvey Milk. 'Here, Harvey, there's some money in your pocket, but I don't know how it got there. It's not from me.'"

Though Harvey didn't use drugs anymore, he and Dennis were close friends and associates. He held staff meetings and threw parties at the Island. That Dennis might have slipped him a little something for the campaign seems not at all unlikely.

The next time Mer stopped at the Island, Dennis wanted to talk volume. "How many of these lovely treats can you whip up?" he said. "You bake 'em, I can move 'em."

He invited her up to the Big Top to see what he'd created, but Mer demurred. Her gut wasn't giving her the green light. Later, she tossed hexagrams about selling at the Big Top. The results seemed risky. She trusted Dennis personally, but he'd been busted before, and the cops would have their eye on him. She decided to proceed with great caution. She avoided going into the Island and the Big Top. Instead, Dennis would send his lover to meet her in a parking lot, and Mer would have everything set to do the transaction swiftly. And she always tossed hexagrams beforehand, trusting the *I Ching* to keep her safe.

The official line in San Francisco was tolerance and equality. The gay and lesbian community — now flexing muscles as a voting bloc — had allies in high places. Foremost among them was Mayor Moscone, who'd championed the 1975 Consenting Adult Sex Bill that decriminalized sodomy in California. There was also the chief of police, Charles Gain, who told the *Bay Area Reporter*, "If I had a gay policeman who came out, I would support him 100%."

Both Moscone and Gain were on shaky ground with the SFPD rank and file. Looking back, retired sergeant Jerry D'Elia tells me, "From a police officer's point of view, Moscone was one of the biggest double crossers in the history of the police department, because he had promised us that if we supported him, he would choose a chief from within the ranks. And the first thing he did was get Gain."

Charles Gain was the first chief in fifty years who'd never served on the SFPD. Originally from Texas, he had been chief of police in Oakland during the racially dynamic years that gave rise to the Black Panther Party for Self-Defense. His conciliatory posture toward black activists earned him a reputation for being forward-thinking — along with a no-confidence vote from his own force. Moscone brought him in as a reformer, and Gain wasted no time. He banned drinking on the job and made examples of those who disobeyed. And he encouraged racial minorities and gay people to join the force. He also ordered the department's black-and-white patrol cars painted white and baby-blue, which he thought projected a more humanistic image — much to the embarrassment of old-timers on the force.

The SFPD was predominantly Irish Catholic, conservative, and resistant to change (despite efforts toward racial integration, Josh Sides points out, the force remained 85 percent white and 95 percent male as late as 1979). Cops took their grievances to the press. "First he calls us alcoholics," one officer grumbled. "Now he's calling us fruits." Some policemen called their chief Gloria Gain behind his back.

On the county side, Sheriff Hongisto had also proven himself a gay ally, causing chagrin among his men. He had used personal vacation time to travel to Florida and campaign against Anita Bryant's referendum. While he was away, the 250-member San Francisco Deputy Sheriffs' Association composed a telegram to Anita Bryant. "We consider your opinion to be a sacred right," it said. "We applaud the stand you have taken and admire your courage." The president of the association told the *San Francisco Chronicle*, "We're not trying to buck the sheriff . . . He's supporting the Coalition for Homosexual Rights [*sic*] and that's his thing. We can say what we'd like to say."

The liberal attitudes were being imposed from the top down.

D'Elia recalls that during his patrolman days, back when his beat included a stretch of gay establishments South of Market, he'd sometimes take flak from other officers. "How can you go into those fag bars?" D'Elia shook it off. "First of all," he tells me, "it was my job. Second of all, I couldn't care less, you know, as long as everybody's okay with it." D'Elia admits that he was more open-minded than many of his colleagues, some of whom had "stupid hostility" toward gays and lesbians.

Meanwhile, violent attacks were spiking. "By 1977," wrote journalist Warren Hinckle, "a decade after the famous hippie 'summer of love' in the Haight Ashbury, gays were experiencing a summer of terror in the cradle of the counterculture." He cited reports of thirty to forty muggings and stabbings per month by "street toughs" targeting gays. Given the unfriendly history between law enforcement and the City's homosexuals, victims were sometimes reluctant to turn to police for help when gay bashers marauded. Castro locals organized street patrols and handed out police whistles for people to summon help from neighbors in case of an attack.

On June 14, 1977, a state senator from Orange County named John Briggs stood on the granite steps of San Francisco's city hall and announced his plan to get homosexuals banned from working in California schools. Briggs hoped to run for governor the following season and was looking for buzz, so he borrowed rhetoric from Anita Bryant. His team notified gay activist groups in advance of the press conference to draw a hostile crowd for the cameras.

A week later, four youths attacked a gay couple near Whiz-Burger Drive-In a few blocks from the Sticky Fingers warehouse. A nineteen-year-old stabbed Robert Hillsborough fifteen times in the chest, stomach, and face while screaming, "Faggot! Faggot!" long after the man was dead.

Hillsborough, a thirty-two-year-old city gardener whom local kids affectionately called Mr. Greenjeans because of the grass stains on his work clothes, became a martyr to rally around that summer. Thousands attended his memorial service.

Mer could hear the motors revving long before they came into view: dozens of tough-looking women decked out in leather and bandannas riding double on motorcycles. Signs read DYKES ON BIKES and WOMEN'S CONTINGENT. Applause swelled. In the crowd, Mer linked arms with Doug.

The 1977 Gay Freedom Day Parade was the biggest it had ever been. There seemed to be a million banners for a million clubs. Ministers for Human Rights, East Bay Lesbians, San Jose Gays, Straights for Gay Rights, Gay Socialists, Gay Teachers, the Gay Yacht Club. There was a gay marching band with baton twirlers, gay cowboys on horseback, even a contingent of gay Republicans. Dressed head-to-toe in white with a flower behind his ear, Sylvester rode in the back of a convertible looking as prim as a black Queen of England.

A row of giant signs aligned Anita Bryant's smugly wholesome face with images of Hitler, Stalin, Idi Amin, and burning crosses. Throughout the parade, people carried flowers to pile on the steps of city hall in memoriam to the gardener who'd been murdered near Whiz-Burger.

Mer, who lived for color, cheered loudest for the more lavish, sparkling floats. Drag queens in headdresses and elaborate gowns, a peacock with a six-foot tail fanning behind her, a shimmering mermaid surrounded by an undersea tableau, a pharaoh among glittering pyramids.

And then, coolest of the cool, Grace Jones cruised by, swathed in fiery orange fabric. Her oiled body and shaved head gleamed like obsidian as she sang her hit single, "I Need a Man," in a resonant growl. An endless disco procession followed her.

Newspapers would estimate a crowd of 250,000 — all walking in the same direction, toward freedom, responding to the hate-mongering with renewed strength. Watching the community come together filled Mer with hope. She felt increasingly confident that this was the right time and place to have a baby. The world was becoming freer. Their son could be who he wanted to be, love whom he wanted to love. She enlaced her fingers with Doug's; he squeezed her hand. They smiled together out at the sea of determined lovers.

CHILD OF LIFE'S LONG LABOR

STICKY FINGERS
BROWNIES

Child of Life's Long Labor

Doug awoke in the dark. He fumbled for the legal pad and pen on his nightstand. His eyes adjusted, capturing streams of watery blue drifting down from the skylights. His dream had started to fade, but he wrote what he could remember. When his pen ran off the right-hand side of the page, he used his finger to follow the indentations back across, and began a new line.

Doug had dreamed that he was in a collapsing building. He ran with a group of people from room to room, looking for an escape. Then he saw the spirit-child, his golden-haired son, standing calm and unafraid. The child's blue eyes penetrated the illusion. *I'm dreaming*, Doug thought, and stopped running. Then they were in a summery field in the country. Looking at each other, smiling. The child said something to him. A name.

Doug strained to remember. It was an ancient name, one he'd heard before. But it had already fallen into the slipstream, back into his subconscious.

Meridy snored beside him. Her form hulked under the blankets, a she-bear in hibernation, her breathing labored under the extra weight of the unborn child inside her womb. Doug rolled onto his back and took a deep breath. If he stopped trying to remember the name, it might come back on its own.

In a few months, Doug would become a dad. Fatherlessness had defined his youth. His own dad had drowned when he was five, leaving him with scant memories, mere flashes of the time *be-*

fore. He remembered a moment of riding on his dad's shoulders, as high as a bird. Another moment of perching on his dad's knee, settling into the safe cage of his arms on Christmas morning. His dad's indescribably unique smell swirled with that of his mother's fresh-baked cookies. Then there was the endless time *after.* The boat ride to England with his brother and mother and her captain friend—how alone he'd felt even with them. The cold stone halls of Holmewood House, the housemaster who'd spanked his bare ass with a sneaker, and the headmaster who'd used a cricket paddle; Doug couldn't remember his transgressions, only the beatings. His mother never remarried, never fell in love again. He'd had no positive male role models. Nobody to show him how to be a man.

This, Doug believed, was at the root of the attraction he sometimes felt toward other men: an old yearning for his father. Like a broken bone that hadn't been set properly and ached from time to time. This child was Doug's karmic contract, his destiny. He would experience the relationship he'd missed out on but in reverse. The father would raise the child; the child would heal the father.

Doug rolled onto his side and rested his palm on his wife's stomach — hard with pregnancy, tacky with sweat. He felt it rise and fall with her breath. This was no ordinary child, no doubt about that. He would be a healer. And then, a whisper in his mind, *Galen.*

Galen, the ancient physician, one of the Greeks. Being careful not to wake Mer, Doug got up and padded into the kitchen, where a book of baby names sat beside a rolling tray. He flicked the lighter and looked up the name. It meant *calm.*

A healer of men, a healer for the people, for the world. Bearer of peace in a time of tumult. The calm eye at the center of a storm.

Warehouse life was chaotic. The only dependable routine was the production of brownies, but even that involved half a dozen people coming and going, smoking and drinking, laughing and arguing. Mer felt increasingly testy. There was plenty of space in the warehouse but no privacy. Sometimes she wished for a door to close.

One afternoon, she and Doug were walking around Stow Lake in Golden Gate Park. The wedding ring Jeep made was a little large for her finger. It had slipped off and Doug was holding it — but not holding it, exactly. He was playing with it, tossing it into the air, then catching it. "Come on, you're going to drop it," Mer cautioned as they started across a footbridge.

Doug ignored her, apparently enjoying ruffling her feathers. He never knew when to stop.

In the air, the ring caught light as it spun and fell smoothly into his palm.

He tossed it up again. The ring bounced off the rail and *plink!* A glimmer as it sank out of reach beneath the greasy green surface.

Mer was furious. They fought for days. By the end of it, Doug had agreed to build Mer her own room. He and Jeep erected walls and helped her set up her armoire and chest of drawers and a queen-size bed she bought secondhand. She still slept in Doug's bed under *The Eye of God*, but when the pregnancy wore her out and messed with her moods, she liked to stretch out in her own space and read.

That autumn, the book was *Dune* by Frank Herbert. Mer didn't usually go for science fiction, but Doug had read it over the summer and assured her that it was more than space gadgetry and aliens. She loved it. The characters all had unique philosophies and mantras that fascinated her. They used psychedelic drugs to enhance telepathy. Mer especially dug the Bene Gesserit, a powerful order of women whose psychic mastery ran centuries deep. Men feared them, believing them witches, but still depended on their insights and strength. Meanwhile, the Bene Gesserit used the men to further their own political ends.

Midway through the story, a Bene Gesserit named Lady Jessica disobeys taboos and drinks the psychotropic Water of Life while pregnant. Awakened by the drug, the fetus inside Jessica's womb absorbs the memories of her ancestors. Baby Alia is born speaking complete sentences and is so powerful and strange that even the other Bene Gesserit are terrified.

"Alia." Meridy said the name aloud. It had music. The character was a little dark, but what a powerhouse! They were having a boy; Doug was certain of that, and Mer believed him; Galen it would be.

Still, she wrote *Alia* on a scrap of paper and tucked it in the back pocket of her maternity jeans. From time to time, she came across the scrap and whispered the name to herself before shoving it deeper into her pocket.

Any pregnant hippie worth her salt chose a natural birth. It would be painful, of course. But Mer didn't want to be numb when Galen entered the world; she wanted to be present and clear.

She and Doug signed up for weekly Bradley method classes at nearby General Hospital, which was dabbling in some of the more mainstream New Age methods amid high demand. According to the Bradley teacher, a plump midwestern midwife, 90 percent of mothers who used the method gave birth with no medication at all, having learned to control pain through deep relaxation, breathing, and physical preparation. Physical preparation, Mer learned, meant squatting.

Squatting and meditation. Meditation and squatting. Kegel clenches and hoot breathing. Bland, healthy food. And plenty of rest. She tried to stick to the regimen. She ate all the vegetables and brown rice she could handle. She hooted and squatted and clenched. But rest? That wasn't her style.

Mer took figure-drawing classes at the San Francisco Art Institute. She went dancing with Doug or Donald. She micromanaged the baking routine. Then she loaded herself with some thirty pounds of brownies and lumbered around the Castro on Fridays,

the wharf and North Beach on Saturdays   returning to the warehouse achy and exhausted.

Castro Street was buzzing with news on July 22: the Big Top Marijuana Supermarket had gotten raided two nights before and a cop
had shot Dennis Peron. Mer picked up bits of the story at different stops. Details varied as to how badly Dennis was hurt, who else
had been arrested with him, and how much they'd confiscated.
Mer finished her run feeling woozy.

The *San Francisco Chronicle* ran a front-page story along with
a photo of Dennis recovering from a shattered femur in the hospital, wearing his usual scraggly hairdo and mischievous smile. And
damned if he wasn't pinching what looked like a joint between his
fingers.

According to the article, Officer Paul Makaveckas had originally claimed he opened fire because Dennis pointed a gun at
him When no gun was found, the story changed; now Dennis
had hurled a five-gallon glass water bottle down the stairs at him.
The cop then shot him in the thigh in self-defense. The SFPD vice
squad arrested Dennis along with thirteen other people, a combination of employees and customers, and seized a serious quantity
of pot along with hashish, hash oil, LSD, mushrooms, marijuana
plants, $8,000 in cash, Big Top records, and letterhead stationery.

Dennis's memory of his 1977 bust strays from the official take.
"This guy with a gun was coming up the stairs," Dennis says. "He
had on a fatigue jacket, big hair, and a hat." The Big Top had been
robbed twice before, so Dennis panicked. Instinctively, he grabbed
an empty Alhambra water bottle from the landing — a pathetic excuse for a weapon, but he was a peacenik and it was all he had.
Then Dennis felt an explosion of pressure in his thigh. Collapsing backward, he dropped the bottle behind him. A second bullet
whizzed past his ear.

Dennis still believed he was getting robbed. *I'm going to die over money,* he remembers thinking. *It's so mindless!* He started pulling cash out of his pocket, yelling, "Take the money!"

When uniformed police came in behind the shooter, Dennis's first reaction was relief. *The cops are here — good.* Then they thundered up the stairs and handcuffed Dennis while he bled on the landing. He didn't learn until later that the gunman was a plainclothes officer. They had a warrant. Dennis had sold weed and LSD to a narc.

The *San Francisco Chronicle* reported that police had confiscated "between 30 and 150 pounds of pot" — a perplexing range. Dennis claims they actually took two hundred pounds, but a "mouse" kept eating it in the evidence room. "More like a rat," he jokes darkly. "It was Colombian pot, so this was a very selective rat."

Decades later, in 2015, the cop who shot Dennis would go to prison for accepting bribes from would-be taxi drivers. For the moment, he was a hero; the Police Officers Association awarded Paul Makaveckas a Silver Medal of Valor for his bravery while being "attacked by a man with a five-gallon water bottle."

Dennis's bust left Meridy shaken. She had come so close to selling at the Big Top. Thirteen of Dennis's associates had been picked up in the raid. If the *I Ching* hadn't steered her away, Mer could have been among them. She didn't want to have this baby in jail, but the brownies were their only source of income.

It was a close-enough call to make Mer worry — particularly about the ledger Doug insisted on keeping, meticulously logging the details of their business each week: how much money they'd earned, how much they'd paid Carmen and the Wrapettes, how many dozens they'd sold, how much pot they'd used. Money coming and going.

"Doug, we need to get rid of that ledger."

"This again?"

"Records are *bad*. Records could put us away."

"You're generating an awful lot of negative energy around this."

Mer considered stealing the ledger and getting rid of it herself, but it would cross a line of trust in their relationship. She turned to her hexagrams. Every Friday and Saturday before leaving the warehouse, Mer consulted the oracle for warning signs. Then she packed her duffels and headed out into the City to work her magic.

Late July, a monthly magazine called *New West* published an ex- posé by Marshall Kilduff and Phil Tracy on some disturbing goings-on within the Peoples Temple. Ten temple defectors were accusing Jim Jones of conducting fake healings, bilking money and property from his congregation, subjecting temple members to brutal public beatings and humiliation, and manipulating po- litical elections.

In the months leading up to publication, *New West* had received as many as fifty phone calls and seventy letters *per day* begging them not to run the article. Temple spokespeople went to the press with rebuttals before the article even came out. By the time the piece ran, Jim Jones was already gone, having absconded to the church's agricultural mission in Guyana.

What most people — my parents included — wouldn't under- stand until later was how deeply Jim Jones had insinuated himself and his followers into the liberal power structure. Jones counted among his supporters the likes of Governor Jerry Brown, Assem- blyman Willie Brown, and Lieutenant Governor Mervyn Dymally. Even First Lady Rosalynn Carter and Vice President Walter Mon- dale had taken time to meet with Jones personally.

Back in spring of 1977, two Temple defectors had taken their allegations to the police. To work on the case, District Attorney Joe Freitas had assigned a deputy district attorney named Tim Stoen as his liaison. Freitas would later claim that he had no idea

that Tim Stoen was Jim Jones's personal lawyer and a prominent
member of the Peoples Temple.

Freitas had also assigned Tim Stoen to oversee the investigation
into the voter fraud alleged in the 1975 election. Not only did Freitas direct the investigation into voter fraud alleged *in the election
that had brought him to power,* but he did so with the assistance of
a high-ranking member of the organization accused of perpetrat-
ing that fraud. As historian David Talbot puts it, "The foxes had
free run of the henhouse, and they left only feathers."

In 1979, after the Jonestown nightmare had played out, federal investigators would ask to see the voting rosters from the 1975
election — only to find some one hundred voter registration books
missing. According to the *San Francisco Chronicle,* Freitas's office
had notified the registrar that the records were "no longer needed."

Whether the Peoples Temple stole the 1975 election for Moscone
and his cohort may never be known for certain. One can only guess
whether cantankerous John Barbagelata — if he'd become mayor
instead — could have done anything to stop Jim Jones or save his
followers.

Even Harvey Milk, though less implicated than others, had
shown his face at Temple services. He had also utilized the group
to help distribute campaign materials. Once, Cleve Jones recalls,
Harvey wanted a last-minute crowd for a midday press conference
and told Cleve to call the Peoples Temple. Forty-five minutes later,
three school buses pulled up carrying conservatively dressed African Americans. Jones didn't appear that day himself. The crowd
seemed to take cues from a muscular black man in mirrored
shades who stood at the front of the group. When he clapped, they
clapped; when he stopped, they stopped. Cleve found it chilling.

Patrolman Jerry D'Elia remembers those school buses well. "We
used to laugh," he says. "You know, in San Francisco at that time,
we had over three hundred protests a year or something. And
anytime they wanted a turnout for whatever the cause was, these

buses would pull up . . . The Peoples Temple would show up and it would be like, *Oh, here they are again!"*

They even came in the dead of night. When hundreds of San Francisco deputies, police officers, and mounted patrol descended on the International Hotel to finally evict the two hundred elderly people who lived there, they found themselves faced — at 3:18 a.m. — with an estimated three thousand protesters, largely from the Peoples Temple. Authorities bypassed the human barricade by using a hook-and-ladder rig to access the roof, but it was a showdown.

Who else could produce a crowd like that on a moment's notice?

Supervisor Barbagelata remained convinced that he'd been robbed of the mayoral seat by a "coalition of liberals and radicals." In May 1977, he'd collected enough signatures to require a special referendum that stood to effectively recall Mayor Moscone, Sheriff Hongisto, and District Attorney Joe Freitas — all in one swoop. On August 2, San Francisco voted two-to-one against Barbagelata's recall attempt; they also voted to sally forth with the district elections, which would benefit Harvey. Whether or not there had been shenanigans in the 1975 mayoral race, voters chose decisively to stick with their current leadership. Moscone joked to the press, "I just finished my midterm exams and I got pretty good grades."

Mer had promised her dad that she would bring her husband to Milwaukee at the first opportunity. In October, she made good. Milwaukee displayed its finest features in autumn, the air crisp but not frigid, the trees ablaze with oranges and reds. Bill was overjoyed to learn he had a grandson on the way; even Florence, in moments of lucidity, seemed happy.

In pictures from that visit, my mom looks oddly childlike, hair in tight Shirley Temple curls. Her outfit, a maternity shirt with a high neckline and horizontal stripes, seems girlish and conservative compared with her usual style from that period — kimonos, harem pants, turbans, and her leather bomber jacket. Doug is playing it square, too, dressed in a beige and navy-blue rugby shirt with a white collar, the only rainbow being the one around his ring finger. Though Bill disliked using his prosthetic leg, he's broken it out for the occasion and stands with a cane. Florence squints through coke-bottle glasses, her expression confused, hair unruly, Alzheimer's in bloom.

Even in Milwaukee, Mer's wheels kept turning. She needed to plan for time off when the baby came. Doug had his routes in Noe Valley and the Haight, but his sales were never great. Mer wouldn't have said it to his face, but she didn't think he'd do well in the Castro. (It's possible that Mer sensed a certain awkwardness Doug sometimes felt around gay men that stemmed from the urges she didn't know he was suppressing.) He was too blunt, too serious for that party scene. Barb was out of the picture, gone to Boston to open a costume business with an old friend. While staying with her parents, Mer decided to look up another old Milwaukee pal who might help.

Cheryl Beno stood six feet one in sock feet, with mile-long legs, sharp elbows, elegant cheekbones, and brunette hair in a Cleopatra bob. She had a brassy Milwaukee accent, and when she laughed, she'd jut her chin forward, open her mouth wide, and squawk, "HA!" Or occasionally, "AAAH-ha!" A fun, startling, uncouth sound. And Cheryl knew her way around drug culture.

To hear Cheryl tell it, she and Mer first met outside of a friend's house back in 1970. Minutes into their conversation, Mer looked Cheryl dead in the eye, and said, "You and I could be really great friends." In Mer's version, they met at a party around the same time. Cheryl walked in wearing a floor-length raccoon coat, spun on black beauties, and accompanied by a rude rock 'n' roller in fringed leather pants.

Either way, they remained casual acquaintances for a year or so until a stolen cake of hash brought them together. The hash incident happened during the mellow period after Patrolman Buxbaum's accident. A friend had given Mer the hash, which she was slowly selling to friends. She didn't consider herself a dealer then, but maybe she was dipping a toe in the water. Mer kept her stash in an antique beaded purse hanging on her wall. One afternoon, she made the rookie mistake of letting a customer, a rich kid who hung around the Eastside, see her hiding place. The purse vanished later that night.

Mer knew who the thief was, but he'd disappeared. She would have shrugged it off — easy come, easy go — but she kept running into her stolen stash all over town. She'd go to a party and someone would pass her a pipe loaded with familiar-tasting hash. Annoyed, she asked around. So-and-so got it from so-and-so, who got it from so-and-so. The crumbs led to the door of a man I'll call Victor.

Victor was a tall skinny speed dealer — the guy you phoned if you wanted black beauties or bennies. When Mer showed up at his place looking for her hash, his live-in girlfriend answered the door: Cheryl.

As it turned out, the thief owed Victor money for speed pills and had used Mer's hash to satisfy the debt. Victor believed in karma. So, feeling pretty sure that the hash was stolen, he'd been giving it away for free.

Victor gracefully paid Mer for the hash and even threw in some black beauties for no hard feelings. After that, the three of them became tight. Victor was a devotee of the *I Ching*, and though Mer already knew the basics, he got her into the habit of using it regularly. Cheryl was an ace thrift shopper. She and Mer would thumb through musty racks all afternoon, then get dolled up in their new-old outfits and hit the blues clubs.

Victor eventually went to prison for dealing. By then, Cheryl was pregnant with his baby. She didn't have a car, so Mer would drive her three hours to the prison and read in the parking lot while the couple visited. The romance survived Victor's sentence only to dissolve when he got out.

Fall 1977, Mer found Cheryl living with roommates and raising her toddler son alone. "Why don't you bring your son out to San Francisco for a few months?" Mer said. "You can stay with us in the warehouse and take over my sales routes while I recuperate."

Cheryl said yes without blinking. She would take the train to San Francisco after Thanksgiving.

One Friday shortly after returning to the City, Mer walked into a dive on Castro Street called the Nothing Special. The after-work crowd was out. Business types loosened ties and rolled up French cuffs while chatting up lumberjack clones. Baby Galen kicked Mer's belly in time with the thumping disco beat; he always seemed to get excited as her run wound down. Mer was finishing a deal with the bartender when a guy in a leather jacket burst through the door. "They got her!" he yelled.

"Who?" the bartender said.

"Anita Bryant! She got pied!"

The bar crowd hooted and applauded.

"What flavor?" someone inquired.

"Banana cream, of course!" And he was off to the next bar.

The pie sniping, which took place in Des Moines, Iowa, had been the work of four Minneapolis activists. But news traveled fast, especially on gossipy Castro Street. Mer heard cheers erupting as the story spread up the street. At the Nothing Special, the bartender poured a round of Anita Bryants on the house — apple juice and vodka (Mer toasted with plain apple juice). The rest of her run, she moved through crowds giddy with schadenfreude.

The next night, there it was on *Saturday Night Live*'s "Weekend Update." Anita, with her imperious cheekbones and back-swept coiffure, was speaking at a press conference about a recent appearance that had been "met with protest and all kinds of problems, and—"

Splat.

Cream filling bulged around the tin as it slid slowly down her face. Obscene white gobs clung to her eyebrows. The camera panned to a man in a tweed sport coat holding his hands over his head. Security moved to apprehend the pie sniper, but Bryant's husband said, "No, let him stay. Let him stay."

Wiping cream from her eyes, Anita quipped, "Well, at least it's a fruit pie."

Bryant's husband called her to seriousness. "Let's pray for him right now, Anita. Let's pray."

"Father, we want to thank you . . ." she began, then burst into sobs. Creamy tears streamed down her cheeks.

Back to Jane Curtin: "Fortunately, Miss Bryant, who was not injured, enjoyed a good laugh and said it was okay if the assailant dated her husband."

On November 8, 1977, Harvey Milk captured a definitive victory in his district. Legend would affix Harvey as the first "upfront gay" elected to public office. This wasn't true; two openly lesbian women and one gay man had been elected in other states during the early 1970s, though to little fanfare. Harvey's charisma combined with increasingly splashy media battles against the antigay crusaders made him a national icon in a way his predecessors had not been.

After eleven on the night of the election, Harvey rode back to Castro Camera from city hall on the back of a motorcycle driven by a striking leather-clad lesbian. Sheriff Hongisto rode beside him on a motorbike of his own. A crowd of some three hundred waited in the street. Harvey held court at Castro Camera through the night while friends and colleagues streamed through and beer flowed freely. The image of the politicians tearing around town on motorcycles made front-page news.

For his next brownie-bag design, Doug drew six swimming geese, heads and necks above water. One goose's head is burned black, sending up little squiggles of smoke, and the words *Your goose is cooked.* It was a message to the conservative old guard. On the ragged left edge of the country, free spirits seemed to be firmly in charge.

But nothing is simple.

The same night Harvey and friends thundered up Market Street, a voice from that other San Francisco also made itself heard. A handsome thirty-one-year-old named Dan White won in his district of Visitacion Valley, an Irish Catholic neighborhood two miles south of the Castro. With his square jaw, cleft chin, and tidy haircut, White was the image of a young conservative Democrat.

Both an ex-cop and an ex-fireman, Dan White presented himself as the law-and-order candidate. He gave a voice to San Franciscans who felt morally outraged, edged out, and dispossessed. Those who wanted to reclaim their hometown.

"I'm not going to be forced out of San Francisco by splinter groups of radicals, social deviates, and incorrigibles," his campaign literature promised. "You must realize there are thousands upon thousands of frustrated, angry people such as yourselves waiting to unleash a fury that can and will eradicate the malignancies which blight our beautiful city."

Patrolman Jerry D'Elia, whose brother had gone to school with Dan White, thought the young supervisor-elect was too idealistic for his own good. "Dan White was Don Quixote if he ever lived," D'Elia says. "He was looking for perfect. He was looking for Utopia in a very nonperfect world."

Ironically, Harvey Milk, who was in many ways Dan White's polar opposite, also liked to compare himself to Don Quixote. In speeches, he sometimes said that he couldn't tell whether he was wearing the helmet of Mambrino or a barber's bowl on his head. "Maybe I see dragons where there are windmills," he once told a crowd. "But something tells me the dragons are for real, and if I shatter a lance or two on a whirling blade, maybe I'll catch a dragon in the bargain."

The two quixotic crusaders — one representing old San Francisco values, the other rising from the new city — were on a collision course.

Since early in Doug's involvement in Sticky Fingers, he'd been drawing a unique doodle every week, then copying it onto hundreds of Zee brand paper lunch sacks in various colors — each of which neatly held a dozen brownies. Repeating his designs by hand took many hours. And the drawings were getting more complicated.

In November, he drew a humanoid form perched inside a circle, eyes closed, one foot extended. The figure is hairless and sexless, its features half-formed. An umbilical cord winds up from its belly. Arcing over its head are the words, *Child of Life's Long Labor.*

Among Doug's stops in Noe Valley was a small print shop staffed by artists his age. Flyers and posters covered the walls floor to ceiling. Doug found the smell of ink and the clacking noises of the printing presses intoxicating. The printmaker was impressed with Doug's fetus drawing. "Are you doing all of these by hand?"

"That's right."

"You know, we could print these for you."

"You can print on lunch bags?"

They could.

Doug arranged to trade brownies for printing services. He returned home elated. Now his designs could become intricate and more meaningful, each bag carrying a unique message to the City's freaks. The weed would carry the word.

To this day, when people wax nostalgic about Sticky Fingers Brownies, the artful designs on the bags are invariably among the first things mentioned. Some customers prided themselves on having deep chronological collections. An underground comic from an underground bakery.

Shortly thereafter, Doug found a screen printer to make T-shirts. He chose a photograph of Mer in the early days of her pregnancy, spent a week sketching at his drafting table, and came up with an extraordinary piece of stoner art for the logo.

Meridy, rendered in black ink, appears in the center of a round frame, looking like a mirror or a clock face. She eyes the viewer with a sidelong come-hither look, hair curling around her cheeks. Her left hand extends a plate of fresh brownies out of the frame, as if to say, "Take one." Her right hand lifts a brownie to her parted lips for a satisfying bite. Light is exploding around her. Looping above Mer's head, elaborate script reads, *Sticky Fingers Brownies*. The letters ooze and drip. Along the upper arc of the frame are the words, *Eat it, Baby!*

Customers began wearing them around town. Only the coolest of the cool cats knew what they were about.

Meridy was thirty-seven weeks pregnant when Cheryl took a train from Milwaukee to San Francisco with her son, Noel, a towheaded two-year-old with intense black eyes. She made the classic newbie mistake of bringing light clothing to San Francisco, assuming that the lack of snow meant warm weather. Then she froze her skinny ass off during the first cold snap in the unheated warehouse. She and Noel settled in Mer's middle room. They folded instantly into the Sticky Fingers family.

Mer was barely waddling through her runs by then. Galen was a watermelon sitting on her bladder. She suffered backaches and heartburn, and was plagued by Braxton Hicks contractions — agonizing abdominal clenches that felt like real labor but bore no results. She and Cheryl did the Castro and wharf runs together once, then Cheryl took over. Mer still didn't know how to relax. She'd sit up in bed with a TV tray and wrap brownies in the stretches between her Braxton Hicks torture sessions. Even in late pregnancy, she was like a downhill freight train with bad brakes.

Salen's batch

Sticky Fingers Brownies

12

Galen's Batch

M er went into labor on a gray Tuesday, December 13, two
weeks after Galen's due date. Doug drove her the six
blocks to San Francisco General, but after a cursory exam,
the midwife sent her back home with instructions to return when
the contractions were four minutes apart. Mer passed the day deep
breathing and timing contractions that made her curl around the
baby and groan. She smoked occasional joints for pain. The build
was annoyingly slow, minutes creaking into hours. "Time to wake
up, kiddo," she said, patting her strained abdomen. "It's your birthday."

A brownie bag Doug had designed would serve as their birth
announcement: the words *galen's batch* in fanciful bubble letters.
Cheryl dropped off the design at the print shop, took Noel to a
babysitter, and returned wearing a conical happy birthday hat.

Mer's anticipation mounted through the hours. Finally, at
eleven at night, the contractions reached four-minute intervals.
Doug pulled the VW around, and Cheryl helped Mer waddle out
to it. The moon was obscured by rainclouds the gray-green of a
chalkboard.

The nurses settled her into a private room in the alternative
birth center: floral-print wallpaper, innocuous landscape paintings, and an armchair with throw pillows. Like a movie set of a
small-town motel room.

The midwife wanted her to walk and walk and walk. She walked
with Doug then walked with Cheryl. Then Jeep showed up and

she walked with him. Up and down the halls of the maternity ward. The hours lost shape. Other women bellowed and grunted and screamed while fathers-to-be chain-smoked in the hall. When contractions hit, Mer gripped the wall and did her hoot breaths.

She labored through that sleepless night and the following day. The second night was ablaze. Lightning shot brilliant white light around the blinds in the birthing room — which was disorienting, because when was the last time anyone had seen lightning in San Francisco? The taiko-drum boom of thunder rattled the fixtures. It seemed to Mer as though the elements had gathered to usher in this child.

Later, a brownie customer would give Mer a photograph taken from above Dolores Park that night. The San Francisco skyline appears in silhouette, the Transamerica Pyramid and Coit Tower clearly distinguishable before a lavender sky. A tremendous lightning bolt jitters from a high purple cloud and splits into four distinct tines that strike the bay behind the buildings.

The pain mounted, peaked, subsided, climbed again. Gusts lashed the old brick hospital and shook the windowpanes. When the rain finally came, it came all at once, like a spigot turned on full force. And with that, Mer entered the transition phase, the wrenching apart of the birth canal. The Bradley teacher had warned her, "You might want to leave your body right about now." Doug was hunched beside the bed doing his coaching routine — the eye contact, the breathe-with-me's — while she gasped like a hooked fish and lightning strobed the room.

A nurse listened for the baby's heartbeat, and Mer caught a glance between her and the midwife. "It's posterior," she said.

The midwife nodded, businesslike. "We need to rotate your baby," she said to Mer. A nurse wheeled in a monitor that showed her contractions as a tiny white light rising and falling with her pain. They tried different positions: all fours, knees to chest, on one side, then the other. Nothing worked. Galen was still upside down when he started to crown. "You'll to have to birth him this way, honey," the midwife said. "Time to push!" There were hours of pushing in all positions. One foot up on Cheryl, the other on the midwife. Galen was stuck.

Toward dawn, the baby's heartbeat showed signs of distress. The midwife sent the nurse scrambling for a doctor. They wheeled Mer out of the soft light of the alternative birth center. When the next contraction hit and the midwife told her to refrain from pushing so they could wheel her to another ward, Mer howled. Banks of fluorescent lights streaked overhead.

Doug tried to ground his energy. He snapped a shower cap over his head and tied a medical mask over his nose and mouth. Beneath the scrubs he'd been given, his button-down shirt was drenched with nervous sweat and clinging to his body.

"Christ, what a day," Cheryl said, her voice muffled through her own mask. "Or *two* days. Poor Meridy, my God." None of them had slept.

"I know she's going to get through it," Doug said. "And Galen's going to get through it. This has been clear from the beginning."

It had been clear to him from the moment he'd laid eyes on Meridy standing at the top of her staircase in the Haight with light streaming around her. They were meant to bring this child through. Galen was in a dark tunnel now, but he would come into the light soon, and he would shine.

The delivery room had much harsher energy than the alternative birth center. White walls, gleaming stainless steel, headache lighting. A new doctor stood at the foot of Mer's bed, an elderly Asian man Doug had never seen before.

"Who's this guy?" Mer moaned, face blotchy and dripping. "Where's my midwife?"

"Just relax, Mrs. Volz," the doctor said. He peered between Meridy's legs, palpated her abdomen, shook his head. "I need to do an episiotomy and turn the baby around," he said. "I want to numb you for that, okay?"

Mer's head lolled. "Numb me or shoot me."

The doctor rolled Meridy onto her side. Doug watched the needle enter his wife's spine. He saw the scalpel gleaming in the doctor's gloved hand, then the sex organ being sliced and parting around the opalescent skin of Galen's pale crown. Then the doctor produced a glass and rubber apparatus that looked like a cross between bagpipes and a Shop-Vac.

"Wait a second," Doug said, snapping to attention. "What the hell is that?"

"It's a birthing vacuum."

One end of the hose was shaped like a toilet plunger; Doug realized that it would fit on the baby's head. "No way in hell are you using that *thing* on my baby! Absolutely not."

"Maybe you ought to step out, Doug," Cheryl said. "Let him do his job."

The doctor rolled his eyes, and he shoved the Frankenstein device aside. "Fine," he said. "Forceps."

Bile rose in Doug's throat as the doctor forced elongated tongs into the bleeding gash, the flesh peeling open like the rind of some alien fruit, then clamped them around Galen's little head. He rotated the tongs as if turning a heavy log in a fire while Mer made guttural buffalo sounds.

Later, Mer would tell Doug that the epidural had numbed her pelvis and legs but not her uterus or birth canal; she could feel everything.

The delivery room became thick with odors from the inside of Mer's body. The cloying iron tang of blood clashed with prickly antiseptic.

Suddenly, Galen moved. His shoulders emerged and his body spilled into the nurse's arms with a gush of fluid. His skin was an eerie shade of lavender. The baby remained silent. There were seconds spent teetering on a cliff's edge. Doug heard his wife panting, the *snick* of the cord being cut, liquid dripping into a metal pan. Then Galen opened his maw and wailed.

"Congratulations!" the nurse beamed. "It's a girl."

Mer collapsed back on the hospital bed, her relief like a sledge-hammer.

That was her child crying, tinny and *alive*. She tried to watch, but they had the baby on a table to the side. Taking measurements, checking the heart rate, wiping away the fluids.

Wait. A girl?

"Eight pounds, eight ounces," the nurse said, placing the baby on Mer's chest. "She's big!"

And there was this hot, wet creature making little croaking-crying sounds. Calm settled over Mer after the long struggle. Then, too quickly, the nurse snatched the baby away. Mer felt a vague prick in her arm, and the room swam into a spinning blackness.

Her eyes opened onto a different room. She blinked, saw that she was alone, drifted again. A different nurse woke her soon after and told her not to sit up because of the epidural. She came back with the infant swaddled in a pink blanket and laid her across Mer's belly. The baby mewled and snorted — a new personality in the world — while the nurse showed her how to breastfeed. It took some trying, but when the baby latched on, Mer felt a loosening of mind and body that felt like the first hit of opiated hash.

She vaguely noticed that Doug wasn't around, but it didn't matter. Because here was this gently squirming baby with strawberry blonde hair. Alive. A girl. Alia.

Every year on my birthday, my mom calls me, and says, "Guess what I was doing ____ years ago." Then she screams into the phone at the top of her lungs.

Having been down this road before, I know to hold the phone away from my ear so she won't deafen me. When she's done screaming, she'll say, "So I go for a natural birth, no drugs —*first*

time in my life I'm not taking drugs! And you were late, which is
so *typical* of you, and you were as big as a house and facing the
wrong way so, of course, you got stuck. You just couldn't do it like
everyone else, could you? Thank you very much, goddamn it."

"Sorry, Mom," I'll say.

"You could hear me screaming from one end of that county hospital to the other."

"I can still hear you."

She'll laugh like it's the first time we've done this. Then she'll
say, "Ask me if I'd do natural childbirth again," and I'll hear her
smiling around the words.

"Would you?" I always oblige.

"Are you *fucking* kidding me? No way! Fuck that noise. Kumba-
fucking-ya, my ass. Really, honey, I'd recommend the drugs."

Doug rushed out of the hospital. He left because the linoleum
floor felt unreal beneath his feet, because he'd been awake for two
nights straight. He left to clear the hospital stink from his nose,
to shake the shock of seeing his wife turned inside out. He left because his dreams had lied.

He walked through the waning storm as the sun rose on December 15, 1977. Water dripped from his nose. Listening to his
boots striking the concrete, Doug tried to reenter his body after
having been thrown a mile clear of himself. He wondered if, by
showing him Galen, then sending him someone else, the Universe
was fucking with him. Was this punishment for hubris? Galen was
to have been the golden thread connecting him to his own dad.
The son to heal the father.

I don't think he meant to go where he went that morning. There
were so many gay bathhouses and sex clubs back then, at least a
dozen within walking distance of the hospital, who even knows
which one he ended up at. Whether he went there on purpose or
simply found himself outside a door behind which lay a certain
kind of relief, he walked through it as if in a dream.

"I know I came as a surprise," I say to my dad on the phone. "You were expecting Galen."

"Oh, yes!" he says, his tone jokey and self-mocking. "I knew for sure that my child was going to be a boy. Right up until *she* was born."

I take a deep breath and plunge. "Do you remember leaving the hospital for a bathhouse, like right after I was born?"

"What?" he says. He sounds genuinely baffled. "No, I can't imagine doing that."

I tell him what I know: that he disappeared from the hospital right after the birth; that he later confessed to Cheryl about going to a gay bathhouse on the morning I was born; that, later still, he told my mom about it during a fight — and that this was the first she'd heard about his desire for men. "Do you remember *not* doing that?" I press. "Did you return to the hospital? Did you go somewhere else?"

He's silent for a time. "I don't remember anything," he says finally, his voice somber. "I'm sorry, it's blank."

My dad was sexually confused — torturously so — and afraid. He was married to a woman with a huge personality, and he fought for his identity in reckless, sometimes brutal ways. He wasn't strong enough to match wills with my mom. Nor was he suited to the quantities and types of drugs they did; with severe epilepsy and memory problems, he should have kept his distance from cocaine and LSD.

"Meridy and Cheryl both say that happened?" he asks after a while.

"I'm afraid so," I say.

"Oh, boy."

We take deep breaths. The story hangs between us. I feel the urge to apologize for bringing this up, but I swallow it. "Well," he says finally. "If they both say that's what happened, I guess it must be true."

When we talk again a couple of weeks later, my dad says he can't stop thinking about what I told him. "It hurts my heart to know that I did that," he says. "One thing I can tell you is that I fell in love with you at first sight. Maybe I was upset at first that I didn't get my way. But you were astounding. I felt very blessed to have you as my daughter. So full of light. An incredibly vibrant individual."

I believe him. I've seen it in pictures. There's one of us on a picnic blanket in Golden Gate Park on a sunny day. I look squishy and damp and pink, eyes unfocused, arms and legs splayed in that helpless way of very new babies. My dad, shirtless, lies beside me, his fingers curled by his cheek. He's grinning with his whole face. He looks utterly amazed both at himself and at me just for being there on a blanket in the sun.

"You were always traveling around him," my mom says over the phone. "Except he thought you were someone else. Mr. Psychic says to me, 'We're having a son. I dreamed it and therefore it is so.' He was so sure! And we were contracted to have a baby, definitely. Except that it was *my* contract to have you."

When I came out a girl, my mom claimed me as her own, no going back. It's always been that way between us.

Of the 104 brownie bags in the family archive, *galen's batch* is the only one that never circulated through the City. The child unborn. The design shelved. They'd printed hundreds of copies of the bag, then I showed up with my double-x chromosomes.

Sometime between my Thursday morning birth and Cheryl's Friday afternoon Castro run, my dad designed a replacement bag: the name *Alia* in ornate lettering. Where *galen's batch* is drawn in playful bubble lettering, *Alia* is solid black, the lines sharp, elegant, and . . . witchy.

I hold the two bags, *galen's batch* and *Alia*, one in each hand, and wonder about the spirit-child from my dad's visions. The blond boy Doug thought would be a beacon of light for mankind. The little healer.

My birth was a betrayal of my dad's vision; it called his power into question. I can't help but wonder: If I'd been born a boy, would I be as much his child as my mom's?

Meridy's episiotomy did not heal well or quickly. The nurse stuffed the wound full of gauze, which Doug was supposed to pull out one inch per day. It felt like sandpaper on her shredded flesh. Mer turned to a naturopathic healer, who made a poultice out of pounded comfrey root that Doug applied twice a day. It was a chilly winter in the uninsulated warehouse. Rain streaked the skylights and pattered on the tin roof for weeks on end. Space heaters proved useless with the thirty-foot ceilings. My mom and I spent those first months huddled under an electric blanket. Or bundled beside the Wedgewood oven while Carmen baked — cementing in my mind an early sensory association between the smell of marijuana and chocolate in the oven and the safety of my mom's arms.

Doug bought a Christmas tree and decorated it with multicolored lights and ornaments his grandmother had made from dismantled egg cartons, beads, and gold paint. Mer loved the tree's fragrance and twinkling lights. And the smells of a new infant: milk drying on clothes, baby powder, newly formed skin. Something in that first Christmas lodged in her psyche because she — a Jewish girl with pagan leanings — became a Yuletide nut forevermore.

PART III

THE
DEVIL'S
PLAYGROUND

Sticky Fingers
Brownies.

13

The Devil's Playground

The rain continued into 1978, the two-year drought lost to a slushy winter. Mer's birth wounds slowly healed. She signed up for dance classes: Bob Fosse–style jazz with lots of body rolls, splayed fingers, and aggressive snapping. Doug joined a modern dance group, all geometric shapes and tumbling.

On January 9, Harvey Milk walked the two miles from Castro Camera to his swearing-in ceremony at city hall in a drizzle, arm around his lover, brownie regular Jack Lira. A spontaneous procession of about 150 celebrants followed them. Anita Bryant, who'd told *People* magazine that God had personally summoned her, claimed that California's two-year water shortage was heavenly retribution for the 1975 Consenting Adult Sex Bill — the bill coauthored by George Moscone to decriminalize sodomy and oral sex. As he was sworn in under an umbrella, Harvey smiled up at the sky. "Anita Bryant said gay people brought the drought to California. Looks to me like it's finally started raining."

Dan White also joined the board of supervisors that morning, though to less fanfare. The *Bay Area Reporter* had recently described White as "somewhat to the political right of Attila the Hun," but no one could have imagined how profoundly the handsome young supervisor would change San Francisco by the end of the year.

Early 1978 had the attitude of a tequila sunrise and a joint. The recession was fading into memory. There were no immediate international threats. Carter had begun advocating for decriminal-

ization of possession of up to an ounce of weed — the first US president to openly discuss easing up since the beginning of cannabis
prohibition. His drug czar and close friend, a psychiatrist named
Dr. Peter Bourne, had volunteered at the Haight-Ashbury Free
Clinic in San Francisco in 1967. Bourne believed that treatment
was a more effective response to drug use than criminal punishment. Yet, according to the National Organization for the Reform
of Marijuana Laws, better known as NORML, 457,000 people
had been arrested on marijuana charges in the United States in
1977 — the greatest number of arrests in a single year to that point.
Bourne argued that jailing pot users for simple possession was a
waste of resources; civil penalties (fines) would be more appropriate and much less expensive. Carter agreed. "Penalties against possession of a drug should not be more damaging to the individual
than the use of the drug itself," he told Congress in August 1977.
"And where they are, they should be changed."

John Travolta was king; the Bee Gees' "Stayin' Alive" topped
charts throughout February. People dressed like Travolta, danced
like Travolta, strutted like Travolta.

Mer resumed her Castro run on February 24, now with a wiggling, crying, pooping little person hanging from her neck in a rebozo-style sling.

She'd designed a brownie bag, her first, in honor of the *I Ching*
hexagram "61. *Chung Fu*/Inner Truth." It's a graceful, subtle design: Chinese characters rendered in calligraphy before a background of woven bamboo bordered in cherry blossoms. The hexagram spoke to influencing others through internal balance and
clarity — although schlepping two army duffels full of brownies,
a ten-pound baby, and a satchel of cloth diapers and extra clothes
hardly suggests an image of balance.

"Of course, you were always with me," she says. "First through
pregnancy. Then once you were born, I carried you in a front carrier — with all the fucking brownies. Then in a Gerry carrier on my
back, which was nice because it freed my arms, and you were coo-

ing in my ear; I loved that. Eventually, a stroller worked because I
could put some of the brownies in the stroller."

"Seriously?" I say, vaguely disturbed by the idea of my mom
dealing out of my pram.

"Not *in*," she says. "But, you know, hanging off the back. They
were heavy, so if you were out of the stroller, it would tip backward.
Here I was with a beautiful baby and brownies and all dressed up.
People loved us."

There it is: they loved *us*. My mom wasn't the type of druggie
who neglected her child; she was the type who took her child on
deals. If I was her "karmic contract" — as she's still fond of saying all these years later — that meant she was also mine. At two
and a half months old, I became her accomplice. Cruising along
with her from business to business loaded with contraband. Getting my diaper changed in supply closets and break rooms. Being
greeted with squeals of delight and having my little piggy toes wiggled by customers while my mom dished out the goods. Smelling,
I'm quite sure, like a Rastafarian in a chocolate shop with notes of
sour milk and pee.

Here's another thing I know: I liked it.

True, I was too young for specific memories. My prelinguistic
brain had no way of cataloging my experiences or the people we
encountered. But something from these early forays into the City
stays with me like an aftertaste.

It's a peculiar type of nostalgia, undiluted, raw, separate from
my remembrances of later years. A feeling more than a narrative.
A sense of belonging. I somehow understood, even then, that my
mom and I loved San Francisco and that San Francisco loved us
back.

Cheryl experienced her first months in California like a trip down
the rabbit hole to Wonderland. "San Francisco was the most fabulous city you could ever go to," she says, looking back. "I mean,
what compares? It really is like a carnival." Her plan had been to

return to Wisconsin once Mer got back on her feet, but she was having too much fun. Rather than become superfluous, Cheryl proposed breaking in new turf, beginning with Polk Gulch.

The area was frothy. It bordered the Tenderloin, a vice district since the early 1900s. An abundance of cheap residential hotels and containment policing made it both a ghetto and a haven for the City's more marginalized residents: recent immigrants, transgender women, hustlers and prostitutes, drug addicts and alcoholics, and the elderly and impoverished. In 1966, as historian Susan Stryker points out, the management of an all-night Tenderloin diner called Gene Compton's Cafeteria called the police to roust a group of noisy queens who were hanging around without spending much money. When a cop grabbed one by the arm, she threw hot coffee in his face. Others joined the fray, smashing windows and overturning tables. The ensuing riot consumed several blocks and lasted two days — three years before Stonewall.

A short walk from the heart of the Tenderloin was the mile-long strip of bars, restaurants, and boutiques locals affectionately called Polk Strasse. It had been a "gayborhood" back when Eureka Valley was still working-class and Catholic. Both the annual Halloween street party and the Gay Freedom Day parade (now Pride) had started on Polk. And it didn't have that upwardly mobile, same-sameness of streets thronged with Castro clones. Sex workers of all genders turned tricks in doorways and alleys. Historian Josh Sides quotes a transgender woman named Regina McQueen: "One side would be men standing out there posing, luscious little creatures — oh! And on the other side of the street would be women dressed in evening gowns with feather boas and big hair and lots of makeup. And the next night, some of the boys would be over there on the other side of the street in femme drag and vice versa." If the Castro was gay uptown, this was gay downtown. Cheryl got a kick out of the funkiness and the sexually charged air. Even the name, Polk Gulch, sounded like the title of a porno flick.

Until then, Cheryl had followed Mer's established routes. Now she had to walk into rooms cold and sell drugs to strangers. It helped that Sticky Fingers had a wide reputation.

She'd open with "Hey, ever heard of Sticky Fingers Brownies?" Often, the response would be "Oh, are you the Brownie Lady?" Why, yes, she was.

It could be that easy, though not everyone went for it. When Cheryl got turned down, she'd smile sweetly, and say, "I won't bother you again," on her way out the door.

Cheryl dressed to party; it helped her get in the mood. Sequined blouses, tight satin pants, high heels or strappy platforms, 1940s hats, and Jackie O. glasses. Sometimes she teased her hair into a giant triangle like a hot version of Roseanne Roseannadanna from *Saturday Night Live*. One day, she dressed up in a real Girl Scout Brownie uniform that fit her like a micromini — complete with activity patches, pigtails, and knee socks. Clicking down Polk, Cheryl felt sexy and subversive. Customers greeted her with flirtation, laughter, and cash.

Once, when she was covering Mer's run in the Castro, she wore a sparkling gold trench coat and high heels and nothing underneath, and when she walked into Hot Flash of America, everyone stopped what they were doing to applaud her entrance.

At six feet one (six feet five in certain shoes), Cheryl got noticed walking into a room. She had yards of skinny limbs, a rawness in the visible tendons and joints. When sitting, she tended to fold herself so her elbows and knees formed isosceles triangles like an origami crane. When she wore blouses unbuttoned to her waist (in fashion then), her upper ribs rippled beneath her cleavage, looking both sexy and savage. Not pretty in a girlish way but gorgeous and strange.

People had been telling Cheryl since high school that she should model, but she'd lacked the confidence. She thought that her nose was too wide, her face too long. She'd never felt especially graceful in her movements. But here she was, cutting a high profile in San Francisco and relishing it. She enrolled in modeling classes at the

Barbizon school downtown. Most of the other students were too young to drink in bars; Cheryl was twenty-seven and the mother of a toddler. She thought of the classes less in terms of starting a new career than cranking up the volume of her natural assets.

At Barbizon, she learned how to vary her hairstyles — permanents, updos, disco puffs, Farah Fawcett flips. How to use bronzer to slenderize her nose and accentuate her intense cheekbones. How to work the camera with slinky, provocative poses and geometric shapes. How to high step into a room and own it.

She got everyone at the warehouse involved. Before each sales run, she'd yell, "PHOTOSHOOT!" in a brassy Wisconsin yowl. Mer, Cheryl, and Doug took turns posing using the warehouse's

Cheryl.

ample props and patchwork spaces, and drawing inspiration from fashion magazines, dance classes, and one another. Cheryl challenged herself to never repeat a look on her brownie run, a game all three salespeople started playing. They shopped while they dealt. You could trade almost anything for brownies: taxi rides, meals, other drugs, massages, concert and theater tickets, and clothes and jewelry from shops on your route. Anything traded was fair game.

The crew prodded one another, conjuring increasingly dramatic versions of themselves for the camera, exploring themes. Furs, hats, feathers, signs and statement pieces, face and body paint. Doug — always striving for order (a Sisyphean task in the Sticky Fingers world) — began a chronological photo archive of their weekly looks that he housed in five oversize photo albums decorated with Egyptian hieroglyphs — what we in the family call the Brownie Books.

The clothing wasn't merely about looking good, it became an art form. Sometimes they dressed in theme: one day, all three went for a 1930s picnic look; another time, they all wore head-to-toe orange. Often, the outfits reflected the brownie bag designs. Distributing the product was their exhibition; the City was their gallery.

Customers loved it. "It was like an explosion of color and glitter coming down the street," says Patricia Rodriguez, aka "Sunshine," a punk photographer who day-jobbed as a cook at the Neon Chicken, a diner on Mer's route. "I remember, very distinctly, there always being a baby. I remember the stroller and ribbons and balloons and glitter and wild outfits . . . I thought to myself, *Man, not only are they here selling brownies, but they're, like, making a big deal out of it. Not on the down-low or anything.*"

It was gutsy to draw attention to oneself while committing a felony. But my folks had another way of looking at it: They wanted to be so obvious that cops wouldn't suspect them. They'd hide in plain sight.

If you saw a woman dressed to the nines on a weekend afternoon trundling a happy blonde baby down the street in a stroller with balloons streaming off the back, would your first thought be *drug dealer?*

Part of the weekly fun was hearing about the mischief customers had gotten into.

Eating a whole Sticky Fingers brownie wasn't usually a great idea; the recommended dose was a quarter. But people didn't always listen. Hence, many a story started with *I ate the whole thing and . . . ended up in Las Vegas* or *passed out at my brother's wedding* or *let my boss take me to an orgy.*

Bette Herscowitz from Mendel's in the Haight, now Doug's route, liked to keep extra brownies in her freezer. Once, while Bette was vacationing in Thailand, her mother happened upon the stash. She noticed that the brownie tasted funny but ate it anyway. An hour later, her lips became rubbery and numb, and she couldn't think coherently. Bette's mother was in her late sixties and thought she was having a stroke. She went to the hospital. The doctors kept her overnight, running tests. By the time they pronounced her healthy, she was feeling fine again. Overdoses — though not physically dangerous — were common.

Sunshine still remembers figuring out her ideal amount. "I never ate a whole one," she says. "They were too strong. And if I ate a half, I would feel like I wanted to pass out. And a quarter was a little bit too small. But a third was a perfect dose. I could function and still do things. It was a lot of bang for your buck."

Even if you were careful, the high could be unpredictable. Today, California cannabis products are precisely labeled with THC and CBD proportions as clear as nutritional information on packaged foods. Not so in the 1970s. Plus, since Sticky Fingers sourced their shake from multiple sinsemilla growers, the intensity of the active ingredient varied from week to week. Their best gauge of the product were the anecdotes that came back.

———

The warehouse was a playground for the Sticky Fingers kids. Children's toys accumulated: a wooden rocking horse, handmade stuffed animals, wagons and dolls and dump trucks. Two-year-old Noel stomped around in his first cowboy boots. Fridays, when Carmen and Susan Vigil came to bake and wrap, their toddler got into the mix; Marcus and Noel had epic indoor tricycle races.

In a vast, booming space where none of the rooms had ceilings, it got loud. Jeep moved out to live with bachelor friends in the Haight; it was one thing to be kept awake by roommates arguing or having sex, and another to be kept awake by squalling babies. So Cheryl and Noel moved into Jeep's old loft overlooking the kitchen. Cheryl could walk out onto the rafters, high above the floor, and look down into different areas. She sometimes "visited" Mer in her middle room and talked to her from above.

"It was nuts to be in that place with a baby," my mom says. The mulchy wood floors were full of splinters. There were exposed wires and carpentry tools, jars of turpentine and palettes of wet oil paint. The rickety stairs up to the loft lacked a guardrail. Cockroaches scuttled in the corners. No heat or insulation from the Pacific chill. With one door and no windows, it was a fire trap.

And why not address the brontosaurus in the room? Weed was everywhere: green clouds engulfed my dad when he prepared the ghee, coating dishes and utensils; dank buds lolled on rolling trays and in unlocked stash boxes; joints smoldered between our parents' fingers, then shriveled in ashtrays already heaped with roaches; brownie crumbs blanketed the floor where we played. Between second-hand smoke, secret finger swipes of batter, and stolen crumbs, we tots consumed a significant amount of cannabis. It is, I suppose, a testament to the drug's natural mildness that all three of us have developed into capable, healthy adults.

Meridy swore she wouldn't be like her mother — domineering, critical, resentful, and depressed over suppressing her own desires to tend a family. She knew what she *didn't* want to do, but what did the alternative look like?

In the 1970s, a lot of parents were asking themselves this question. Mer joined a group of new mothers that met every week to
share ideas and discuss quandaries in improvised parenting. They
were artists and writers and activists exploring new concepts in
child-rearing, determined to raise kids without sacrificing their
own dreams — a revolutionary notion for women who'd grown up
in 1950s households.

A series of photos documents a wind-whipped afternoon at Fort
Funston. My folks and a bunch of other adults sit in a circle amid
sand dunes and ice plants for some sort of ritual led by a woman
swathed in billowing pink plastic and wearing an Egyptian-style
headdress. It's hard to tell what's going on, but it involves people
shouting into abandoned bunkers while the woman in the headdress dances in the wind. My dad has painted the Eye of Horus on
his face. I'm there, too: a pudgy pink baby, looking like a figment
of someone's acid reverie.

My parents didn't let me slow them down. They simply carried
me along through the tornado of their lives.

Doug still believed in his duty to carry out the Berkeley Psychic
Institute word. He gave readings and shared off-the-cuff observations with friends, brownie clients, and sometimes strangers. His
famous phrase was "I just have to tell you . . ." followed by whatever he thought you ought to confront about yourself, your blind
spots and weaknesses. He'd call people out on pessimism, denial,
hypocrisy, addiction. In Mer's case, her fluctuating weight. He was
everyone's self-appointed magic mirror.

The reactions were mixed. Maybe Doug's impromptu readings
stung because they hit home. He *was* perceptive, but he lacked social grace. Instead of waiting for a private moment, he'd dress people down in the middle of a party, in front of friends and lovers, or
while trying to sell them brownies — confident that he was doing
them a favor by being honest.

Some people found Doug's candor refreshing. Like Stannous

Flouride, the punk counterman at Acme Café in Noe Valley. Stannous had come to San Francisco to be a hippie in the late sixties but found the flower children mealy. Punk culture had all the hedonism and playfulness of the era minus the cheery mood. It offered Stannous a delicious outlet for his manic energy and the internal *fuck you* he'd been nursing since childhood.

Doug couldn't wrap his head around punk. The music made him cringe, and the poster art disturbed him. But despite their opposing aesthetics, Doug and Stannous found common ground. They were both intellectual, artistic, and iconoclastic. Both got a buzz from freaking people out. Doug would ask one of his confrontational questions like "What do you get out of projecting hostility into the world?" and instead of taking offense, Stannous would challenge him back. They indulged in long debates about discordance as an art form, the role of violence in social change, and, of course, the Nuns vs. the Bee Gees.

A friendship bloomed. Stannous started hanging out at the warehouse. "I had been buying brownies for a long time before I was ever around during production," he says, "because production was such a serious operation and the guys who were cooking and stuff wanted to keep it low-key. When I realized the extent of what they were doing, it was like *whoa*." Stannous eventually designed two brownie bags, one of which depicts a champagne bottle with the cork popping off, and says, *If all the world's a stage, San Francisco is the cast party!*

Stannous had thought the business model was smart from the beginning, but he hadn't pictured the high volume. "The nature of the distribution made it so that people think, *Oh, yeah, the bakery was in Noe Valley,* because we were in Noe Valley and we thought it was local," he says. "I don't think most people realized that it was citywide, that it was as large as it was."

By spring of 1978, the brownies were all over town, though few people knew where they came from. Even today, many former customers are surprised to learn the size of the operation. If you were

on Polk Street, Cheryl was the Brownie Lady. If you were on the
wharf, it was Mer. Why would you expect multiple salespeople
working different routes simultaneously?

Doug carefully measured out a thirty-foot-by-thirty-foot square
on the warehouse floor. He'd borrowed a power sander from a
friend who worked in construction and spent the afternoon shav-
ing away layers of splintery wood. Mer was in Milwaukee introducing her parents to their granddaughter — leaving Doug with
much-needed time alone.

It felt good to work with his hands. The roar of the sander, saw-
dust kicking into the air as he erased old hoofmarks and gouges.
He finished the edges meticulously by hand, making clean right
angles in the corners. He didn't have to think, and no one was talking. Beautiful wordless time.

Cheryl and Noel came and went, and he ignored them, deep in
his work, eyes on the lines. Later, he suggested they leave again so
he could apply thick layers of toxic varnish to seal in the splinters
that plagued the rest of the warehouse. Then he installed a bal-
let barre that he'd found dumpster diving and hung large mirrors.
Their own home dance studio.

The dance floor was a gift for Mer. She was bigger than ever after the pregnancy. She took dance classes three days a week but
didn't exercise on the off days. And if Doug didn't stay on her case,
she reverted to eating unhealthy foods. Doug couldn't figure it out:
Why did she choose to be fat?

As the *I Ching* hexagram "43. *Kuai*/Break-through (Resolute-
ness)" said, "The best way to fight evil is to make energetic progress in the good." So here he was, focusing on a positive outcome.

The dance floor would be the centerpiece for amazing parties.
And with this in the house, Mer would have no excuse not to exercise daily. It would be a superb surface for the kids, a no-splinter
zone for crawling and sliding. A boon to the whole Sticky Fingers
family.

With the project finished and Mer still in Milwaukee, Doug allowed himself one small indulgence — an experiment he'd wanted to try for a long while.

"After we became friends," Stannous Flouride tells me, "your dad took me to see *Women in Love* at the Castro Theatre. He wanted me to see it because of the wrestling scene. Have you ever seen *Women in Love*? It should be called *Men in Love* because it's actually about the relationship between these two men. And there's a scene in it where they wrestle. Your dad wanted to see that because he wanted to do that. I was a little taller, but we were both about the same weight. And it was nothing. Get the person down until they say 'Give' and then let them up. And then, you know, do it again. And I mean for several hours."

I ask Stannous if he and my dad were lovers. He gives me a wry, one-sided smile that I've noticed is prominent in his facial repertoire. Very punk.

"He and I were probably both . . . I don't know about bi . . . but sluts at that time in our lives. But this was physical, and it was romantic without being sexual. It was, you know, a chance to be physically intimate with somebody in a nonsexual manner. Wrestling puts you so tightly and so closely into contact."

Women in Love, a 1969 British melodrama directed by Ken Russell and based on the D. H. Lawrence novel, follows two male friends — Gerald and Rupert — who fall in love with each other and try to make sense of their feelings while surrounded by women. The Castro screened it on March 16, 1978, along with a gay coming-of-age comedy from France, a double bill the theater called "The Search for Sexual Identity."

I imagine my dad taking Stannous to that resplendent old film house with its gilded statues, velvet curtains, and imposing deco chandelier. Sneaking glances at his companion's face in the darkened theater, trying to gauge his reactions.

The wrestling scene takes place in a lavish drawing room in

front of a crackling fire. "I have a feeling," Gerald says, eyeing his friend, "that if I don't watch myself I might do something silly."

"Why not do it?" Rupert says.

They flirt for another beat. Rupert mentions that he used to do a little "Japanese-style wrestling."

"How do you start?" Gerald asks.

"Well, you can't do much in a stuffed shirt."

Cut to a lock being turned in an ornate door. Cut to the men, now buck naked, circling each other in front of the fire: sculpted abs and biceps, swinging dicks, hairy balls.

The men box lightly. Then one bear-hugs the other and slams him to the ground. They rise and fall again. Grabbing and twisting and rolling. Muscles flex; sweat glistens. There's the slap of flesh on flesh, the groans and grunts. Dramatic, dark music swells to a fearsome crescendo.

Afterward, resting on a polar bear rug, Rupert pants, "We ought to swear to love each other, you and I, implicitly, perfectly, finally, without any possibility of ever going back on it. Shall we swear to each other one day?"

They nearly kiss. Then Gerald squeezes his friend's shoulder instead — a restrained, fraternal gesture — and says, "Wait until I understand it better."

The scene is both erotic and poignant. One feels Gerald's tumult, the struggle between passion and intellect, his war against his instincts. How he doesn't want to want what he wants.

The bag Doug designed that week depicts the grinning face of Satan — pointy Vulcan ears, reptilian eyes, sharp tongue protruding from a seductive smile. Text beside his face reads, *The Devil's Playground*. From the Devil's left eye pours a river of naked, writhing bodies copulating in every imaginable combination and forming the words *Sticky Fingers Brownies*.

Doug had an affinity for cycles of sin and expiation, dissolution and rebirth. His next bag — for his wife's return the following week

—was a portrait of a haloed Jesus Christ along with a quote from John 3:3: *And JESUS said; Except a man be born again, he cannot see the Kingdom of God.*

Mer was delighted by the dance floor. She stepped into the center and tried out a few moves on the slick surface. She loved to dance, and Doug's idea of bringing that into the home filled her with optimism. They would groove together, to their own music, melding their styles.

Doug twirled her into a dip.

They began planning a summer bash.

At first, Mer didn't see that the dance floor might be a booby-trap. That she would be goaded to exercise constantly whether she had the time and energy or not, that she'd be shamed if she skipped a day. She didn't immediately notice something back-handed in the gift.

Nor did she know about Doug's wrestling date with Stamnous or his occasional erotic adventures in the men's sauna at Finnila's Finnish Baths. She sometimes got jealous when she caught him eyeing thinner women, but she failed to notice his attraction to men.

For the last weekend of March, Mer designed a bag based on an image from her tarot deck: a sweet-faced young man wandering over a grassy hill.

The Fool.

sticky fingers brownies

Mick

14

Off My Cloud

Summer of 1978, if you weren't looking for a party, you'd come to the wrong town. And if you were here long before this party started and wanted nothing to do with it, too bad.

Michael Maletta, a hairdresser and disco promoter on Mer's Castro route, threw a series of outrageous bashes. Michael was a handsome New York transplant with a sarcastic wit, a fanciful imagination, and a disbelief in limits. Friends nicknamed him the P. T. Barnum of the '70s.

Late May, Michael invited Mer to sell brownies at a mega party called *Stars*. "You'll need a can opener," he said, handing her a cylindrical tin akin to a soup can. On the label was an image of three prancing unicorns. OPEN CAN AND GET READY, it said. MAY 27, 1978, BE A STAR. Mer cracked into it at home. Inside was a baby-blue T-shirt silk-screened with a red star, along with typed instructions for mailing in photographs to be used for your *Stars* passport, and a slide of yourself "looking and feeling like a star."

Stars took place in a huge wooden warehouse at a defunct pier on a desolate stretch of the waterfront. When the taxi driver got lost, Mer rolled down her window and they followed a thumping bass to its source. The bouncer seemed surprised to see a woman with a *Stars* passport. "I'm the Brownie Lady," Mer said, handing him a freebie. He waved her in.

The sound inside was colossal — an octave-jumping bass line and strings surging through climax after climax. The air was jungle hot and steamy, pungent with male sweat and the chemical tang of poppers. Most boys had already stripped off their shirts, and some were down to jock straps and boots. Slick bodies gleamed in strobing lights.

Mer stood on a chair to get her bearings. Erotic images projected onto billowing fabric on the walls alternated with the cheesecake photos men from the audience had sent in. In one corner, a tower of fresh strawberries rose above a moat of flowing chocolate, and behind that Mer could make out an orgy in progress. Men stood in line on a raised platform over the dance floor. It took a moment to identify that they were pissing into a trough dozens of feet long.

Mer seemed to be the only female in the room. Still breastfeeding and avoiding uppers, she stayed for only an hour, long enough to sell out her duffel of brownies. But she heard that the party went until noon the next day. People talked about it for weeks afterward.

On the business front, the expansion continued. Once Cheryl had found her footing on Polk, she traversed Nob Hill to the tony boutiques lining Union Street in the Marina, the upper-crusty-but-still-sort-of-bohemian neighborhood Armistead Maupin often featured in his daily "Tales of the City" serial — where the Marina Safeway and a corner laundromat were depicted as the hottest spots for straights to pick up dates. It was a less obvious match for Sticky Fingers than Polk Gulch. But just because some of the businesses catered to snooty clientele didn't mean the people who worked in them were squares.

North Beach Leathers became the highlight of Cheryl's run. Founded in 1967, they utilized snakeskin, buckskin, furry hides, and ample fringe to produce custom leather outfits for Elvis Presley, Jimi Hendrix, Sonny Barger of the Hells Angels, Jim Morrison, Tina Turner, Huey Newton of the Black Panther Party for Self-Defense, Janis Joplin, and, of course, the Rolling Stones. The original workshop was in North Beach, but the Marina storefront catered to socialites gone wild.

The salespeople were all smoking-hot, leather-clad bad boys. For Cheryl, this was a dangerous kind of heaven. "The first time I walked into North Beach Leather on Union Street," she says, "Afghan Face grabbed me and gave me a big kiss right on the lips." The guy she calls Afghan Face was a wiry Englishman with a long narrow face, hair in a silver shag. He looked a bit like his dog, an Afghan hound, hence her nickname for him. "I mean, he completely swept me off my feet the first time I walked in there," she says. "He didn't even know what I was there for yet. Long live rock and roll and tight pants!"

Since the Milwaukee days, Cheryl had had a thing for guys who wore leather and did mountains of drugs. While Cheryl sold him brownies, Afghan Face laid out rails of coke in the store's back room. The cherry on top: he knew the Rolling Stones personally. Cheryl nursed a crush for weeks. They eventually slept together.

Later that summer, the Rolling Stones — Cheryl's favorite — came through on their *Some Girls* tour and played in Oakland. Afghan Face had backstage passes and asked Cheryl to be his date. She didn't go. "I didn't understand him," she says in an exasperated tone. "There was a language barrier and I didn't actually find out that he'd invited me until afterward. He was telling me about the show, and I was like, 'Oh, that must have been wonderful! I wish I could have gone!' And he said, 'Well, I asked you if you wanted to go.' My heart dropped to the floor. His accent was so thick, I probably understood an eighth of what he said to me at any point, but I was in love. Then our romance was over, you know, because he wasn't used to being turned down by women."

Customers often tried to score other drugs from Sticky Fingers — cocaine, quaaludes, heroin — but the answer was no. In Cheryl's mind, the fact that they dealt only wholesome herbal brownies was their karmic shield. "We always felt really righteous about it," she says. "You know, like we weren't really drug dealers."

Most of Union Street was more buttoned-up. Cheryl had to break businesses in cautiously, on high alert. Customers gave tacit signals indicating how to operate in their workplaces. She often followed them into back rooms or supply closets, but some did transactions right in the open in front of shoppers. So long as no one acted paranoid, the straight world wouldn't be the wiser. A lot was communicated through nods of the head, hand gestures, shifting glances; it was important to read between the lines.

Once, when Mer was wrapping up a deal at a cash register in a magic shop, her customer cried out, "Oh, hello, Officer! How are you today?"

Glancing behind her, Mer spotted a man in a drab sport coat circulating around the store — a plainclothes cop. She grabbed a novelty item from beside the cash register, paid for it with money the cashier had just handed her, and walked casually out the door. Only after she'd put distance between herself and the narc did she glance at her purchase: a phony dollar bill that — *presto chango!* — turned into a hundred.

The Castro Street run had reached what Mer calls "gigantor proportions." She'd start every Friday at around two p.m., first by car, double-parking outside various businesses to drop off individual grocery bags that had been prepacked with advance orders. She'd then load herself down with two army duffels of brownies and hang more off the stroller. With the baby supplies and extra clothes, maneuvering through a crowd with that much stuff was exhausting.

Then Kissie, the waitress at the Village Deli, said, "You know, you could leave some brownies here in the kitchen and come back when you need to restock. Don't worry, we'll keep an eye on it." She winked. "For that matter, we could probably sell some for you. The whole damn neighborhood comes through here anyway."

Mer started doing exactly that: leaving a duffel of loose brownies and a stack of brownie bags at the café for Kissie to sell. Soon thereafter, the Village Deli hired Dan Clowry, a bookish twenty-six-year-old from Pennsylvania, as the new manager.

Dan had recently moved to San Francisco and come out of the closet in one breath. When he arrived, Sylvester's "You Make Me Feel (Mighty Real)" was becoming an international hit. The song had two verses: the first about meeting someone on a dance floor and wanting more to happen, the second about the thrill of a first kiss when the new lovers find themselves together in the dark. But mostly it was Sylvester doing a gospel-style vamp about how *real* he felt. Dan considered it his "welcoming song."

"Within a week or two," Dan says, "I was in a gang right in the heart of things. It was pretty amazing in this community. There was a feeling of closeness brought together by people being unable to come out to their families and creating their own families."

By the time he started at the Village Deli, Dan remembers, Kissie was selling a full gross of Sticky Fingers brownies every Friday afternoon. "Then we got up to two gross!" he says. That's 288 brownies, which seems like a lot to sell from the counter of a café in one afternoon. "People were buying them for the bags as well," Dan adds. "Some people would just buy two or three [brownies] as long as they could get a bag. It was part of the whole feeling of that time."

Mer didn't arrive with the brownies until late afternoon on Fridays, but Dan says that as soon as the café opened in the morning people would start asking, "Hey, did the brownies come in yet?" and "What's the bag like this week?"

Mer gave the Village Deli crew a deal and never asked if they marked the price up for resale; she didn't care. "I'd drop off a duffel of brownies," she says. "Two or three hours later, I'd pick the duffel up again. Instead of brownies, it would be full of cash." After a while, she stopped counting the money. She trusted Kissie and Dan, and they didn't let her down.

Another fixture at the Village Deli in those days was Cleve Jones, the twenty-four-year-old activist from Arizona. He had curly brown hair, rosy lips, and naturally pink cheeks; behind the baby face was a lefty spitfire.

When he first met Harvey Milk, Cleve tells me, he wasn't impressed. Being middle-aged and a businessowner put Harvey in a category with the Man. It was only after Anita Bryant and the evangelicals began attacking gay rights that the young activist joined Harvey's campaign. Cleve had a knack for the mechanics of large protests; he became the supervisor's protégé and street-level organizer.

Cleve lived in a small shotgun flat with roommates, one wall phone, and no privacy. The Village Deli became his de facto office. He'd claim a small table near the counter, and Kissie and Dan would let him use their phone to plan demonstrations. Looking back, he remembers the heavy traffic on Fridays when people streamed in looking for brownies — though he rarely bought them himself. "I never knew when it was going to hit, you know, so I would eat some and then I wouldn't feel it, and then I'd eat more, and three hours later it's like I'm on bad acid. They were very potent."

The antigay crusaders had been on a roll all spring, successfully repealing city gay rights ordinances in St. Paul, Wichita, and Eugene. As soon as news of each repeal broke, Cleve would muster forces at the intersection of Market and Castro. The crowd would march two miles down to city hall, up Polk Street to California, and up a steeper hill to Grace Cathedral — growing larger and louder along the way. They would then stampede down Powell Street into touristy Union Square.

The organizers called this the "disaster route," and it was deliberate. "You didn't have to activate the telephone tree or put up posters," Cleve explains. "People would know, *Oh, shit, something's going down. Go to Castro right now*. It was very, very intentional."

Carmen and Cheryl.

The fast-paced, hilly marches were also a strategy for avoiding violence; they left the protesters too tired to riot. And the rapid assembly and circuitous route kept the SFPD off guard. "They *hated* it. I never took out a permit for anything." Cleve smiles. "I have my permit: it's called the Constitution."

Doug shifted grinding the pot to Wednesday so baking could start on Thursday and continue through Saturday. Carmen churned out batch after gooey batch, averaging forty pans per workday — about 2,800 brownies per week. He stacked the pans perpendicularly in tall wobbly towers while they cooled enough to be wrapped.

One of the Wrapettes designed a bag depicting the Keebler Elf version of the Sticky Fingers baking team. Carmen is pudgy and cute in a giant chef's hat and overalls, his patchy black beard and sideburns curling around his face. Wearing roller skates and miniskirts, the Wrapettes zoom through the frame with improbable pyramids of brownies piled on trays. The kitchen walls are curved and textured like the hollow inside of a tree, with a hole opening onto rolling hills at sunrise. As if the brownies came from a distant fairy land instead of a ramshackle Mission warehouse.

Hardly anyone knew where Sticky Fingers came from, making a bust less likely. But in the summer of 1978, shortly after the *Carmen and the Wrapettes* bag, they let that advantage slip away.

Cheryl began selling brownies at the warehouse. It started slowly, with close friends stopping by to make purchases, and gradually expanded to include close friends of close friends, then friends of *those* friends. To avoid having people show up unexpectedly, Cheryl set a time — four p.m. to seven p.m. on Fridays — when customers could visit. She enjoyed holding court at home for a change, passing doobies and sipping wine.

Of all the risks they took, I can't wrap my head around this one.

It had backfired on Dennis Peron. After his 1977 bust, Dennis told a reporter, "I didn't know the narco I let in, but I got good vibes from her." He'd trusted his gut like my parents trusted theirs. Then the vice squad showed up at his door and a cop shot him through the thigh.

To produce their current volume of around ten thousand brownies per month, Sticky Fingers needed one hundred pounds of raw shake, approximately ten large garbage bags full. It would be impossible to pass as a small operation. Plus, Doug was writing everything down; he'd already filled one ledger and begun a second one. With so much evidence lying around, a raid could have sent my parents to prison — and me, a baby, into the foster system.

When I ask my mom why they did the home sales anyway, she says, "I did a lot of things that made me nervous back then. But if you're not a little nervous, you make mistakes. You have to understand we were always very careful to consult the *I Ching* before doing anything like that."

Sticky Fingers decided to throw a summer shindig — a Kings and Queens costume party to spark up the dance floor. Unlike today, one couldn't resort to mass-produced costumes from Amazon. Creativity was king, playfulness was queen.

Mer settled on Cleopatra. Egyptian fever was sweeping the nation as the *Treasures of Tutankhamun* exhibit made its slow tour of the United States. She hand-sewed an ornate golden headdress out of lamé, vintage coins, and metallic mesh, with a wired gold cobra rearing above her forehead. Cheryl was the Roller Derby Queen in red satin short shorts, knee-high socks, a sparkling crash helmet, knee and elbow pads, and, of course, roller skates. Doug became the Rainbow King in a headdress made from a baby toy: plastic donuts of gradating sizes and colors stacked to form a rainbow cone on top of his head. Strands of rainbow electrical wire jittered out from the base of the cone like static.

They laid a refreshment table with hundreds of brownies cut into quarters and hired a rock band as well as a doorman to collect the three-dollar admission and make sure no one got in without a full costume. No exceptions.

Some five hundred people came: jugglers and dancers and magicians and mimes from the wharf; radical theater freaks from the Angels of Light, Project Artaud, and *Beach Blanket Babylon;* Al Fellahin, a genderfuck belly dance troupe in gypsy garb; leathermen and leatherdykes; and strippers who danced on the rafters in stiletto heels.

"Usually, you'd go to a party and it would be all gay guys or all North Beach types," says Stannous Flouride, who came as the King of Marvin Gardens, head-to-toe in canary yellow with a crown and a shirt silk-screened with RENT $24 WITH ONE HOUSE. "The [Sticky Fingers] parties really reflected the diversity of their clientele. You would have straight white people from Union Street, you'd have freaks from Noe Valley, and gays from the Castro and Polk and that kind of stuff. It was this total cross section of the City — or the stoner population of the City."

Some people brought exploding bags of confetti and glitter. The mulchy wood grabbed the sparkles and wouldn't let go. After that first party, the warehouse floors always shone in sunlight as if the wood were inlaid with gemstones.

Mid-June, Barb blew through town on tour with *A Chorus Line*. (Her costume business hadn't worked out in Boston, and she'd moved on.) She had a layover at SFO between cities and spent it at the warehouse.

In a sleeve of photos labeled BARB'S FIVE-HOUR VISIT, I find shots of her and my dad doing cocaine off a pocket mirror, their jaws and brows tense. Cheryl mugs with a small lampshade hanging from her ear. I'm there, too, a bubbly six-month-old in a striped yellow shirt and white moccasins. First in my mom's arms (who doesn't appear to be doing coke), then on Barb's lap. Sometime during the visit, my mom asked Barb to be my godmother.

In yolk-yellow afternoon light, Barb took me for a walk up the block propped on her hip. Seeing our shadows crisp against the wall of a nearby building, Barb lifted my baby hand and waved it — which she says made me squeal in amazement as I recognized my shadow for the first time.

Later, Doug brought Barb into his studio to see *We Are All One. We Are None the Same*, which he'd finished over the winter. He'd done the portraits in a meticulous photo-realistic style, but he'd also taken some liberty: he had shrunk Mer to a thinner size.

Barb folded her arms across her chest. Doug had painted her wearing a bulky, unflattering sweater. Her cheeks looked chipmunky. "Jeez, Doug," she said. "If you were going to slim Mer down, why'd you keep me fat?"

"Tell you the truth," he said. "I think I did you a favor by showing you as you really are."

"Yeah, well, don't do me any more favors."

Decades later, Barb is still pissed about that painting.

And my dad still believes his honesty was a gift. "My mistake
was in shrinking your mother down," he says. "She wanted to be
thin, so I made her that way. But you don't help someone by telling them what they want to hear."

None of the Sticky Fingers women had a positive body image.
Even Cheryl, always skinny, rode an anorexic edge. She'd barely
eat for days, then binge alone in her room, scarfing boxes of cookies before burying the evidence in the garbage.

The dance floor became the locus of weight-loss mania. Mornings, Cheryl zipped herself into an ankle-length green-velour
housecoat with a hood, piled sweatshirts over that, cranked the
music, and ran in place for an hour, sweat streaking her face. Then
she dropped to the floor for bicycle crunches, push-ups, and log
lifts.

Mer occasionally joined in, but she hated it. Hated jogging,
hated sit-ups, hated feeling obligated. She dieted, fasted, and took
saunas at Finnila's. She loved to dance. But she was never one of
those my-body-is-a-temple people. Her body was a box, a con-
tainer, a house.

Swaggering though the middle of this was Doug with his John
Travolta physique. He could eat heaping plates of spaghetti, seconds and thirds of Chinese takeout, double scoops of ice cream
— and always look trim. A natural advantage he used for leverage
when he felt weak in other ways.

Even people beyond the immediate circle noticed. "They would
talk about stuff in front of us," says Alice Charap, a chiroprac-
tor who sometimes hung out at the warehouse. "Doug might say,
'If Meridy would just shape up, she'd be so much better off.' He
seemed to be very critical. And yet, he was with her by choice. You

couldn't help but think that he'd selected a plump woman. She was always talking about her weight and always on some new regimen. Always looking gorgeous, by the way, but she wasn't happy."

June tended to be gray and damp as hot inland temperatures sucked fog in from the Pacific to loiter over the bay. But a dour weather forecast was no match for hundreds of thousands of cheerful gays and lesbians. As soon as the Gay Freedom Day parade started inching along Market Street on June 25, 1978, the clouds parted, as if some queeny angel were elbowing through to watch muscles flex and sequins sparkle.

Mer and Doug found a spot in the throng. With me in a Gerry carrier, they bobbed along to disco blaring from passing floats and soaked up the sunshine.

The *Los Angeles Times* would report 375,000 in attendance. Even if that overshot the mark, it was likely the largest gathering in San Francisco during the entire 1970s. "A sense of gay manifest destiny gripped San Francisco by 1978," Randy Shilts wrote, "as if it were ordained that homosexuals should people the city from sea to shining bay." An army vet-*cum*-activist named Gilbert Baker had designed and hand-sewn a pair of enormous rainbow flags. This international symbol for LGBTQ+ diversity debuted that day in San Francisco.

Harvey Milk sat atop his gray Volvo with his legs dangling through the sunroof. He wore a ringer T-shirt, a lei of fresh flowers, and a black armband with the pink triangle symbol used to mark homosexuals during the Holocaust. Milk wasn't messing around. In his first months in government, he had secured passage of an ordinance prohibiting discrimination against gays in housing and employment (for which the sole opposing vote had come from Supervisor Dan White, apparently in retaliation for an earlier vote of Milk's); he'd taken on greedy real estate developers with an antispeculation bill; and he'd introduced a pooper-scooper bill to force dog owners to clean up after their pets.

Unbeknownst to the public, Harvey had received dozens of death threats leading up to the parade, including a typed postcard that read, "You get the first bullet the minute you stand at the microphone." Harvey often wisecracked to friends about being assassinated. Cleve teased him about it. "Who do you think you are?" he prodded. "Martin Luther King? Malcolm X? You're just a gay shopkeeper." Joking aside, Harvey had already recorded three tapes at his lawyer's office that expressed his last wishes in the event of an assassination. As the death threats rolled in, close friends had tried to talk Harvey out of appearing at the parade, but he'd shrugged them off and declined a police escort. Today was too important.

If gays and lesbians seemed to have clout within the glitter-swirled snow globe of San Francisco, the glass was thin. Antigay crusader Anita Bryant had been named Most Admired Woman by readers of *Good Housekeeping*. She'd nearly lost her $100,000-per-year contract with Florida Citrus, then won it back as her popularity surged. In a lengthy *Playboy* magazine interview in May, she'd shared her opinion that people should be locked up for at least twenty years if convicted of a homosexual act. "Any time you water down the law, it just makes it easier for immorality to be tolerated," she told the interviewer. "They'll have plenty of time to think in prison."

The evangelicals had yet to lose a ballot-box fight. Now they were coming for California. Senator John Briggs had gotten Proposition 6 on the ballot for November 1978. Briggs's rhetoric played on fear, linking homosexuality to pedophilia. Most anyone would agree that children should be protected from predators. Therefore, gays shouldn't be allowed near kids. The language of Proposition 6, however, made no mention of pedophilia or molestation.

> Provides for filing charges against schoolteachers, teachers' aides, school administrators or counselors for advocating, soliciting, imposing, encouraging or promoting private or public sexual acts . . . between persons of the same sex in a manner likely to come to the

attention of other employees or students; or publicly and indiscreetly engaging in said acts.

Even heterosexuals accused of "advocating," "promoting," or "encouraging" homosexuality could lose their jobs. It would be left up to school boards and district courts to decide what these broad terms meant. The Briggs Initiative laid the groundwork for a witch hunt. And it had an early lead in the polls.

Increasingly, Harvey framed coming out of the closet as less a personal decision and more as a political imperative. "You must come out," Harvey would say in his Gay Freedom Day speech later that afternoon. "Come out to your parents, your relatives. I know that it is hard and that it will hurt them, but think of how they will hurt you at the voting booth! Come out to your friends . . . to your neighbors, to your coworkers, to the people who work where you eat and shop . . . [B]reak down the myths; destroy the lies and distortions for your own sake, for their sake, for the sake of the youngsters who are being terrified by the votes coming from Dade County to Eugene."

Defying the assassination threats, Harvey sat tall on the roof of that Volvo and whipped his arm overhead like a cowboy swinging a lasso.

Supervisor Dan White was also in the crowd that afternoon, granting interviews from the sidelines. He'd been the sole supervisor to vote against closing Market Street for the annual parade. "The vast majority of people in this city don't want public displays of sexuality," he'd said. White wasn't alone in this sentiment. "I think it offends a lot of people because it's just *blatant*," a young man with a bristly mustache said in a man-on-the-street interview. An elderly woman chimed in, "I don't want people to make a mockery out of themselves."

One woman who grew up in Eureka Valley in the 1970s still remembers men walking past her stoop wearing assless chaps—

clearly unbothered that there were kids like her nearby. There were dozens of bathhouses operating in San Francisco in 1978, plus playrooms, glory holes, and dungeons in many discos. There were water-sports parties, mass orgies, and anonymous sex in public parks at all hours. "Men come and go like food," wrote diarist Mark Abramson, "and a store is always open when you need one." Sexuality had reached a high boil and the lid was rattling.

For the bakery, keeping up with demand that summer required frequent expeditions into the Humboldt wilderness, a four-hour drive on the highway before starting down dirt roads. By July, their usual suppliers had run dry and harvest was still months away. Buying trips became more complicated, leading deeper into the backwoods. The roads were perilous and often unmarked; growers didn't want to be found. More than once, they'd been greeted with a rifle.

Then Doug and Mer got lucky.

In hippiedom, picking up hitchhikers is considered good karma. One afternoon, Doug and Mer offered a ride to a longhair in Marin, a back-to-the-lander heading to the City for the weekend. Introducing himself as John Schaeffer, their passenger proffered a joint of powerful sinsemilla.

John talked excitedly about his new business venture. He'd been living on a rural commune near the tiny town of Philo and commuting forty miles each way to his job as a computer operator for Mendocino County (back when computers took up entire rooms and were controlled with punch cards). Folks from John's commune would give him long shopping lists — kerosene lamps, tools, books — and he'd have to stop at five different stores to gather it all. John drove a Volkswagen convertible with a redwood stump for a front seat. Driving back to the commune, he'd smoke a joint and let his mind wander. One night, it hit him: *What if you could get all this stuff in one place?* He opened Real Goods in the town of Willits, three hours north of San Francisco. It was among the first supply stores in the state that catered specifically to back-to-the-land hippies.

The conversation stuck with Mer. Back-to-the-landers might mean growers.

On the next trip to Humboldt, Doug and Mer were passing through Willits, so they stopped at Real Goods and gave John a sample brownie. "Say," Mer said. "You wouldn't know anyone who has shake lying around, would you?"

As it turned out, John did.

The market for California sinsemilla had exploded since Mer's first trip up to Humboldt in 1976. The *San Francisco Examiner* reported in 1978 that California sinsemilla was selling for $1,500 per pound within the state (equivalent to $5,892 in 2019) and more in other parts of the country. The high dollar amount attracted both thieves and drug enforcement. Sheriff's deputies in Humboldt county claimed to have "seized pot worth as much as $5 million in a single day of raids on hidden gardens."

Farmers were eager to move their product quickly. As one grower told a reporter, "It's constant paranoia until it's all gone." A dusty truck loaded with typical growing supplies — rolls of chicken wire, irrigation pipes, fertilizer — could draw unwanted attention. Always innovative, John had thought of a system to help his customers stay under the radar. He had them arrive in the evening with shopping lists and park in the loading area. John's crew worked overnight to fill orders. Customers returned in the wee hours, paid for their goods, and hit the road before sunrise with supplies secreted beneath tarps.

Simple to add one more step. Now, twice a month, growers brought bags of unwanted shake for John's crew to set aside for Sticky Fingers Brownies. The price was fifty dollars a pound: cheap for the bakery and extra cash for the growers, many of whom usually burned or composted their shake. John didn't make any money from brokering these deals, though there were always a dozen brownies in it for him. He saw it as a service to his valued customers, a favor to his new San Francisco friends, and a way to amass extra karma — which, according to his beliefs, was a kind of currency.

This was a huge break for the bakery. No more rutted dirt roads, no more getting lost. And John seemed to have an endless contact list; it wasn't unusual for him to have fifty pounds ready for Doug and Mer to cram into their car and transport — slowly, carefully — to San Francisco.

These bimonthly drives awakened something in Doug. He'd see a red-tailed hawk circling overhead and feel his spirit soar with it. He relished the fresh air, the lazy sprawl of oaks, the sweet taste of water from a natural spring. His muscles unwound. He found

Doug in Willits.

himself looking forward to the bucolic beauty, quietude, and *right-
ness* he experienced on these bimonthly trips. City life could be
thrilling, but he envied John a little bit.

Mer saw Willits as fuel for their urban lifestyles; Doug felt like
he was visiting his future.

Decades later, John Schaeffer marvels at the brazenness of collecting that much weed in his store. "I tried to arrange it so it came
just in time," he says. "Even though it was shake, which seemed
like it was a little more legal than buds." He starts laughing. "But
it probably wasn't."

A pound is a pound is a pound.

I think about the stories we tell ourselves in order to feel se-
cure when we aren't safe at all. Like Cheryl deciding she wasn't
really a drug dealer since it was only pot. Like Doug thinking he
could bring order to his chaotic life by writing numbers in ledgers.
Like Mer deciding she wasn't in danger because she'd consulted
the *I Ching*.

John's extra karma seems to have paid off, however. He explains
that a few months after he connected with my parents, a stranger
pulled up to Real Goods with a nine-watt photovoltaic panel in
the trunk of his Porsche. The driver, a guy named David Lemm,
was looking for a buyer for solar panels rejected from the space
program. John bought one panel, tinkered with it, and resold it to
a grower for $900. He ordered ten more panels, then a hundred,
then a thousand — likely becoming America's first retailer of solar
panels for private homes. "Soon," John says, "we had execs flying in
from ARCO Solar to try and figure out why all these panels were
selling in Willits, of all places."

One word: weed.

Solar helped the illicit farmers stay off the grid. "In hindsight,"
John says, "it was a synergistic coevolution between cannabis and
solar. Because the cannabis growers in the woods needed solar to
support their lifestyles . . . which enabled them to grow their mari-

juana. At the same time, these same growers, because of their income, were the only ones who could afford these solar panels . . . These two industries were inextricably linked for a time."

Real Goods celebrated its fortieth anniversary in 2018. Along with its sister business, the Solar Living Institute, it remains core to California's alternative energy industry.

My parents were also thinking ahead.

People often asked for the secret recipe — which Sticky Fingers withheld as a matter of policy. If they played their hand right, maybe they could patent it and cash in down the road. They joked about selling it to Betty Crocker once marijuana finally became legal — which, with the commander in chief advocating for decriminalization, seemed to them not a matter of *if* but *when*.

But how did one patent a recipe that depended on an illegal ingredient? Could it be done? One of Mer's customers on her Castro route was a lawyer — I'll call him Goran — who'd handled some intellectual property cases, so she broached the subject with him. He offered to come by and talk it over.

Goran was a flamboyant Yugoslavian who kept a tank of nitrous oxide in the trunk of his car and balloons in his pocket. When he came to the warehouse to discuss patenting, he brought the tank in with him. He periodically filled a balloon for Mer, Cheryl, or Doug, or huffed one himself, his voice dropping and expanding, so it was like hearing a Yugoslavian Barry White talk patent law.

Even with Goran's help (such as it was), patenting an illegal recipe would be delicate — if not impossible. They decided to hold off for the time being and see what would come from Carter's interest in marijuana reform.

On July 20, 1978, the president's drug czar, Dr. Peter Bourne, got caught writing his administrative assistant a prescription for quaaludes under a phony name. Days later, Bourne was accused of snorting cocaine at a benefit for NORML. The drug czar resigned in disgrace. Then seven junior aides told the press that they smoked pot regularly (though never at work), leading to wide-spread reporting on "drug abuse" in the White House. Faced with a public relations horror show, Carter issued severe warnings to his staff about marijuana use. All talk of decriminalization ceased. (The next US president to publicly discuss softening federal cannabis regulations would be Barack Obama three decades later; even then, the talk would amount to nothing.)

For the time being, Sticky Fingers settled for what they made on the street. Mer was returning from her Friday runs having peddled eight hundred to a thousand brownies. Saturdays on the wharf — with stops in North Beach and South of Market on the way — could be nearly as good. Between Polk and Union streets and Friday sales at the warehouse, Cheryl was pulling in similar numbers. Doug was not.

"He never did very well with it," my mom says. "And was always freaked out that he didn't do very well, you know . . . I remember coming in and he would've sold two dozen. Period."

In Cheryl's words, "He couldn't make a dime. Not a damn dime."

Doug had better weeks and worse weeks. But he was cut from a different cloth than Mer or Cheryl. "It's like I got on a Disney ride," he says, looking back. "That's what life was like. It was all about *fun*, you know? It's not very realistic. It's not grounded. I'm going to say it's not very honorable. You don't have a lot of self-esteem if you're running around life like that."

At the same time, Doug didn't like being bested. He'd stew over the disparity in numbers, saying things like "Well, *you* were in the Castro, so of course you're going to do well there."

Cheryl might chime in, "Then why did I do so well on Union Street, Doug?"

They'd fall into three-way spats. Or Doug would brood in his studio, then launch a counterattack later, turning his attention more sharply toward Mer's weight.

For the time being, there was bounty to go around. After Carmen and the Wrapettes were paid and funds set aside for ingredients, the remaining amount got divided evenly between the three salespeople, who each netted around $1,000 per week. As a couple, my parents were earning five or six times the average household income in 1978. They had a pile of cash to count every week.

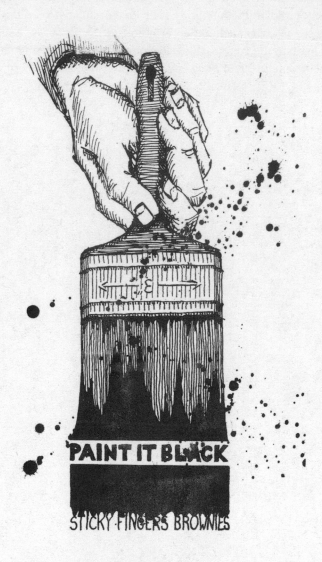

PAINT IT BLACK

STICKY FINGERS BROWNIES

Paint It Black

I n Barb's dream, three men stood in the warehouse facing away from her. Single file, like they were waiting in line for tickets at a movie theater. She didn't know who they were or why they were there, couldn't see their faces. The man at the rear raised his arm. In his hand, a glint of metal: a gun. Before Barb could react, he shot the person ahead of him point-blank in the back of the head. With the jerky movement of an automaton, he stepped over the body to shoot the third man, who hit the floor with a thud that shook the walls.

She awoke with blood pounding in her ears, her skin tingling. Her eyes adjusted slowly, picking out bluish rectangles high above: skylights. *I'm in the warehouse. In bed. It was just a dream.*

Barb called to Boogie in a whisper. She heard his claws click across the wood floor and his panting draw near. She felt for her cigarettes in the dark, then smoked one while stroking Boogie's shaggy ears. She heard overlapping snores: from the back of the warehouse where Doug and Mer and the baby slept, and from Cheryl and Noel's loft in front. Everyone was all right. Boogie snuffled, settling on the floor by the bed.

Barb had landed back in San Francisco after her summer on the road with *A Chorus Line* and was staying in the warehouse while looking for her own place. Having fantasized about starting her own clothing line for some time, she'd enrolled at the San Francisco School of Fashion Design to learn about merchandising. *Maybe*, she thought, *the rootlessness is starting to get to me.*

The next morning, Barb mentioned her nightmare to Doug. "This building used to be a livery stable, like after the 1906 quake," he said. "There could have been a shoot-out here long ago. Maybe you're picking up old vibes."

Barb stirred cream into her coffee. "I have been *really* psychic lately," she said. "It's almost too much."

She blamed this on her new boyfriend, a real estate agent named Mike White. She'd met him at a party — tall, sandy-haired, kind eyes — then bumped into him again at a Scientology meeting. When they met a third time on the street, Mike asked her out. He was divorced and had a son who lived out of state. One evening, out of the blue, Barb said, "I think your mother's going to call tonight. Something about your son. He wants to live with you again." Mike's phone rang a little later, and guess who it was. Within weeks, Mike's thirteen-year-old son had moved back to the City. Ever since they'd started dating, Barb's antenna had been picking up signals from all over the place.

She sipped her coffee, smiled at Doug. "Guess I'm pulling stuff out of the air."

But the dream lingered, remaining vivid as weeks passed.

Late September, my parents packed their blue plastic suitcases and my portable stroller for a trip to Europe. This would be their honeymoon. Barb and Cheryl would handle brownie sales until we returned in mid-November.

In my baby passport picture, my dad's knobby hands hold me up in front of a screen. I'm wearing a little milkmaid outfit and smiling. The first stamp, on September 30, 1978, is an entrance to Paris. From there, we toured Switzerland, Italy, and Spain. Trains, planes, automobiles. Four countries over six weeks with a baby in diapers. My mom had already decided that motherhood wouldn't knock the adventure out of her life; I would be part of the fun. And it's true that I look cheerful in pictures from the trip, all toothless smiles and balled fists. My parents wear stylish travel outfits — Mer in an off-the-shoulder sweater and a burgundy beret; Doug in his leather cowboy hat and a denim shirt Barb had embroidered with an image of a falcon flying over a river valley.

Art had brought Doug and Mer together, and it would be the focus of the trip. Museums in every city. At the Uffizi in Florence, my mom says we sat for an hour in the Botticelli room while I baby-talked to the cherubs in *The Birth of Venus*. I'm told I took my first baby steps in my grandmother's garden in Mijas, Spain, where on clear days you could see Morocco like a mirage across the water.

The City was not quiet while we were away. Senator John Briggs was stumping for Proposition 6, stirring the pot at every opportunity. He campaigned throughout the state but focused especially on San Francisco, which he liked to describe as the "moral garbage dump of homosexuality in this country." He gave California's more conservative elements a platform. For those in San Francisco who'd been displaced by gay gentrification — families who couldn't compete economically against newcomers with two incomes and no kids — Prop. 6 offered a chance to punch back. And it was working. A widely published September poll had the measure leading 61 percent to 31 percent, with only 8 percent undecided.

But San Francisco's lesbians and gays were ready for battle. Harvey, who'd just lost his lover Jack Lira to suicide, threw himself into the campaign like a man on fire leaping into a swimming pool. The community rallied around him. There were televised debates, marches, and fundraisers. Everyone seemed to have an opinion. Even punks got into it; the Mab threw a September benefit party called Save the Homos featuring performances by DV8, the Dils, and the Offs!, all proceeds going to Harvey's anti-Briggs fund.

Bay Area activists bused to the most rural nooks of the state, hoping that if people could speak face to face with real homosexuals the monster image would crumble. This was classic Harvey, who insisted that people were innately good and intelligent, just educated differently. He thought anyone could be won over if you were earnest and friendly and open.

Meanwhile, Dennis Peron was running a campaign of his own. Dennis had been out on bail, with his trial over the Big Top bust ongoing, when he'd marched into the registrar's office — flanked by dozens of supporters and a bugle player for dramatic flair — and announced that he had 20,800 signatures to get Proposition W on the ballot: *toot-tootle-oo!*

Prop. W stated: *We, the people of San Francisco, demand that the District Attorney, along with the Chief of Police, cease the arrest and prosecution of individuals involved in the cultivation, transfer, or possession of marijuana.*

Toward the end of Dennis's trial, his defense received a major boost from an unlikely source: Dennis's own irrepressible mouth. Whenever he saw the cop who'd shot him in the hall outside the courtroom, Dennis made catty remarks, complimenting Makaveckas's footwear or hairstyle in a queeny tone. One day, according to Dennis, the cop snapped. "You motherfucking faggot! I wish I'd killed you," he said. "One less faggot in San Francisco." The judge happened to overhear. In court later that day, when asked to demonstrate how he'd angled his gun during the raid, Makaveckas pulled out his service revolver and aimed it at Dennis for some thirty seconds. Outraged, the judge threw out the policeman's testimony, stripping the prosecution of their key witness. Dennis got a light sentence of six months in county jail followed by four years of probation.

Once the verdict came down and Dennis started doing his time, he went right on fighting for Prop. W — from jail. He also launched a campaign for a seat on the city charter revision commission. The press seemed amused. "[Peron] has determined that 200 of his 2500 fellow inmates at San Bruno are registered voters of San Francisco," one reporter wrote. "And he is forced to confine his electioneering largely to them."

Mer was impressed, if a bit baffled. "Dennis was fearless," she says. "Just absolutely fearless. Such a sweet guy, you know, Dennis wouldn't harm a fly. But he had balls of iron! I was pretty brave but never like that."

My parents had cast absentee ballots before leaving for Europe. They wouldn't learn the results until our return in mid-November.

Barb had a second dream in the middle of October that was almost identical to the first. Again, she saw three men standing in a line with their backs to her and felt a surge of adrenaline. Again, the man in back shot his two companions. A pool of dark blood swamped her feet. The name *White* drifted through her mind.

She awoke panting. What the hell did Mike White have to do with this? She knew he kept guns; she'd seen them in a glass cabinet at his house. They had a date the next night, so she decided to confront him.

"This is going to sound weird," she said to him at dinner. "I'm having these really vivid dreams where you're shooting people."

Mike squinted. "What?"

"I'm getting your name in the dream, too. I just . . . I feel like something bad is going to happen to you. Or maybe you're going to do something bad."

"That's a rotten thing to say."

Barb leveled her gaze. "Well, I *know* you have guns. I've seen them."

"So what! I inherited them, okay? My father was a cop. I don't . . . *shoot* people, Barbara."

Mike brooded through dinner. Barb didn't hear from him for days after that. When he finally called, it was to break up. "I'm sorry," he said. "But this psychic stuff with you is too much."

Barb felt defeated; she was fond of Mike. But she decided that the dreams must have been a warning to steer clear of him. She would ask for an aura cleansing from Doug when he and Mer got back from Europe. She'd gotten too hooked into Mike White's psyche somehow.

Halloween night 1978, Senator John Briggs tried to prank San Francisco's gay community. He called the SFPD early that evening to say that he was heading to Polk Street (which would be cordoned off for the annual street party). He also notified the press, obviously angling for publicity. "I'm here because this is a children's night and I'm interested in children," he said. A gaggle of journalists turned up for the expected confrontation between the homo-hating senator and some 80,000 queens on their high holiday.

Mayor Moscone caught wind of the planned shenanigans and intervened. Instead of delivering Briggs to Polk Street, a police cruiser escorted him to nearby Larkin Street, where he was met by the mayor, supervisors Milk and Silver, and Police Chief Gain, along with some twenty-five cops under orders to keep him out of Polk Gulch. A handful of years before, the SFPD had routinely arrested and often brutalized flagrant homosexuals. Now, some of the same cops were being used to protect them from an outside agitator. This didn't help the mayor's abysmal relationship with the SFPD rank and file.

On November 7, the Briggs Initiative got walloped in the voting booths — definitively and permanently crushed. Prop. 6 lost two-to-one statewide. When the results were announced, the San Francisco Gay Freedom Day Marching Band took to the streets with baton twirlers. So many people flooded the Castro for an impromptu dance party that the police had to block traffic until four in the morning.

The following week, we returned from Europe.

To Mer, the news seemed good on all fronts. Not only had Briggs failed, but Dennis's weed proposition had blazed to an easy victory. The city measure was nonbinding, but it would send a message about the people's will: leave stoners alone.

Mer decided to put a call in to Goran the nitrous oxide–huffing lawyer to discuss the next step. She thought the moment to take the brownies aboveboard might be imminent.

She was wrong. In the chaos of the coming weeks, Prop. W would be lost in the shuffle. It would take Peron nearly two more decades to push the next piece of pro-pot legislation through. By then, marijuana would no longer be a good-time drug; it would be medicine.

My mom still believed we were cruising on the upside of a wave. But there was gravity to consider.

Mer hit the wharf on November 18, 1978, with me in the stroller — her first brownie run since Europe. It was an exquisite day on the waterfront, with fresh salt breezes sailing in from the Pacific to nudge wispy clouds inland. The vermilion bridge looked particularly majestic, its height and breadth accentuated by Mer's sea-level view.

Pier 39, a new shopping center-*cum*-tourist attraction, had launched with a big whoopty-do while she was away. Mer was eager to check it out and had brought extra brownies to use as samples for new customers. After doing her usual route around Aquatic Park, Ghirardelli Square, the Cannery, and along Jefferson Street, she made her way toward the white and blue flags marking the entrance of the new mall. Maneuvering the stroller through a pushy crowd, she entered a multilevel complex of shops, restaurants, and entertainment, all with a nautical aesthetic — like a Disney version of the pier that had been there before.

Hundreds of people staffed the new stores and attractions. And if they were dealing with throngs of tourists from morning until night, Mer figured they'd want to get high. It wasn't easy to navigate Pier 39's wooden staircases with a stroller, but Mer managed to give out sample brownies at several new shops and concession stands.

Among her first customers on the pier was a unicycle-riding juggler and funnyman named Robert Armstrong Nelson III, better known as the Butterfly Man. Decades later, Butterfly would remember that first day clearly. "I was at [Pier 39] on day one; Meridy was probably there on day two. She was young and not so innocent, and she was hungry in those days or she wouldn't have been out there pounding the road like I was. She was living by her wits; I was living by mine." Butterfly had gotten a giant monarch tattooed on his prematurely bald pate as a commitment to juggling. (Who would hire him for anything else?) He saw Mer as one of his kind. "Your mother became an icon because of her choice of nomenclature — the Brownie Lady — and the way she approached it," he says. "She had this look that she gave you. She had these beautiful eyes and she was so commanding in her presence. She'd say, 'Would you like to buy some brownies?' And she never veered from your gaze. You felt like you were being read by a psychic. She became a staple of our subculture."

With dedicated areas for busking, Pier 39 was an extension of the vaudevillian street-performing scene that had erupted on the wharf in the early seventies. It was also an evolution. Two levels of balconies surrounded the main stage, bringing a vertical aspect to theater in the round. Shows got bigger and splashier. One stage converted into a nine-foot-deep pool, and a high-dive team performed dizzying leaps from an eighty-seven-foot ladder.

Pier 39 had been controversial from the start — rife with accusations of bribery and political favoritism, and complaints from those who wanted to preserve what little remained of the working-class waterfront. By the time the complex opened, the FBI had already launched an investigation into whether a certain supervisor got a food concession in exchange for pushing permits through. The subject of the investigation was the straitlaced thirty-two-year-old from Visitacion Valley, Dan White.

Having given up a fireman's salary to begin his new job, White was struggling to support his wife and infant son on a supervisor's modest income of $9,600 per year. At the new Pier 39, he opened the Hot Potato, a fried-spud stand. The week prior, on November 10, he'd tendered his resignation to Mayor Moscone, explaining that the potato stand was consuming too much time but that he needed the money.

If on that Saturday, my mom had offered a sample brownie to Dan White at the Hot Potato, she would've been met with a cold reception — if not a call to the police. Most likely, she took one look at White's anchorman haircut and pushed the stroller right past, barely noticing his all-American good looks. The world would know that face soon enough.

That very afternoon, in a steaming jungle 4,396 miles away, the Reverend Jim Jones gave orders for the Jonestown medical doctor to mix tranquilizers and potassium cyanide into a vat of Flavor Aid.

News trickled out of Guyana slowly; it would take a full week for the public to learn the extent of what happened that Saturday. The first word, Sunday morning, was that California Congressman Leo Ryan had been shot on a tiny airstrip several miles from the Jonestown settlement. (He'd been investigating the Peoples Temple for nearly a year and had flown down to Guyana at the behest of constituents who were worried about their relatives at the agricultural mission.) By nightfall, Ryan was confirmed dead along with three reporters and a woman who'd tried to escape the settlement with Ryan's group. Another Peoples Temple member living in Guyana's capital had gruesomely slain her three children with a butcher knife before killing herself.

Monday-morning headlines screamed 400 DEAD IN GUYANA. Gory details emerged. A carpet of decomposing corpses, many beyond identification. People standing in line to drink poison while others writhed and seized on the ground and those who resisted were forcibly injected. On TV and in newspapers, "experts" waxed about suicide cults while the many politicians who'd enjoyed Jones's support — like Mayor Moscone — scrambled to cover their asses. Some news reports described up to five hundred people escaping into the jungle.

In San Francisco, especially within the predominantly black Fillmore district where many of the Jonestown settlers had lived, vigils stretched through the week in hope that loved ones would emerge from the Guyanese wilds. Fog smothered San Francisco like wet wool, erasing bridges and buildings. Foghorns lowed in the bay. There were terrifying rumors. One Jonestown survivor warned reporters that temple snipers would "seek out their enemies one by one and kill them." Some feared a large-scale terrorist attack (not far-fetched; Jones had reluctantly abandoned a plan to crash an airplane into the Golden Gate Bridge). Police guarded the Peoples Temple on Geary around the clock to both protect the remaining members from vigilantes and watch their every move. People stayed home, glued to television sets. Bars kept the music low and the news on while drinkers grimly sipped beers or saluted wordlessly with shots of the strong stuff.

Saturday brought devastating news: the whereabouts of the missing five hundred. The corpses thought to be strewn on the dirt actually lay on top of more corpses — piled four deep in places. On the bottom layer, the most profoundly decomposed, were children and babies. Snowplows had to be flown into the jungle to scrape up the remains. Guyanese officials detained only two people related to the killings. Nearly everyone else was dead, including Jim Jones. A week after the massacre, the total body count settled at 918.

My folks didn't know anyone personally who'd gone to Jonestown. But Mer had lived a couple blocks from the Peoples Temple in the early days of the brownie business and had interacted with temple members on the street. She thought of faces from the neighborhood. The civilian death toll was among the highest in American history, not to be exceeded until 9/11.

An almost seismic shifting, a crack rent into reality.

Doug had designed a lighthearted brownie bag that week, but as the Jonestown tragedy deepened, he threw it out. Instead of having new bags printed at the shop, he decided to do them himself; he needed the release. He glopped acrylic paint onto a board in primary colors and used a dry paint roller to apply broken layers of pigment to bag after bag, doing hundreds of them in a fog of despair.

Doug had never given the Peoples Temple much thought. He'd heard about some of the scandals but mostly remembered admiring their social projects: the soup kitchen, drug rehab programs, senior centers, and their defense of free speech and racial equality. As Doug understood it, they had gone into the jungle to build a new kind of society. He'd idly wondered, now and again, *Would I have the fortitude for that? Could I give up my comforts?*

Staggering to think that this had mutated into something so evil.

Layers of red, layers of blue, slashes of yellow. Moments of vivid color, moments of hideous murk. He thought about the choices people had made. The pain of the human condition that might draw someone, step by step, to follow a madman to their death. In seeking, in devotion to public service, in striving for equality, those who'd joined the Peoples Temple seemed to express mankind's finer attributes. It had seemed like the ultimate utopian experiment.

Demise disguised as salvation; an ending disguised as a beginning. He called the bag *Camouflage*.

Mayor George Moscone vomited when he heard the news. He spent days on the phone calling relatives of people in Jonestown.

Jim Jones had become profoundly ensconced in the San Francisco political structure. Numerous politicians were implicated but none as conspicuously as the mayor — who'd already fought off a recall attempt over his relationship with the Peoples Temple. Moscone had appointed Jim Jones chairman of the San Francisco Housing Authority in 1976. The massacre at Jonestown could well have wrecked Moscone's career. But the mayor wouldn't live long enough for that.

The same week as the horror of Jonestown slowly unfolded, a small drama was brewing at city hall, though it didn't draw much attention at the time. Dan White, who'd resigned as supervisor to run the Hot Potato at Pier 39, wanted his job back. It would later emerge that members of the Police Officers Association were leaning heavily on White, as was the Association of Realtors. White was their conservative bulwark against a liberal majority on the board of supervisors. Moscone initially told White he could come back. But after hearing complaints from White's own constituents and a rousing pitch from Harvey for all they could accomplish with an unimpeded liberal board, the mayor changed his mind.

White huffed to reporters, "The gloves are off."

On November 27, Barb had a third violent nightmare. She floated down a long hallway. A man walked in front of her, whom she could see only from the elbows down, as if viewing him from a fixed camera angle. She watched his shoes moving across the floor, his hands swinging at his sides. He entered a room and approached a large wooden desk that made Barb think of a hotel. Another man sat behind the desk; Barb could see his suit and tie and his hands folded in front of him. The person she followed pulled a gun and shot the man at the desk. Then he passed through a door into another room and slaughtered a second man.

Barb sat bolt upright in bed with the name *White* burning bright in her mind.

She was living in her own place by then, a flat close to the warehouse. She checked her bedside clock; it was past three. The dreams were growing more detailed, solidifying.

Barb had already been thinking about Mike White that week. He had once mentioned that he'd helped broker the sale when Jim Jones bought the Peoples Temple building on Geary. Now there were rumors about Temple snipers planning to attack. Had Mike gotten tangled up in this somehow? She couldn't ignore the feeling of dread.

Her hands shook as she dialed.

Mike answered, his voice thick with sleep.

"Uh, Mike? It's Barb."

"Jesus, what time is it?"

"I had that dream again, the one where you're shooting people."

"Look, I don't know what kind of drugs you're on, but don't call here again. Leave me the fuck alone. Or I will call the police."

Unable to sleep, Barb chain-smoked until it was time to head downtown for class. A long day of sewing stretched ahead of her. It was an overcast morning, yellowish and windless. Too warm for late November. Two women were talking about it on the bus. "Earthquake weather," one said.

At school, Barb dove into her sewing project and let the train-like drone of the machine calm her. She commented to a classmate that awful dreams had kept her awake.

"That's funny," her friend said. "I had a nightmare, too. Something in the air I guess."

"Mm-hmm," Barb murmured. "Earthquake weather."

At 11:20, an emergency bulletin interrupted the music on the radio at their shared table. Dianne Feinstein spoke: "As president of the board of supervisors, it is my duty to make this announcement," she said haltingly. "Both Mayor Moscone and Supervisor Harvey Milk have been shot and killed."

In the sewing room, someone screamed.

"The suspect," Feinstein continued, "is Supervisor Dan White."

Patrolman Jerry D'Elia was buying a hot dog at the Doggie Diner on Van Ness Avenue when a high-priority call came in over dispatch. He and his partner jumped into their cruiser and sped the three blocks to city hall. D'Elia ran up the marble stairs to the lavish rotunda. A sergeant he recognized from another station gestured toward the mayor's office. D'Elia walked in and saw Moscone sprawled in a pool of blood. The office was already crowded with police, so he hurried back out to find the sergeant. "What can I do? Where do you need me?"

"Go down the other end. Harvey Milk's been shot."

The situation felt unreal to D'Elia, like some sort of elaborate prank. As he started toward the supervisors' chambers, he turned, and said, "Hey, Sarge, do you have any suspects?"

"Yeah," he answered. "Dan White."

Decades later, D'Elia recognizes that he'd entered a kind of denial. "I started laughing," he says. "I thought, *Here's this time of crisis, and he can come up with a joke* . . . I won't add all the adjectives he called me. But he let me know he wasn't kidding."

Mer had just gotten back from dance class and was changing out of her sweaty clothes when the phone rang. It was Donald, who'd come back to the City and was living with roommates in the Haight. He was crying so hard that Mer could barely make out the words, and when she did, they didn't make sense.

She thought of Harvey as she'd last seen him, walking loose-limbed down Castro Street one Friday before she'd left for Europe, talking with a younger man and casually waving to people they passed. Mer remembered noticing how long and expressive his fingers were and thinking he'd be interesting to draw or paint sometime — she loved doing unique hands. *Maybe*, she thought,

I'll pitch that idea to him if the opportunity comes up. When their paths crossed that day, Harvey nodded and smiled but seemed engrossed in his conversation. Mer smiled back and continued with her brownie run. Now he was dead.

She sat there, still pantsless, her skin tacky on the wooden chair, and felt a wave of collective sadness roll toward her like the aftershock of an earthquake. It hit her in the solar plexus, seemed to lift her out of the chair for a moment, then drop her back into it.

Our wave, she thought, *it's crashing.*

There was no manhunt, no mystery. The details came out all at once on the day of the killings.

At 10:25 in the morning, Dan White had crawled into city hall through a basement window to avoid metal detectors, walked to George Moscone's office on the second floor, exchanged words briefly. When the mayor turned to fix him a conciliatory drink, White produced his revolver. He shot the mayor four times, once in the shoulder, once in the pectoral, and twice point-blank to the head. He then reloaded his .38-caliber Smith & Wesson Model 36 with hollow-point bullets and hurried to the other side of city hall. White popped his head into the office where Harvey Milk was talking with a colleague. "Say, Harv, can I see you a minute?"

White led Harvey across the hall, into the office that had been his until recently, closed the door behind them, and pulled out his gun. Harvey raised his right hand in a defensive gesture. White shot him once through the wrist, twice in the chest, then twice to the back of his skull.

George Moscone was forty-nine. Harvey Milk was forty-eight.

Some who heard the gunshots thought a car was backfiring outside. Feinstein recognized the sound of gunfire and ran to Harvey's office, finding him on the floor. When she picked up his wrist to feel for a pulse, her finger slid into a bullet wound.

Amid the confusion, Dan White exited city hall unobstructed. He drove to a nearby phone booth and arranged to meet his wife at Saint Mary's Cathedral. The couple walked together to the same police station where Dan White had worked in his days on the force. He turned himself in.

Jonestown took a week to emerge, but the murders at city hall took minutes. Both tragedies were impossible to accept and impossible to erase. The brutality of those two gestures. A one-two punch that left the City reeling.

Cleve Jones was picketing with the Local 2 union when an acquaintance yelled to him from a bus window: "Cleve, it's on the radio, they shot Mayor Moscone!" He caught a taxi to city hall. Time seemed to slow down, his footsteps echoing eerily off the marble as he hurried toward the supervisors' offices to look for Harvey.

Not until he saw his mentor's secondhand wingtip shoes protruding from Dan White's old office did he realize that Harvey had been hurt. Cleve reached the door just as a cop was turning the body over; Harvey's face was a horrific shade of purple, his skull blasted apart. Blood and brain matter on the walls.

It's over, Cleve thought. *It's all over.*

He felt his emotions shutting down even as another part of his mind kicked into autopilot. Cleve made his way back to Castro Street and quickly put together flyers for a candlelight vigil. People were milling around the neighborhood, some in apparent shock, some weeping. At the Village Deli, Dan Clowry handed out candles and paper cups until they had no more, then shuttered the café.

The crowd grew to hundreds, then thousands, then tens of thousands.

Cleve's flyers had hardly been necessary. The "disaster route" the Castro activists had strategically introduced that summer was working. Everyone knew where to take their grief.

———

Word spreads on Castro Street.

Doug and Mer packed a baby bag and bundled me into a stroller. By the time they made their way to the corner of Market and Castro, most nearby businesses were dark, some with hastily written tributes to Harvey in the windows. Candles glowed in waxed paper cups. At nightfall, the crowd moved toward city hall as one body — some 30,000 people, newspapers would say — walking in near silence. A river of tiny flickering lights keeping pace with a spare drumbeat as steady as a heart. At city hall, the half-mast flags hung limply, the air unusually still.

Dianne Feinstein, who'd been catapulted automatically from president of the board of supervisors to interim mayor, addressed the crowd briefly. Various speakers groped for words. Joan Baez played "Kumbaya" and other folk dirges. Finally, someone held a tape recorder up to the mic and replayed Harvey Milk's victory speech from a rally held after defeating the Briggs Initiative three weeks before. A short time ago but suddenly a very different time. His voice with the tinny Long Island accent, the bravado and humor, left the crowd cheering and sobbing. The next morning, the statue of Abraham Lincoln was glazed in the wax of hundreds of candles left to gutter out.

Moscone had been the people's mayor — that was how Mer thought of him. A native San Franciscan who seemed unperturbed by the young people who thronged to his hometown in search of freedom. From old San Francisco but not of it. A guy who wanted to see women and minorities in government, and who didn't so much mind if people smoked weed. And Harvey, well . . . if Moscone was the head of liberal San Francisco, Milk was its heart. Now the City had lost both.

Doug, Mer, and Cheryl talked about closing Sticky Fingers until the new year but thought better of it. People would need to be soothed. Doug's next bag was a prayer for those lost and a message of hope for those left behind. He drew a mandala composed of maybe a hundred humanoid bodies radiating outward from a circle of light. Other bodies floated up from the void to join the web. It read, *Returning in Pure Compassion to the Wheel.*

The City limped toward the year's end like a crash victim. A hitch in its step, a stagger, not quite itself, but somehow still alive. You think you won't go on, but you do go on.

Around Christmas, Mer suggested they throw a party to put some closure on the year. "Let's get the energy flowing in a different direction."

Sticky Fingers gave a New Year's bash. In pictures from that night, everyone looks manic and pale, a little desperate, eyes bulging over gritted smiles. Confetti dusts their hair like ash from a house fire. Mer, who was no longer breastfeeding, looks coked out. Cheryl is mostly absent from the pictures; she'd broken her own rule about dosage, eaten half a dozen brownies, and passed out in the middle of the party.

There is a picture of me the next day. One year old, zipped into a flannel onesie and crawling through drifts of confetti past empty bottles of cheap champagne, looking dazed and nervous.

1979 had begun.

16

No Peace

K ILL FAGS! DAN WHITE FOR MAYOR! Sprayed in foot-high
lettering on a wall by Dolores Park, the graffiti stopped Mer
in her tracks. Early 1979: a new world, a dark gray day.
Closer to Castro Street, she saw FREE DAN WHITE! in the same
rough scrawl.

The dismay must have shown on Mer's face when she ducked
into Main Line Gifts on Castro Street.

"Like the new mural?" her customer Roger said.

"Why do people have to be so ugly?"

He smirked. "We had the bigots scared for a while, but they're
getting frisky again."

Mer knew homophobia existed in San Francisco, like everywhere else in America. But when your social circle was an echo
chamber, you could pretend. Easy to imagine this pretty city as
a bubble floating above ignorance and intolerance. Dan White
might have acted alone like the papers said, but he wasn't alone
in his hatred. A whole side of San Francisco that Mer had barely
noticed before — old-school conservative, morally outraged — was
showing its teeth. People who'd been disregarded, first by a hundred thousand or so hippie kids, then by a hundred thousand or so
gays and lesbians.

Roger twirled the metal police whistle he wore around his neck.
"Fashion statement of the season."

On Castro Street, people talked about the uptick in violence:
brutal attacks in alleys; police harassment in lesbian and gay bars

under flimsy pretenses; teens prowling in muscle cars, throwing garbage and picking fights. There were articles about it, and not only in the gay press and local papers; the *Washington Post* ran a piece under the headline, ANTI-GAY SENTIMENTS TURN VIO-LENT IN AFTERMATH OF MOSCONE-MILK KILLINGS.

Mer might not have known that in the weeks following the as-sassinations police and firefighters had jointly raised $100,000 for Dan White's defense. Or that White had been greeted with a friendly ass pat when he turned himself in at Northern Station, as if he were a baseball player returning to the dugout after a home run. Or that some cops had sung "Danny Boy" over the police scanner when the assassin's identity was revealed. Or that the offi-cer who'd taken White's confession had known him since grammar school and softballed the interrogation. But she could see that her friends were scared.

Roger bought two dozen brownies. Looking at the bag design, he scrunched his forehead. "Is everything okay with you?"

It was one of Doug's bags: a furiously scribbled drawing of a woman (obviously her) and a man (obviously him) facing away from each other with a malevolent demon sneering between them, and the words, *It's Not Me, It's My Brownie.*

Mer shrugged it off — "The joys of marriage!" — and continued on her way. Everything wasn't okay, but she'd rather not advertise it. Unlike Doug, apparently.

He'd been going off his Dilantin again. Mer had woken up after midnight to an earthquake — no matter how many times it hap-pened, it always felt like a goddamn earthquake. Realizing it was another seizure, she'd forced her arm under Doug's jolting body and rolled him onto his side to prevent choking. The commotion woke the toddlers, who both started howling. Then the whole household was up. Mer had spent the morning bringing Doug cold washcloths for his headache while he vomited brown bile.

She wished episodes like this would keep him on his meds. Doug would take his Dilantin for a while, then secretly taper off again. Always testing, trying to prove he had the power to control his own epilepsy.

They fought about that. And about the ten pounds Mer couldn't seem to lose, and the ledgers Doug insisted on keeping, and music and movies and art and their friends and pretty much everything else.

Mer was wearing an outfit inspired by Han Solo from *Star Wars* — khaki vest, black blouse, harem pants, knee-high leather boots, and a black beret. A militant look, but it suited the gunmetal weather. And her mood. She'd decided to do her run alone that afternoon — easier to negotiate stairs and tight spaces without a stroller — but she missed the guileless joy. The duffels of brownies seemed to weigh two tons as she trudged to her next stop. Boys were still cruising at Hibernia Beach, but there was a singed, burned-toast vibe.

The neighborhood seemed somehow stripped of its innocence. Because even in its most hard-core sexuality — the relentless cruising, the bathhouses and sex clubs, the orgies her friends told her about, even the S & M scene that Mer never quite understood — something about it had always seemed gleeful and immature, like teenage lust. Adding grief to the equation made the bawdiness so . . . intentional, like people were trying too hard to have fun.

Early 1979 clicked by with mounting tension, like a roller coaster climbing the first incline before the inevitable plummet and loop the loops. As anger and frustration intensified at the warehouse and in the City at large, so did the frenetic partying.

The photos of the Sticky Fingers crew from this period reveal a shift in attitude. The flamboyance rocketed into outer space. Especially in shots of my dad, whose outfits became dares. One week, he wore elaborate black eye makeup, shiny red spandex pants, and a women's red satin blouse open to his navel and cinched at the waist. The next week, Stannous Flouride helped him dress up as a punk in torn slacks, plaid jacket, black nail polish, and a fake bloody wound on his face so he could experiment with nihilism for a day. Another week, Doug imitated the Chicano men he saw in the Mission wearing high-waisted black pants, a white wifebeater, and a panama hat. On the bus to Noe Valley, the dirty looks he got from real Chicanos convinced him never to try that again.

One Saturday, Stannous accompanied Doug on a sales run. Doug wore white martial-arts pajamas with his skin and hair painted entirely white so he appeared to glow; Stannous wore all black, with face paint and mirrored sunglasses. They sold brownies in those getups: the silent wraith shadowing the movements of the shining man.

Even in San Francisco in the seventies, where fashion sometimes verged on costume, this would've raised eyebrows. I appreciate that my dad saw his sales runs as performance art. But from my distance of decades, I feel like I'm seeing him begin to slip, his grip on reality loosening. The bags he designed became stranger. One featured a nude man ripping his chest cavity open, spraying blood in all directions. *The heart is an organ, too*, it read, *so why not let it breathe?*

For the vernal equinox on March 21, my dad proposed a party to celebrate the rebirth he hoped would follow a winter so marked by death. San Francisco had been vanquished before in earthquakes and fires. Each time, the City had risen from its own ashes, renewed. The phoenix was a bird that combusted whenever it sensed death approaching; a new phoenix always rose from the ashes. It was the symbol of San Francisco, the image on the municipal flag.

He and Mer choreographed a dance together, fusing her jazz moves and his modern moves, their styles not parallel but intersecting. Five women would represent fire. Four men would embody the smoke and ashes. Doug would be the phoenix. Together, they'd perform a rite to welcome the cycle of new life that would accompany spring. They called it *Phoenix Rising*.

Of the friends they recruited to perform, not one of them was a trained dancer.

Stannous and Doug dressed to sell.

The memory makes my mom laugh. "John Battle was even in it, that oaf. He was gigantic and a total klutz. And we had him, like, leaping all around. Hundreds of people came to this party. I don't know what we were thinking."

I was too young to remember *Phoenix Rising*, but part of me would sacrifice a lesser tooth to see a video of my parents and their friends — not a serious dancer among them — pretending to be fire birds and flames and raining ash.

In the wee hours of March 31, the dregs of a bachelor party showed up at a low-key lesbian dive in the Avenues called Peg's Place. According to a firsthand account published in the *Bay Area Reporter*, some of the eight or so men arrived carrying open beers, so the female bouncer denied them entrance. When the men tried to muscle past her, she yelled for the bartender to call the cops.

"We are the cops," one of the men said. "And we'll do as we damn well please." He hit her in the chest. Someone in the group yelled, "Get the dykes!" as the men forced their way into the bar. One guy put the bar's owner — a woman who was already disabled from a back injury — in a choke hold; she was later hospitalized. Another guy clobbered the bouncer's head with a pool cue.

Two of the brawlers turned out to be off-duty police officers. The women tried to press charges, but no arrests were made.

Dianne Feinstein was so slow to discipline the rowdy police that she lost credibility with many in the lesbian and gay communities. Some were already upset because she'd been sluggish about filling Milk's seat and had bypassed a neighborhood favorite, Harvey's former aide and campaign manager, Anne Kronenberg. And Feinstein had won herself no friends by telling the *Ladies' Home Journal*, "The right of an individual to live as he or she chooses can become offensive — the gay community is going to have to face this." DUMP DIANNE T-shirts and pinbacks became a fad. Meanwhile, rumor had it that some cops wore FREE DAN WHITE shirts under their uniforms, as if this were a secret superhero identity.

Cleve Jones was in a bar on Castro Street when half a dozen cops came in, demanded IDs, and roughed people up, apparently for kicks. Shortly thereafter, Cleve was sitting on his own stoop in the middle of the day when an officer strolling by whacked him on the shin with a billy club, "Get moving."

"I live here," Cleve said, rubbing his leg.

"I told you to *get moving*."

Cleve headed inside and locked the door behind him.

Dan White consumed the news throughout spring. The defense was wily and innovative; the prosecution was weirdly limp — hobbled by politics (including District Attorney Freitas's unflattering ties to Jim Jones). Before being selected as prosecutor, attorney

Tom Norman allegedly commented to a colleague that he hoped he wouldn't be assigned to the city hall murders because he felt sorry for the accused. White got an entirely heterosexual, predominantly white Catholic jury, one of whom was a retired cop, and half of whom lived near the area where White had grown up — the demographic most likely to share his frustrations over what he called "radicals, social deviates, and incorrigibles."

The open-and-shut case grew slippery. To get first-degree murder convictions, the prosecutor had to prove that White had acted with premeditation and malice aforethought. But instead of laying out that crucial angle, Norman belabored ballistics and other details of the killings that weren't even being disputed. Homophobia was *never discussed* in court nor was the political jockeying between Milk and White. Both issues could have been used in a malice argument but not without exposing broader corruption within city government and law enforcement.

Some mainstream reporters took pains to describe White in sympathetic tones, waxing at length about the loss of his father at a young age, his athleticism in school, military record, heroism as a former firefighter and police officer, and his devotion to family — while managing rarely to mention the wife and four children mourning Moscone or the vast community grieving for Milk. Toward the end of the trial, one reporter for the *Sunday Examiner & Chronicle* went so far as to conclude that "there were three victims of the terrible events in City Hall Nov. 27: George Moscone, Harvey Milk, and Dan White."

Even so, Mer felt sure that the only real question was whether Dan White was going to get the death penalty (which he, ironically, had helped reinstate for crimes like his in California) or life in prison. Because how could someone — anyone — walk into city hall in broad daylight, execute two elected politicians, boldly confess to pulling the trigger, and not spend the rest of his days behind bars?

———

Tension was ratcheting up. At the same time, spring of 1979 saw some of the decade's most opulent parties as well as an obsession with all things shiny and gold. *The Treasures of Tutankhamun* would come to San Francisco's de Young museum in June, drawing record crowds and becoming one of the most popular exhibits of all time. The hoopla started months in advance: there were movies, camp theater, and academic seminars; fashion leaned heavily on draped fabric and gold serpent bracelets; a new seventeen-scene Egyptian exhibit opened at the Wax Museum at Fisherman's Wharf. In April, Barb landed a gig costuming an elaborate Egyptian-themed benefit for Children's Hospital, a spare-no-expense, gala-*cum*-all-night-disco extravaganza.

To costume the event, Barb rented pieces from the American Conservatory Theater and created others out of gold lamé, painted leather, beads, and glass gemstones. Cyril Magnin, the elderly magnate behind the I. Magnin department stores, embodied the pharaoh perched on a golden throne borrowed from Twentieth Century Fox. To portray the pharaoh's royal court, Barb recruited the Sticky Fingers crew; Doug, Mer, Cheryl, Carmen, and Susan appeared dripping in gold jewelry and wrapped in muslin. Even the brownie babies — Noel, Marcus, and I — shuffled around in tiny white togas and little headdresses.

Camels were hauled in from Marine World/Africa USA to roam the dance floor along with pythons and brightly plumed parrots. There were live bands and deejays, belly dancers, and hors d'oeuvres sprinkled with flakes of real gold. Sand dunes and statuary flanked the entrance of the South of Market Galleria event center. It was a high-society ball straight from the satirical "Tales of the City" column.

Cultural insensitivity abounded: heavy brown bronzer and thick black eyeliner was fair game for an "Egyptian look," and blonde toddlers in togas could belong to the royal family of a nation on continental Africa. No one worried about the mental health of live camels forced to prance around a crowded disco with

Sticky Fingers kids, left to right: Noel, Alia, and Marcus.

flashing lights and pounding music. All of it done in the name of something so unimpeachably respectable as children's health care. There was, perhaps, a hint of desperation in the extravagance, as if people sensed they'd better get their kicks while they could; the seventies were ending.

And there we were, interlopers from the fringe of society. My parents were in orbit, their kohl-ringed eyes bulging from cocaine. Old Cyril Magnin surveyed the revelry from his golden throne.

Mer drew a king on a throne. In his right hand, a sword. In his left, the scales of justice. With a verdict on Dan White expected any day, she based her brownie bag for May 18 on the tarot card *Justice*.

She thought closure would do everyone good. The assassinations had revealed festering ugliness; it was as if a rock had been moved, exposing a world of creepy crawlies. She hoped they could kick some dirt over it and move on.

The verdict landed like a fist to the jaw at 5:28 p.m. on May 21: two counts of voluntary manslaughter carrying a maximum sentence of eight years. With good behavior, Dan White could be free in under five years.

"Lord God," White's defense attorney had said in his closing statement. "Nobody could say that the things that were happening to him wouldn't make a reasonable man mad . . . A good man, a man with a fine background, does not cold-bloodedly go down and kill two people. That just doesn't happen." White was simply an earnest, patriotic San Franciscan who'd been pushed too far by conniving liberals, lost too much sleep to depression, and, yes, ate too much sugar. Anyone in his position might have done the same.

Contrary to popular belief, the defense hadn't argued that overdosing on Twinkies had driven Dan White insane. His plea wasn't one of insanity, but rather that he'd suffered a brief period of impairment caused by long-term undiagnosed depression and insomnia. Eating sugary food was held up as a symptom of his malaise (not the cause). But some clever journalist coined the term "Twinkie Defense," and it caught on. The voluntary manslaughter conviction was so improbable given the facts (the deliberate reloading of his gun before killing Milk, for example) that you might as well blame it on sugar.

James Denman, the undersheriff who held Dan White during the seventy-two hours after his arrest, described his prisoner to journalist Warren Hinckle as "perfunctory and businesslike" and without an "iota of remorse." And when the supposedly impaired White entered the state prison in Soledad to begin his sentence, the psychiatrists who examined him decided against prescribing therapy, finding "no apparent signs" of mental disorder.

Cleve was in his apartment when a city hall reporter called. He stretched the cord of his kitchen phone into the bathroom and closed the door for privacy. When the reporter told him the verdict, Cleve leaned over the toilet and puked.

"Are you there?" the reporter asked. "Do you have anything to say?"

He wiped his mouth. The verdict had shown Cleve that the justice system wouldn't protect even the most powerful among them. "This means that in America it's okay to kill gay people," he said.

Cleve's roommate pounded on the door to say that lesbian activists Del Martin and Phyllis Lyon were waiting in front of the Twin Peaks Tavern with some reporters. Cleve grabbed his jacket and ran downstairs for an impromptu press conference.

A local TV news reporter said, "You have a permit to close Castro Street tomorrow to celebrate Harvey Milk's birthday. Is that when the community will react to this verdict?"

Cleve looked dramatically into the camera. "No," he said. "The reaction will be tonight. It will be *now*."

Days before, Cleve had walked down to the Mission Station with two other activists to warn the SFPD that if Dan White got off the neighborhood was going to explode; they should prepare for a riot.

"You people aren't really violent," Captain George Jeffries told him. "If a crowd gathers, you'll march them down Market Street like you always do." The captain's smile was so condescending that Cleve thought he might get a pat on the head.

Now the scenario Cleve had predicted was underway. He ran back to his flat to get ready. Paramount in his mind was something Harvey had said in the lead-up to the Briggs vote: "Don't burn down your own neighborhood." He'd taken note of the destruction in Watts and other black neighborhoods after Dr. King was assassinated. "If there's going to be a riot," Harvey said, "take it downtown. Burn the banks. Don't let it happen where we live."

Cleve grabbed his jacket and a bullhorn Harvey had given him. By the time he got back on the street, hundreds of people had already gathered in the intersection.

———

Doug and Mer consulted the *I Ching* about joining the protest that night, but the hexagram warned of violence and possible bloodshed; with a baby to protect, they decided to sit this one out. Later, at about ten that night, Barb called the warehouse. "They're rioting at city hall. It's on the news."

Some five thousand people had marched to Civic Center chanting, "Dan White was a cop!" and "Avenge Harvey Milk!" Chief Gain —the Moscone appointee who'd had the police cruisers painted baby blue—ordered his men to hold their ground without using force against the protesters, a stance many of the rank and file resented. This would later cost the chief his job; the San Francisco Police Officers Association would vote "no confidence" in Gain the following month, and Feinstein would eventually give in and appoint a good old boy who would promptly repaint the squad cars black and white.

The crowd broke through police lines, tore the elegant ironwork off the doors of city hall, and used it to break windows. They set dumpster fires and trashed nearby buildings. Police attacked with tear gas and batons, while rioters threw rocks and bottles. Several policemen had to be rescued after getting trapped inside city hall when the crowd surrounded the building. By the end of the night, twelve squad cars had gone up in flames, their melting sirens moaning like wounded animals.

Reporter Warren Hinckle was on Castro Street when rogue squad cars rolled up: "They came in marked cars, first in twos, then in threes," he wrote in the *San Francisco Chronicle.* "The cars were sardine-full of cops; three in the back seat, sometimes three in the front." Never mind that many of the people who'd stayed in that neighborhood were the ones *not* rioting at city hall. Officers were heard yelling "Banzai!" as they charged into the Elephant Walk—one of Mer's regular brownie stops and a favorite performance venue of Sylvester's. Cops bludgeoned patrons and employees, broke windows and chairs, and shattered the artful elephant-motif stained glass, raining shards onto those cowering behind the bar. As one bar patron who was hospitalized with five broken ribs and a partially collapsed lung commented later, "They were down here to crack a few heads open."

A former police inspector who'd tagged along with Hinckle that night found Captain Jeffries directing troops, and confronted him: "It was all quiet before you sent these guys in here. You're provoking these kids and putting a lot of cops in danger. What kind of police work is this?"

"We lost the battle at city hall," the captain snapped. "We aren't going to lose this one."

Patrolman Jerry D'Elia, a single dad, had just come home to his kids after a long day on Muni transit detail when the call came in to go back on duty. D'Elia assumed it was a prank and hung up. The dispatcher called back and explained that there was a problem with the White verdict and that all hands were needed. They had even put out a mutual aid request for surrounding counties to send available officers.

By the time D'Elia got to Castro Street after putting his kids to bed, the melee had escalated. Police were getting pelted with beer bottles and debris. D'Elia wasn't close enough to the Elephant Walk to see what happened there. "But tensions were running pretty high by then," he says, thinking back. "The cops were really heated because Gain muzzled everybody. We were a really well-trained big department and he wouldn't let us clear the streets or anything. So once that happened — once they knew we weren't going to do anything — well, we kind of became piñatas for them."

D'Elia joined a skirmish line on Market Street. He remembers glancing down the line and seeing a group of Castro guys poking his deputy chief in the chest, and saying, "You take *one more step* . . ." At another point, he struggled to process a surreal vision of flaming car tires rolling downhill toward him and the other police.

At about two in the morning, D'Elia and some of his colleagues decided of their own volition to disperse. "We were so disgusted, we left," he says. "Just one by one, the whole thing dissolved. We didn't cross their line and I guess they got tired, too. Everybody went home to fight another day."

Most news outlets reported that sixty-one police officers and more than one hundred civilians were injured that night. The Police Officers Association claimed it was the other way around, with twice as many cops hospitalized as civilians. Either way, people got hurt.

When Dan Clowry got to work the next morning, he was stunned to see the Elephant Walk's windows boarded up and glass all over the sidewalk. He had marched to city hall with everyone else but left when things started getting broken. One of his regulars came in for coffee after being released from the ER. He had pins in his arm from getting whaled on with nightsticks. "They beat him into a corner," Dan recalls. "And then they beat him some more."

Mayor Feinstein thought the manslaughter verdict was a miscarriage of justice, but she could not abide rioting. She gathered prominent gays and lesbians in her office the next morning. Permits had already been issued for a street party to celebrate Harvey Milk's birthday later that night. According to Cleve Jones, Feinstein had assembled them to explain her decision to summon the National Guard. Convinced that this would only escalate violence, he dissuaded her by lying. "I have five hundred trained monitors ready to keep the peace on Castro tonight," he bluffed. "If you keep the police away, there will be no violence."

The fib worked. Activists spent the day teaching last-minute volunteers how to monitor a crowd. They planned escape routes in case people needed to scatter. Finally, Cleve marshaled the ultimate peacekeeping weapon: he asked Sylvester to perform.

That night, some people showed up for the celebration wearing helmets and carrying baseball bats. The mood was tense. But when Sylvester started to groove, the crowd got high and danced in the street. The cops maintained their distance, and no harm was done.

At one point, someone in the crowd burst out screaming, "He's dead! He's dead and he's never coming back!" People surrounded and embraced the man, holding him as a group, while Sylvester led the crowd in singing "Happy Birthday" to Harvey Milk.

When Mer did her run later that week, some businesses were still boarded up. People wore their injuries like badges of honor. Doug had designed a beautiful bag that week: a Buddha-like face in meditation, with the *I Ching* hexagram "11. *T'ai*/Peace" on his forehead. Mer thought Castro Street looked more like a war zone.

New graffiti in the neighborhood struck a different chord than before. One wall read, DAN WHITE & CO. YOU WILL NOT ESCAPE, FOR VIOLENT FAIRIES WILL VISIT YOU EVEN IN YOUR DREAMS.

"We were swaggering," Cleve says about the mood following what became known as the White Night Riots. "Yeah, we were swaggering." He brings up something Allen Ginsberg told the *Village Voice* after the 1969 uprising at the Stonewall Inn: "They've lost that wounded look that fags all had 10 years ago."

The cops didn't come around so much after that.

As 1979 careened into summer, Sticky Fingers reached a degree of notoriety that sometimes unnerved Mer. Everyone seemed to know who they were, and thanks to the raucous costume parties and Cheryl's Friday-night warehouse sales, a growing number of people also knew where they operated.

Early June, one of Mer's wharf customers told her that the extra brownies he was buying were for a friend heading to the SALT II talks in Vienna; he planned to smuggle them in his suitcase. Another customer said that the famed columnist Herb Caen was purchasing brownies through a friend. "Cool," Mer said. "So long as he doesn't put us in his column."

Sticky Fingers had been courted by writers — one who wanted to include the Brownie Ladies in a book on iconic San Francisco women — and a few journalists hoping to write articles, but the hexagrams were never right, so the brownie crew demurred.

A photojournalist named Laurence Cherniak convinced them to reconsider. He had some impressive bona fides — like founding what was probably the world's first head shop in Toronto in 1965 (predating San Francisco's legendary Psychedelic Shop by several months). Cherniak also marketed his own line of purple-and-red-speckled rolling papers, which were popular then. He'd been documenting hashish production worldwide since the 1960s, and his sensual images often graced the pages of *High Times*. Now he was launching *The Great Books of Hashish*, the first in a planned trilogy to be published by And/Or Press in Berkeley. The first book focused on the Middle East, but the second one would include a section on the United States, and Laurence's editor sent him to find the famous Sticky Fingers Brownies.

Dennis Peron made the introduction. Cherniak was handsome and loquacious, with a shock of dark hair and olive skin. He promised to refer to Sticky Fingers only by their business title and exclude personal information and identifiable photos. He came to the warehouse bearing an astounding hunk of opiated Nepalese Temple Ball hash to share.

As usual, hexagrams had the final say. This time the oracle gave a green light.

Between June and August 1979, Cherniak hung around the warehouse, photographing the baking process. Mer even brought him along on a Saturday sales route.

"They were producing thousands of brownies at that time," Cherniak says, looking back. "And I remember standing over the warm stove as the butter was melting, and then stirring in the cannabis and carefully mixing each ingredient in. How much care went into each stage of preparation. So when we carried the brownies up to the twentysomething floor of the Transamerica building to deliver them, that love was present. I saw the joy and gratitude come over the faces of their customers, who returned that love. That's what it's all about."

When I ask Laurence if, in his extensive travels through the underground cannabis world of the 1970s, he ever encountered an operation like Sticky Fingers — either in scope or in the relationship they had with their community — he doesn't hesitate. "Absolutely not," he says. "If it wasn't happening in California, it wasn't happening in the United States at all. This was where it was revolutionary. That's why I came several times to photograph the process. And why I have that wonderful picture of you in my book."

The picture Laurence is referring to appears in *The Great Books of Cannabis,* his second volume, which begins with a preface by Timothy Leary. You see a pan of gooey, freshly baked brownies along with a brick of weed, a small pile of homegrown, an array of wrapped brownies, and — invading one corner of the frame — my blonde head and one curious blue eye staring straight into Laurence Cherniak's lens.

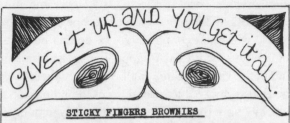

GiVE it UP aND YOU GET it ALL.

STICKY FINGERS BROWNIES

8oz. Magic (oven-dried, powdered in a food
processor, sifted, California-grown
sin semilla leaf. Note: Chaff may
be used later for grass oil.)
5 sticks butter
16 eggs/6 cups sugar
3 cups flour
3 tbsp. baking powder
1.3 tsp. salt
16oz, unsweetened baking chocolate

1. Melt butter in a double boiler, and stir in
   the magic. This is the "Ghee."
2. Combine eggs and sugar in a large bowl.
3. Slowly melt chocolate in another double boiler.
4. When the Ghee has cooked for 30 min., add
   flour, powder, salt to eggs and sugar. Then
   add the Ghee and the chocolate.
5. Pour into four 9"x12" greased baking pans.
6. Bake at 400F, patting down the batter several times with a spatula to keep it from
   rising. When the brownies are solid, but still
   very moist, remove from oven and cover with
   a towel to keep moisture in.
              ....Yields 8 dozen 2"x2" brownies..

Power to the People !
We love you ...
   — Sticky Fingers Brownies

Give It Up and You Get It All

D oug dreamed of an earthquake. Crevasses opened in city streets. Buildings collapsed, sending dust plumes into the sky. A gleaming tidal wave reared so high that the Transamerica Pyramid looked like a child's toy. People swam in water poisoned by their own sewage. There would be famine because we'd forgotten how to grow food, disease because too many people lived in close proximity. Waking up, he thought, *Mother Earth is pissed. And we had better be ready for her wrath.*

To survive our karma, mankind would have to return to simplicity. Go back to the land, restore harmony. The meltdown at the Three Mile Island power plant in Pennsylvania that March should have been a wake-up call. Lawrence Livermore National Laboratory was a mere fifty miles from San Francisco. What sort of fools built a nuclear weapons research facility on a major tectonic fault?

Doug had recently seen in an article that major earthquakes came in cycles of roughly eighty years. The 1906 quake had hit seventy-three years ago. Sometimes Doug felt like the only lemming in the pack to look around and say, *Hey, guys, isn't that a cliff up ahead?*

The big one was coming. Doug did not want to be in a crowded city when it hit.

"The big one is always coming," Mer argued, exasperated. "You're just freaked out because you had a seizure. And if you would take your damn Dilantin like you're supposed to, this wouldn't happen so often." They were having coffee in the kitchen. The kids were playing with a Playskool vacuum that sounded like a cross between a popcorn maker and a machine gun.

"It's not the fucking epilepsy," Doug countered. "People aren't supposed to live piled up on top of one another."

Maybe Doug didn't see the pattern, but Mer did. He'd have a grand mal seizure in bed, and in the days and weeks that followed, his dreams would become apocalyptic. Even when he wouldn't admit he'd had an attack, she could tell from his behavior. The spaciness, the brooding, the scary pronouncements.

Doug talked about "getting out of the rat race" more and more since they'd been making trips to Willits. Mer could see that he loved it up there, how he relaxed and brightened. Maybe it would be good for their marriage to get Doug away from the pressures of city life. It could be good for raising a child, too. Open fields, blue skies, and all that.

But Mer wasn't a country girl.

"Look," Doug said. "Maybe you think earthquakes are no big deal because we've been through a couple of shakers. But we haven't seen shit. Tens of thousands of people are going to be wiped out by what's coming."

Mer didn't know what to think. Sure, there could be a big earthquake. But was that a reason to move? You didn't leave Hawaii because there might be another tsunami. You didn't abandon Kansas because your house could get picked up in a twister. Doug was psychic but not infallible. Were the apocalyptic dreams fears? Hopes? Visions of the future?

Mer, meanwhile, had been having nightmares about a bust: police kicked down the door while Carmen baked and the Wrapettes gossiped at the table; three cops dressed all in black slipped in like ninjas during the night to steal Doug's ledgers; a customer reached into a pocket for money and instead came out with a badge. There were dreams of losing her family. Dreams that ended in prison.

Early July, Dan Clowry at the Village Deli told Mer about an unsettling incident at the café. An unfamiliar man had come to the counter and ordered a brownie. Dan put a regular chocolate brownie on a plate for him.

"Don't you have magic brownies here?" the guy said.

Dan feigned surprise. "Gosh, not that I know of! We're just a café."

The guy blinked pointedly, paid for his unmagical brownie, and ate it on the way out the door.

"I don't know why," Dan told Mer. "But I knew he was police. Anyway, he wasn't one of us."

As usual when anxiety kicked in, Mer lay on the barge in her room and tossed hexagrams. *What is my inspiration for this week's brownie run?* and *What are the effects of continuing to sell at the Village Deli?* Indications were all right, so she sallied forth.

Now that Mer was no longer breastfeeding, there was more blow in the house — and that bothered Doug. Not just for occasional parties anymore, but for the pre parties and post parties and between parties. The ladies would bring stuff home from their brownie runs. *Look what so-and-so traded me!*

On coke, Mer and Cheryl buzzed with ideas and humor, but the drug had a stiffening effect on Doug. It left him stressed and edgy, electricity fizzing in his brain. Late one night, he blew his nose in the bathroom and saw red streaks on his handkerchief. Suddenly, blood gushed from his nose down over his mustache and lips. In the bathroom mirror, his face looked drawn and somehow jagged. He heard Mer and Cheryl cackling uproariously in the kitchen, and thought, *This is not my divine path.*

Thereafter, he worked against party plans — which made him the bad guy.

Once, he came home to find Mer giggling hysterically on her bed with some flaming gay guy Doug didn't even know. Doug thought, *Why the fuck is this man in bed with my wife?* He knew she wasn't cheating, but it chafed him to see her in tears of laugh-

ter with a stranger while their own conversations drifted into frequent arguments, the joy draining out of their shared life.

Doug sealed himself behind the copper doors of his studio. His
paintings came slowly, laboriously. Art, for him, was about revealing paths toward enlightenment. The message had to be perfect.
Sometimes he'd cover an inch of canvas in a whole day. Sometimes
all he did was undo his work from the day before. Sometimes all
he could do was think.

Meridy, on the other hand, turned out drawings and paintings in a kind of ecstatic frenzy. She didn't have her own studio
but worked wherever, whenever. If she didn't work, she became
touchy and overwrought; but as long as she applied pigment to a
surface, she seemed pleased with herself at the end of the day. It
was all so easy for her.

Summer 1979, a book came out that would have a major impact on
my dad's life. To this day, he keeps a copy prominently displayed on
his bookshelf: *Sexual Secrets: The Alchemy of Ecstasy.* The spine
is cracked, pages worn from being referenced repeatedly over the
years. (I remember this book being around throughout my childhood; our copy bears crayon marks from when I colored a detailed
drawing of a blow job in grass green.)

Sexual Secrets is a compendium of sex and mysticism rooted
in Eastern traditions. The jacket copy describes it as the "distil-
lation of more than two thousand years of practical techniques
for enhancing sexual awareness and achieving the transcendental experience of unity." The author, Nik Douglas, had studied for
eight years in the Himalayas and did many of his own translations
from Sanskrit. The text — scholarly, dry, research heavy — appears
alongside hundreds of original illustrations by collaborator Penny
Slinger as well as reprints from pillow books and sacred texts.

The book was an instant hit among spiritual seekers like my
dad. I imagine him reading it in the armchair in his studio surrounded by his own paintings, which incorporated symbols of

Hinduism, Taoism, Tantra, and Native American religions. Not just paging through the erotic drawings but carefully reading the text. How spiritually serious he was, how sincerely he wished for enlightenment.

I envision him arriving at page 336 and beginning the section "Male Homosexuality" with a mixture of trepidation and thrill.

Nik Douglas depicts homosexuality as a perversion of the natural balance between masculine and feminine energy—an abomination. He claims it's the negative result of aggressive copulation between the parents, an unhealthy pregnancy, or a childhood without male role models. The author describes gay men as having the "hormonal chemistry and minds of women" and anal sex as "unnatural, unhealthy and potentially damaging to the psyche." He waxes at length about various religions that have condemned homosexuality for one reason or another.

He also argues that flourishing homosexuality has preceded the collapse of several world civilizations. "An excessively homosexual society will quickly annihilate itself," he writes. "No amount of theorizing can alter this fact, which has been demonstrated throughout history."

Toward the end of the section, he lays out "practical techniques for overcoming the wiles of destiny," which include yoga postures, breathing, and meditation. "Tantra teaches that when the creative attitude is brought to bear on any problem, there are no obstacles that cannot be overcome."

This doesn't sound any healthier or more feasible to me than Christian-based conversion therapy. I imagine these words entering my dad's consciousness and doing their work there, making him ashamed and also strengthening his resolve to change his nature by force of will, to cleanse himself.

Maybe that's why he decided to confess.

He told Cheryl first.

Doug doesn't remember this moment, but Cheryl does. They

were in the baked-goods aisle of Cala Foods buying brownie supplies when Doug brought it up. "I have to tell you something."

Cheryl thought, *Uh-oh*.

"Remember how I was so sure Alia was going to be a boy?"

"Oh, yeah," she laughed. "You were convinced."

"Well, I kind of freaked out when things didn't go the way I expected. And I left the hospital and I went to a bathhouse . . . you
know, to be with men."

Cheryl eyed him sideways. "I don't know why you're telling me
this."

"Because I think I should tell Meridy. It was wrong, and I need
to come clean."

"No. Doug, you do *not* have to tell Meridy. What is that going to
accomplish? You two fight enough already."

Doug squinted at her, head slightly cocked.

"We need butter." Cheryl turned and moved quickly toward the
dairy aisle in the too-bright store.

He did tell Meridy. Not gently or carefully but in the middle of a
fight about something else.

She was dumbfounded. She'd suffered through thirty-two hours
of labor, merciless contractions, and slicing and dicing, and he'd
taken that opportunity to indulge a fantasy. "You were out screw-
ing some guy?"

"I didn't have intercourse if that's what you're asking. But I did
do other things."

The shock gave way to rage. Though six inches shorter than
Doug, she stood on her toes to get up in his face and yell at the
top of her lungs. At some point, Doug tried to shoo her away. She
turned toward him, and the flat of his palm accidentally whapped
the side of her head. Mer felt a sharp pain deep in her ear followed
by a rushing sound like television static.

"What the fuck did you do?" she wailed, and there was something wrong with how the words sounded inside her head. Cot-

tony. Smothered. Like someone wanted to hush her with a *shh* in her ear.

A General Hospital ER doctor confirmed that Mer's eardrum had ruptured. He referred her to a specialist who patched the tear, warned her to avoid airplanes and water for a while, and sent her home. It healed within a couple of weeks, no infection or permanent damage.

In the aftermath, Doug was contrite and ready with promises. They had long-overdue heart-to-heart talks.

"So," Mer asked quietly. "Are you gay?"

"No," Doug answered firmly. "I am definitely not gay. I'm attracted to women."

Mer might have preferred to hear *I'm attracted to you,* but he kept going and she listened.

"In *Sexual Secrets,* they talk about what can cause a masculine-feminine imbalance. One of the main things is growing up without a father. A boy needs a father to show him how to be a man, and I didn't get that. Then watching you go through that birthing process — how incredibly strong you were — and being wrong about Alia. I guess it made me feel like a child. And I wanted my dad. So I went looking for that."

This was heartfelt; Doug was confused. And the sympathy Mer responded with was real. The notion that he might be bisexual didn't enter their conversation then. Bisexuality was not yet broadly accepted as a unique orientation. (The initialism LGBTQ+ wouldn't begin to acquire its B for bisexual until the late 1980s.) In Doug's mind, the fact that women aroused him was proof that he wasn't homosexual — only wounded and in need of healing. He would cling to the idea that he could be "fixed" for decades.

In July, a performance artist who lived in a big loft next door, Diana Marto, offered to hold an exhibition of Doug's and Mer's work in her space. She had beautiful white walls and was hooked into a different art scene than they were. It would be good exposure, motivation to organize the work they'd each been doing, and a chance to focus on the positive.

The two poured thousands into framing the pieces they'd created in the two years they'd been together — both an affirmation of their love and mutual inspiration, and an investment in their future.

They planned the show for a month later, August 3, 1979.

Mid-July, Dennis Peron got busted — again. He had scarcely begun his four years of probation for the 1977 arrest. But he had gone right back to dealing, opening a new pot shop at a friend's house on Fell Street. He had also announced that he was running for supervisor of District 5 — Harvey's old district. Dennis felt he owed this to his slain friend.

The Big Top bust had taught Dennis not to do business in his home. Since Dennis didn't live at the house where the deals were going down this time, and was physically nowhere near the location when the sting happened, the charges wouldn't stick. The case ultimately got dropped due to weak evidence but not before entangling Dennis in months of legal hassles. "I want to call a truce with the narcotics officers," he told a *San Francisco Chronicle* reporter. "But I'm too afraid to walk up to them and say it. They don't really care for me." Privately, Dennis suspected that this bust was more about political intimidation over his bid for supervisor than a serious effort to put him behind bars.

Meridy sighed over the news. But one detail made her heart gallop. Police bragged to reporters about confiscating Peron's address book, which they said contained the names of more than two thousand customers and associates; Mer had no doubt that her name and phone number were among them.

"For the last time, Doug," she said. "We have got to get rid of those fucking ledgers."

It was the same fight they'd had a thousand times, but now there was desperation behind it. "This is not a game!" Mer shouted. "They have Dennis's address book."

"I'm not discussing this again. Period! That's it!"

"But you name *names*, for Chrissake. You like all those Willits people so much? Then don't rat them out with your asinine ledgers!"

Cheryl was fed up with the fighting. She felt that the frequency and intensity with which Doug berated Mer for her weight amounted to abuse. She thought Mer was a fool for staying with him despite a flock of red flags.

Mer and Doug would start yelling, which would scare the kids, so they'd scream. The warehouse was big but not big enough for that kind of drama. Cheryl took her son and moved in with Barb up the street. Nearby but far enough away not to hear Doug and Meridy yell.

Occasionally, when Mer felt lost in the relationship, she phoned Paula, Doug's grandmother in Long Island, to ask her advice. Ever since her visit before marrying Doug, Mer had thought of the older psychic as a guiding light. Paula had known Doug his whole life; she understood him well enough to be critical without judging.

"Funny you should call today," Paula said. "I was watching Lawrence Welk and he had a psychic named Irene Hughes on as his guest. Do you know of her?"

"I may have heard the name . . ."

"She's famous for predicting Robert Kennedy's assassination, you know. She also foresaw the exact number of inches that would fall in the Chicago blizzard."

"That's right!" Mer said. The same blizzard had hit Madison while she was in college. She did remember Irene Hughes.

"Well, she said something today that troubles me. She feels very strongly that San Francisco is going to suffer a terrible earthquake the likes of which has not been seen in our lifetime. It will put the 1906 quake to shame. And it's going to happen in January of 1980."

Mer told Paula about Doug's earthquake dreams, the apocalyptic visions, her frustrations with him for refusing his medication, the seizures, the fights.

"You know," Paula said, "my grandson is quite a talented psychic — I can't imagine where he gets it from!" She giggled. "The trouble is that he picks up too much information and can't always tell what's true. One must separate the wheat from the chaff."

Should they worry about an earthquake, a nuclear meltdown, a bust, or nothing at all?

Irene Hughes, sweet faced and grandmotherly, was making the talk-show rounds with a variety of predictions. She said, for example, that Jimmy Carter would get reelected for a second term on a ticket with a black vice president. And that voices from outer space would shock the world in 1986. Over time, Hughes would produce a mixture of hits and misses — with enough of the former to maintain a following.

For Mer, the *what ifs* became more insistent. One Wednesday in late July, Mer was resting on the barge in her middle room. She unsnapped the pocket of her leather-bound *I Ching* and slipped out her three tarnished coins for her usual weekly hexagram. *What is our course for this week?*

Six. Yang. Yin. Yin. Yang. Six.

This was bad. Opening her book, she fanned the pages to "29. *K'an*/The Abysmal (Water)." This was never a pleasant hexagram to get, but what really hit her was the changing line she'd rolled, six at the top.

> *Bound with cords and ropes,*
> *Shut in between thorn-hedged prison walls:*
> *For three years one does not find the way.*
> *Misfortune.*

Mer charged out of her room to read the interpretation of that line to Doug. "Listen to this: 'A man who is in the extremity of danger has lost the right way and is irremediably entangled in his sins has no prospect of escape. He is like a criminal who sits shackled behind thorn-hedged prison walls.'"

"Ew," Doug said. "That's not good."

"That sure sounds like a bust, doesn't it?"

They sat together at the kitchen table while Mer threw hexagram after hexagram looking for an exit. *What is it to operate through the summer and then leave? What do we realize by taking a break and then resuming? Is it in accordance with natural law for Sticky Fingers to continue?*

All bad.

Not just a little bad, but the most disturbing imagery the *I Ching* had to offer. "A hundred thousand times you lose your treasures . . ." "The bed is split to the skin . . ." "You've let your magic tortoise go . . ." "Waiting in a pit of blood . . ." "The nose and lips cut off . . . ." "Misfortune from within and without . . ." No matter how Mer phrased her questions, no matter how fervently she hoped for better results, the oracle was clear: dark days were coming.

Then Doug said, "Ask what it is for us to move up to the country."

"All right." She closed her eyes, took a deep breath, and muttered her question while throwing the coins six times. The oracle gave her "40. *Hsieh*/Deliverance."

Thunder and rain set in:
The image of DELIVERANCE.
Thus the superior man pardons mistakes
And forgives misdeeds

The country.

Willits.

It wasn't what Mer wanted, but it was a way out. Cheryl, also an *I Ching* devotee, agreed that the message was unequivocal: it was time to close. Rent for the warehouse, which wasn't zoned for residential use anyway, was paid month to month in cash; Doug phoned the landlord and gave notice. Mer broke the news to Carmen and the Wrapettes. Nobody was thrilled, but no one wanted to get busted either.

With a decision made, the feeling of impending doom receded. More hexagrams followed. Doug and Mer concluded that they should operate for two more weeks and make as much money as possible. But a third week would bring a rain of misfortune.

A hexagram had started Sticky Fingers Brownies on July 4, 1976, and now a hexagram would end it. If you believed that magic could open doors, you had to accept when it closed them.

On the next brownie run, customers bought in a panic. Folks who usually wanted two dozen put in orders for the weekly maximum of ten dozen to stock their freezers.

"We didn't know what we were going to do," says Dan from the Village Deli. "It was such a tragedy! Truly the end of an era." He and Kissie spent a stoned night asking themselves, *Why is this happening?*

Doug called his bag that week *The Age of Kali.* The dark Hindu goddess of transcendence, keeper of the rhythm of time, essence of female sexual power, Kali protected Mother Nature from the evils of mankind. She could be ruthless when disrespected. Though she is often portrayed with skulls around her neck, Doug drew a more visceral version of Kali wearing a belt made from the severed heads of businessmen; blood pours from their necks down her thighs.

On his route through the Haight and Noe Valley, Doug felt full of portent. While telling customers of their closure, he also warned them. "If you're smart, you'll get out," he told people. "And if you don't get out, get ready."

He was right.

Not about the massive earthquake. But about untold suffering and loss of life. A new virus was already lurking in the blood and spreading unchecked through the community. Some men would later look back at 1979 and remember a strange fever that came and went without explanation. Kali was indeed coming to San Francisco.

———————

The next week, Doug and Mer drove the three hours to Willits to lease a small two-bedroom farmhouse on a country road near town. Nothing fancy, but the landlord took their cash with no questions. They returned to the warehouse the same night and started packing.

To fill the huge orders, Carmen started baking on Tuesday of the final week and didn't stop until Saturday afternoon. Throughout, Doug, Mer, and Cheryl debated what to do with the thriving underground network of customers they'd cultivated. A few people had expressed interest in buying the business. Should they cash in? Hexagrams brought lines about greed and overreaching. Giving it to Cheryl or a trusted friend like Stannous looked even worse — like it would bring the law down on all their heads. Each option was weighed and ultimately discarded.

Then, as she and Doug were settling into bed, a favorite axiom floated into Mer's mind. "You know," she said, rolling to face Doug. "We always say that if you really want something you should let it go, right? If it's meant to be yours, it'll come back."

"If you love it, set it free," Doug said.

"So, let's give it away."

Doug shook his head. "We looked into giving it to someone and that wasn't good."

"I mean to everyone. What if Sticky Fingers isn't ours to keep? Maybe it belongs to San Francisco. Let's print the recipe on the bag."

She and Doug connected in that moment with a zap of the electricity that had brought them together.

"I like the way you're thinking," Doug said finally.

"That feels right, doesn't it?" Mer beamed. "Give it up and you get it all."

Then they laughed. Laughed and laughed.

On the final bag, above the recipe, Mer wrote, *Give it up and you get it all!* in ornate script. Lettering across the bottom said, *Power to the people! We love you, Sticky Fingers Brownies.*

The art show they had been planning at Diana Marto's doubled as a bon voyage party where, as my mom describes it now, her art "sold like a motherfucker" and his didn't.

Oh, I can see this so clearly. My mom with her social ease, laughing confidently, proud of her work but acting casual about it. She'd framed dozens of figure drawings and priced them low enough for people to buy without having to sleep on it first. Doug, with his social awkwardness, standing beside his expensive opuses. Not letting the paintings speak for themselves but asking anyone who looked, "So, what do you think this painting is trying to tell you?" then explaining the correct answer. Each piece was priced in the thousands, as if this were a New York gallery opening instead of a San Francisco studio party.

The next morning, Doug would seethe while Mer would silently gloat as she pretended to be humble.

With Sticky Fingers officially closed, Doug consented to burning the ledgers that had been such a point of contention. Mer, giddy with relief, wanted to do it immediately, before he changed his mind. She called Cheryl over, and the three of them went together to Baker Beach to burn the ledgers in an ocean-side firepit.

That night, they said prayers of thanks, prayers of goodbye, prayers of hope for fruitful futures. As waves tumbled roughly onto the shore, the pages curled and caught fire, sending tiny bright sparks into the frigid Pacific wind.

The bakery had begun, only three years before, with breads and muffins that the Rainbow Lady had carried in her basket while saving to visit Findhorn. Now Sticky Fingers was turning out more than ten thousand brownies per month. It had bloomed into the largest known cannabis-food business at that time in California — if not the world, as Laurence Cherniak believed — and the first to offer weed edibles through a high-volume delivery service.

Fast-forward four decades, and their industry, now called can-

Meridy, Doug, and Cheryl off to burn the ledgers.

nabusiness, is a booming semilegal market that exceeded $10 billion in the United States in 2018. Though projections vary, most predict at least double that value in the next few years. This was all new in the 1970s, and the risks were real. At each turn, Sticky Fingers Brownies grew organically through serendipity and their belief in magic. It was a home-baked revolution.

Monday morning, the phone was ringing like mad.

"Have you seen it? Get a newspaper!"

Herb Caen, the beloved columnist, had written about their decision in his weekly spot in the *San Francisco Chronicle*.

HEAD SET: "Thank God It's Friday" had a hollow ring in certain parts of town last Friday, for THAT bakery in the Mission went out of business. THAT bakery made only one product — marijuana brownies, individually wrapped "to insure freshness and quality control" — which brought happiness to hundreds of office-workers each Friday for the past two years . . . In this city of wagging tongues, the secret of the Brownie Ladies and the Mission bakery

Alia in *The Great Books of Cannabis.*

never got to the law, but the owners decided not to push their pot luck. Fridays will never be the same.

Any other week, this kind of press would have sent the crew into a panic. But Caen nailed the essential detail: they had closed. This would send a message to the vice squad that if they'd hoped to pinch Sticky Fingers they were too late. Bark up a different tree, boys. *Good old Herb,* Mer thought. *He waited until we were safe.*

Doug and Mer had just finished reading the article together shortly past ten a.m. and were getting ready to dig into their last big day of packing when the warehouse jolted. The old wood creaked, dishes rattled, a coffee mug tumbled off the counter and shattered. Measuring 5.7 on the Richter scale, it was the largest earthquake in sixty-eight years. Aftershocks rolled throughout the morning. They couldn't pack fast enough.

My parents took me across the Golden Gate, and we vanished into the countryside.

PART IV

REINSTATING THE DRAFT - CHEMICAL POISONING
NUCLEAR WASTE - PARAQUAT - SACHARYN - DCIO's
THE FALL OF SKYLAB - DEFEATIST ATTITUDES -
ARTIFICIAL COLORING - MICROWAVE OVENS - CARTELS
EXPLODING WHALES - RADIO DISC JOCKEYS - TV ASSES
HUMAN STERILIZATION - RONALD McDONALD - D.D.T.
NUCLEAR REACTORS ON EARTHQUAKE FAULTS - LANDFILL
BUBONIC PLAGUE - TEST TUBE BABIES - LAETRILE BAN
HIJACKING AIRPLANES - HOMOPHOBIA - PLUTONIUM -
CHEMICAL WASTES -   POISONED KOOL-AID -
ENDANGERED SPECIES   NITRITES / NITRATES

at the crossroads ∞ *of infinity ~*

VOYAGER SPACECRAFT   THE RAINBOW FESTIVAL
  DREAMS AND VISIONS   FINNILLA'S STEAM BATHS
  DR. BRONNER'S PURE PEPPERMINT CASTILE SOAP -
 THE LEGALIZATION OF MARIJUANA - BODY AWARENESS
FEMININE STRENGTH - MALE GENTILITY - THE DANCE
  CHILDREN'S LAUGHTER - CARE FOR THE ELDERLY -
BENTONITE AND PSYLLIUM SEED - SHARE THE WEALTH
HOME-GROWN TOPS FOR CITY HEADS - BUD'S ICE CREAM
  PSYCHIC HEALING - THE I'CHING - MEDITATION *
  TAKING CARE OF YOUR OWN SHIT - FUNKY MUSIC -
STICKY FINGERS BROWNIES - KEEP THE PEOPLE HIGH !

The Crossroads of Infinity

L ate on a golden afternoon in August 1979, Doug turned the twenty-six-foot moving truck onto an unpaved driveway on East Hill Road — a country highway that traversed the Willits valley toward Pine Mountain, where dozens of growers lived. Among the items in the tightly packed truck were the dance mirrors from the warehouse along with the drawings and paintings that had been framed at great expense for the art show. The little farmhouse emerged between oak trees. "Home sweet home!" Doug crowed, failing to notice a gigantic tree root hiding a deep pothole.

As Mer would describe it later, "You could hear every single piece of glass shatter."

I don't think there's a culture in the world that would deem the shattering of two giant mirrors on the final approach to your new home a good omen.

It was a bland house: not old enough to have character, not new enough to be nice. After a tumultuous season, peaceful domestic life seemed exotic to Doug and Mer. The stillness of that first night was stunning. There was the occasional rumble of a pickup heading into the hills, the cluck of the neighbor's chickens, the hoot of a barn owl. Nobody arguing on the sidewalk, no Friday-night lowriders, no friends stopping by to get high. No Cheryl with her honking laugh, no Noel stomping on plank floors. No Carmen and the Wrapettes. Just a fat silver moon hanging over the fields like the pendulum of a stopped clock. A quiet so profound you could hear the old oaks creak in the breeze.

Doug looking at Mer, Mer looking at Doug. Me, the toddler, watching them both for clues.

All of a sudden, an ordinary family.

The first clear memory I have from Willits is of chasing the neighbor's chickens that ran free in the dirt lot next to our house. I was swinging a toy rake over my head. The hens darted on spindly legs, fluffed their butts, and made silly gurgling noises. I thought this game hilarious until the monster-size rooster flapped into the air and zinged toward me. With a scream lodged in my throat, I scrambled for the house, but my foot snagged on a loop of baling wire and I fell. The rooster raised his talons above my face . . . and that's where the memory ends.

My mom says she "had a heart attack" when I came into the kitchen with blood streaming down my face. New to country living, she was still trying to figure out how much leeway to give a two-year-old to play outside. She thought I'd been blinded. Luckily, the wounds were superficial, no permanent harm done, though I still have a small scar above my right eyebrow.

Before the chickens, I have flashes of memory of San Francisco. There's a vivid image of my feet in striped tights and satin Chinese slippers stomping in a warm puddle on the sidewalk in front of the warehouse. "Don't play in that," my mom said. "It might be pee!" I recall isolated moments, emotions, smells. But mostly it's a feeling of being elemental to the world we lived in, as if there were no difference between me and the City itself. That all changed in Willits. I remember standing alone in the yard, aware of myself as distinct from my parents and a stranger to my environment. I remember being *me*.

Early memories are tricky. There are long blank stretches. I don't, for example, recall almost dying several months later when an allergic reaction to baby aspirin ate a hole in my stomach and I vomited so much blood that I had to be rushed by ambulance to San Francisco for a transfusion. That apparently paled in comparison to getting spurred by a rooster. Sometimes it's hard to tell how much of what I associate with those days is shaped by what my parents have told me. But the chicken incident is mine. It was my first story: beginning, middle, end. The moral, of course, is that if you're going to taunt the hens you'd better be ready for the rooster.

Willits boasted one of the longest-running rodeos in California: Frontier Days, held every July since 1927. That and a train museum were the primary attractions of this town of 4,008 inhabitants, many of whom lived in the surrounding hills. Route 101 cut right down Main Street, stoplights slowing traffic to a crawl. "Downtown" consisted of a family drug store, a battered saloon, a single-screen movie theater, and a strip of old-timey buildings with a few New Age galleries and a little bookstore. Businesses scraped by on the trickle of locals, and motorists who stopped to pee.

The town had redneck roots, complete with a semifamous shootout and a dying logging industry. But the hills were alive with hippies. Tree huggers and tree killers living together, with predictable tensions between them. Rural families came to town for groceries and banking, and to pick up their mail from PO boxes; many were growing marijuana and didn't want their home addresses known. If my parents hoped to get out of the weed business, they chose an inopportune location.

We would stay in Willits for eight years, a fat chunk of my childhood, but these would be tough years. Before Sticky Fingers, Doug had done a little carpentry and psychic work, and Mer had illustrated children's books; neither had experience with straight jobs. They wanted to live on their artwork. Eventually, they would even open a gallery on Main Street, but it would fail. In an obscure highway town with an already disproportionate population of artists, who would buy the work?

The local job market offered few opportunities. Doug worked briefly for John Schaeffer at Real Goods but either quit or got fired over some now-forgotten argument. Their financial situation soon became dire.

I have often thought that my parents' plan for making a living in Willits was unrealistic. Now I realize that it's not that they had a bad plan; it's that they had *no* plan. No idea how to survive without dealing. It hits home for the first time just how hasty our exit was, how scared of getting busted my parents must have been to move so quickly.

Cheryl, meanwhile, was trying to kick-start a modeling career through a contact in Milwaukee. Perhaps this was a stretch at twenty-eight, but after the Sticky Fingers adventure, she felt herself crackling with power; she could do anything. Cheryl returned to Milwaukee thinking that Noel's father, Victor, would provide childcare while she went after gigs. But Victor wanted nothing to do with such a plan. Cheryl blazed through the money she'd saved from the brownies. Frustrated, she started drinking heavily. When she caught herself adding brandy to her morning coffee, she knew something had to change.

Cheryl took Noel up to Tomahawk, Wisconsin, a tiny lakeside town where she used to spend summers with her family. It was mid-October. The sky looked like a concrete wall behind trees in autumnal flame. Noel trolled for seashells by the lakeshore (she didn't have the heart to tell him there were none), his fingers bright pink from the frigid water. The wind was beginning to get mean. Cheryl's bones rattled under layers of wool. What the hell was she doing back in Wisconsin?

She drafted a letter to Meridy: "I feel like I need to come back," she wrote. "I thought I was rich, but I'm not rich. Maybe we should do the business again."

Then she hightailed it back to the City before the first snow-
fall. She arrived at a friend's house where she and Noel would be
staying until they found a new place. There was a message already
waiting for her: *Call Meridy.*

"How did you get my letter so fast?" Cheryl said when Mer
picked up. "I just sent it."

"I didn't get a letter," Mer said. "Barb told me you were coming
back."

"So, what did you want to talk about?"

"I've been looking at hexagrams," Mer said. "I think we should
open the biz again but on a smaller scale."

Cheryl laughed. They had read each other's minds.

They agreed to share the work: Cheryl would bake and wrap
twenty batches at her friend's house, Doug and Mer would prepare twenty batches in Willits, and Mer would drive them down
by herself. The Brownie Ladies would sell, and they'd split the
proceeds three ways. Lower volume, abbreviated runs — better
than broke. By the time Cheryl's missive reached Willits a few
days later, Doug was already grinding shake for a weekend round
of brownies.

Crossing the Golden Gate Bridge, Mer rolled down her window
and inhaled deeply. The bracing moisture, a slap across the cheek
— *snap out of it!* She'd missed that cool salt air.

She rented a room at Beck's Motor Lodge, a seedy Market Street
motel on the edge of the Castro. Three stories in horseshoe formation around a parking lot. She splurged on the "fireplace suite" at
the rear of the building because a corner in the hallway ensured
that office staff wouldn't see people coming and going from her
room.

Friday afternoon, she did a small Castro run, stopping by the
Village Deli, Sylvester's flat, and a few other favorites. She let the
other neighborhood runs go by the wayside to keep a lower profile. Customers complimented her Indian-summer tan and sun-

bleached hair. Mer savored being back on the street, shaking off the country dust, feeling the urban vibrations around her. While Mer worked the Castro, Cheryl did a little run on Polk and Union. Then they met back at Beck's and held court on the motel bed while customers came to them.

The Beck's weekends were a risky way to do business — the long drive loaded with contraband, dozens of people passing through the motel room — but they made enough for one month's rent and bills. From then on, Mer straddled two worlds: the dry, quiet country life and the raucous escapades in the City every fourth weekend (when rent came due). Sometimes I went along. Or she'd go alone, returning to the boondocks with a stack of fifties and twenties like a mama bird bringing food to her chicks.

In late April 1980, Mer got a call from Milwaukee: Bill was in the hospital with congestive heart failure. For years, he'd been wheelchair bound but mentally very sharp. Florence was deep in dementia but could follow simple instructions. Between his mind and her legs, they'd managed. Now Bill's organs were shutting down. Mer booked a flight.

In Milwaukee, she hovered at her dad's bedside, reading him passages from *The World According to Garp* while he went in and out of consciousness. Bill had always been cool, collected, and connected in tough situations; he was Mer's anchor and her safety net. Seeing him like that — intubated, catheterized, half-lucid — felt like a violation of natural law. Late at night on May 3, 1980, Bill Domnitz died. He was sixty-two years old.

It hit her weeks after she got back to Willits: deep, wet heaves that rolled and rolled. Meridy came to think of grief as water. An ocean. An endless river. A faucet that you could learn to turn off, though it was always ready to gush.

She still misses him today. "He would do anything to make me laugh," she tells me in the honeyed tone she reserves for Bill. "His

humor wasn't highbrow. You know, rolling around in his wheelchair with a mop on his head. Or doing a hula dance in the kitchen
on his one leg. He never judged me no matter *what* I got myself
into."

I don't remember meeting my grandfather when I was a baby.
But I understand the relationship my mom describes because I've
experienced it myself. In elementary school, for example, I got in
trouble for calling my teacher a bitch. "Mrs. Ahearn *is* a bitch," my
mom said. "You're not wrong. But if you say it to her face, we have
to hassle with the principal." Later, during my teenage punk phase,
when I was running around and partying all night, I knew I could
call her for help at any hour and she'd never be angry. And when I
lost my virginity at fifteen, she gave me her copy of the *Kama Su-
tra*. No reason to keep secrets or tell lies. She was unflappable and
always available. Having a parent like that in your corner, you feel
safe — whether or not you actually are.

On November 4, 1980, Ronald Reagan crushed Jimmy Carter in
the presidential election. It had been a lousy year for Carter. In-
flation was up; jobs declined. The Iranian Revolution provoked
a second oil crisis in the US and created long lines at the pumps.
Carter's reluctant decision to let the deposed Shah receive emergency medical treatment in New York outraged the revolutionar-
ies. In November 1979, an extremist group took over the US Em-
bassy in Tehran, holding fifty-two Americans hostage. Nightly
news reports led with the updated count: 110 days, 280 days, 443
days. While Reagan was a guns-blazing, can-do optimist, Carter
could be depressing, always going on about oil addiction — ahead
of his time, as it turned out. He'd even installed solar panels on the
White House, which Reagan dismantled once in office, comment-
ing that the program "hasn't produced a quart of oil or a lump of
coal."

Carter had been the first US president to advocate decriminalizing cannabis — and he'd paid the price. Reagan doubled down on Nixon-era rhetoric. "Leading medical researchers are coming to the conclusion that marijuana — pot, grass, whatever you want to call it — is probably the most dangerous drug in the United States," he said while stumping in 1980. "We haven't begun to find out all of the ill-effects, but they are permanent ill-effects." In coming years, Reagan would wage a literal war on California's marijuana farmers and dealers.

A month after the election, John Lennon was shot to death by an obsessed stranger outside his New York apartment. Doug, who'd spent painful childhood years in England before coming to California and becoming a hippie, knew the whole Beatles canon by heart as well as the solo albums and Lennon's collaborations with Yoko Ono. He had idolized Lennon; the death hit him hard. That such a peace-loving man would meet such a violent end felt like a harbinger of worse things to come.

Back in San Francisco, Cheryl was renting a room for her and Noel from a longtime brownie customer. She struggled with single motherhood and became adamant that Noel should spend time with his deadbeat dad. Cheryl bought her five-year-old son a plane ticket, duct taped a giant N on his suitcase, stuffed a wad of cash in his pocket, and put him on a flight to Milwaukee to see the father he barely knew.

While Noel was away, Cheryl visited Willits for some fresh air and ended up having a fling with a grower more than twenty years her senior. Cheryl didn't think much of it at first. But when she returned to the City, he sent a love letter inviting her and Noel to live with him on his pot farm. Though Cheryl wasn't head over heels, he promised to take care of them — and that sounded good. By the time Noel returned from the week with his dad, Cheryl was packing their belongings. Though Noel would eventually bond deeply with his mother's boyfriend, he recalls the initial shock of suddenly moving into the deep, secretive woods. No electricity or phone lines, no immediate neighbors, and a brand-new father figure.

In early 1981, my folks moved us to an eccentric house in the unincorporated community of Hearst on the Willits outskirts. Built in the 1890s as a stagecoach stop, it had fourteen bedrooms and a great room with a wraparound balcony like in a Wild West cathouse. A flock of peacocks nested under the porch, littering the property with their magnificent feathers and squawking like vuvuzelas. The house was situated in an isolated field on several acres of untamed land. Forests of manzanita, oceans of poison oak, blackberries to pick in summer. A mile down the dirt road, we had a private beach on the languid Eel River. With no one around for miles, we usually swam nude. A hippie paradise.

Naturally, the house was in disrepair: drafty, moldy, and in need of stripping and patching. Peeling the rotting wallpaper from the laundry room revealed layers of German-language newspapers from the nineteenth century. In a triangular closet under a staircase, Doug was stunned to discover a small cache of gay porn magazines left behind by a previous tenant. The desire he'd hoped to escape seemed to be following him.

My parents believed the old stagecoach stop was haunted. One room stayed noticeably colder than the rest of the house, and if Mer passed by quickly, she sometimes saw an old woman in a rocking chair out of the corner of her eye. They invited friends to skinny-dip in the river and held Ouija board seances in the great room at night, often contacting the ghost of a sea captain.

At three and four years old, I was supposed to be asleep during the seances, but I'd watch through the balcony rails until I got ushered back to bed. I don't recall being afraid of ghosts, though I believed in them. It was always like that with me: if my parents were cool, I was cool.

At Hearst, my memories tilt toward galloping through tall

grasses, inventing games to play with imaginary companions. There was my blooming obsession with horses, and my blooming loneliness as an only child in the woods. But mostly I think of summer. The box freezer where we'd keep organic juice until we could eat it with a fork by the lazy green river. There was a high boulder my dad would scale to huck himself into the water; beside that was a smaller rock that I could jump from wearing my floaties. I remember sitting in my mom's arms in the gentle rapids beyond our swimming hole and how we had to wipe tiny leeches off afterward. The long afternoons, the sunburns. The dusty manzanita and the deep silence.

My mom in the woods makes as much sense as a bear in the city.

She has always been clumsy on uneven terrain and would never hike to the top of a mountain *for fun*. Confronted with natural beauty, she'll rock on her heels, tilt her head, and squint. "Pretty," she'll say, fluttering her long bright fingernails. She seems to regard nature as two-dimensional. As if a misty meadow were actually a *painting* of a misty meadow.

Most Willits women were "earth mother" types, but Meridy wasn't into meditation or sunrises or gardening. So she tried to citify Willits. Mer taught her own brand of jazzercise classes at the local gym and cofounded the Willits Dance Coalition, a spandexy troupe that performed throughout the county to raise funds for antinuke actions. Mer also cocreated a political affinity group called the Rainbow Light Brigade and became the area's primary nonviolent-resistance trainer and action coordinator for protests at the Diablo Canyon Power Plant and the Lawrence Livermore National Laboratory. She and her friends joined massive demonstrations and chained themselves to fences. During this time, the brownie bags for monthly runs were often antinuke-themed. Between 1981 and 1986, Mer would get herself cuffed eleven times for civil disobedience. Once, heading to a Diablo protest, Mer sewed packets of prenatal vitamins and herbs into the lining of her bomber jacket so she could smuggle them to pregnant women in the holding camp when she got arrested. She didn't feel like herself unless she was bucking the system.

Then there were the "shows," annual fundraising extravaganzas that involved half the town and drew sold-out crowds from throughout the Emerald Triangle (the tricounty area sometimes called the "cannabis breadbasket"). Mer had her fingers in every aspect of production: auditioning, directing, writing, choreographing, and creating special effects. She made costumes by hand at our kitchen table.

To this day, some Willits people talk about the "Meridy years" as a unique epoch in the community's history. She blew into that little town like a hurricane.

Mer adapted in some ways. She wore less makeup and let her hair grow long and frizzy. Tie-dye crept into her wardrobe as did long flowing skirts. We ate tofu instead of meat, carob instead of chocolate. Once, for an ill-fated round of brownies, Doug and Mer tried substituting carob, molasses, and wheat flour for the usual baking ingredients, but the result was disgusting. In pictures from this period, she always looks slightly cramped, like a kid in a school picture.

My dad, on the other hand, felt he could finally relax into his skin. During the hundred-plus-degree summers, he'd hike into the golden hills to draw bearded oaks *en plein air*. Drum circles excited him, and he picked up enough guitar to write folk songs. He took mushrooms and acid, and camped alone in the woods.

Late 1981, Doug decided that he needed a new name.

The idea came from a friend named Morningstar. She was a classic nature hippie, with long graying hair, clear eyes, and wide hips. Her name had once been Susan Smith, but she'd changed it through a Native American–inspired vision quest. Doug found it spectacular that she could go from an ordinary handle to such a magnificent one. He coveted an experience like that for himself.

One autumn evening, Morningstar and Doug tromped into the woods with a sack of psilocybin mushrooms, ate them together, then parted ways to wait for their respective inspirations. Late that night, Doug awoke in his sleeping bag to a vision of a feather on fire floating in the sky overhead.

Firefeather.

What does it mean?

Ask my dad now, and you'll get a long and complicated answer that has something to do with the abundance of Scorpio in his astrological chart coupled with his Sagittarius sun sign; something to do with his belief that his art will guide people to higher consciousness someday; something to do with having no choice but to bear the torch of illumination.

When I press him to translate his name into one statement, he makes a couple of false starts, then says, "Hidden self that is emerging from dark water, being reborn, and becoming highly visible."

Soon after the vision quest, my dad wrote to Social Security and made it official. He changed his name to Douglas Firefeather and asked everyone to call him by the new last name.

December 1981, Mer did a pre-Christmas brownie run. She was making her way up Castro Street toward Market when she saw a small crowd studying a poster outside the Star Pharmacy. She leaned in to check it out.

GAY CANCER it said across the top. Below that was a series of graphic Polaroid photos of sores on a man's legs, feet, and arms. The back of Mer's neck prickled. Hadn't she seen one of those little spots on Roger's wrist that afternoon? *Weird,* she thought, as she continued on to do the next deal.

The flyers were the work of Bobbi Campbell, a handsome

twenty-nine-year-old registered nurse studying to be a nurse practitioner who specialized in gay men's health. Mer had occasionally sold Bobbi brownies at Café Flore. A couple of days prior, Cleve Jones had been walking past the Twin Peaks Tavern when a friend tapped on the window and motioned him inside. Bobbi was there. He took off his shoes and socks. Small purple sores covered his feet and calves. That same day, Cleve helped Bobbi photograph his lesions for the poster he wanted to make.

Bobbi Campbell was among the first people diagnosed with Kaposi's sarcoma. He was also one of the first in the country to sense the enormity of the danger. As a public health nurse, he was not going to sit back and watch. Declaring himself the Kaposi's sarcoma poster boy, Bobbi began a column in the *San Francisco Sentinel*, a gay newspaper, detailing his experiences. His first piece, "I WILL SURVIVE!" ran that month. The tone of the column was buoyant and witty, but it dispensed crucial information. And although Bobbi would not, in fact, survive — he would die within four years — he became a hero of the AIDS epidemic.

Until that point, there had been a few AP articles buried with other low-priority news. Rare skin cancer seen in young homosexuals. Fatal pneumonia caused by a common fungus. It was enough to interest a couple of journalists and concern some doctors — one of whom, Dr. Marcus Conant, would contact Cleve several weeks later to warn him. But there were still fewer than three hundred identified cases nationwide.

It started in that small way: whispers, rumors. Something going around. People feeling fatigued and vaguely ill. A recurring flu. A stomach bug that wouldn't quit. Those painless purple spots showing up out of nowhere.

It was still business as usual in the Castro.

And business was good enough. With Mer coming down once a month (sometimes with Cheryl or me, sometimes solo), customers stocked up on larger quantities of brownies. Beck's Motor Lodge could be rowdy on weekends, popular among Castro boys for both cruising and tricking for money. On the plus side, that meant people came and went for various reasons, which Mer thought gave her cover. Safe to say, Beck's personnel didn't want to know what people did in their rooms.

Sunshine, a photographer and cook who'd been a customer for years, usually bought five or six dozen; she'd sell some to friends and keep the rest in her freezer to last through the next visit. Sunshine remembers approaching Beck's and seeing a buck-naked guy standing in the picture window overlooking Market Street. She thought it was weird, so she mentioned it to Mer, who shrugged it off. Apparently, it was this guy's deal to hang out nude in the front window so he could cruise without ever having to put clothes on or walk down to the street; his tricks could come up and find him. Sunshine also remembers there "always being a child there." She'd enter the motel room, and Mer would whisper, "Shh, Alia's sleeping."

It's not true that I was there every time. But I adored going to the City with my mom. As we sailed through puffs of fog crossing the bridge, we'd belt out, "San Francisco, here we come! Da-da-da! Right back where we started from!" I loved the sound of traffic below the motel windows. I loved customers waltzing through the door with a singsong "Hello, darlings!" How the damp night air would trail them, clinging to their leather jackets and smelling of the street and the ocean. How their hair was never shaggy like up north but spiked and dyed bright colors or coiffed into artful shapes. I loved that everyone told me how tall I'd gotten since the last time. I loved shrill city laughter, the boldness of it. The magic of carelessly caring so much about everything. I loved going to Sylvester's, that sumptuous wonderland of fabric and antiques and music. But I especially loved the barge — which was any bed my mom captained. Just floating along on a squeaky motel bed with the grown-ups. The whisper of money in my mom's hands, the dry

Meridy and Alia on a brownie run.

snap of rubber bands when she counted it out at the end of the weekend.

If that environment was too much for a girl of four and five, I didn't notice.

My mom was there. I was safe.

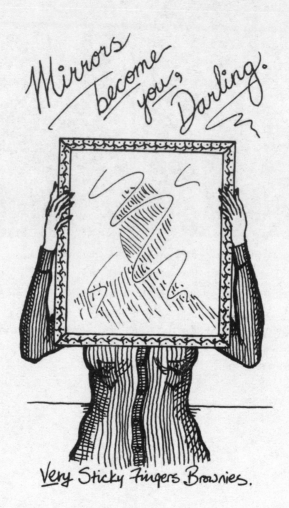

Mirrors become you, Darling.

Very Sticky Fingers Brownies.

19

Mirrors Become You

On January 14, 1981, policemen knocked on the door of a Victorian flat in the Castro. A plump woman with curly gray hair and owlish glasses answered. "I figured you guys were coming," she said sweetly, as the cops filed in. They nabbed fifty-four dozen brownies, eighteen pounds of pot, a half ounce of psilocybin mushrooms, thirty-five pounds of margarine, fifty pounds each of flour and sugar, twenty-two dozen eggs, and twenty-one thousand feet of plastic wrap.

Mary Jane Rathbun had been a waitress for forty-three years until she fell while working the graveyard shift at IHOP. She told reporters — and later the courts — that she'd been selling marijuana brownies for the past six months to supplement her Social Security income. Calling herself Brownie Mary, she'd posted flyers on telephone poles around the Castro offering "magically delicious" baked goods and listing her phone number and regular business hours. She'd been an easy catch for narcs, who only had to phone and ask for her address.

It's possible that Mary had been baking with weed longer than she admitted (Dennis Peron later said he'd carried her treats at his Big Top Marijuana Supermarket for a while during the late 1970s). But if Mary's version is true, she began peddling brownies in the Castro several months after Sticky Fingers left for the country. She'd found a hungry market.

This was how Mer the Brownie Lady became conflated with

Brownie Mary. Both women sold high-grade sinsemilla brownies in the Castro. They didn't look alike — Mer favored glitzy outfits and vampy makeup while Mary, twenty-five years older, wore Hawaiian-print shirts and polyester slacks — but they were both full-figured white women with curly hair. Sticky Fingers closed right before Brownie Mary opened shop. Then Mer reopened for monthly stints at Beck's just as Mary's home sales were expanding. Who *wouldn't* get confused?

"People in the neighborhood would ask for her [Brownie Mary's] brownies," says Dan Clowry of the Village Deli. "Even though we had Sticky Fingers and knew that name, people would come in and say, 'Do you have Brownie Mary's brownies?'" He didn't bother correcting them.

Anyone getting busted was bad news. At the same time, Mer had to imagine that if any cops had been eyeing her since the warehouse days they would now assume that they'd found the real culprit.

Mary Rathbun stepped boldly into the limelight after her arrest. What she lacked in subtlety she made up for in charm. Though only fifty-seven, she gave off serious granny vibes. She spoke in a warbly voice and hobbled on bad knees. Her only daughter had died in a car accident in 1974; you couldn't help but sympathize. There was something irresistible about Mary Rathbun, and she knew it. "I was pretty blatant, to say the least," she told the *San Francisco Chronicle*. "But who's gonna mess with me — a little old lady who fell on her butt and baked health food brownies to supplement her income?"

The press was smitten.

The courts didn't seem to know what to do with such a likeable dealer. Mary fretted to one interviewer that she was looking at fifteen-to-twenty years in the slammer; but as an elderly white woman with no previous record, she got off with a thirty-day suspended sentence, three years on probation, and five hundred hours of community service.

The community service turned out to be life-changing for Mary. She started in the soup kitchen at St. Martin de Porres House of Hospitality but soon switched to the Shanti Project, an organization offering end-of-life counseling and hospice care. Shanti was beginning to look after the young men coming down with gay cancer — many of whom were outcasts from their birth families. After finishing her court-ordered service, Mary went right on volunteering. She found a home for her soul among the City's lost boys. As Dennis later wrote, "Mary had lost her only daughter in an auto accident . . . and now she adopted every kid in San Francisco as her own."

Mary noticed that cannabis helped with a variety of gay cancer symptoms — notably nausea, appetite loss, insomnia, pain, and depression. In defiance of the court, she went back to what she did best: baking. In December 1982, one of the same narcs who'd originally arrested Mary caught her with four dozen brownies. Rathbun explained that she had baked them for a friend suffering from cancer. She was charged with multiple counts of possession and violation of her probation.

By now, Mary's reputation had grown, and the community rallied — circulating petitions, fundraising, and writing letters. Mid-1983, the district attorney bucked convention and dropped the charges against her.

From the beginning, Brownie Mary had described weed as "health food" or "medicine" for her sore back and knees — never as a drug. Though ganja lovers had been extolling the medicinal value of cannabis for ages, Mary was among the first to successfully sell that notion to the US media. Maybe America needed someone grandmotherly to do it — especially with ultramaternal Nancy Reagan adopting the War on Drugs as her FLOTUS pet project. Mary was sweet and earthy. Her tireless volunteerism won hearts. People could disagree with her, but it was impossible to paint Mary Rathbun as a villain.

———

The tenor of the Castro was changing. Boys were still on the street, cruising, looking good, laughing. But there was something in the air, snaking through the crowds. A new scent.

Fear.

Everyone knew someone who had gay cancer.

Mer saw it on her monthly runs. Those little purple spots. Roger had one, then Michael had two, then Patrick had five. Pudgy Ronald, who was always trying fad diets to lose weight, seemed excited to have found a regimen that really worked; a month later, his collarbones protruded. When Mer phoned Rick to say she was in town, he apologized that he wasn't feeling up to company — down with the flu again. What the hell was going on? Were these a bunch of little problems or one big one? Could it have something to do with the poppers everyone was into at the discos and sex clubs? Was someone poisoning the liquid soap in the bathhouses? Was the CIA in on it? Some guys started eating healthier, taking more vitamins, going out less. Others played harder, leaning heavier on cocaine and poppers, and spending night after night at the baths — might as well have fun.

Bobbi Campbell, the nurse who'd made the gay cancer poster, joined an order of drag nuns-*cum*-activists called the Sisters of Perpetual Indulgence. Reinventing himself as Sister Florence Nightmare, RN, Campbell encouraged the group to draw attention to the illness with its rambunctious brand of street theater. In June 1982, the Sisters hosted a campy dog show at Hibernia Beach, drawing a crowd of some five hundred people with both the dogs and the owners in costume. It was the Sisters' second annual dog show. This year, however, all proceeds went to the new Kaposi's Sarcoma Research and Education Foundation — possibly the world's first fundraiser to fight gay cancer.

Two months later, Mer's friend and customer Michael Maletta died.

When Mer heard the news at Beck's, it hit her right in the third eye, spun her momentarily out of her body. "Jesus," she gasped. "But he's so young."

Not only young but *vibrant*. A stylish and handsome New Yorker with strawberry blond hair and a wicked wit. One of those people who seemed more alive than others around him. In the warehouse days, Mer had sold him brownies every week at his in-home hair salon on Market Street. Michael was known for throwing lavish all-night happenings; the outrageous *Stars* party, where Mer had sold brownies in 1978, had been Michael's doing. He'd been diagnosed with Kaposi's sarcoma a mere nine months before dying in hospice care. Mer hadn't seen him in a while, but it hadn't occurred to her to worry. Now he was dead.

A couple of months later, in November, Patrick Cowley, Sylvester's synth player and the producer of *Step II* — the album that had rocketed the singer to international disco stardom — died from *Pneumocystis carinii* pneumonia. Mer had smoked pot with Patrick at Sylvester's house and chatted with him at gigs. He was a pale willowy blond. A little bookish, quietly sarcastic, someone who always seemed like the smartest guy in the room. In the last year of his life, aware that he was dying, Patrick worked against the clock. He cofounded Megatone Records, and wrote, arranged, and recorded three complete albums as well as two dance-club hits. Patrick would be lauded posthumously as a key innovator of electronic music; decades later, his tracks would be collected and reissued. He died at thirty-two.

By the end of 1982, the San Francisco Department of Public Health had recorded forty-six deaths from what was now being called acquired immunodeficiency syndrome. Nationwide, some nine hundred cases had been reported to the CDC. A former brownie customer, Ellen Freed, was now working as a medical assistant in an STD clinic with gay clientele. At night, when she went dancing at the Stud, friends would bounce up to her: "Hey, Ellen, look at this spot on my arm. Do I have the gay cancer?" She would squint at their skin under the strobing disco lights and suggest they make an appointment for a proper exam. Then they'd go back to dancing.

Few could fathom the enormity of what was coming — least of all a five-year-old. With that capacity young humans have for absorbing new realities, I gathered that some of my mom's friends were sick — the suddenly skinny ones, the frail and hunched ones — though the gravity escaped me. Nothing changed how much I loved coming to the City.

I was more comfortable hanging out with stoned adults than with other children. I'd twirl around the motel room, tell jokes I'd made up myself, wiggle loose teeth with my tongue — and they rewarded me with laughter and attention. Kids were heavy and baffling, but grown-ups loved me.

By early 1983, we had moved from Hearst to a smaller ranch house closer to town. My parents enrolled me in a Waldorf school where we learned basic math by drawing gnomes who gathered and lost gemstones. I did well in class but poorly on the playground. I'm not sure what alienated me from other children so early, but I imagine it had to do with being socialized in such a peculiar environment. Perhaps learning to keep secrets at a young age made me cagey. There must have been a moment when my parents sat me down and explained that their business was illegal — that I'd have to lie to protect them — but I don't remember it. That knowledge seems to have always been with me. By five, I understood very well that if I told anyone about the family business — the garbage bags of pot, the gooey brownies, our thrilling weekends at Beck's — my parents would go to jail.

I was an early and avid reader, hiding books under my bed to read by my dim night-light when I was supposed to be sleeping. My favorite was *Alice's Adventures in Wonderland*. Looking back, it makes sense. Consciousness began in the warehouse with its parade of curious characters: Day-Glo punks, leather daddies, cross-dressing belly dancers. On brownie runs in the stroller, I ogled jugglers and drag queens and tap-dancing nuns. We'd visit Sylvester; in my memory, he's draped languidly on his divan in glittery robes and turbans, smoking a fat joint: the stoned caterpillar in human form.

And, of course, I was Alice. Admitted to the inner circle without really belonging. Too young to understand the jokes but keen enough to pick up on the mood and always allowed to listen. Like Alice stumbling into the Mad Hatter's unbirthday party and the Red Queen's croquet match, I'd find myself in the middle of the action but a few steps behind the plot . . . curiouser and curiouser. By then, long blonde curls hung in tangled waves down my back. I had large blue eyes and snaggleteeth. My favorite dress was a square-dance number with puffy sleeves and a faux apron that I loved precisely because it resembled Alice's.

San Francisco was my Wonderland. I must have sensed a growing darkness, but that didn't make me want to stay away. Alice's dreams were scary, too.

In Willits, money problems were ongoing. Mer scraped together rent but rarely without stress. From her perspective, Firefeather wasn't doing much to help. He'd never excelled at sales, but back in the warehouse days, he had walked his route and taken the same risks as she and Cheryl. With money flowing abundantly, it had been enough.

Now that things were tight, she expected more effort. Firefeather took odd work and construction gigs, but opportunities were scarce and the work he found didn't suit him. Eventually, he'd offend someone or get fed up with whatever the work-culture bullshit was and quit. He also had rotten luck — like when a kitchen fire destroyed the restaurant where he'd begun waiting tables. Nothing lasted. Mer had never worked a straight job either, but she hustled when it was time to hustle. She thought Firefeather was being a prima donna. She wanted him to get a job, *any* job, so the pressure wouldn't sit so heavily on her shoulders.

Firefeather felt both frustrated and emasculated, ill-equipped to support his family. His best wasn't good enough. He had always been critical of Mer's extra cushion, but during the warehouse days, the margin had been small — ten or twenty stubborn pounds. Now, in the nowhere of Willits, Mer began to pack it on in earnest. The more Firefeather rode her about it, the uglier she felt and the more she sought comfort in binge-eating. Twenty pounds became fifty, then seventy-five, then a hundred.

The familiar arguments worsened.

When are you gonna make some money?

When are you gonna lose some weight?

They fought prodigiously, impressively, endlessly.

Mer's artwork intensified. She painted *impasto,* using a palette knife to create Van Gogh–esque swirls, piling her pigments an inch thick in places. Instead of flesh tones, her figures vibrated with yellows, purples, and greens. She unleashed her frustrations on old mirrors, which she piled into a burlap sack and bashed repeatedly with a sledgehammer, growling and cursing. Then she pressed the shards into the deep wet paint on a life-size depiction of a spinning belly dancer. Standing in front of it, you'd see your face reflected in deconstructed slivers, your features scattered and multiplied.

Summer of 1983, Firefeather signed up with a crew of men heading to Shasta, California, some four hours northeast. The plan was to camp for a week during which they'd harvest pine cones for the rich, expensive nuts. This involved climbing tall evergreens and dangling from harnesses while gathering the cones.

As much as Mer wanted him to work, the image of Firefeather climbing trees dozens of feet tall turned her stomach. She suspected he was messing with his meds again. "What if you have a seizure up in a tree? You could *die.*"

"I won't have a seizure." Firefeather was sick and tired of being nagged about money, and the organizer promised a lucrative return. They bickered, as they bickered about everything. Then he left.

The job turned out to be a scam. The crew had to provide their own food, transportation, and camping supplies. The work was high-risk and physically strenuous, and in the end, no one got paid what they'd been promised. A close friend of Firefeather's who also went on the trip, Jeff Crawford, would later sue the organizer over unpaid work.

When I ask my dad about this now, that's all he remembers: that he went to Shasta to pick pine cones and never got paid properly. The rest of the story is blank to him.

But according to Jeff Crawford, on the second or third night of camping, Firefeather vanished from the campsite without a word. The men called out to him in the woods, foliage absorbing their voices. In the morning, they searched the nearby forest.

Hours later, Firefeather wandered back to camp. He was pale and shaky, scraped and bruised as though he'd fallen. He told Jeff that a spirit had awoken him during the night and led him through the woods on a vision quest. A seeker himself, Jeff respected his friend's spirituality; it wasn't *what* Firefeather said that concerned him but the look in his eyes, the unsettling gaze. His pupils were dilated like someone on an acid trip, though Firefeather swore he'd only smoked a little pot the night before. Jeff would later describe the episode as "some kind of psychological-spiritual meltdown."

No way Firefeather should climb trees in that shape.

Meridy was furious when she got the phone call. *I knew it,* she thought. *He went and had a fucking seizure and now he's delusional.* She found a babysitter, then drove the four hours to Shasta to collect her husband. Upon arriving, Mer found him rambling semi-incoherently. He claimed he'd been bitten on the leg by a rattlesnake, but when he pulled up his pant leg to show her the wound, all she saw were some scratches from wandering in the woods.

Firefeather's seizures generally began with a radiant, prismatic mandala floating in his peripheral vision. The attacks could leave him confused or delusional. He lost chunks of memory. But the preseizure aura was so inspiring that it *almost* made the consequences worthwhile.

Even today, when my dad talks about his epilepsy, it's not with the voice of someone who feels afflicted. "Light," he says, "is nothing but the fabric of life pulled aside to reveal the true splendor of the Absolute or the Divine. [By taking Dilantin] I felt like I was turning my back on something extremely exciting. Why would I want to deny myself that?"

My dad is not alone in romanticizing his epilepsy. Fyodor Dostoevsky experienced his seizures as holy gifts. "For a few seconds of such bliss," he wrote, "I would give ten or more years of my life, even my whole life."

According to science writer Sam Kean, a lot depends on where in the brain the seizures happen. If the short-circuit occurs in the temporal lobe — possibly the case with my dad — the experience can be spiritually charged — what's called "ecstatic epilepsy." Some temporal-lobe epileptics, Kean writes, "feel their 'souls' uniting with whatever godhead they believe in."

Mandalas featured prominently in Firefeather's artwork. He spent untold hours hunched at his drafting table with his compass, ruler, and colored pencils producing vivid, kaleidoscopic images. They plastered the walls of our home. He began a series of twelve visionary oil paintings he called the Light Series, representing the "twelve steps of spiritual awakening" and featuring rivers of energy, exploding rainbows, and multiethnic spiritual symbols.

What Firefeather wanted was to explore his preseizure auras without suffering the consequences of a grand mal attack. In the early 1980s, Firefeather landed on what he thought of as an effective method for controlling the seizures without medication. He found that if he turned his eyes firmly *away* from the mandala he'd eventually feel a little *pop*, and the orb would float away like a balloon on a broken string. But many of his seizures came late at night when he wasn't conscious enough to control his impulses. And sometimes, even when he was awake, he couldn't resist the magnificent visions.

I vividly recall my dad showing me his rattlesnake bite when my parents got home from Shasta. Even though it had been his hallucination, I *saw* weeping fang marks on his calf—the puncture marks surrounded by yellowish waxy flesh. I panicked, thinking he might die. At five, I still accepted his delusions as truth, and my imagination supplied the missing details. Not until recently did I learn that my dad has never in his life been bitten by a snake. This is a pitfall of growing up with an unstable parent: his unreality made my reality dubious.

What I call the "mandala snakes" must have started then. In bed at night, as I tried to fall asleep, multicolored circles spun behind my closed eyelids and transformed into jeweled snakes that unfurled in the dark and swam toward my face, fanged mouths gaping to swallow my head. This terrified me as a little girl. Even now, when I'm battling insomnia, I'll sometimes slip into an unpleasant loop of imagining colorful snakes winding toward my face.

My dad recalls little of the Shasta episode. "It's so strange hearing about all these things that I did that I just don't remember at all," he says.

Sometime in the 1990s, he switched to Tegretol, an anticonvulsant that he likes better and takes regularly. He hasn't had an attack in nearly twenty years. But I sense that a part of him misses it a little bit. "My life sure is boring now by comparison," he says.

On December 15, 1983, my mom tied a blindfold over my eyes during my sixth birthday party. I heard unusual noises and gasps from

The big reveal.

the other kids. My mom whispered, "Happy birthday, baby," and untied the blindfold. Standing in front of me was a shaggy Shetland pony, brown with white splotches, wearing a red bow in his forelock.

Meridy gave me a pony for my birthday.

I had been obsessed with horses since I could remember and had started taking kiddie riding lessons at four from a woman named Susan. I saved pennies and nickels in a jar labeled PONY FUND. My mom had scrounged up a few hundred dollars and splurged. I named the pony Acorn, and we housed him at my riding teacher's ranch.

In truth, Acorn was too unruly for a kid my age. He bucked and bit and took off galloping. I had neither the muscles nor the skill to earn the respect of a mean little pony like Acorn. I did better with Susan's gentle school horses.

After six months or so, money got tight again, and my parents ended up selling Acorn, with promises to buy me a bigger horse when I was old enough to take care of one myself. From the beginning, the plan had been unfeasible. Giving a child gifts you really can't afford seems irresponsible when I think of it now. I'm sure I was brokenhearted. And yet, I don't remember that part. What stands out in my memory is the great reveal. That moment of pure magic when my mom made my most treasured dream — a surprise pony for my birthday — come true.

She was like that with me: encouraging, dazzling, unrealistic.

My mom kept her cocaine grinder on top of her highboy. I remember a brown plastic cylinder with a little crank and a film of white dust around the cracks. A pocket-size makeup mirror sat beside it along with a crusty little straw. I knew where these things were kept, and I knew they weren't toys.

She must have acted differently when high — tense and overexcited and self-absorbed — though it wasn't obvious to me back then. Since babyhood, I had been surrounded by adults in altered states. Mushroom trips, LSD trips, brownie highs, cocaine highs, occasional periods of delusion. The air in our home was always thick with pot smoke.

It was an atypical, looking-glass childhood, but it wasn't a bad one. I kept up with riding lessons. I went to Wavy Gravy's circus camp one summer and a horse camp the next. I swam in rivers and ran through sunstruck fields. I experienced the vibrant intensity of urban life, too. My parents could be self-involved and erratic but not neglectful. I never went without food or shelter or someone to comfort me when I cried.

Spring of 1984, Firefeather tried his hand at growing pot. He planted twelve seedlings in white five-gallon buckets and later transferred them into a small clearing in the woods near our house. Throughout the summer, he hauled buckets of water into the woods, two at a time, then trudged back up to the spigot for refills. Hot sun pounding on his neck, blue sky spinning overhead.

The price of Mendocino bud was climbing. If this starter crop worked out, he planned to go bigger next season.

I'd tag along when he watered, scampering to keep up with his long legs. I knew marijuana in other phases — the Dr. Seuss silhouettes of uprooted plants drying on clotheslines, the gooey buds that left miniature crystals on my fingers, the avocado-green dust that went into brownies — but our weed babies were different. Leaning close to the leaves, I whispered encouragement until they swayed above my head. I remember looking up at the jungle-green star points haloed in sunlight. And the tight fists of new buds huddled close to the stalks.

Then the caterpillars came.

Alice had one bigmouth caterpillar to deal with, but our plants shivered under a writhing mass of thousands of blue and yellow bodies. Beautiful and gruesome, they wrapped themselves around stems, dangled from leaves, and squirmed over one another.

My dad gawked in dismay, his skin rinsing pink. He hurled the water bucket against the trunk of a nearby tree. "Goddamn it!"

I trapped a wriggling caterpillar in my cupped hands and scurried home. Tiny sticky feet. Delicate bright fur tickling my palms. My mom poked holes in the lid of a pickle jar. The next morning, I sneaked to the clearing and saw that my dad had torn the plants from the ground, leaving a wasteland of holes. Their corpses lay in a heap, dirt clinging to their naked roots, stripped almost bare by the caterpillars. I gathered scraps of pot leaves from the ground and sprinted home to feed my pet his favorite food. I hoped he would build a cocoon and turn into a butterfly, but he died in my glass trap.

Firefeather took the caterpillar invasion as a sign that he wasn't meant to be a grower. Despite the fighting and financial pressure at home, this might have been for the best. It was becoming increasingly dangerous.

Reagan had promised a new war on drugs; in July 1983, he'd lobbed the first grenade — at California's pot growers. The Campaign Against Marijuana Planting, known as CAMP, was a coalition of local, state, and federal agencies tasked with stamping out cannabis cultivation in California. To explain his targeting of rural hippies, Reagan trotted out the old "gateway drug" theory — the statistically unsupported notion that marijuana would lead people to heavier drugs.

There was a more mercenary reason for targeting pot farmers. The Sentencing Reform Act of 1984 expanded antiracketeering laws that allowed the government to confiscate property used in committing a federal crime — and auction it for revenue. The administration talked plainly about it. "The biggest focus of what we're doing is going to be on land seizures," deputy commander of CAMP William Ruzzamenti told journalist Ray Raphael. "Anybody who is growing marijuana on their land, we're going to take their land. It's as simple as that."

Astoundingly, law enforcement didn't need proof of criminal activity to confiscate property; they didn't even have to file charges. They could now take everything simply by asserting "probable cause." The new laws presumed that anything purchased "within a reasonable time" of a suspected drug deal was bought with drug money — which made it subject to forfeiture. Not only land, but also cars, computers, and jewelry. Even when the accused was later found not guilty, the legislation offered no roadmap for reclaiming what the government grabbed. In a searing 1991 exposé based on a review of 25,000 seizures nationwide, the *Pittsburgh Press* reported that 80 percent of the people whose property was taken were never even charged with a crime.

Under these new provisions, the feds were encouraged to divvy proceeds with local law enforcement; a lion's share of the take flowed right back to police departments. Busting suspected drug offenders suddenly became lucrative in a way that fighting violent crimes — robberies, rapes, murders — was not.

During the Reagan years, CAMP mushroomed into the largest law enforcement task force in US history up to that point, involv-

ing more than one hundred agencies, and they all got a piece. In its
first six years of operation, CAMP reported seizing $19.7 million in
assets (equal to about $40.7 million in 2019) along with cash and
thousands of vehicles. On the national level, a fund was created in
1986 to collect and dole out drug war money; by 1990, the kitty
held $1.5 billion.

Reagan also championed a program to funnel disused military
equipment — U-2 spy planes and helicopters, automatic weaponry, infrared imaging, armored vehicles, flash bang grenades — to
local police for use *against citizens*. Increasingly, "Ronnie's Raid-
ers" turned to aggressive no-knock tactics — busting doors down
unannounced at all hours without giving the occupants a chance
to get dressed or comfort children.

Gone were the days when police had knocked politely on Mary
Rathbun's door.

With CAMP, California became the testing ground for drug
war tactics that soon spread throughout the country. The inclusion of military-grade weaponry and profit-sharing between the
feds and local police became standard. Harking back to the Nixon
era, when the drug war's targets were the "antiwar left and black
people," the Reagan administration put crosshairs on its perceived
enemies: counterculture holdouts in rural areas and urban communities of color.

Crack made the scene in the mid-1980s, inspiring waves of sensationalized media coverage. From the beginning, it was portrayed
as a black drug, despite similar usage rates across races. The Anti-
Drug Abuse Act of 1986 laid out grossly unequal sentencing for
powder cocaine and crack, even though the chemical makeup is
the same. The mandatory minimum sentence of five years in federal prison applied to dealers caught with *five hundred* grams of
powder cocaine or just *five* grams of crack.

Drug arrests doubled during Reagan's tenure. Defense attorneys in drug cases were soon required to report any fees received

in cash as well as payments exceeding $10,000. The federal government could then seize those assets and destroy the attorney-client relationship. Think of it this way: If someone accused of murder had the means, he or she could hire top-notch defense lawyers, but defendants in penny-ante drug cases were stuck with overburdened public defenders.

This was the dawn of mass incarceration, which today imprisons nearly 2.3 million people in the United States. Almost 80 percent of people in the federal prison system and 60 percent of those incarcerated at the state level on drug offenses are black or Latino. One in every thirteen black adults has been stripped of his or her right to vote by a felony conviction.

CAMP, aimed at California growers, was the first salvo in this new War on Drugs. If the goal of those operations was to fatten coffers, militarize police, strip rural hippies of their land, and populate new private prisons with people of color, CAMP was an unequivocal success. But if the goal was to reduce the amount of California homegrown flowing through America, it didn't work.

The pot-growing community banded together for support. They shared tips (like planting near bright manzanita to confuse infrared cameras) and used CBs and phone trees to warn one another when CAMP was prowling.

Busts drove up the market price. According to CAMP's annual reporting, California sinsemilla brought an average wholesale price of $3,400 per pound in 1986, more than double what it had been at the beginning of the decade. Who could afford *not* to either grow or traffic weed? Especially in places like Willits, where legal jobs were scarce and paid little. Before CAMP came along, Mer had mostly stuck to selling brownies. Pot was bulky, odoriferous, and dangerous to transport. She had to bring a triple-beam scale in the car, making her intent to sell patently obvious. But it had become too lucrative to pass up.

These forces were beyond my comprehension as a child, though

I knew that our kind was being hunted. I remember the helicopters pounding above our house, the U-2 spy planes cutting arcs overhead. My parents would point to the sky and whisper, "CAMP," a simple statement of evil.

By 1984, Mer's trips to the City had become heartbreaking and surreal.

People physically transformed between visits: from a handsome thirty-year-old to a frail seventy-year-old within months. *Act normal,* she'd think, struggling to mask her shock. *Say something funny . . .*

She can't remember who among her friends was next to go after Michael and Patrick. AIDS took out so many people so quickly that it sometimes seemed more like a natural disaster — a tidal wave, a volcanic eruption, a flood — than a disease. Brownie customers disappeared from the shops and restaurants and bars where they'd worked for years. One month, a regular would be there buying his usual dozen. The next month, someone new would be working his shift.

From his post at the Village Deli, Dan Clowry watched his community change. Other waiters at the café began to miss shifts. Sometimes, when customers showed visible signs of illness, Dan's coworkers would be too scared to serve them. Dan understood this less as a fear of contagion than a fear of confronting their own futures.

All these years later, Dan still thinks about a café regular who always dressed in spiffy 1940s military uniforms. One day, the guy came in with his entire head swollen and discolored "like a big purple balloon." Nevertheless, he had put on his crisp uniform and plopped the little sailor cap on top of his suddenly enormous head. The other waiter on shift was freaked out, but Dan walked right over and sat down with his customer. "Honey," he said. "You look fabulous today."

Two revelations hit Dan that afternoon.

First, that he'd missed his calling; he should have gone into health care.

Second, that they were all in deep, deep shit.

San Francisco General had been the first hospital in the country to open a dedicated AIDS clinic back in 1983. It soon expanded into three wards. Scared of exposure to a disease about which so little was understood, some health practitioners refused to treat AIDS patients. The list of ailments grew longer and more bizarre — including infections normally suffered by cats, birds, sheep, and deer. The doctors and nurses who staffed wards 86 (outpatient) and 5B/5A (inpatient) volunteered to work those posts, running unknown risks. One nurse famously became infected via a needle stick and went right on nursing. These were days of true heroism. But nothing slowed the dying. "I haven't cured anybody yet," a nurse told journalist Carol Pogash. "And that's tough."

Doctors and nurses at General eschewed hazmat suits, face masks, and gloves — insisting that human touch was an essential component of treatment. Practitioners were encouraged to hug their patients, cry with their patients, feel and express love. "I don't want them to think they're like lepers," one nurse said in an interview with the *San Francisco Chronicle*. "That nobody wants to come near them." Visitors could stay on the ward all night, and patients were empowered to decide who was welcome, defying the tradition of prioritizing blood relatives. Eventually, practitioners from around the world visited General to study "patient-centered care"; even Mother Teresa took a tour. Not everyone was on board. Four nurses filed complaints with Cal/OSHA but lost their case. The network that arose between public health officials, doctors, community organizers, and patients became known internationally as the San Francisco Model.

The first blood test for human immunodeficiency virus, the cause of AIDS, was developed in 1984 and became widely available in 1985. Brownie customer and editor in chief of *Drummer* magazine Jack Fritscher remembers the sudden maturity the test demanded. "You look at your lover you've been with for all these years, and you think, *Should we even get tested? What if one of us has it and one of us doesn't?*" Before visiting the clinic, he and his lover sat down to write up a game plan for each possible outcome. These were end-of-life decisions, normally the purview of couples entering their golden years, forced upon people in their twenties and thirties.

Even with the mode of transmission understood, confusion and paranoia persisted. Was it safe to hug and kiss? Were some kinds of sex okay and others not? Could you eat from the same plate of food? In 1985, the *New York Times* reported that 51 percent of survey respondents supported quarantining AIDS patients, 48 percent supported issuing identity cards, and 15 percent thought that people with HIV should be forcibly tattooed.

I ask my mom if she worried about contagion on the weekends she spent with sick friends at Beck's. She answers with an anecdote. When she was five, her appendix burst, and she had to spend some time in the hospital. She got bored and somehow slipped past the nurses. After a frantic search, they found her on another floor, playing with kids in the polio ward. "I guess I knew on a gut level that it was okay," she says about AIDS. "I worried a lot about my friends, but never about that."

It's hard to fathom the apathy with which the Reagan administration met the AIDS epidemic. Journalist Lester Kinsolving had asked the first-ever AIDS-related question at a White House press briefing in 1982. He wanted to know the president's reaction to the CDC's announcement that the "gay plague" was an epidemic with more than six hundred cases.

Reagan's press secretary, Larry Speakes, teased the reporter: "I don't have it," he quipped, getting a laugh from the press pool. "Do you?"

Kinsolving tried repeatedly over subsequent years to get the

White House to answer seriously. Speakes mocked his interest in "fairies" and insinuated that he must have the virus himself to be so curious.

That AIDS wasn't exclusively attacking gays was a known fact; by late 1982, the illness had also been reported among IV drug users, hemophiliacs who received frequent transfusions, Haitian immigrants, and babies born to infected mothers. But voices within the power structure continued to frame AIDS as a gay affliction: the price of hedonism and perversion. Pat Buchanan, whom Reagan would later appoint as his communications director, wrote, "The poor homosexuals. They have declared war on nature, and now nature is exacting an awful retribution."

Reagan had made his own views on homosexuality apparent early on. As governor of California in the early 1970s, he'd vowed to veto attempts to reform an 1872 law prescribing felony penalties for "crimes against nature." Willie Brown and George Moscone had had to wait for his departure to push the 1975 Consenting Adult Sex Bill through. A man who believed sodomy should be a felony was now presiding over the onset of the AIDS epidemic.

Worse, the epidemic erupted during an era of fiscal conservatism, in which both the CDC and NIH were chronically understaffed and underfunded. Annually, like clockwork, the White House budget proposal either lowballed or slashed AIDS funding. Time and again, Congress forced Reagan's hand to increase the amounts.

The surgeon general, C. Everett Koop, despite being staunchly antiabortion and deeply religious, thought moralizing had no place in a public health crisis of such magnitude. But his superiors within the administration forbade him from speaking about it. "For an astonishing five and a half years, I was completely cut off from AIDS," Koop later wrote. "The conservative politics of the middle and late years of the Reagan Administration attempted to thwart my attempts to educate the public about AIDS and tried to stir up hostility toward its victims." Not until after Reagan's personal friend Rock Hudson died did the president allow Koop to mail an informational pamphlet about AIDS to American households. Fellow conservatives were scandalized when the surgeon general advocated condom use (abstention being the official line) and sex education in schools.

Reagan himself did not utter the word "AIDS" publicly until September 1985 when he was pushed by another persistent journalist. Adopting a defensive tone, the president characterized AIDS as "one of our top priorities," and said, "I *have* been supporting it for over four years now." His administration had just proposed reducing AIDS spending again. Congress, as before, would goose the number back up.

Reagan wouldn't deliver his first speech on the epidemic until 1987 when he addressed the American Foundation for AIDS Research, an organization that Rock Hudson had helped launch in his last months. During the entire eighteen-minute talk, Reagan artfully managed not to say "gay" or "homosexual" once, instead focusing on babies born with the virus, hemophiliacs infected via blood transfusion, and spouses unaware of their partners' shady pasts — the perceived innocent victims of the gay plague.

By that point, 36,058 Americans had been diagnosed with the disease; 20,849 had died.

San Francisco took care of its own.

Mayor Feinstein rose to the occasion. According to historian David Talbot, when Supervisor Harry Britt showed her the first requests for research funding in 1982, Feinstein said simply, "Fund everything." Throughout the eighties, California consistently dedicated more resources to AIDS annually than any other state.

Community organizing was reborn. "We had to do it ourselves," Cleve Jones says. "Our friends were starving to death because they were too weak to go out, so we had to create systems to bring them food. Landlords were evicting them because they were afraid of them, so we had to create systems to house them. We had to do our own research. We had to smuggle in medications."

Organizations arose to help the sick and dying. Bill Pandolf, a longtime brownie customer, volunteered to drive patients to medical appointments through a "buddy" program. Project Open Hand and Meals on Wheels delivered hot food to those too sick to cook for themselves. Shanti Project and other hospice groups provided in-home care, counseling, and end-of-life housing. Project Inform kept people abreast of the latest drug trials, while the AIDS Emergency Fund paid late rent and overdue electric bills.

The plague manifested among white gay men first, but it shifted over time, cutting cruel swaths through neighborhoods of color and other marginalized groups. Transgender women were hit especially hard in a situation compounded by employment discrimination and poverty-related sex work. Where separatist movements of the 1970s had sometimes put lesbians, gay men, bisexuals, and transgender people at odds, the pandemic demanded collaboration. Lesbians, especially, did a lot of heavy lifting during the worst years. "I counted on my women friends to live forever," Mark Abramson wrote, "to cheer us on, to take care of us as we slid from our deathbeds into our graves."

Activists learned to fundraise on a new scale. "I don't remember what Harvey's budget was for his [1977] campaign," Cleve Jones says. "But it was about $25,000, which at that point seemed an astronomical sum. Within years, gay communities all across the country were routinely raising and spending millions of dollars. And then tens of millions of dollars." The Sisters of Perpetual Indulgence, which had begun as an Easter prank in San Francisco in 1979, blossomed into an international HIV/AIDS education and fundraising organism.

Drummer, the magazine that had most defined San Francisco's hard-core leather scene, reimagined itself through a lens of education. "We turned to fetishes as an idea of how to approach sex without having bodily fluids," says Jack Fritscher. "We began to teach safe sex and the glories of solo sex through articles and videos."

On ward 5B, a dancer named Rita Rockett brought home-cooked meals every Sunday using money she raised by passing the hat at community events. Dressed in showgirl garb, she tap-danced for patients and spent hours just hanging out. When diagnosis was a death sentence, people like Rita tried to make dying less lonely.

Brownie Mary volunteered as a nurse's assistant and runner on ward 86, logging so many hours that she was named Volunteer of the Year. Convinced that cannabis eased a variety of AIDS-related symptoms, Mary sneaked dosed brownies and cookies to patients on the ward. With scant treatment options, doctors and nurses turned a blind eye.

Dennis Peron and others donated pot so Mary could distribute her goodies on the ward for free. At her maximum, Mary allegedly baked up to 15,000 marijuana treats per month. It wasn't enough.

On monthly visits to the City, Mer watched the Castro empty out. Suddenly, there was ample parking, vacancies where there'd been a housing crisis, half-empty restaurants. Amid much controversy, the health department began shutting down bathhouses in 1984. Parties evolved into memorials and fundraisers. When local TV news interviewed Dan Clowry about the new challenges facing merchants in San Francisco's gay corridors, he said, "Business is dying off," and immediately regretted his word choice.

In January 1984, Dan White was released from prison after serving less than five years for assassinating Harvey Milk and George Moscone. Protests erupted; some demonstrators wore buttons that said, DAN WHITE'S HIT SQUAD. Authorities paroled him to Los Angeles to avoid bloodshed, but he slipped back into his hometown. In October 1985, he ran a garden hose from the exhaust pipe of his 1973 Buick LeSabre into its front window and killed himself. Reporters who went looking for vindictive comments from Castro residents were met with something akin to a shrug. "I'm glad his conscience caught up with him," one said. There were bigger fish to fry.

Mer's customers still bought their multiple dozens of brownies at Beck's or the Village Deli. She still did large deals in parking lots with Dennis's lover. And much like the old days, the brownies wound their way through the community, with each person buying for their friends and loved ones. But now, along with new wave clubs, discos, and house parties, Sticky Fingers appeared beside sickbeds.

Cleve Jones hadn't been a big Sticky Fingers customer in the warehouse days because he found the brownies too potent. AIDS changed that. When he tested positive in late 1985, he was frightened but not surprised. He'd begun experiencing fatigue and flu-like symptoms as early as 1979 — long before anyone knew what was happening. He'd suffered shingles on his scalp that made him feel like his hair was on fire and bouts of respiratory infections and digestive distress. Like many people, he found cannabis helpful with his sleep, pain, depression, and nausea, but recurrent pneumonia had left his lungs too delicate for smoking. He switched to edibles, which he sometimes bought from Mer at Beck's.

Nearly everyone on Mer's route was either dying, nursing someone who was dying, or mourning the death of a good friend or lover. Canes and walkers were commonplace. Young men shuffled around in wool coats and scarves even in warm weather.

The Castro had warped into a funhouse-mirror distortion of itself. It seems ironic that AIDS would take root in a community that so highly prized physical beauty — ravaging bodies and faces, eviscerating the cult of youth worship. Strength of spirit shone through death masks.

There's nothing superficial about fighting a plague.

!! ELLA–VAY–SHUN !!

STICKY FINGERS BROWNIES
?

20

Ella-Vay-Shun

There's a photo of my mom in a wheelchair, wearing a neck brace, full-leg cast, and dark sunglasses. She's bloated and pale, hair in an Einstein frizz.

The accident happened in November 1986. She was driving through Willits when she got distracted by a pedestrian sporting hot-pink pants and slammed into the car ahead of her. My mom, who hadn't buckled her seat belt, slid under the steering wheel, mangling the soft tissue around her right ankle and knee. She spent months in a wheelchair or on crutches. Downed-out on Percodan, depressed. The car was totaled, so no trips to the City. My dad wasn't working. There was no money coming in at all.

My parents had already separated for a few months during which my mom and I lived in a tract home and she attended *Women Who Love Too Much* meetings. In their attempt at reconciliation, my parents had rented a fancy yellow house with a swimming pool in the middle of town, but it didn't help. Their fights shook the windows. My mom screamed herself hoarse; my dad broke furniture.

At eight going on nine, I became convinced that the yellow house was haunted. It looked the part: a hulking Victorian on a corner lot, with a picket fence, rose garden, and an attic with peaked dormer windows. It had asymmetrical rooms and staircases leading to nooks that served no purpose. Despite its size and amenities, the rent was low when we'd moved there earlier in 1986 — and in scary movies, weren't haunted houses always cheap?

There were nice moments. Camping out by the pool to watch Halley's Comet streak slowly overhead. Splashing around on an inflatable pool toy that was supposed to be a horse, though it looked like a giant sausage. But in my bedroom at night, mandala snakes swam toward my face. I felt sure a clown lived under my bed. I had nightmares and insomnia, and sometimes wet the bed because I was scared to walk down the hall; its slanted ceiling played tricks on my eyes.

In retrospect, the house was probably fine. But my family wasn't.

Early December, my dad announced to us that he was quitting his epilepsy medication permanently. Then he climbed to his studio in the attic and stayed for days, coming down only for food. Stuck in her wheelchair on the ground floor, my mom would send me up with messages. I'd find my dad bent over his drafting table, absorbed in bright, intricate designs. Mandalas plastered the walls.

Mer felt like she'd been carrying the family's financial burden for eons. Now that she was unable to earn money — unable to walk — she needed Firefeather's help. But instead of stepping up, he isolated himself in his attic and went off his meds.

On top of everything, a certain somebody's ninth birthday was coming up, and she'd promised to throw a slumber party. When your kid has trouble making friends, birthdays become overblown with excitement and anxiety. So she rolled her wheelchair up to the kitchen table and spent days hot gluing feathers and flowers to party hats and candy baskets. It felt good, at least, to do *something*.

December 15, the day of the party, Firefeather came down to raid the fridge. As he passed her, Mer heard him say, very quietly, "I thought you'd want to know: I'm Joseph. You're Mary. And Alia is the baby Jesus."

"Are you kidding me?" Mer called after him as he climbed back up to his tower.

He didn't answer.

Kids showed up. Meridy wheeled herself around, popping popcorn, putting *The Last Unicorn* in the VCR yet again. In the early evening, Firefeather brought his knapsack and bedroll downstairs. "The Dalai Lama is speaking in San Francisco," he said. "I need to see him. He has a message for me."

"Now?" Mer hissed. "On Alia's birthday? While we have a house full of kids and I'm in a fucking wheelchair?"

"I need to do this," he said.

"The car's totaled."

"I'll hitchhike."

She caught his eyes and stared hard, trying to find the bond that was once so strong between them. He stared back, eyes glittering like ice chips. He did not look like himself.

"Doug," she said, trying his given name. "Don't go."

He went.

Terrible scenarios flashed through Mer's mind: Firefeather could have a seizure on the road, hit his head, forget who he was; he'd end up homeless on the streets of San Francisco. He'd gone too far this time.

Quietly, she made phone calls, getting one friend to chaperone the party while another drove her to the police station to fill out forms for an involuntary psychiatric hold. If Firefeather got picked up for acting disruptively, she wanted the police to know not to put him in jail. He needed a hospital and Dilantin. She cried in the car. Then she collected herself and returned to the party.

I recall the lead-up to my ninth birthday: my dad drawing in his tower; my mom surrounded by feathers and garlands, joking that the "froof bomb" had gone off. From the party, I remember lying in sleeping bags in wheel-spoke formation, maybe six kids, and telling ghost stories. I remember pepperoni pizza. I don't remember my dad disappearing. Either I've blocked that part out or my mom managed to shield me from what was happening. It wouldn't have been the first time.

Mer focused her freight-train energy on being Super Mom while my dad chased his spirituality over a cliff.

The Dalai Lama wasn't scheduled to be in San Francisco then; he was in Bylakuppe, India. But Firefeather didn't get far enough to find that out.

He stood beside Highway 101 with his thumb out for an hour or so, then said to himself, *Maybe I'm not supposed to go seeking the Dalai Lama. Maybe I already have the consciousness I need within myself.* Deciding to embark on a vision quest instead, he set out to circumnavigate the Willits valley.

Firefeather now acknowledges that this was unrealistic, though it made sense to him at the time. There was no hiking trail around Willits. Even if there had been, it would've taken days, and he carried no food or water.

Firefeather climbed straight up into hills thick with scrub and poison oak. At some point, he stowed his knapsack and bedroll inside a hollow tree and promptly forgot where they were. When the temperature dropped, he took shelter in an abandoned shed. Later, he became certain that something violent had happened there, and he set off again into the night. He soon found himself flailing down a steep hill through oak branches and brush before emerging onto a country road.

Two cop cars were waiting.

An area neighbor had heard somebody crashing around in the woods and phoned it in.

Firefeather explained to the officers that he'd been hitchhiking to see the Dalai Lama but decided to walk in the hills instead — which they must have found concerning enough to confirm the alert Meridy had put out. They sent Firefeather to a psychiatric ward in a neighboring town for an involuntary seventy-two-hour hold.

According to Firefeather, he stayed in a communal room with about twenty patients, some of whom were clearly disturbed. He felt sure he didn't belong there; this was all a misunderstanding.

One woman walked circles around him, drawing close to his body and muttering gibberish. Her smell seemed wrong, more like rotting flesh than human body odor.

Eventually, Firefeather was taken to speak with the head psychiatrist. He answered the doctor's questions carefully. Looking back, he recalls feeling confident that he would be released. "Because obviously I was perfectly clear thinking and everybody else around me was not." He was stunned when the doctor told him they still needed to keep him under observation.

When Firefeather explained this to another patient in the communal room, the guy said, "I knew it! This place is a coven of witches and the man running it is the warlock. They'll keep you here as long as they can. That's how they do it."

That made sense to Firefeather, and it infuriated him. Forcing himself to remain calm, he asked to speak with the psychiatrist once more.

"You need to understand something," he told the doctor. "I am a graduate of the Berkeley Psychic Institute and I am a reverend of the Church of Divine Man. I demand to be released. Right. Now."

As my dad remembers it, he was out of that facility and breathing fresh air within five minutes. To this day, his perception is that he secured his freedom from a hospital controlled by witches by announcing himself as a trained psychic. "Then," he says, "I went back to Willits and back to normalcy."

By the time he came home, my mom had taken me into hiding.

She explained to me that when my dad stopped taking his medication he sometimes "got a little weird." And this time he was weirder than usual. We stayed with my mom's friend Kathy, whose daughter Karma was two years older than I was. There are pictures of us girls wearing splotchy makeup and high heels that don't fit, and blowing kisses in front of a Christmas tree. Through the holidays and into the new year, Karma pretended to be the sister I'd always wanted.

I didn't know it then, but my dad, who was living alone in the yellow house, was leaving messages with mutual friends and on community bulletin boards. *Tell Meridy that I want to see Alia so I can give her my Christmas presents.* My mom called him a couple of times, but he kept describing us as the Holy Family reincarnated — which scared her. What if he harmed himself? What if he harmed us?

She finally asked her therapist to visit him and assess the situation.

"He's having a full-blown psychotic episode," the therapist said afterward. "I can't guarantee it's safe."

By January, I was begging to see him. I was over the novelty of a fake sister. I wanted my dad.

In the end, of course, it was an *I Ching* hexagram that convinced my mom to risk a visit. Her therapist coordinated with the police, so if Mer called 911 from the yellow house, they would come without asking many questions.

The image of my dad opening the door is seared into my mind. His blue eyes gleamed from a naked face. No eyebrows, head as shiny as a beach ball, chin vulnerable without his red beard. Despite the January chill, he wore a sarong knotted at the waist, his freshly shaven chest and arms bare. When we hugged, his skin felt prickly and unfamiliar, though I recognized his smell.

My mom, still hobbling in a soft cast, followed me inside and sat beside the phone.

I gave my dad a wool sweater and was relieved when he pulled it over his bald torso. He gave me a board game called *Wildlife Adventure,* which involved matching endangered species to their habitats. He read the rules aloud, pronouncing each word precisely in the same tone and cadence that he'd used to read me *Alice's Adventures in Wonderland* when I was younger. I watched the colored lights blink and let his voice carry me to a safer Christmas.

The psychosis eventually passed, but my mom was fed up. She

moved us into a double-wide near Kathy and Karma's. Her paintings stacked against the faux wooden walls left little room to move. I slept under a heap of stuffed animals.

We would never live with my dad again.

So when my dad says decades later that he "went back to normalcy" after the psychiatric hospital, I'm taken aback. I remind him that we weren't there when he returned to the yellow house. That our little family broke.

"Interesting," he says. "I didn't realize those events were connected."

My dad recounts his ill-fated trip to see the Dalai Lama with a level of detail that's unusual for his damaged memory. From the measured way he delivers the story, I feel sure that he's told it before. That he's not only remembering what happened but also how he's described it to other people. But in his version, he didn't leave on his daughter's birthday and come home to an empty house. He doesn't see the experience as a psychotic break, though he can't explain some of his actions.

In his telling, the most important part of the story is using his psychic prowess to escape the witches. In my telling, the most important part is losing my dad.

Unable to sell brownies or pot since the accident, Mer had no income and was borrowing money. Cheryl's boyfriend took up a collection among the Willits growers to buy her a dented mustard-yellow Honda. Nothing fancy, but it would get her to the City. In March 1987, she and Kathy baked and wrapped forty dozen brownies (and it says something about my mom's level of desperation that she baked). Leaving me with Kathy, she drove down with a loaded trunk and settled at Beck's for the weekend.

Mer had been away for only five months—but they had been plague months. Each time someone knocked, she girded herself for the possibility that her friend or customer had wasted to bones, curled into himself, been taken over by KS lesions, lost his mobility, his lover, his beauty, his humor. Catching up meant discovering which mutual acquaintances had died and speculating about who would be next. Even making phone calls to tell people she was in town was nerve-racking.

A drug called AZT had just hit the market. It was the first AIDS medication to gain FDA approval. At a cost of about $10,000 per year, it was also the most expensive prescription medicine in history. To protest the cost, a newly minted activist group called the AIDS Coalition to Unleash Power — or ACT UP — staged a dramatic protest on Wall Street, accusing the pharmaceutical company of profiteering and the FDA of ignoring other promising drugs. AZT would turn out to be ineffective over the long term, though it extended some people's lives. It was highly toxic, causing severe anemia, dizziness, headaches, vomiting, and diarrhea. Many patients couldn't tolerate it at all. For some, weed helped mitigate side effects.

On Sunday, Mer met Dennis Peron in a rooftop parking lot above Café Flore. Decades later, she can still picture Dennis leaning on a railing overlooking the Castro, his prematurely silver-white hair ruffling in a breeze.

Dennis bought all the brownies she had left.

When Mer told him she and Firefeather were divorcing, Dennis said, "You could always come back. You know what people keep telling me? They say, 'Dennis, if it wasn't for this joint, or this brownie, I wouldn't be out of bed today. It's keeping me going.' Brownie Mary is baking her ass off for the guys on the AIDS ward. She's been pulling names out of a cookie jar. There's too much need."

Medical marijuana wasn't a new idea — but it was still a radical one.

Veteran potheads like Dennis and my mom trusted their guts

about the healing potential of cannabis. That it had legitimate medical properties came as no surprise to them.

What's more surprising — and disheartening — is that the government knew it, too. Back in 1974, the Nixon administration had created the National Institute on Drug Addiction. NIDA acted both as a research-funding machine and as gatekeeper. Its mandate was to develop and conduct research "for the prevention and treatment of drug abuse and for the rehabilitation of drug abusers." But scientists kept stumbling on good news about pot instead: that it decreased ocular pressure (1971) and reversed glaucoma damage (1976); that it slowed the growth of Lewis lung tumors and leukemia in mice (1975); that THC was an effective analgesic for patients suffering pain related to cancer (1975); and studies during the seventies and eighties showed that THC minimized nausea and vomiting in chemotherapy patients.

Subsequent research has uncovered palliative and curative potential for an astonishing range of conditions. But human clinical trials are still scant in the United States, limited by legal hurdles. It's sobering to note that the first indications that cannabinoids might be harnessed to treat such illnesses as leukemia appeared in peer-reviewed journals more than forty years ago. Instead of chasing those leads, the government prioritized drug-war messaging over science. Because NIDA was the sole legal source of cannabis for researchers in the United States, only studies that served the administration's agenda were likely to move forward.

Marijuana has been classified as a Schedule 1 narcotic since 1970 — defined by the DEA as having "no currently accepted medical use and a high potential for abuse." It's worth repeating that this classification never had a scientific basis. The attorney general placed marijuana under Schedule 1 as a stopgap while Nixon's blue-ribbon commission investigated. But when the report recommended decriminalization and further exploration of medicinal value, Nixon rejected it flatly, and the temporary scheduling became permanent. That cannabis is more severely restricted than methamphetamines and oxycodone (both of which doctors can legally prescribe) has always been political — not scientific.

In 1976, a glaucoma patient named Robert Randall smoked a joint with friends and discovered, quite by accident, that marijuana eased the ocular pressure that was blinding him at twenty-five. He soon got busted for growing four plants for personal use. In preparing his defense, Randall contacted scientists at NIDA, the DEA, and the FDA, and was appalled to learn that studies had already demonstrated marijuana's effectiveness in fighting glaucoma. The government *knew* pot could help people like him. He decided to base his case on medical necessity, a defense that had never been used successfully.

Realizing that even if he won in court he'd just get busted again, Randall audaciously petitioned the government to supply his weed from its own experimental farm. And to stop them from hiding the research from other glaucoma patients, he took his story to CBS News. Amazingly, Randall's strategy worked; the government provided him with ten joints per day for the rest of his life.

Randall's case forced the FDA to create the Compassionate Investigational New Drug program to supply legal pot to people who could prove medical necessity. Distributing marijuana through Compassionate IND was a de facto admission that cannabis *had* therapeutic value — despite ongoing Schedule 1 classification. But they kept the program quiet. Moreover, the red tape was so elaborate, expensive, and exhausting to navigate that few clawed through to certification; at the program's height, it served fifteen people.

In 1986, the FDA approved a synthetic THC capsule, marketed under the brand name Marinol, as an antiemetic for chemotherapy-induced nausea and vomiting; it would soon be approved for AIDS-related wasting syndrome as well. Unlike homegrown pot, synthetic THC could be patented and marketed by pharmaceutical companies. But it was not without side effects; Marinol came on like a speeding train, leaving some people too stoned and paranoid to function. (Some ongoing research suggests that other cannabinoids — like CBD — may naturally counteract the psychoactive intensity; Marinol was a pure slug of synthetic THC.) Many patients found a couple of puffs from a joint equally effective and less punishing.

Some AIDS doctors saw in marijuana a missed opportunity. First as a fellow in oncology-hematology at the UCSF Cancer Research Institute, then as assistant director of the AIDS ward at San Francisco General, Dr. Donald Abrams had been on the frontlines since the beginning of the epidemic. Abrams found AZT unimpressive. He dissuaded his own ailing lover, Mark, from taking it, though it was the only approved treatment for AIDS at the time. What Mark did do, according to Abrams, was smoke pot every day.

Abrams watched his lover outlive the other patients in three separate support groups at Davies Medical Center. When Mark died in 1989, having surpassed his prognosis by three years, Abrams was left with the impression that cannabis might have helped. At General, he'd heard the rumors about Brownie Mary sneaking pot-infused desserts onto ward 86 to fight wasting, and some of his patients admitted to smoking illegal weed to help with a variety of symptoms. He thought they could be on to something.

A couple of years later, a medical-marijuana research advocate sent a letter challenging Abrams to collaborate on a study to evaluate cannabis as a treatment for AIDS-related nausea and anorexia. He suggested that the proposal should come from "Brownie Mary's institution." Looking back, Abrams laughs. "As if she were the dean!"

The letter made an impression nonetheless. "I remembered Mark because he had done so well using cannabis," Abrams says. Very little clinical research had been conducted into marijuana's therapeutic potential, but as Abrams has written, "The absence of evidence is not evidence of absence of effect."

Abrams and his collaborators secured a research grant. But to access marijuana legally, he needed approval from the FDA, the DEA, NIDA, and various other agencies. Over five years, he got the bureaucratic runaround while thousands died. At the height of his frustration, the usually unflappable doctor wrote an open letter to the director of NIDA. "You had an opportunity to do a service to the community of people living with AIDS. You and your Institute failed. In the words of the AIDS activist community: SHAME!"

Finally, the NIDA director told Abrams in person that his organization was the National Institute *on* Drug Abuse, not *for* drug abuse. NIDA's congressional mandate didn't allow it to support studies into marijuana's therapeutic attributes.

It was a moment of revelation. Abrams reframed his study: instead of looking for possible benefits, he would investigate whether marijuana *harmed* immune-compromised patients by interfering with their ability to process protease inhibitors. That got approved in 1997. Abrams eventually concluded that smoking cannabis helped AIDS patients gain weight while showing no adverse effects on viral load or interference with other medications. In a subsequent study, he found that marijuana eased the otherwise untreatable AIDS-related neuropathy. He was only able to get there by tricking the system.

For many people with AIDS, using marijuana to treat their symptoms was common sense especially when it came to fighting nausea and stimulating appetite. Cleve Jones remembers traveling to Sacramento sometime in the early nineties to speak before the state senate in favor of compassionate marijuana. A witness from law enforcement testified that there was no conclusive evidence that cannabis was an effective appetite stimulant. Waiting to testify, Cleve rolled his eyes. "There's a word in the English language that exists solely because of this phenomenon," he said when his turn came. "That word, Senator, is 'munchies.'"

Faced with bureaucratic rigidity, people with AIDS broke the law to self-medicate with marijuana. Dealers became healers.

Back in the stuffy double-wide, Mer stared up at the faux-wood ceiling and thought, *What the hell am I doing here?* When the school year ended, we moved back to San Francisco.

After eight years in Willits, Mer had direct access to pricey sinsemilla. Charging market rate for bud subsidized the brownies, which were still made with inexpensive shake. She didn't give brownies away like Mary Rathbun at General Hospital, but she stuck to her 1970s prices — a dollar or two for a brownie that most people split into three or four doses.

She rented us a spacious three-bedroom flat on Fourteenth Avenue, walking distance from Golden Gate Park. It had high ceilings and hardwood floors, French doors, a sunroom, and a scrubby backyard. Mer set up her studio in the living room and began a series of impasto paintings so large that she had to stand on a ladder. In coming years, her work would begin winning awards and being shown in West Coast museums. With new freedom, she stretched more fully into herself.

We had moved seven times since leaving the warehouse. The flat on Fourteenth Avenue became home.

On Market Street one day, Mer noticed new activity in the cavernous space that had housed Castro Camera in the months leading up to Harvey's assassination. A sheet of butcher paper taped in the window read, THIS IS THE NEW HOME OF THE NAMES PROJECT, followed by a wish list that included sewing machines, fabric, sequins, back rubs, hugs, and money. Mer ducked through the door. Inside, music competed with the thrumming of sewing machines. Bolts of bright fabric reared from bins and cascaded from shelves. This, Mer learned, was Cleve Jones's new project, the AIDS Memorial Quilt. From then on, Mer stopped in regularly with brownies for the sewers.

Cleve had been nursing the notion of a quilt since the 1985 Milk/Moscone candlelight vigil when he'd asked the crowd to write the

names of lost loved ones on their cardboard signs and tape them
to the wall of the San Francisco Federal Building; the visual reminded him of a patchwork quilt. Friends teased him, dismissing
the idea as too steeped in Americana. But for Cleve, wholesome-
ness was the point. He wanted to create an avenue for people who
weren't radicals to join the conversation about AIDS.

The project started small. But after the first viewing on the National Mall in D.C. in the fall of 1987, panels would pour in from all
over the country along with invitations to display the quilt. Cleve
would embark on a twenty-city national tour, bringing him into
intimate contact with grieving families from all walks of life, far
beyond the Castro. "America came to know her gay children at the
time of our greatest suffering," he says. "A lot of parents discovered for the first time that their son was gay when he came home
tell them that he was going to die. And some of those parents responded horribly, and those stories are often told, but most parents would never abandon their child."

Cleve had experienced this transformation firsthand. When he
came out to his family as a teenager, his own father had snarled,
"What do you like best, getting fucked in the ass or sucking cock?"
They didn't speak for years after that. But when Cleve called home
to say that he was sick, his dad started going to quilt displays and
marches.

"People who had never knowingly been around gay people suddenly had gay people coming into their homes to care for their
kids," Cleve says. "They saw the compassion, they saw the solidar-
ity, they saw the incredible courage, and their hearts were touched
by it."

Today, the quilt includes more than 48,000 panels from all over
the globe. It was nominated for a Nobel Peace Prize in 1989, by
which point HIV cases had been reported from every region of the
world. The AIDS Memorial Quilt remains the world's largest community art project.

Moving made the divorce feel permanent. I loved San Francisco —
the salt-lick smell, foghorn serenades, everyone in leather jackets.
I wanted to be there, but I wanted my dad, too.

Whenever he phoned, I'd careen around the house screeching
"Daddy!" at full volume. In my new bedroom, I arranged an altar to him, decorated with photos and mementos. For visits, my
mom drove me halfway to Willits and did the handoff at a roadside
diner. I remember howling in the parking lot, gripping one parent
with each hand and forcing them to touch.

Summer of 1987, my dad was renting a tiny loft in Willits. We
played *Wildlife Adventure* sitting cross-legged on a braided rug
that had been in our home since my earliest memories. That part
is vivid: the divided furniture, records, knickknacks. The sensation of visiting objects from a childhood that had suddenly ended.
How my dad's smell grew muskier in isolation. I inhaled lungfuls
of him, like taking final breaths before diving underwater.

One night, he kneeled to feed a log to the woodstove and collapsed backward. His fingers curled into claws. His eyes flashed
white. Saliva bubbled from his lips. I didn't know what to do without my mom there, how to bring him back. I hovered over his
trembling body, holding my breath while he sputtered. After the
seizure had passed on its own, he went to bed with a cold wash-
cloth on his forehead. I lay awake for hours, watching shadows on
the ceiling.

Maybe six months after the divorce, my dad moved in with a
new woman, Ruthanne.

Ruthanne was studying to become a child and family therapist.
She was tough and maternal, which clearly scratched an itch for
Firefeather. She was also overweight. But she was good for him
in ways my mom wasn't. She had firm boundaries, insisting that
he pursue a profession with a steady income even if it only paid
minimum wage. Firefeather had become fascinated with tantric
teachings about exposure to death and dying as a way of understanding life's impermanence, so he took a job as an orderly in a

nursing home. His relationship with Ruthanne would last more than twenty years.

I despised Ruthanne.

She couldn't seem to resist practicing her therapist-in-training techniques on me. When my dad and I argued, she stepped in to mediate — which infuriated me. A few times, I came home from visiting them with a migraine and the dry heaves. An unsubtle reaction to the trauma of a broken family.

Resentments festered between my parents. Firefeather blamed Mer for taking me so far that visits meant gas money and wear and tear to his beater car. Mer blamed Firefeather for never paying child support. Either one could have pressed their issues in court, but neither did. My dad would later say that, in addition to financial and geographic obstacles, it became emotionally painful for him to see me. Our visits dwindled to two or three per year. Phone calls became infrequent.

I blamed my mom, mostly because she was available for blaming. She taught me to cuss, and I used my harsh new words on her. When rage boiled over — occasionally hers, usually mine — we'd yell and slam doors like a warring couple. After the fury passed, we'd sit on the barge and talk things out until we were ready to hug and "start the day over." Then we'd slather microwaved popcorn in butter and nutritional yeast, and watch *Night Court* or *ALF*.

Mer sought guidance from a single parents' support group, a private therapist, and books like *The Drama of the Gifted Child*. For a while, she sent me to a therapist, too. Having been conditioned since toddlerhood to dodge prying questions — especially from adults — I clamped my mouth shut, tinkered with figurines in the therapist's sandbox, and waited for the hour to tick by. My mom tried to convince me to talk about everything *except* her source of income, but I couldn't relax. The therapist finally admitted that she wasn't getting anywhere. I dropped therapy and started riding lessons in Golden Gate Park.

Cooking, as we know, was not in my mom's repertoire.

Sian, a longtime customer and friend, would later recall peeking into our kitchen and seeing stacks of pizza boxes. "Meridy," he gasped. "How the fuck can you cook for your kid in here? Look at the stove, it's all pizza boxes!"

To which she responded, "Why would I cook?"

The only thing warming in the oven were pot brownies.

At nine, I was old enough to help. Baking was my rite of passage. We did it together, giggling at our awkwardness like Lucy and Ethel. I relished the toasty kitchen, the mess, the silliness, and the fragrance of chocolate and weed amalgamating, a smell I would always associate with family.

I soon knew the steps by heart.

Melt unsalted butter in a double boiler. Dump in the powdered weed and heat slowly for thirty minutes, skimming the foam. Break bars of unsweetened chocolate and swirl them into the green butter until it's velvety and tempting. Don't lick your fingers, looks like chocolate fondue, tastes like hell. Crack sixteen eggs into a mixing bowl. Smile because they're sunny. Beat together with a heap of white sugar, then pour in your chocolaty ghee. If you dunk your fingers now, it tastes delicious, but you risk salmonella poisoning. Add flour, baking powder, salt. Go to town with an electric mixer, trying not to splatter the walls; cackle when you splatter them anyway. When it looks like fresh cow poop, you're ready to bake. Divide the batter into greased pans and slide them into the oven. Close your windows to keep the neighbors out of the loop and relish the aroma blooming in your kitchen. After fifteen minutes, pat the brownies with a spatula to arrest rising. Bake another five to ten minutes until a crispy top layer coats the molten center. *Ta-da!*

I was an honest kid and I knew not to eat pot brownies, so sometimes we made a pan of "straight" brownies for me. My favorite part was wrapping, the intimacy of sitting with my mom for hours, entertaining each other with stories, hands busy. *Place a brownie on a square of cellophane. Fold the top down, the bottom up. Pull the sides tight so no air gets in . . .*

We became more like best friends or sisters than mother and daughter. We argued, negotiated, and made decisions as a team, an army of two. There were drawbacks, of course. I lacked security and structure. I was a nine-year-old kid playing adult games.

When I started fourth grade at Sutro Elementary School in the fall of 1987, I was in for culture shock. In Willits, my schoolmates were mainly hippie spawn like me, but most Sutro kids came from conservative Asian American households. They'd grown up on cartoons and video games. Desperate to blend in, I wore black leggings, Keds, and bulky sweatshirts like the other kids. Once, a classmate invited me to play *Super Mario Bros.* after school. I remember being amazed by how sterile her home seemed — everything tidy and beige, no art anywhere. Her mom brought us a tray of snacks like in a sitcom. I tried to act normal, but the weirdness must have leaked out somehow. The girl's mom later told her we couldn't be friends. I didn't ask why. I felt like an alien from another planet.

Schoolyard dynamics mystified me. During recess one day, a popular kid named Jerry called another boy a fag. "There's nothing wrong with being gay," I said. So Jerry ran around the tetherball court screaming that I had AIDS and was trying to give it to him. Other kids joined in — including the one Jerry had called a fag in the first place. We talked about AIDS at home, so I knew you couldn't catch it like a cold. Jerry was an idiot, but that didn't make it less embarrassing. I locked myself in the girls' bathroom to read until recess ended.

At night, real fags came over, and I loved them. Sian, who had spiky platinum-blond hair and pierced eyebrows, was wickedly funny. He nicknamed me Womb Unit (Wombie for short) because he'd known my mom since she was pregnant. His lover, Abel, was shy and beautiful, and had the longest eyelashes imaginable. There was Barry the cabaret crooner and Gino the salsa deejay with his snappy tropical style. There was my mom's new best friend, Phillip, whose infectious laugh began deep in his chest and ended in a twitter.

This was the era of the most magical barge. A world unto itself. My mom handled customers she didn't know well in the dining room, but friends came to her bedroom and stayed for a doobie. I loved listening to their conversations and trying to laugh at the right moments. "You were this little girl with these big eyes," Sian says about me as a nine-year-old. "Abel and I would come in and you were, like, *quiet*. Eyes open, just looking at everything."

My mom's adult friends were kind, but the children I knew seemed monstrous. When my mom tried to throw me a tenth birthday party, I sat by the front window for hours. No one came.

I retreated into books, especially horror novels. During free-reading period at school, while other girls read the Sweet Valley High series, I dove into *The Stand* by Stephen King — an 823-page opus about a plague that wipes out most of humanity. It gave my kid brain a way of processing terror and grief from the safety of a fantasy with a happyish ending.

Most regulars came to our flat. But my mom did short weekly runs and a growing number of house calls to customers who were too sick to go out. Sometimes I'd tag along. After school one day, we delivered brownies to a wedding-cake Victorian up a steep side street in the Castro. These were new customers, my mom said, friends of Sylvester's. I remember the door swinging open by itself — controlled by an old-fashioned automatic butler.

A man's voice called, "Come on up, dear."

He stood on the landing backlit by alcove windows. When my eyes adjusted, my breath snagged. He was shirtless, chest sunken like he'd been hit by a flying bowling ball. His sweatpants hung from protruding hip bones. Purple lesions dappled his chest and neck. Up near his collarbone, sores had grown together into a large butterfly. I'd seen KS plenty of times but not like this. I remember feeling embarrassed. Not by his scant clothing but by his scant flesh.

He seemed startled to see a kid. "Forgive me for not dressing up. Fashion's the first thing to go."

"That's okay, sweetie," my mom said. "I'm a pajamas-around-the-house girl, too. This is my daughter, Alia." Then she added, "Don't worry, she's cool."

"Alia, what a unique name," he said. "I wish my parents had come up with something more exotic than David. It's so pedestrian. *Enchanté.*"

When David turned to lead us toward the living room, my mom locked eyes with me, her expression a little frantic. Then we were in a large overheated room with gleaming hardwood floors and soaring ceilings.

"Sylvester raves about your brownies," David said. "Food has gotten so . . . *blech.*"

"Dessert first," my mom said brightly. "Guaranteed munchies."

Near a pretty bay window, a hospital bed was cocked to a half-sitting position. It appeared empty until I realized that the small gray tangle of blankets was a person. Eyes closed, cheeks so paper thin that I could make out his teeth. Pale blond hair fanned behind his shoulders.

I knew he was dying.

"Keith, honey, wake up for a sec," David said. "I want you to meet someone."

An IV bag dangled from a hook above the bed, and my eyes followed the yellowish snake of tubing to Keith's hand, the bruising around the needle, the bulge of his wrist bones. One finger twitched. He murmured.

"What's that, baby?" David leaned close to his lover's lips. He placed his palm gently on Keith's cheek. Another murmur. "Okay, in a moment. I'm getting us those magic brownies."

David faced us with a smile that wasn't a smile. "He's having a bad day."

While they did the deal, I wandered around the room. A framed photograph sat on the mantel. Two men, shirtless on a beach, arms slung around each other. One looked like Tom Selleck without the chest fur, and the other had beachy surfer hair and bright blue eyes. Both were tanned and muscular, shoulders flecked with sand. I began to sweat.

"Now, don't eat too much," my mom was saying. "Start with a quarter of a brownie and give that forty-five minutes before taking more. I'm serious, they'll have to peel you off the ceiling."

"More like the floor," David said with a rich laugh. The contours of his face softened. His teeth gleamed white. For a moment, he was handsome, almost Tom Selleck.

That radiance was the worst part.

In the car afterward, my mom put her hands on the steering wheel but didn't start the engine. "Wow," she said. "You okay?"

"Sure," I lied.

"I wouldn't have brought you in . . ." She put her clammy hand over mine. Her chin trembled and collapsed. I didn't want to watch her cry, so I focused on the rooftops scattered below us like jigsaw puzzle pieces in a box top. You could see all the way to downtown. The Transamerica Pyramid rising above the stubby skyline, the gray Bay Bridge loping across the water to Oakland.

As we descended the hill, a van bearing the logo of Project Open Hand — a charity that delivered hot food to sick people — was heading up. "Would you look at that?" my mom said. "They're bringing the food, and we're bringing medicine to help the food stay down." I felt her eyes on me. "You know we're helping these guys, right?"

Blood pounded in my ears. The whole fourth grade had been ushered into the cafeteria, where a uniformed policeman was waiting. I was sure he'd come for me.

The cop introduced himself and explained that we'd be spending a lot of time together that semester.

We were going to learn how to Just Say No to drugs.

Once each week, amid the reek of old meatloaf, Juicy Fruit gum, and prepubescent body odor, I sat through lectures about the dangers of illegal narcotics like marijuana. About how to handle peer pressure and how to recognize dealers.

The program's real name was Drug Awareness Resistance Education, but we all called it "D.A.R.E. to keep kids off drugs" — the slogan emblazoned on the bookmarks, notebooks, and T-shirts we could win by tattling on classmates the cop recruited to playact as dealers. They used corny lines like "Hey, little girl, want to buy some marijuana? It'll make you look really cool . . ."

I could've told them that this wasn't how it worked.

Instead, I circled the correct answers on D.A.R.E. quizzes, and chanted, "Just say no!" But it never occurred to me — not for a second — that the smiling policeman in the cafeteria could be anything but my mortal enemy. I still remembered the helicopters thundering over our house in Willits.

In the kitchen at home, I held an egg above a metal mixing bowl. "This is your brain," I said, mimicking an antidrug commercial that was everywhere that year. I cracked the egg on the rim, and the golden yolk joined fifteen others atop a bed of white sugar. I clicked the electric beater on high, scrambling the mess together. "This is your brain on drugs!"

My mom cracked up.

I knew we were the good guys.

Even if it meant lying to police, therapists, teachers, other kids, everyone, really.

By this point, Meridy had been delivering brownies to Sylvester for ten years. First to a cluttered flat in the Castro, then to the flashy multifloor affair on Twin Peaks. Sometime in 1987, he moved down off the hill into a modest apartment on Collingwood.

There had never been a closet big enough for Sylvester. From the acid-drenched genderfuck theater scene that launched the late

1960s into outer space through the übermasculine Castro clone era and deep into the AIDS years, Sylvester was *himself.* A hippie and a disco superstar and a jazz crooner. A fabulous diva and a strong black man. Royalty parading down the street with his blond borzois and an entourage of boys — but also approachable and funny and generous. He was exceptional in the same way that the City could be exceptional for people chasing freedom.

Sylvester was Rubenesque. He'd do crash diets from time to time and his weight fluctuated, but he'd always been *substantial.* Late 1987, he started looking too thin. Mer worried. He was performing less, going out less. People gossiped.

One week, someone from Sylvester's inner circle came downstairs to do the transaction with Mer at the door instead of inviting her up like usual. "Is he okay?" she asked.

"Oh, you know, just tied up."

She kept delivering every Friday. But she never saw Sylvester again.

On Lesbian & Gay Freedom Day 1988, Sylvester made his illness public by leading the People with ARC/AIDS contingent of the parade. Riding in a wheelchair pushed by a friend, he wore a large black sun hat and held a single balloon in his lap. Mer didn't attend that year. ("Too sad," she says.) Others who were present described the crowd's confusion: a long pause before recognizing Sylvester in his emaciated state, an audible gasp, a cheer, a sob, more cheering. By August, when Sylvester usually headlined the Castro Street Fair, he was too frail to leave his apartment. A crowd gathered nearby and chanted his name so he could hear from his bed.

A chamber of San Francisco's heart shut permanently when Sylvester died on December 16, 1988. It was the full stop at the end of an era.

RETURNING IN PURE COMPASSION TO THE WHEEL

Sticky Fingers Brownies

21

The Wheel

O n October 6, 1989, a gray Friday, Mer had wrapped up her run in the Castro and was driving to a customer's house with a delivery when she passed a protest at city hall. The pink-triangle logo of ACT UP caught her eye. There was a parking space, so she snatched it. She could spare an hour.

ACT UP, the raucous, radical activist group that had roared to life in New York two years before, had now spread to several major cities. Even within the gay community, some people found them too extreme, but Mer admired their chutzpah. She didn't attend meetings, but she sometimes joined protests. ACT UP coupled the serious study of potential new treatments with disruptive actions. They stormed news programs, heckled bureaucrats, burned effigies, and doused themselves in fake blood. Demands included transparency in FDA approval processes, early access to experimental medications, inclusion of women and minorities in drug trials, and involvement of activists in designing those trials to ensure that patients' needs would be prioritized over the interests of scientists and pharmaceutical companies.

In time, the combination of headline-grabbing drama and procedural innovation would produce tangible changes — including expanded access to unapproved drugs for terminally ill patients. The FDA usually took about nine years to approve new drugs — a death sentence for many people with AIDS. In the depths of the plague, what was there to lose?

Mer eased into the crowd and soon ran into friends. Some of

the protesters looked very frail; a few were in wheelchairs. Mer got swept up in chanting. Demonstrators wearing skeleton masks unfurled a large black banner reading, BASEBALL = DEATH, a reaction to Mayor Art Agnos's proposal to spend hundreds of millions of dollars on a new ballpark for the Giants — funds the activists wanted spent on treatment. The rally wasn't huge, maybe two hundred people, but there seemed to be as many police as protesters.

The cops weren't being friendly.

When the group marched up Market toward the Castro, police hemmed them onto the sidewalk, rapping the shin of anyone who stepped into the street. The crowd thickened as they moved, joined by the after-work crowd and people like Mer who couldn't resist a protest. At Castro Street, Mer split off and headed back to the car to finish her deliveries. It was after she left that the night went mad.

Mer heard about it the next day. ACT UP had held a die-in, with some forty protesters sprawling in the street while others painted crime-scene outlines around their bodies. Another fifty people sat in the intersection and refused to move until the cops dragged them into paddy wagons. Demonstrators blew whistles and taunted the police.

The tipping point was undefinable. Suddenly, police were laying into people with billy clubs and kicking them with heavy boots. Like any Friday evening, the Castro was thronged with folks heading home or out to dinner, but the cops weren't differentiating between protesters and bystanders. "They hit me with their billy clubs when I went to help a woman," one man told a reporter. "I was just on my way home from work. I wasn't even part of the protest." Police forced people to line up against walls and trapped patrons inside shops and restaurants. After dark, a phalanx of officers in riot regalia marched up and down Castro Street, threatening to arrest anyone out of doors. One cop was heard repeatedly yelling, "We declare martial law!"

The *Bay Area Reporter* ran a multipage spread under the all-caps headline, CASTRO HELD HOSTAGE. Over subsequent days, reports about police using homophobic slurs and excessive force flooded the Office of Citizen Complaints. Though ACT UP was far from universally popular, riot cops stomping down Castro Street seemed like something from a totalitarian nightmare.

"I have been in San Francisco since 1977, marched with Harvey Milk and have participated in many (if not all) public demonstrations since. The police haven't reacted like this since the White Night Riots of spring 1979," wrote Sister Vicious Power Hungry Bitch, a founding mother of the Sisters of Perpetual Indulgence. This harked back to the night of Dan White's manslaughter verdict when police had marauded in the Castro. "Whoever orchestrated the crackdown on ACT UP Friday night lost more than they gained," the Sister concluded. "There is nothing that will make a queen more radical than having to sit in a police van for two hours without her nail polish!"

The Castro in 1989 stood in stark contrast to the prior decade. Harvey Milk was a martyr from a distant yesterday; death was now an everyday occurrence in a community powered by the sobering resilience of the sick and grieving. Anita Bryant and her cohort were mosquitos compared with this Goliath epidemic. Yet bigotry was still so much a part of it — because anyone could see that the plague would have been taken seriously from the start if the early victims had been suburban housewives instead of gay men. And at the end of the day, overzealous cops still cracked queer heads.

Later that month, I was stretched out on my mom's bed in our Fourteenth Avenue flat getting ready to watch game three of the World Series. A bookish, awkward eleven-year-old, I couldn't have cared less about baseball. But the Giants were battling the Oakland A's, our neighbors from across the bay, and even non-sportspeople like me had to see it.

My mom was hustling around the room, getting ready to leave

for dance class. She had changed a lot since we'd seen Oprah Winfrey — rail skinny in tight jeans and a black turtleneck — strut across the TV screen pulling a Radio Flyer wagon heaped with jiggling pig fat. Oprah had lost sixty-seven pounds on the OPTIFAST diet. My mom signed up.

Between January and October of 1989, she didn't chew so much as a sprig of parsley. Breakfast, lunch, and dinner were shakes made from little packets of powder and eight ounces of water. Between "meals," she sipped broth. It was one thing having a mother who didn't cook, and another having a mother who didn't eat. I watched her melt away, losing eighty-nine pounds in nine months.

Now she was reintroducing tiny portions of bland food. My mom adopted a new style for her thinner figure. She clamped on heavy silver jewelry, slung wide leather belts with giant flying saucer buckles low around her hips, and sawed the necks out of her shirts so her shoulders showed. She got an asymmetrical haircut like Sheila E.'s and lined her blue-green-amber eyes with kohl and purple eyeshadow. She sweated through dance classes five days a week.

Meanwhile, I still lived on microwaved meals and pizza delivery. For the baseball game, I had nuked a bag of popcorn and drowned it in I Can't Believe It's Not Butter.

My mom adjusted her leg warmers. She bent to kiss me goodbye just as jittery white lines began scrolling down the TV screen. The sound seemed to come from the south: a deep, resonant rumble that grew thunderous, like a stampede of buffalo in a western. The house began to dance.

"Get in the doorway!" my mom yelled.

I hurried over with her, my feet uncertain on shaking ground, and braced myself in the doorjamb like they taught us in earthquake drills in school. I don't remember fear so much as the sensation of being wide awake. This was both impossible and inevitable: the Big One. The world was breaking open and it was insane and horrible and somehow wonderful — that something so surprising could happen on a banal Tuesday. I heard crashes from around the house: a large ceramic cat tumbling to her death, dishes leaping from cabinets, my model horses diving to the floor. The quake rocked itself out. An eerie silence followed.

We picked our way down the hallway to the front door. Outside, the high gray sky seemed to spin overhead. Then one distant siren multiplied into many. We rode out the first aftershock standing in the street, a rough jittering of the asphalt. The world blurring because my eyes couldn't keep up. The electricity was out, and the phone lines were jammed. We sat on our stoop, my mom still in her leg warmers, until dusk stirred cold winds that chased us inside, where we lit candles and unrolled sleeping bags on the living room floor. The earth shuddered as aftershocks rolled through the night.

Measuring 6.9 on the Richter scale and lasting fifteen seconds, the Loma Prieta earthquake was the biggest to hit San Francisco since 1906. More than a mile of an Oakland freeway's upper deck collapsed onto the lower deck, trapping motorists. Once power was restored, we watched endless aerial footage of the pancaked stretch of freeway, crunched cars visible through the cracks. There were dramatic rescues, interviews with stunned survivors, tears for those who didn't make it. Sixty-three people died — forty-two of them on the collapsed freeway. Thousands were injured. Newscasters kept marveling about baseball having saved an untold number of lives since people were positioned in front of televisions at 5:04 instead of driving in rush-hour traffic.

Hardest hit in the City was the Marina, a clean, ritzy neighborhood, the natural habitat of the San Francisco yuppie. It was also the birthplace of Sticky Fingers Brownies back in 1976 when the Rainbow Lady had peddled magic brownies from a pouch over her shoulder on Fisherman's Wharf. That area had been constructed on landfill — some of it rubble from the 1906 quake — which dissolved. My mom and I volunteered at a makeshift shelter in a Marina school, serving food to rich people suddenly rendered homeless. Nature didn't care about wealth. The plague didn't care either. Beauty, talent, affluence, kindness, taste, smarts, determination, love — none of these things kept people safe.

The quake of 1989 was the exclamation point at the end of a devastating decade. Sister Vicious Power Hungry Bitch was right to raise the specter of Bloody October — that awful month in 1978 when Jonestown and the assassinations of Milk and Moscone sent the City staggering into the violent spring of 1979. The seventies had died with gunshots and a riot; the 1980s died with a riot and an earthquake.

Even now, when I close my eyes and think of home, I envision San Francisco as seen from the Golden Gate Bridge. The Transamerica Pyramid towers above a modest, low-slung skyline blurred by a veil of mist. Our skyline doesn't look like that anymore; it has morphed into an ice-cube tray of office buildings like any ordinary city. Our tallest building, the Salesforce Tower (what many locals refer to as the "sky dildo") is the first bit of skyline you'll see from almost anywhere in town as well as from the Marin Headlands and the Oakland Hills and probably outer space.

When I consider what my hometown has become — the homogeneity, the wealth, the cultural sterility — I think of AIDS. So much death all at once left a vacuum. There were vacancies ready to be filled by tech innovators and money makers, a fresh wave of newcomers who arrived during the first dot-com bubble of the 1990s. This new gold rush economy would burst in 2001 only to balloon again a few years later.

When I tell people I was born in the City, the typical response is a variation on a theme: "I *never* meet San Francisco natives!" or "You're a unicorn!"

I'm first generation, nothing special; I know people whose families run five generations deep. But I still see techies as an invading force — here to colonize, pillage, vanquish. In a city limited in size by its geography (as Manhattan is, too), when new people arrive, others must leave. Change is always violent to what came before.

Today, I live near our old Fourteenth Avenue flat. Maseratis prowl our formerly low-key district. My immediate neighbors, a white heterosexual couple with two young daughters, own a late-model Audi, a new BMW, *and* two SUVs. My hometown becomes less recognizable every day. I'm irked by the money, the flashy cars, the e-scooters, the souped-up strollers. And yet, those strollers carry home-baked San Franciscans, native sons and daughters like me. They may grow up feeling inseparable from this new San Francisco as I felt inseparable from the city that made me. Someday they'll be usurped, too. People like us seem to be part of every era here: locals who watch helplessly while their hometown is stolen by outsiders. Knowing that San Francisco thrives on cycles of mass migration and collapse doesn't make the loss less keen.

My dad was in Willits when the earthquake hit, too far north to feel the tremors. Unable to reach us by phone, he watched the news cycles closely. Undoubtedly, he saw Kali in the rubble — the Hindu goddess of nature's wrath. After all, he'd been expecting a massive earthquake since the seventies. I'm sure he was worried about me. We must have spoken as soon as the phone lines opened, though I don't remember the conversation.

I don't recall much of him from this period at all. I visited a few times a year, but those weekends blur in my mind. I remember a shifting series of houses in Willits, none of which were home to me. I remember Ruthanne's overstuffed oatmeal couch, its unpleasant softness. And my dad's record collection, always in the same window-paned cabinet that had housed it since I was a baby.

In health care, he'd found a calling and a career that would sustain him for decades. First as an orderly, then as an LVN, and finally as a home-care nurse, he put in long hours on his feet. He complained bitterly about my mom's "easy drug money" and "un-realistic lifestyle" — how a poor workingman couldn't compete.

Mostly, I remember his absence. An empty space shaped like him. I remember the ache of needing someone who didn't seem to need me as much. He was my first heartbreak.

My mom doubled down on our relationship. We took mother-daughter road trips, had salon dates, and spent foggy afternoons at the old-timey arcade behind the Cliff House, where a nickel would send toy racehorses galloping around a track or make a miniature lion tamer crack his whip.

Late in 1989, Mer received a small inheritance from her mother's death three years before. Together, we discussed what to do with the money while driving around between deliveries. I could get braces to fix a widening gap between my front teeth. We could upgrade our beater car. Or we could take an extended trip to Mexico, just the two of us.

Of the three options, we settled on the least practical one — also the most whimsical, magical, and adventurous. My mom met individually with each of my sixth-grade teachers and convinced them to assign my schoolwork in advance so I could do it on the beach.

For six weeks, we lived in a small cabana in Zihuantanejo, Mexico, upstairs from a beach with gentle waves. We rode horses, bounced on banana boats, worked on our tans, and bought each other dozens of inexpensive tchotchkes for Christmas, which we wrapped sitting back-to-back on the Mexico version of the barge: *la barcaza*. We took water taxis to Ixtapa and crashed fancy resort pools, sipping virgin piña coladas with our pinkies in the air.

Months after our Mexico trip, my mom came through on a promise she'd made when I was six years old. Ever since we'd sold Acorn, I'd harbored a fantasy of having my own horse. I'd kept up with weekly riding lessons in Golden Gate Park and periodically brought up the subject, wheedling, swearing that I was totally responsible enough. Finally, my mom agreed that if she sold a significant painting in an upcoming show we'd get a horse with the money.

"Of course," she says now. "I didn't expect it to happen right away." A week later to the day, a self-portrait sold from the gallery for five thousand dollars.

We bought Tango, a scrappy pinto mare with a marking shaped like a goose on her face, and boarded her at a ramshackle barn on the outskirts of the City. Trails snaked to a wind-whipped stretch of beach. Every day after school, my mom drove me half an hour to the barn and returned for me at dusk. My mare, who was a little high-strung, would tremble as soon as her hooves touched the beach. I'd contain her until we got to the water's edge where the sand was packed hard and turn her loose. We'd thunder through the surf at a dead gallop, Tango's mane whipping my arms, icy Pacific water splashing my thighs. I fell off countless times, sometimes trudging all the way back to the barn from the beach. But it didn't matter; I'd found my place in the world.

Tango's board, feed, vitamins, vet bills, farrier bills, and tack cost hundreds of dollars a month. After a while, I started competing. Then came professional trainers and expensive horse shows and specialized gear. "Well," my mom sometimes quipped. "It's cheaper than a lifetime of therapy." Of course, I owed the horse to drug money. That and a mother who didn't trivialize her kid's dreams.

We weren't rich, at least not usually. When money was tight — what my mom called "scrapey" — she stressed and schemed and tossed hexagrams and made phone calls until something gave way. When money flowed, we spent it. One Christmas, we went to Civic Center and handed out one hundred five-dollar bills to homeless people.

There was no savings account, no medical insurance, no college fund; we had no credit cards and no assets. We never bought a house, a new car, designer clothes, or the latest technology. I never did get those braces. But when I needed a horse, I got a horse.

Rummaging through a box of my mom's photos, we find her old address book from this period. She flips through it, muttering, "Dead . . . dead . . . almost certainly dead . . . dead . . ." She pauses. "Hmm . . . What happened to Mark? I *think* he died, but we can try looking on Facebook." She shakes her head, scans the next page, then stops, her brow furrowing. "Aww . . . oh boy . . ." Her eyes, huge and watery, find mine. "Remember Phillip? My good friend?"

I do. After we moved back to San Francisco in 1987, Phillip Gas-

Phillip, oil pastel on paper. Meridy Volz, 1990.

ton became my mom's handsome go-to date for comedy clubs or nights at the opera. Tall and sturdy, with wavy blond hair and dimples and a smile that consumed his whole face, Phillip looked like an actor from a soap opera. He favored classy blazers and polished leather shoes. He'd been HIV positive for years but remained healthy. I remember when that changed. Bouts of clumsiness and disorientation led to a diagnosis of progressive multifocal leukoencephalopathy. Extremely rare prior to AIDS, PML attacked the myelin coating that protected the brain's nerve fibers, causing dementia and loss of motor functions almost like a series of strokes. Phillip died about six weeks after his diagnosis. He didn't waste away or suffer KS lesions. He died beautiful, senile, unable to walk or form words. It hit my mom hard.

"I can't do this right now," she says. "Too depressing."

She puts the address book back in the box.

I remember the dismay I felt as a child at seeing loving couples who'd been together in my earliest memories split in half. Barry lost Gino, his musical collaborator and life partner. Sian lost his beautiful Abel and never got over it. Decades later, he still goes into seclusion for weeks around the anniversary of Abel's death.

My mom often describes the "phenomenon of the last man standing." How out of a big group of close friends, there would be one guy left alive to carry all the memories, all the guilt.

"It's just, you know, difficult," says Lou Briasco, a longtime brownie customer. "Because I didn't expect to be here now." For thirty-four years, he ran the same tiny luggage shop on Market Street that he and a friend (deceased) opened in 1982. Lou was diagnosed HIV positive in the mid-1980s and thought for sure he was a goner. But he survived. And kept surviving while the people in his social circle died. Lou, who lived with his dog in a small apartment above the shop, kept the business going mostly to stay busy. Lou's lease came up in 2016; faced with the inevitable rent hike, he finally decided to close. He says he's lost more than fifty friends to AIDS.

That number seems to be common among the survivors I know: fifty loved ones dead.

Problems arose that you might not imagine. Like the super-abundance of stuff: antiques and knickknacks passing from friend to lover to friend, collections growing exponentially as more people died. The last man standing would find himself buried beneath an avalanche of keepsakes.

When Wayne Whelan arrived in San Francisco in 1986, he was amazed at the quality furniture and antiques abandoned in dumpsters and on street corners. In need of cash, he began collecting and reselling found treasures at flea markets. Among his new neighbors was Val DuVal, an occasional drag performer who ran a chaotic custom dress shop out of his cluttered home. Wayne rented a window in Val's space to sell some of his antiques, and the two became close. When Val's health gave out, Wayne helped nurse him through his painful last weeks and ended up inheriting the shop — which he renamed Therapy. For years, Wayne gathered and sold the beautiful trinkets and stylish furniture left behind by the dead, eventually moving into a larger space on Valencia Street. Some objects passed through Therapy multiple times when customers who'd bought them also succumbed to the plague. At estate sales, Wayne would find himself staring at the peculiar mementos kept at bedsides near the end. *Why this button or this teacup?* he'd wonder. *What was important about this?* A day came when Wayne couldn't take it anymore. His store was full of ghosts, everything saturated in heartbreak. He gave up on antiques and switched to new merchandise.

Dan Clowry left the Village Deli after a change of ownership. When a good friend fell ill, Dan became his caretaker. The disease kept coming for more friends until Dan was running himself ragged trying to help them all and still support himself. Finally, he figured, *What the hell,* and went back to school to become a nurse. He helped launch the AIDS unit at Mount Zion hospital, which soon shifted to UCSF.

Back in the warehouse days, Dan and Kissie would sell two gross of Sticky Fingers brownies while Mer did her Castro run. Now Dan kept a reserve of brownies in his freezer to sneak into the AIDS ward for patients who were wasting. "They came up with a medication that was supposed to stimulate appetite," he recalls. "But because it was new, they were being very cautious with the dosing. And I was like, 'This doesn't do anything, just give them pot.'" He and some other nurses also let patients smoke weed out the windows of their hospital rooms. "We were lucky that we had windows that opened," Dan says. "We got some complaints now and then, but I didn't care."

I ask if the doctors on the ward knew about this. He feels sure they did, though it was something no one spoke about. "What was [pot] going to do," Dan says, "kill them?"

January 25, 1990, at around 1 a.m., ten narcs with sledgehammers and a search warrant burst into Dennis Peron's flat on Seventeenth Street. The cops ordered Dennis and his lover of more than ten years, Jonathan West, to lie on the kitchen floor while they ransacked the house for weed. Jonathan was emaciated and covered in KS lesions, so the cops made a show of putting on latex gloves before touching him. "Do you know what AIDS means?" one officer said. "Asshole in deep shit." Upon noticing a framed photograph of Peron with Harvey Milk, an older cop launched into a rant about how much he'd hated "that fag" back then.

At first, SFPD told reporters they'd found between two and three pounds of marijuana in Dennis's flat but later admitted that it was only four ounces of bud — no scales or packing equipment. Nevertheless, they booked Peron for possession with intent to sell and carted him to jail, leaving Jonathan alone in the flat.

A few hours later, narcs raided 663-A Castro Street, where Dennis's associate, Steve Heselton, was living with another friend. That search was more fertile, turning up "40 pounds of marijuana, two pounds of hashish, a pound of 'magic mushrooms,' and about

$6,000 in cash," according to the *San Francisco Chronicle*. This was, of course, Dennis's stash, but he'd learned long ago that he was too hot a target to risk keeping his product at home.

Dennis spent the night in jail worrying about Jonathan. When he finally slept, he dreamed about a large room full of sick people, some in wheelchairs. He saw men and women, young and old, all races, sitting together, laughing, and sharing cannabis. Dennis awoke convinced that he'd had a vision of the future. He would create a public medical-marijuana dispensary where people like Jonathan could gather with friends to smoke pot, unashamed of their infirmities.

When Dennis's case came to trial ten months later, Jonathan testified. By then, he weighed about ninety pounds and could barely walk to the witness stand. In a hoarse whisper, Jonathan insisted that the weed had been his, and that Dennis, as his caretaker, had kept it and rolled joints for him.

The judge let Peron off with one year of probation, citing a lack of evidence that the four ounces of marijuana were for sale. According to Dennis, she also scolded the arresting officers, telling them she never wanted to see another case like that again.

Two weeks later, Jonathan died. He was twenty-nine.

This was the year that AIDS became the leading cause of death in the United States for men aged twenty-five to forty-four.

Dennis vowed to spend the rest of his life fighting to legalize marijuana for "all the other suffering Jonathans of the world."

"Marijuana in its natural form is one of the safest therapeutically active substances known to man." This bold statement came from the DEA's own chief administrative law judge, Francis L. Young, in September 1988. "By any measure of rational analysis, marijuana can be safely used within supervised routine medical care."

This ended a sixteen-year court battle to remove marijuana from Schedule 1 classification. After considering extensive testimony from doctors, patients, law enforcement, and policy wonks,

Judge Young wrote an unequivocal sixty-nine-page decision concluding that marijuana must be moved to Schedule 2 at the federal level.

It was a powerful moment in weed history. Reclassification would enable doctors to prescribe marijuana when medically appropriate. American researchers could finally explore its potential (most studies related to cannabis as treatment were happening in Israel, Brazil, and elsewhere). Everything seemed poised to change.

But an administrative law judge can only make recommendations about federal policy; they can't force the government's hand. And this wasn't what the new Bush administration wanted to hear from the DEA's leading judge. Bush and his cronies ignored the decision, clung stubbornly to Schedule 1 classification, and continued the tradition of stonewalling medical marijuana.

That same year, the first cannabinoid receptor was identified in the brain of a rat, followed in 1992 by the major discovery of the endocannabinoid system — a complex network of receptors and transmitters found throughout the animal kingdom; even sponges have them.

In humans, the endocannabinoid system helps regulate immune activity, pain response, appetite, memory formation, and other functions. Receptors have since been found in the kidneys, lungs, liver, white blood cells, gut, spleen, and central and peripheral nervous systems. To be clear, this system functions whether or not we use cannabis. It just so happens that some chemical compounds in marijuana fit our native receptors like a key in a lock.

Research into the possibilities this presents is still in its infancy. In the United States, it's severely hampered by the federal government's resistance to viewing marijuana as anything other than a party drug. We're left with a plant that appears ideally suited to interacting with the human body and brain — and a government that discourages unlocking its medicinal potential.

Even so, the medical-marijuana movement gained steam all over the country. Not only in San Francisco, and not only among

gays and hippies. In 1990, Harvard University researchers surveyed a third of the country's oncologists. Of the 1,035 who responded, 48 percent said they would prescribe marijuana if it
was legal. Most of those also admitted that they'd already recommended it as an antiemetic.

A hemophiliac from Florida named Kenny Jenks had contracted HIV from a blood transfusion and unknowingly infected
his young wife, Barbara. The Jenkses were both wasting badly
and suffering intolerable nausea. Someone in their AIDS support
group suggested pot. The couple was straitlaced, but they were
starving to death. After smoking the first joint, they found they
could eat a little.

The Jenkses soon got busted for growing two pot plants in their
yard. While awaiting trial, they heard about the Compassionate
IND program — the one created to provide Robert Randall with
marijuana for his glaucoma. It was almost impossible to get certi-
fied. (Only one AIDS patient had been cleared so far, and he'd died
ten days later.) But the Jenkses were perfect candidates: conservative, white, heterosexual, monogamous. They took their plight to
the media. In 1991, the government agreed to supply them with
pot.

The win made headlines. The government was immediately
flooded with applications from AIDS patients clamoring for legal
access to cannabis.

Bush's response was to abruptly shut the Compassionate IND
program down. The handful of people already cleared would continue to receive their government weed, but all pending applications would be cancelled without review.

Back in San Francisco, Dennis Peron was channeling his grief into
action. He'd been an activist for decades, but Jonathan's death
stoked the flame. "It's not just about marijuana," he became fond
of saying. "It's about America. It's about how we treat each other
as people."

In 1991, Dennis got Proposition P on the ballot, a resolution declaring that the city of San Francisco supported medical marijuana. It passed with 79 percent of the vote.

Prop. P was toothless; it had no force of law. But it let city officials know how voters felt. Encouraged, Dennis launched the first San Francisco Cannabis Buyers' Club in a flat on Sanchez Street in the Castro. This endeavor harked back to the Big Top Marijuana Supermarket of the 1970s — but with crucial differences: the new club was staffed by people with AIDS and catered to the needs of the sick; and unlike Dennis's previous ventures, this one operated in the open.

Dennis fully expected to get arrested and make his case in court. But at the apex of the AIDS crisis, city officials were ready to let it slide. By that point, San Francisco had the highest per capita concentration of HIV cases in the western world. On average, thirty-one people were dying of AIDS-related conditions every week in the City. Even Republican Mayor Frank Jordan, a former police chief, signed a resolution ordering the SFPD and the DA to make medical marijuana their lowest priority. Dragging dying people to jail didn't look good.

Peron soon relocated to a more prominent space on Church and Fourteenth streets where he could serve a larger population. As historian Martin A. Lee points out, small underground cannabis clubs sprang up around the country as word spread: New York, Baltimore, Pittsburgh, Cincinnati, Little Rock, Key West, Seattle, and Washington, D.C. But none of these other facilities operated openly — and with the acquiescence of city government — like the one in San Francisco.

Around this time, Cleve Jones's health took a nosedive. He'd been touring frenetically with the quilt, hiding his worsening symptoms and making excuses for canceled appearances. When he could no longer pretend, his family helped him buy a cabin on the Russian River. His T-cell count dropped to a perilous 200 and then tanked to 23 (a healthy range being 500 to 1,600). When his chronic pneumonia developed into the deadly *Pneumocystis carinii* variety in 1994, Cleve figured he was dying.

In a last-ditch effort, his doctor, Marcus Conant, got him into an experimental drug trial through the "expanded access" program ACT UP had wrestled into being. Cleve's regimen combined AZT with two other antiretroviral drugs, ddC and 3TC, plus minuscule amounts of Bactrim; he was horribly allergic to the latter, but he needed it to fight pneumocystis. He vomited relentlessly on this combination, eventually dragging pillows into the bathroom so he could sleep next to the toilet. The pills wouldn't stay in his stomach.

An old friend named Shep, whose lover of many years had recently died, came up from the City to nurse him. "Poor Sheppy was so brave," Cleve says, thinking back. "He knew I was giving up, so he came." Shep knew all sorts of tricks from nursing his partner. To get a little nourishment into his patient, he'd place a tiny cube of chicken, a single broccoli floret, and one ravioli on an oversized plate. "You only have to eat this much," he'd say.

The vomiting persisted. Late one night, Shep brought a lit joint into the bathroom. Cleve, who could barely breathe as it was, waved the joint away. But Shep talked him into a small toke. Cleve coughed painfully, but he stopped retching. With a second careful hit, the nausea receded. After the third puff, Cleve leaned back against the bathtub, and sighed, "Damn, dude, I'm hungry."

He couldn't smoke much because of the pneumonia, but by alternating tiny hits of pot with small portions of edibles, Cleve was able to tolerate the meds, which began to work. A couple of weeks later, he awoke in the early morning to a gentle mist wending between the redwoods surrounding his cabin. He heard birds twittering and felt his stomach growl. He had an erection for the first time in many months.

He was going to live.

Poor Brownie Mary couldn't stay out of jail.

In July 1992, the sixty-nine-year-old got busted yet again for baking with pot — this time at a friend's house in Sonoma County. Instead of taking a plea deal like before, she decided to fight. "If the narcs think I'm gonna stop baking cookies for my kids with AIDS," she famously said at a rally, "they can go fuck themselves in Macy's window."

The old lady baking illegal cookies for the dying made great news copy. With her thirteen years of volunteerism and her grand-motherly cheekiness, she became a press darling. Mary had gotten coverage in California before, but this time her story went international. The London *Times* ran a piece. Dr. Donald Abrams saw the bust covered on TV in a hotel room in Amsterdam. Mary appeared on *The Maury Povich Show* and *Good Morning America*.

When she testified at a hearing on the implementation of Prop. P at city hall in August, Mary received a standing ovation. Supervisor Terence Hallinan called her the "Florence Nightingale of the medical-marijuana movement" and ushered in a resolution proclaiming August 25 Brownie Mary Day in San Francisco.

In November, Sonoma County Municipal Judge Knoel Owen made the unorthodox ruling that Mary could use medical necessity as a defense if she submitted the names and conditions of the patients she supplied with dosed baked goods.

The DA threw in the towel. After dropping the charges, he said, "If her attorneys feel that medical necessity should be a defense to charges of violating the marijuana laws of the state, then they should take their case to the state legislature."

And that's what they did.

Four years later, Proposition 215, coauthored by Dennis Peron, passed a statewide vote in California.

Two months before the vote, the California Bureau of Narcotics

Enforcement had raided the San Francisco Cannabis Buyers' Club, which had relocated to a converted warehouse on Market Street that Dennis liked to call his "five-story felony." The two-year sting had involved fake patients, surveillance, and forged doctors' notes. It culminated with a showy raid by one hundred black-clad state agents using a battering ram. They ransacked the club, demolishing art and furnishings, and wreaking chaos. The club was forced to close, but in November 1996, the proposition won anyway.

The Compassionate Use Act, as it was called, had received support from some surprising corners. Financiers included multibillionaire philanthropist George Soros and CEOs of the Men's Wearhouse clothing chain and the Progressive Corporation. A groundswell of activism was also rising from within communities of color harmed by the drug war. Iconic California rappers like Snoop Dogg, Dr. Dre, and Cypress Hill put smoking chronic back on trend — more fashionable than it had been since the sixties. There were rallies, smoke-ins, and benefit concerts. Undoubtedly, some of the 56 percent of Californians who voted for Prop. 215 cared more about dismantling unjust drug war policies or legalizing weed altogether than about medicinal use. But by centering the debate around compassion for the gravely ill, the medical-marijuana movement tipped the scales.

Because cannabis still was — *and still is at the time of this writing* — a Schedule 1 narcotic, Prop. 215 had to be worded delicately so as not to directly contradict federal marijuana laws. Police officers could still arrest everyone, including terminally ill patients, for any and all marijuana offenses. But the new legislation created a viable defense in court provided that the accused could prove they were using marijuana with a doctor's recommendation. Doctors, meanwhile, couldn't legally *prescribe* cannabis as a Schedule 1 drug, but they could *recommend* it as a matter of free speech.

There were many battles ahead. In response to Prop. 215, the director of the Clinton administration's Office of National Drug Control Policy threatened to bar doctors from participating in

Medicare and Medicaid and revoke their prescription licenses if they recommended cannabis. A group of physicians and patients lead by AIDS doctor Marcus Conant waged a six-year battle for their First Amendment right to discuss marijuana as a treatment option — eventually winning before the Supreme Court. California cannabis clubs, even when left alone by city and state cops, were still subject to federal DEA raids. The legal headaches went on and on. But Prop. 215 was revolutionary; it was the first medical-marijuana legislation in the United States built to stand up in state criminal court.

On the foggy morning of January 15, 1997, a fifty-one-year-old Dennis hosted a tearful reopening ceremony outside the San Francisco Cannabis Buyers' Club at 1444 Market Street — which, at the request of city hall, would become a nonprofit. As the ceremonial ribbon was snipped, Dennis said, "America is never going to be the same!"

He was right. As of 2019, forty-six states have enacted laws supporting medical marijuana; eleven states (plus D.C.) permit adult recreational use. The trend of state-authorized cannabis use grows with every voting cycle.

All of this is in defiance of federal law. But the wall is beginning to crack. A group of determined parents with epileptic children, led by a neuroscientist named Catherine Jacobson, got the FDA to approve a nonpsychoactive CBD-based drug called Epidiolex for two rare forms of epilepsy in June 2018. Three months later, the DEA reclassified Epidiolex under Schedule 5. The rescheduling pertains to this specific drug — no other CBD extracts and nothing containing THC — but it's the first plant-based cannabis drug that doctors can legally prescribe in the United States.

Meanwhile, a quasilegal CBD market booms in states that allow it — from all manner of infused edibles and drinkables to oils, lotions, suppositories, and even supplements for pets. According to the *New York Times*, CVS and Walgreens have both announced plans to carry CBD merchandise in certain areas. A 2017 study documented that 69 percent of the products tested contained either more or less CBD than advertised. Marijuana is sometimes portrayed as a miracle panacea able to prevent — even cure — a dizzying array of illnesses. Although recent revelations about the endocannabinoid system suggest terrific potential, the science is still young and impeded by federal prohibition. Through its unwillingness to *reasonably* regulate cannabis, the federal government may be exposing consumers to irresponsible operators.

In today's San Francisco, where recreational marijuana is permitted, one sometimes sees techies casually vaping cannabis on lunch breaks. If only they knew the wild and heavy history behind that right. The AIDS crisis is painful to conjure, painful to relive. Easier to let the past fade, to toke up and forget. But we would not have legal weed today without yesterday's losses.

Since the first reported deaths in 1981, people had been waiting. Waiting for the cure, the vaccine, the ray of hope. Waiting for the government machine to develop a sense of urgency.

In late 1995 and early 1996, the first protease inhibitors reached the market. This new class of drugs blocked an enzyme necessary for the virus to mature and replicate, arresting its progress in the body. Taken in combination with other medications — what became known as the "cocktail" — protease inhibitors began to extend lives. People rose from their deathbeds, a phenomenon some doctors described as the "Lazarus effect." 1996 was the first year since the epidemic began that the CDC reported fewer AIDS-related deaths than the year before. The tide turned.

Abel, Sian's lover, had died nine months before the first protease inhibitor was released — while the new class of drugs was navigating the layers of FDA testing and bureaucracy. Gino, Barry's partner, died twelve months too soon.

I'm often struck by the waste of potential. The unpainted paintings, the uncomposed music, the undesigned buildings, the unwritten books. "It's very frustrating because here I am at the pinnacle of my career," Randy Shilts told *60 Minutes* a few months before his death in 1994. He'd written *And the Band Played On,* a groundbreaking chronicle of the epidemic's early years. "I could do literally anything I wanted in the world of journalism, and you're left with the strange feeling that your life is somehow finished without being completed."

Protease inhibitors didn't stop the dying in the United States — and certainly not abroad; by late 1996, an estimated 23 million people were living with HIV worldwide. But for those who could obtain the new drugs, survival became one possible outcome. On August 13, 1998, the *Bay Area Reporter* carried a stunning headline in gigantic red print: NO OBITS. It was the first week in seventeen years that San Francisco's major gay paper hadn't received a single obituary to run.

Sometime during the early 1990s, Dennis Peron threw a party. My mom doesn't recall if it was for Christmas or a fundraiser or a birthday, or if it happened at the first or second San Francisco Cannabis Buyers Club. The room was crowded and fogged with skunky smoke. Out of the haze hobbled a pudgy, curly-haired woman in owlish glasses.

"You must be Brownie Mary," my mom said. "I'm Mer, also known as the Brownie Lady."

"Hey, you're the one who never got busted!"

"And you're the one who always did."

They had both, of course, been hearing about each other for years. It was something of a joke among mutual friends that they were never seen in the same room at the same time, like Superman and Clark Kent.

The industry veterans shared a hug and a laugh before the crowd pulled them in different directions.

Someone posts a lovely tribute to Brownie Mary in a nostalgic Facebook group. A long comment thread follows. People share memories of Mary, her kindness, her delicious ganja treats.

I can't help but notice that a few of the comments are actually about Sticky Fingers. One woman writes, "I had PLENTY of her brownies back in the day. She had that storefront in the Mission, and every Friday we would gather a group, and everyone would grab a dozen. The first and best edibles ever, and they were pretty affordable as I recall too, I think 20 or 25 a dozen!! The bags used to have cute sayings on them too, I may have one in storage. RIP Mary."

I decide to respond only because her memory is so specific (and my mom is not dead). "You're thinking of my family's business," I write. "Sticky Fingers Brownies."

The commenter seems dubious. "Ok," she writes, "I know how I can tell for sure. What was the last message printed on the paper bags when they closed?"

That's easy: *Give it up and you get it all.*

Next thing I know, she's messaging me to ask for the recipe. Sure, she can buy all kinds of cannabis products at legal dispensaries now. But as she puts it, "The good old days of edibles is changed."

The Brownie Mary/Brownie Lady confusion pops up regularly, though I almost never say anything. They were part of the same zeitgeist. And if my mom slipped through the cracks of history, that's just fine.

It means she got away with it.

Late one chilly autumn night in 1998, Meridy realized that she was free to move on.

At fifty-one years old, she was living alone in San Francisco, involved in an unsatisfying relationship, and wrestling with a cocaine habit that had gotten out of hand. She had been diagnosed with diabetes and was suffering peripheral neuropathy in her feet

— especially painful on cold nights like this one. Her lifestyle was catching up.

She was still selling weed to make ends meet, but with cannabis clubs proliferating, the marijuana underground was not as lucrative — not as *necessary* — as it used to be. The City seemed full of ghosts, so many friends gone, so many memories. Her child had grown up; I was turning twenty, living with roommates; I had a job and friends, and was chasing my own life.

Mer felt superfluous in more ways than one.

She pictured a warm beach in Mexico. *Maybe*, she thought, *it's time to get out of the biz* . . . Like most of her big decisions, this one came down to three *I Ching* coins rocking and rolling in the palm of her hand.

Mer pulled together $900 and bought a ticket to Puerto Vallarta. She found a small apartment walking distance from a gay beach and set up an easel under a *palapa*. She drew colorful oil pastels of men on the beach and sold them for twenty dollars a pop. Between her gift for gab and hustle, the fine portraits she could turn out while her subjects sunbathed, and a favorable exchange rate, she rustled up enough business to get by. Within a year, she'd found representation and a ritzy gallery to carry her larger paintings, which sold well enough to expats and tourists to support a modest lifestyle. She would stay there for ten years. And she always knew she could unfold her portable easel under a *palapa* if things got "scrapey."

After twenty-two years in the weed business, Mer took a classic page from the dealer playbook and played it clean: escape to a tropical paradise.

She never dealt weed again.

SOUL FOOD - SAINT FRANCIS - SHIT FACED
SNOW FALL - STAGE FRIGHT - SIGMUND FREUD
SOCIAL FUNCTION - SAGGY FANNY - SO FINE
STORE FRONT - SEX FIEND - SILLY FOOL
SMELLY FARTS - SPOILED FRUIT - SURE FIRE
SENATORIAL FILIBUSTER - SWORD FISH
SO FLAKY - STORM FRONT - SPANISH FLY
STRANGE FEELING - SWELL FRIEND -
SPORTS FAN - SWEET FRAGRANCE -
SNA FU - SOLO FLIGHT - STONE FREE
SCARLET FEVER - SWORD FIGHTING -
SIMPLE FACT - SPOON FED - SUPER FLY
SHIT FIT - STRAWBERRY FLAVORING
SINFUL FLESH - SHALLOW FEELINGS
SHIP OF FOOLS — **SF** — SHOW FOLKS
STUPID FIGHT — **SF** — SELLING FAST
SUGAR FREAK — **SF** — SLOW FUCK
SHARP FANGS — **SF** — SAM FRANCIS
SEXUAL FAVORS - SHADY FOREST -
SENSATIONAL FIGURE - SLEEPY FRITZ
STEAL YOUR FREEDOM - SURE FOOTED
SARCASTIC FUCKER - SWELL FRIEND
SALLY FIELDS - SIMPLY FAMISHED -
SECRET FRATERNITY - STUY + FAITH
SPANISH FANDANGO - SAVING FACE
SMALL FRY - SILENT FORTRESS -
SHOCK FACTOR - SEXUAL FANTASY —
SODOMY - FELLATIO - SELL YOUR FACE
SU FI ✳ STICKY FINGERS ✳ SLY FOX
SPANK YO' FANNY - SLEAZY FRIENDS
SAD FACE - SAN FRANCISCO - SORE FOOT
STREET FIGHTER - SCIENCE FICTION

Licking the Spoon

Christmastime 2018, I sit down to lunch with some suspicious characters: my family.

It's unusual for us to get together like this. After years of avoiding being in the same room, my parents have recently softened toward each other. Laughter rises toward the ceiling as we pass a platter of deli sandwiches around the table.

My dad is semiretired from nursing, the years of physical labor having taken a toll on his hips and back. After coming into a modest inheritance, he and my grandmother Jan pooled resources to buy a quirky mid-century modern house on a little hill overlooking glassy Clear Lake about three hours north of San Francisco — where we've gathered for lunch today. Original artwork enlivens every wall: my dad's vivid visionary paintings juxtaposed with the subtle elegance of my grandmother's modernist work. Recent wildfires scorched the surrounding hills, but the home and garden have come through unscathed.

Doug (as my dad now calls himself again) is sitting beside his live-in boyfriend, Rick. At sixty-five, my dad is finally out of the closet as bisexual and in love with a proud gay man. It came as a surprise to ninety-four-year-old Jan, but she's gotten used to it.

Rick is charming and handsome, and takes zero shit from my dad. They kiss in public. This change didn't come to my dad easily; he went through years of therapy, self-help workshops, and earnest introspection. At long last, he seems to have settled into his own skin, and that makes him a pleasure to be around. Rick, Doug, and Jan make an unusual threesome. They bicker, especially over control of the garden, but they also take care of one another and share the labor of running the household.

Today, my godmother Barb — the woman who perfected the Sticky Fingers recipe and introduced my parents — is also here. She has the same apple-cheeked smile and wheat blonde hair as in my earliest memories, and she still smells of cigarettes and the jasmine-scented French perfume she's been wearing since 1973. Now retired from costuming, Barb lives on the other side of Clear Lake with her husband. She still loves to bake.

Sitting beside me is my mom, visiting for the holidays from Desert Hot Springs. A little shorter and rounder than in the old days but no less striking. She dyes her hair burgundy and wears it short. Her blue-green-amber eyes can still arrest you from across the room.

Of the three former outlaws at this table, she's the only one still hustling — not pot these days but art. While Barb and Doug both worked straight jobs for years after Sticky Fingers — accumulating Social Security and retirement benefits — my mom still cobbles together a living from her artwork. She maintains a grueling teaching schedule and spends every morning off painting. "No rest for the wicked," she says. The pace is exhausting, but she's passionate about the work she does.

At seventy-one, she's been talking about moving to New Orleans, where she doesn't know anyone. "I might have one more reinvention in me," she says, eyes wide with possibility.

To look at this group of gentle people, their faces lined by loss and softened by experience, you'd never take them for the master-

Left to right. Alia, Barb, Meridy, Doug.

minds behind a complex outlaw operation. I suppose this is one of the advantages of aging: presumed innocence.

And yet, when Barb arrived today, the first thing she did was hand out cookies wrapped in red cellophane and Christmas ribbon.

"Be forewarned," she said. "They pack a wallop."

Sticky Fingers Brownies began as a lark and grew through friendship, feminist badassery, and hippie magic. Back when it was unequivocally illegal, before tragedy brought pathos and respectability to dealing. Barb innovated a recipe that people still crave today. Doug conceived of the packaging as a means of transmitting messages to the community and spreading awareness through art. Cheryl brought glamour to the operation. Carmen and the Wrapettes mixed and warmed and packaged it with love. The

business model Mer had envisioned at the Ransohoff's Christmas
fair in 1976 metamorphosed naturally when the crisis hit. Working solo through the 1980s and 1990s, she bent through the arc of
necessity to deliver relief to those in need.

"It's kind of fascinating when you think about it," Cleve Jones
said one day. "But your mom and Brownie Mary and Dennis Peron
really are the reason why marijuana is legal now, because no one
had thought of compassionate use."

Cleve was right about that, though my mom's place in cannabis
history is little known. She wasn't a hero of the legalization movement — not like Mary Rathbun or Dennis Peron, both of whom did
jail time, worked the media and the court system, and ultimately
changed laws. But by building that first huge illegal edibles business and sustaining it through the crisis, my mom reshaped the
landscape.

For nearly a quarter of a century, she flew below the radar,
working in the shadows of those who went public in the industry
she helped create. From party drug to panacea. She and her collaborators blazed trails that are still being followed today.

In intervening decades, the rest of the Sticky Fingers family has
scattered. Shari Mueller, the Rainbow Lady who started it all, now
lives with family in Virginia. Donald Palmer, Mer's first partner in
crime, moved back to Wisconsin to teach piano; he died in 2016.
Cheryl Beno lives on a quiet mountaintop near Willits. Mumser
plays harmonica and sings in a rock band in Garberville. Carmen
Vigil has put down roots in Colorado, and his son Marcus started
his own family in Oregon. Eugene "Jeep" Phillips still does his carpentry and art projects in San Francisco. Stannous Flouride is
here, too; he guides tours of Haight-Ashbury. Dan Clowry retired
from nursing in 2015 and has been traveling the world — Hong
Kong, Japan, France. After more than thirty years with the SFPD,
Jerry D'Elia retired as a sergeant in 1999, opting for a mellower
lifestyle north of the City. Cleve Jones has authored two memoirs,
one of which became the subject of an ABC miniseries in 2017. He

remains a committed activist and still leads protests in San Francisco. Mary Jane Rathbun passed away in 1999.

The Prince of Pot, Dennis Peron, died in spring 2018, about a year into California's implementation of fully decriminalized recreational marijuana. Dennis had actually campaigned against Prop. 64, seeing it as a poorly crafted piece of legislation that would harm small farmers. He was not wrong. While legislation included a one-acre limit for the first five years, ostensibly to protect the little guy, a loophole allowed big investors to buy unlimited numbers of these small permits. "Local businesses and nonprofits are all suffering," Mumser says. "People used to make money to give to the fire department or the school." Drive through Willits or Garberville today, and you see businesses shuttered, plywood nailed across windows. Still, I like to imagine that Dennis — who'd fought cannabis prohibition in California for almost five decades — derived at least a little satisfaction from seeing that hurdle cleared in his lifetime.

A new generation of marijuana activists and entrepreneurs is rising to prominence. Mostly millennial and younger, they are sharp, ambitious, and innovative. Some current activism revolves around ensuring that communities of color — hardest hit by the drug war — won't be shut out of what many are calling the "green rush." Financial and bureaucratic hurdles can make cannabusiness licenses available only to the wealthy and connected. Meanwhile, drug busts continue; in late 2018, the FBI reported an average of one marijuana bust every forty-eight seconds. Black Americans are almost six times more likely to be incarcerated for drug-related offenses than their white counterparts despite similar usage rates. And in many locales, prior drug convictions bar people from obtaining cannabusiness licenses. A few cities, including San Francisco, have announced programs to expunge lower-level marijuana convictions from criminal records, but the work in this area is barely beginning.

Still, the rate of change in recent years has been staggering; the laws may shift again by the time this book is released. New products and business models abound, which would have been unthinkable in the 1970s before illegal enterprises like Sticky Fingers Brownies laid the groundwork. My folks took risks that today's cannabusiness innovators don't have to worry about. It's a new era in the world of weed.

In truth, we owe our lavender-scented THC bath salts to activists who fought for access during the AIDS crisis. Many of the people who carried the movement on their backs didn't survive to take credit. Younger generations now enjoy the benefits of decriminalized marijuana heedless of the mortal struggle that brought it to them. I'm glad things have changed, but the collective amnesia disturbs me. According to the CDC, nearly 380,000 Americans had died before Dennis pushed Proposition 215 through — beginning the long process of revamping marijuana's image. That legislation would not have passed if the horrors of the plague hadn't become impossible for California voters to ignore. Cannabusiness crossed a bridge of human bones.

Later, after Barb has gone home, the rest of us retire to the living room. We're all drained from a long afternoon of catching up. Here, a strange thing happens: We watch reruns of *The Golden Girls*.

I look around — my grandmother in a rocking chair, my mom kicked back on a La-Z-Boy, my dad and Rick snuggling on the couch. On TV, Betty White is trying to teach a chicken to play the piano. Everyone laughs.

I don't know what it means, this moment, but it's warm and surreal and it feels like family.

Back in her daily life in Desert Hot Springs, my mom doesn't talk about her role in cannabis history. She never sought credit or notoriety and has been content to keep the stories to herself — frankly relieved to have gotten away with it. She's put those years behind her.

She paints religiously, amassing a vast body of work, which is often shown in galleries and museums in Palm Springs. She teaches art to a range of students, from kids to older retirees. Her favorites are the ones she calls her "naughty kids" — teenagers who've gotten into trouble with the authorities and been classified as "at risk." For my mom, those who push boundaries will always be her kin.

Of course, she doesn't reveal her former life to her students. But some of them seem to sense the history she's hiding. Every so often, they'll try to coax it out. "Hey, Ms. V, were you a hippie in the old days?" one kid prods. "Did you, like, smoke pot?"

"Ask me no questions and I'll tell you no lies," she says, turning back to the easel where she's demonstrating the day's assignment. "Let's just say I've had a colorful life."

ACKNOWLEDGMENTS

It takes a village to write a book about a village. I'm indebted to the many people who confided in me. Some had known me for decades. To others, I was a toddler in diapers suddenly morphed into a grown woman with a lot of questions. I hope I've done right by the memories entrusted to my care. I owe an extra hug to my parents and my godmother for putting up with countless hours of interrogation. I treasured our long conversations, and I believe they did, too — though probably not all my harping about chronology.

I could kiss the feet of the archivists and librarians at the San Francisco Public Library, GLBT Historical Society, the Bay Area Television Archive at San Francisco State University, and the Internet Archive. Not only have they kept the good stuff safe, they've also made much of it available online, almost completely obviating the hell out of microfiche. Thank you, thank you, thank you.

Independent bookstores keep the literary world spinning. I'm especially fortunate to feel at home at Green Apple Books with its creaky stairs, packed shelves, and passionate staff. You're beautiful, don't ever change.

Writing can be a grind; I never expected publishing to be a gas. My sharpshooting agent, Farley Chase, nailed the bull's-eye every time (especially on Mother's Day). Writers fantasize about editors with the grace and acuity of Lauren Wein and Pilar Garcia-Brown; how did I get so lucky in real life? This feeling extends to everyone at Houghton Mifflin Harcourt. It's astounding how many people have to care about a book to bring it to life. I've been fortunate to work with sharp editors, second readers, third readers (eagle-eye Conor!), a design team that knocked my socks off, a production team that got everyone on the bus on time, a quick and careful legal team, a copy editor (David Hough!) who killed 85 percent of my commas so kindly that it barely hurt. Marketing and publicity mavens Hannah Harlow, Emma Gordon, and Lori Glazer got the motor revving. Helen Atsma offered words of encouragement before I knew I needed them. If I seem to glide, it's only because the folks at HMH are carrying me on their fingertips.

Support for this project has come in many forms, and I've needed them all. I'm grateful to Dana Spector for leading the way to Hollywoodland and to Ben Stephenson and Rachel Rusch for the warm welcome; to the MacDowell Colony, the Ucross Foundation, and the Community of Writers at Squaw Valley for time and space in which to work, encouragement, and fairy dust; to everyone at Litquake — especially Jack Boulware — for keeping me in the mix every year (I sometimes think of the day Jack asked if I'd be into dressing up as Slick Ric Flair to read at Bob Calhoun's WWF memoir night as the true beginning of my literary career); to Rod and Sandee Crisp, Robert Mailer Anderson, and Kim Wong-Keltner for the proverbial "cabin in the woods" when I needed it, to the brilliant writers of the Leporine Conspiracy past and present (too many to name here, but especially Jacqueline Doyle, without whom I would sink like a cinder block); to Janice Volz, Rebecca Skloot, Frances Lefkowitz, Laura Lent, Caitlin Myer, Bob Calhoun, Juniper Nichols, Joe Loya, David Talbot, Olga Zilberbourg, Matthew James Decoster, Olivia Griffin, Emily Florence Maloney, Joey and Rachel Tobener, Diane Glazman, Dawn Oberg, Danyka Kosturak, Marie Mutsuki Mockett, and the online community of women and nonbinary writers for friendship, cheerleading, and commiseration on tough days; to Dennis Hearne for the dreamy photographs and to Janet Clyde for the annual celebration at Vesuvio, my favorite night of every year; to Gregory Crouch for the Lyft ride that changed my life; to Karl Soehnlein, Ronnie Johnson, Kyle Sund, and Anastasia Selby for valuable feedback; to the S.F. Elks Lodge No. 3 and the New Eritrea Café for nourishment and relaxation during line edits; to Ron Turner for being nasty and Carol Stevenson for being nice; to Michelle Wildgen for insisting I find the heart; and to Dana Christopher Clarke — who adamantly disbelieved in consciousness after death and won't be able to read this unless he was wrong — for looking at a punk-ass fifteen-year-old and seeing an intellectual.

For daily inspiration, I treasure my partner in crime, Kevin Hunsanger, who cheerfully shared his wife with this book for a decade. Writers are not easy people to live with; we're obsessive, cranky, messy, often solitary, and sometimes terrible at the basic stuff of life. He has picked up the slack and kissed away the frustration. More importantly, he's reminded me time and again to have my own adventures. I can't wait to see what we do next.

Finally, at the end of this road, a blown kiss to the City that once was.

SOURCES

Interviews

Donald Abrams, MD; Harry Anderson; Bess Bair, aka Rosie Radiator; Cheryl Beno; Lou Briasco; Campbell Bruce; Ellen Bunning; Alice Charap; Laurence Cherniak; Bill Clark; Dan Clowry; Matthew Clowry; Jeffery Crawford; Jerry D'Elia; Ellen Freed; Jack Fritscher; Steve Glynn; Gunter Benz; Barbara Hartman-Jencichen; Bette Herscowitz; Steve Heselton; Cleve Jones; Kevin Kearney, aka Stannous Flouride; Howard Lazar; Hank London; Harry Lovecraft; Patricia Lovecraft; Kathy Maples; Rumi Missabu; Shari Mueller; Mumser; Daniel Nicoletta; Robert Armstrong Nelson III, aka the Butterfly Man; Rich Nichols; Noel Odland; Donald Palmer; Bill Pandolf; Dennis Peron; Eugene "Jeep" Phillips, Patricia Rodriguez, aka Sunshine; John Shaeffer; Sian Van Cortlandt; Carmen Vigil; Marcus Vigil; Doug Volz; Janice Volz; Meridy Volz; Wayne Whelan; Carolanne Wildroff; and Bruce York.

Chapter 1: Eat It, Baby!

Asbury, Herbert. *The Barbary Coast.* New York: Alfred A. Knopf, 1947.

Baum, Dan. "Legalize It All: How to Win the War on Drugs." *Harper's Magazine,* April 2016.

——. *Smoke and Mirrors: The War on Drugs and the Politics of Failure.* New York: Little, Brown and Company, 1996.

"Buxbaum, Robert II. 'Bux.'" Obituary. *Milwaukee Journal Sentinel,* July 20, 1999.

"Cannabis and Cannabinoids (PDQ®) — Health Professional Version." NIH *National Cancer Institute,* accessed June 6, 2019, https://www.cancer.gov/about-cancer/treatment/cam/hp/cannabis-pdq#_1.

Coyote, Peter. *Sleeping Where I Fall.* Washington, D.C.: Counterpoint, 1999.

Diekmann, June. "76 Hurt in UW Rioting; Campus Strike Results." *Wisconsin State Journal,* October 19, 1967.

"Four Major Crime Bills Cleared 91st Congress." *CQ Almanac 1970,* 05–125–05–126.

Howard, Jane. "The impact of a 20-year jail sentence." *LIFE,* October 31, 1969.

Lee, Martin A. *Smoke Signals: A Social History of Marijuana — Medical, Recreational, and Scientific.* New York: Scribner, 2013.

"Mail Contains Drug, Young Women Seized." *Milwaukee Journal,* August 22, 1969.

Maraniss, David. *They Marched into Sunlight: War and Peace, Vietnam and America, October 1967.* New York: Simon & Schuster, 2004.

Nixon, Richard M. "Oval Office Conversation: 505–4." Meeting with Nixon and H. R. Haldeman, Washington, D.C., May 26, 1971, https://www.csdp.org/research/nixonpot.txt.

Nixon, Richard M. "Remarks About an Intensified Program for Drug Abuse Prevention and Control." Press briefing, Washington, D.C., June 17, 1971. *The American Presidency Project,* https://www.presidency.ucsb.edu/documents/remarks-about-intensified-program-for-drug-abuse-prevention-andcontrol.

Perry, Charles. *The Haight-Asbury.* New York: Wenner Books, 2005.

Public Law 91–513 — Comprehensive Drug Abuse Prevention and Control Act of 1970. October 27, 1970, https://www.govinfo.gov/content/pkg/STATUTE-84/pdf/STATUTE-84-Pg1236.pdf.

The Report of the National Commission on Marihuana and Drug Abuse. *Marihuana: A Signal of Misunderstanding,* March 1972, http://www.druglibrary.org/schaffer/Library/studies/nc/ncchap2_42.htm.

Sloman, Larry "Ratso." *Reefer Madness: A History of Marijuana.* New York: St. Martin's Griffin, 1998.

State of Wisconsin v. Meridy B. Domnitz, Case No. 2–95998 and H-296 (Wis. 1969), records from August 21, December 3, 8, 12, and 18, 1969; January 6 and 26, March 3, 9, 10, and 20, 1970.

The War at Home. Brown, Barry Alexander and Glenn Silber. Wisconsin Public Television, 1979.

Talbot, David. *Season of the Witch: Enchantment, Terror, and Deliverance in the City of Love.* New York: Free Press, 2013.

Velasquez-Manoff, Moises. "Can CBD Really Do All That? How One Molecule from the Cannabis Plant Came to Be Seen as a Therapeutic Cure-all." *New York Times,* May 14, 2019.

Chapter 2: The Hand

AB489, California Consenting Adult Sex Bill (Ca. 1975), http://www.unmarriedamerica.org/Archives/1975-CA-Consenting-Adults-Act/1975-AB489-CA-Consenting-Adults-Act.pdf.

Abramson, Mark. *Sex, Drugs & Disco: San Francisco Diaries from the Pre-AIDS era.* San Francisco: Wilde City Press, 2015.

Budman, K.B. "A First Report of the Impact of California's New Marijuana Law, SB 95." California Office of Narcotics and Drug Abuse. Sacramento, January 1977, https://www.ncjrs.gov/pdffiles1/Digitization/45532NCJRS.pdf.

Cothran, George. "Barbagelata's Return?" *SF Weekly,* November 18, 1998, https://archives.sfweekly.com/sanfrancisco/cothran/Content?oid=2135846.

Flanagan, Michael. "When Polk Street Exploded: Tear gas, murder and the tradition of the Halloween buses." *Bay Area Reporter,* October 24, 2018.

Guinn, Jeff. *The Road to Jonestown: Jim Jones and Peoples Temple.* New York: Simon & Schuster, 2018.

Hinckle, Warren. *Gayslayer!: The Story of How Dan White Killed Harvey Milk and George Moscone & Got Away with Murder.* Virginia City, Nevada: Silver Dollar Books, 1979.

Kerr, Breena. "San Francisco's Historic Tenderloin May Become World's First Official Trans District." *YES!*, February, 9, 2017.

Maley, Bridget. "Three Temples on Geary: Three bridges, two earthquakes and one zealot." *The New Fillmore,* December 2018.

San Francisco Examiner, November 9, 1975; March 14 and 21, 1976.

San Francisco Chronicle, September 19 and December 14, 1975; January 9, April 13, and July 25, 1976.

San Francisco Sunday Examiner & Chronicle, July 25, 1976.

The San Francisco Street Artists Movement collection. Courtesy of the Bay Area Television Archive at San Francisco State University, https://diva.sfsu.edu/collections/sfbatv/11394.

Sears, Clare. *Arresting Dress: Cross-Dressing, Law, and Fascination in Nineteenth-Century San Francisco.* London: Duke University Press, 2015.

Shilts, Randy. *The Mayor of Castro Street: The Life and Times of Harvey Milk.* New York: St. Martin's Press, 1982.

Talbot, David. "The Peoples Temple's Roots in the Fillmore: Jim Jones moved into the neighborhood at its most vulnerable moment." *The New Fillmore,* September 2013, http://newfillmore.com/wp-content/uploads/2013/08/2013_09.pdf.

Talbot, *Season of the Witch.*

Thompson, Walter. "How Urban Renewal Tried to Rebuild the Fillmore." *Hoodline,* January 10, 2016.

Turner, Wallace. "An Antipolitician Politician Almost Makes It in San Francisco." *New York Times,* December 13 and 14, 1975.

Wilhelm, Richard. *The I Ching or Book of Changes.* Translated by Cary F. Baynes. 3rd ed. Princeton, New Jersey: Princeton University Press, 1967.

The Zebra Murders Collection. Courtesy of the Bay Area Television Archive at San Francisco State University, https://diva.sfsu.edu/collections/sfbatv/bundles/230807.

Chapter 3: If All the World's a Stage

Campbell, Patricia J. *Passing the Hat: Street Performers in America.* New York: Delacorte Press, 1981.

Coyote, *Sleeping Where I Fall.*

Fosburgh, Lacey. "Alcatraz, Now Empty, Silent and Desolate, Is Opened to the Public." *New York Times,* October 27, 1973.

Lee, *Smoke Signals.*

San Francisco Examiner, August 17, 1986.

Stack, Peter. "WHERE ARE THEY NOW? Catching Up With More Local Legends. Find out whatever happened to Phyllis Diller, Eddie Fisher, others." SF-Gate.com, September 26, 1999, https://www.sfgate.com/entertainment/article/WHERE-ARE-THEY-NOW-Catching-Up-With-More-Local-2906483.php.

Pollack, Lisa. "Happy Feat; If ever a record was made to be broken, it seems, it's the one for long-distance tap dancing. A shuffle through 16 years of agony, ecstasy and snappy choreography." *Baltimore Sun*, August 3, 1999.

Talbot, *Season of the Witch*.

Tomashoff, Craig. "The ABCs of CBD." *The Complete Guide to Medical Marijuana*, January 2019.

Werner, Clint. *Marijuana: Gateway to Health*. San Francisco: Dachstar Press, 2011.

Chapter 4: September's Song

Budman, K.B. "A First Report of the Impact of California's New Marijuana Law (SB 95)." California Office of Narcotics and Drug Abuse. Sacramento, January 1977.

Coyote, *Sleeping Where I Fall*.

Lee, *Smoke Signals*.

Lloyd, Pamela. *The Book of Pot*. New York: The Ridge Press/A & W Visual Library, 1976.

Raphael, Ray. *Cash Crop: An American Dream*. Mendocino, CA: The Ridge Times Press, 1985.

Richardson, Jim. Photographs by Arik Woods. *Sinsemilla: Marijuana Flowers*. Berkeley: And/Or Press, 1976.

San Francisco Chronicle, August 26, 1977.

Chapter 5: The Touch

Beren, Peter, and Patricia Roberto. "Zodiac Politics." *Mother Jones*, August 1976.

San Francisco Chronicle, February 11, 1976.

San Francisco Sunday Examiner & Chronicle, February 8, 1976.

Chapter 6: A Zillion and One Raindrops

Gilliam, Harold. *Weather of the San Francisco Bay Region*. Berkeley: University of California Press, 1962.

San Francisco Chronicle, May 28, December 26 and 30, 1976; January 1 and 11, 1977.

San Francisco Examiner, August 3, 1973.

Chapter 7: The Power at Hand

Bay Area Reporter, September 30, 1976; October 13, 1977.

Blando, Sandy. "An American Guru." *Psychic Times*, March 1974.

Caldwell, Earl. "Unlikely Sheriff Elected on Coast." *New York Times*, November 7, 1971.

Kean, Sam. *The Tale of the Dueling Neurosurgeons: The History of the Human Brain as Revealed by True Stories of Trauma, Madness, and Recovery*. New York: Little, Brown and Company, 2014.

Perry, *The Haight-Ashbury*.

San Francisco Chronicle. May 5, 1977; October 27, 1987; February 14, 1988.

San Francisco Examiner, January 9, 1972.

"Sheriff Richard Hongisto, the Notable Exception." *History of the San Francisco Sherriff's Department*, http://www.sfsdhistory.com/eras/sheriff-richard-hong isto-the-notable-exception.

Sides, Josh. *Erotic City: Sexual Revolutions and the Making of Modern San Francisco*. New York: Oxford University Press, 2011.

Talbot, *Season of the Witch*.

Chapter 8: Going Round the Bed

Family archives.

Chapter 9: Kings and Queens

Gómez, Abel R. "San Francisco Pride, Nation's Largest LGBT Celebration, Takes Place on Indigenous Ohlone Land." *Noteworthy — The Journal Blog*, June 3, 2019, https://blog.usejournal.com/san-francisco-pride-nations-largest-lgbt-celebration-takes-place-on-indigenous-ohlone-land-dd4475f47fd5.

"The Gurdjieff Foundation." *Gurdjieff International Review*, February 8, 2019, https://www.gurdjieff.org/foundation.htm.

San Francisco Chronicle, December 14, 1975; May 5, 6, and 26, 1977; November 18, 1998.

San Francisco Examiner, May 1 and 15, 1977.

Sides, *Erotic City*.

Stark, James. *Punk '77: An Inside Look at the San Francisco Rock n' Roll Scene 1977*. 3rd ed. San Francisco: RE/Search, 2006.

Why I Ride: Low and Slow. Directed by Debra Koffler and Vero Majano. Posted to YouTube in September 2011, Part 1: https://www.youtube.com/watch?v=DFR k5Is6qYo, Part 2: https://www.youtube.com/watch?v=-zGsecld51U, Part 3: https://www.youtube.com/watch?v=61HPYBPRMdw.

Chapter 10: Ride That Brownie

Abramson, *Sex, Drugs & Disco*.

Bay Area Reporter, February 5, 1976; June 9 and 23, October 13, 1977.

Berube, Allan. *Coming Out Under Fire: The History of Gay Men and Women in World War Two*. New York: The Free Press, 1990.

Birdsall, John. "The Orange Juice Boycott That Changed America." *Extra Crispy*,

February 6, 2018, https://www.myrecipes.com/extracrispy/the-orange-juice-boycott-that-changed-america.

Black, Jason Edward, and Charles E. Morris III, eds. *An Archive of Hope: Harvey Milk's Speeches and Writings.* Berkeley and Los Angeles, CA: University of California Press, 2013.

The Cockettes. Directed by David Weissman and Bill Weber. Culver City: Strand Releasing, 2002.

Durham, Michael. "Homosexuals in revolt: The year that one liberation movement turned militant." LIFE: The Year in Pictures 1971, December 31, 1971.

Faderman, Lillian. *Harvey Milk: His Lives and Death.* First edition. New Haven, CT: Yale University Press, 2018.

Gamson, Joshua. *The Fabulous Sylvester: The Legend, The Music, The Seventies in San Francisco.* New York: Henry Holt and Company, 2006.

Havemann, Ernest. "Why?" *LIFE*, June 26, 1964.

"Heaven Is on Her Side, Says Anita Bryant, and There's No Sympathy Up There for Gays." *People*, June 6, 1977.

Hinckle, *Gayslayer!*

"Hot Flash Store and Wakefield Poole Interview." Eric Smith, KPIX Eyewitness News. April 16, 1976. Courtesy of the Bay Area Television Archive at San Francisco State University, https://diva.sfsu.edu/collections/sfbatv/bundles/201667.

Jones, Cleve. *When We Rise: My Life in the Movement.* New York: Hachette Books, 2016.

Lagos, Marisa. "Twin Peaks Tavern — Gay Bar, Historic Landmark." SFGate.com, January 19, 2013, https://www.sfgate.com/politics/article/Twin-Peaks-Tavern-gay-bar-historic-landmark-4208442.php.

Neighborhoods: The Hidden Cities of San Francisco: The Castro. Directed by Peter L. Stein. San Francisco: KQED, 1998.

Poole, Wakefield. *Dirty Poole: The Autobiography of a Gay Porn Pioneer.* Los Angeles: Alyson Books, 2000.

San Francisco Chronicle, January 13 and September 23, 1976; May 28, June 8, June 11, June 15, and August 4, 1977; January 3, 1978; August 31, 2018; April 12, 2019.

San Francisco Examiner, June 12, 1977.

Shilts, *The Mayor of Castro Street.*

Sides, *Erotic City.*

Stryker, Susan. "San Francisco." GLBTQ Archives, 2004, http://www.glbtqarchive.com/ssh/san_francisco_S.pdf.

Talbot, *Season of the Witch.*

The Times of Harvey Milk. Directed by Robert Epstein. TC Films International, 1984.

We Were Here. Directed by David Weissman and Bill Weber. Los Angeles: Red Flag Releasing, 2011.

Welch, Paul. "The 'Gay' World Takes to the City Streets." *LIFE*, June 26, 1964.

Chapter 11: Child of Life's Long Labor

Bay Area Reporter. October 13 and 27, November 10, 1977.

Black and Morris, eds. *An Archive of Hope.*

Cannon, Lou. "San Francisco's Moscone Is Buoyed by Vote of Confidence in Bitter Election." *Washington Post,* August 4, 1977.

Faderman, *Harvey Milk.*

Friess, Steve. "The First Openly Gay Person to Win an Election in America Was Not Harvey Milk." Bloomberg.com, December 11, 2015, https://www.bloomberg.com/news/features/2015-12-11/the-first-openly-gay-person-to-win-an-election-in-america-was-not-harvey-milk.

Guinn, *The Road to Jonestown.*

Herbert, Frank. *Dune.* New York: Ace, 2010.

Jones, *When We Rise.*

Kilduff, Marshall, and Phil Tracy. "Inside Peoples Temple." *New West,* August 1, 1977.

Lee, *Smoke Signals.*

Rathbun, Mary, and Dennis Peron. *Brownie Mary's Marijuana Cookbook & Dennis Peron's Recipe for Social Change.* San Francisco: Trail of Smoke Publishing, 1996.

"Sheriff Richard Hongisto, the Notable Exception." *History of the San Francisco Sheriff's Department,* http://www.sfsdhistory.com/eras/sheriff-richard-hongisto-the-notable-exception.

San Francisco Chronicle, July 25, 1976; August 2 and 4, September 6, and November 9, 1977; October 13, 1979; June 20, 1983; September 19, 2015.

San Francisco Examiner. May 15, July 17, and August 7, 1977.

The San Francisco Policeman, March 21, 1978.

San Francisco Voter Information Pamphlet. Special Election, August 2, 1977. SFPL Elections Collection, https://sfpl.org/pdf/main/gic/elections/August2_1977.pdf.

Shilts, *The Mayor of Castro Street.*

Talbot, *Season of the Witch.*

Chapter 12: Galen's Batch

Family archives.

Chapter 13: The Devil's Playground

Bentley, Kevin. *Wild Animals I Have Known: Polk Street Diaries and After.* San Francisco: Green Candy Press, 2002.

"Bournegate Rocks Capitol: White House Dope Scandal." *High Times,* November 1978.

California Consenting Adult Sex Bill (AB489, 1975), http://www.unmarriedamerica.org/Archives/1975-CA-Consenting-Adults-Act/1975-AB489-CA-Consenting-Adults-Act.pdf.

Dokoupil, Tony. *The Last Pirate: A Father, His Son, and the Golden Age of Marijuana.* New York: Anchor Books, 2015.

January 19, 1978: State of the Union Address. Miller Center, https://millercenter.org/the-presidency/presidential-speeches/january-19-1978-state-union-address.

Faderman, *Harvey Milk.*

Gettman, Jon, Ph.D. "Crimes of Indiscretion: Marijuana Arrests in the United States." *National Organization for the Reform of Marijuana Laws,* 2005, https://norml.org/pdf_files/NORML_Crimes_of_Indiscretion.pdf.

Jones, *When We Rise.*

Lee, *Smoke Signals.*

Maupin, Armistead. *Tales of the City.* New York: Harper Perennial, 2007.

Rathbun and Peron. *Brownie Mary's Marijuana Cookbook & Dennis Peron's Recipe for Social Change.*

San Francisco Chronicle, August 4, 1977; January 10, 1978.

Shilts, *The Mayor of Castro Street.*

Stark, *Punk '77.*

Stryker, Susan. *Transgender History: The Roots of Today's Revolution.* 2nd ed. New York: Seal Press, 2017.

Wooten, James T. "Carter Seeks to End Marijuana Penalty for Small Amounts." *New York Times,* August 3, 1977.

Chapter 14: Off My Cloud

Abramson, *Sex, Drugs & Disco.*

Barbash, Fred. "Carter Aide Bourne Resigns Over False Prescription." *Washington Post,* July 21, 1978.

Bay Area Reporter, August 31, 1978.

"Bournegate Rocks Capitol: White House Dope Scandal." *High Times,* November 1978.

Dokoupil, *The Last Pirate.*

Faderman, *Harvey Milk.*

Gamson, *The Fabulous Sylvester.*

"Heaven Is on Her Side, Says Anita Bryant, and There's No Sympathy Up There for Gays." *People,* June 6, 1977.

Hinckle, *Gayslayer!*

Kelley, Ken. "Cruising with Anita." *Playboy,* May 1978.

Poole, *Dirty Poole.*

San Francisco Chronicle, June 10 and 20, August 10, November 5, 1978.

School Employees. Homosexuality. California Proposition 6 (1978). http://repository.uchastings.edu/ca_ballot_props/838.

Shilts, *The Mayor of Castro Street.*

Talbot, *Season of the Witch.*

Chapter 15: Paint It Black

A Closer Look. "Moscone/Milk Assassinations." Television special report. Belva Davis, KQED, November 27, 1978. Courtesy of the Bay Area Television Archive at San Francisco State University, https://diva.sfsu.edu/collections/sfbatv/bundles/235960.

Abramson, *Sex, Drugs & Disco.*

Bay Area Reporter, August 31 and November 9, 1978.

Faderman, *Harvey Milk.*

Guinn, *The Road to Jonestown.*

Hinckle, *Gayslayer!*

Jones, *When We Rise.*

Neighborhoods: The Hidden Cities of San Francisco: The Castro. Directed by Peter L. Stein. San Francisco: KQED, 1998.

San Francisco Chronicle, May 7, August 10, September 12, November 8, 18, 20, 21, 25, and 28, 1978.

San Francisco Examiner, November 19, 1978.

San Francisco Voter Information Pamphlet, General Election, November 7, 1978, https://sfpl.org/pdf/main/gic/elections/November7_1978short.pdf.

School Employees. Homosexuality. California Proposition 6 (1978), http://repository.uchastings.edu/ca_ballot_props/838.

Shilts, *The Mayor of Castro Street.*

Talbot, *Season of the Witch.*

The Times of Harvey Milk. Directed by Robert Epstein. TC Films International, 1984.

Chapter 16: No Peace

Abramson, *Sex, Drugs & Disco.*

Bay Area Reporter, April 12, 1979; May 24, 1979; June 7, 1979.

Black and Morris, eds. *An Archive of Hope.*

Faderman, *Harvey Milk.*

"Gay Police Recruits." KQED News, June 19, 1979, https://diva.sfsu.edu/collections/sfbatv/bundles/189498.

Gilbreth, Edward M. "Forgotten Stonewall Riots Changed Society. *Post and Courier,* September 2, 2014, https://www.postandcourier.com/news/forgotten-stonewall-riots-changed-society/article_1269d59a-a2c0-5b82-a4c1-ce87ec85029c.html.

Grabowicz, Paul. "Anti-Gay Sentiments Turn Violent In Aftermath of Moscone-Milk Killings." *Washington Post,* May 12, 1979

Hinckle, *Gayslayer!*

Jones, *When We Rise.*

Mikkelson, David. "The Twinkie Defense." Snopes.com, Oct. 30, 1999, https://www.snopes.com/fact-check/the-twinkie-defense/.

Pellechia, Thomas. "Legal Cannabis Industry Poised For Big Growth, In North America And Around the World." Forbes.com, March 1, 2018, https://www .forbes.com/sites/thomaspellechia/2018/03/01/double-digit-billions-puts -north-america-in-the-worldwide-cannabis-market-lead/#5a89c2386510.

People's 5. "Gay Power." KPIX, November 24, 1979, https://diva.sfsu.edu/collections /sfbatv/bundles/187731.

San Francisco Chronicle, April 21, May 2, 22, and 23, 1979; July 14, 1983.

San Francisco Examiner, April 22, May 13, 1979.

The San Francisco Policeman, June 1979.

Talbot, *Season of the Witch.*

"White Night Riot Aftermath I-V." KQED, May 22, 1979, https://diva.sfsu.edu/collections/sfbatv/bundles/189781 (through 189785).

"White Night Riots in San Francisco." KPIX, May 21, 1979, https://diva.sfsu.edu/ collections/sfbatv/bundles/190195.

Chapter 17: Give It Up and You Get It All

Abramson, *Sex, Drugs & Disco.*

Cherniak, Laurence. *The Great Books of Hashish.* Vol. 1, bk. 1. Berkeley, CA: And/ Or Press, 1979.

———. *The Great Books of Cannabis.* Vol. 1, bk. 2. Oakland, CA: Cherniak/Damele Publishing, 1982.

Douglas, Nik, and Penny Slinger. *Sexual Secrets: The Alchemy of Ecstasy.* Rochester, VT: Inner Traditions, 1989.

San Francisco Chronicle, March 30, July 13, August 3, 7, and 22, November 7, 1979.

San Francisco Examiner, April 29, 1979.

Wilhelm, *The I Ching or Book of Changes.*

Chapter 18: The Crossroads of Infinity

Aggarwal, Sunil. "'Tis in our nature: taking the human-cannabis relationship seriously in health science and public policy." *Frontiers in Psychiatry,* February 26, 2013.

Balko, Radley. *Rise of the Warrior Cop: The Militarization of America's Police Forces.* New York: PublicAffairs, 2013.

Bay Area Reporter, October 21, 1981.

Biello, David. "Where Did the Carter White House's Solar Panels Go? *Scientific American,* August 6, 2010, https://www.scientificamerican.com/article/carter-white-house-solar-panel-array/.

Campbell, Bobbi. "I WILL SURVIVE!" *San Francisco Sentinel,* December 10, 1981.

Jones, *When We Rise.*

Lee, *Smoke Signals.*

San Francisco Chronicle, November 7, 1979.

Shilts, Randy. *And the Band Played On: Politics, People, and the AIDS Epidemic.* New York: Penguin Books, 1988.

"A Timeline of HIV/AIDS." HIV.gov, last updated December 2018, https://www. hiv.gov/hiv-basics/overview/history/hiv-and-aids-timeline.

Chapter 19: Mirrors Become You

5B. Directed by Dan Krauss. San Francisco, 2018.

Abramson, Mark. *For My Brothers*. San Francisco: Wilde City Press, 2014.

"AIDS: An Incredible Epidemic." San Francisco General Hospital, 1985. Courtesy of the Bay Area Television Archive at San Francisco State University, https:// www.youtube.com/watch?v=cjDIoLlOWQo.

"AIDS Surveillance Report." San Francisco Department of Public Health AIDS Office: AIDS Cases Reported Through August 1993.

Balko, *Rise of the Warrior Cop*.

Baum, *Smoke and Mirrors*.

Bay Area Reporter, January 15 and 16, May 10, June 6, November 5, 1981; March 25, April 22 and 29, May 13, August 12, October 12, November 18, December 8, 1982; May 11 and July 24, 1983; September 17 and November 21, 1984.

Boffey, Philip. "Reagan Defends Financing for AIDS." *New York Times*, September 18, 1985.

Brownie Mary Archive. Courtesy of the Daniel E. Koshland San Francisco History Center at the San Francisco Public Library.

CAMP Headquarters. "CAMP: Final Report, 1983." Courtesy of the Humboldt State University Library — Special Collections.

CAMP Headquarters. "CAMP: Final Report, 1984." Courtesy of the Humboldt State University Library — Special Collections.

CAMP Headquarters. "CAMP: Final Report, 1986." Courtesy of the Humboldt State University Library — Special Collections.

"Earliest CBS Report on AIDS." *CBS News*, June 12, 1982. Courtesy of the Bay Area Television Archive at San Francisco State University, https://diva.sfsu.edu/col lections/sfbatv/bundles/189576.

Flanagan, Michael. "BARchive: Fond Memories of Uranus." *Bay Area Reporter*, June 28, 2015, https://www.ebar.com/entertainment/culture/179890.

"Gay America: Sex, Politics, and The Impact of AIDS." *Newsweek*, August 8, 1983.

Gorney, Cynthia. "Dan White and His City's Tragedy." *Washington Post*, October 23, 1985.

Jones, *When We Rise*.

Kean, Sam, *The Tale of the Dueling Neurosurgeons*.

King, Ryan S., and Marc Mauer. "A 25-Year Quagmire: The War on Drugs and Its Impact on American Society." *Sentencing Project*, September 2007, https:// www.sentencingproject.org/wp-content/uploads/2016/01/A-25-Year-Quag mire-The-War-On-Drugs-and-Its-Impact-on-American-Society.pdf.

Koop, C. Everett. "Introduction to the AIDS Archive." *Profiles in Science: The C. Everett Koop Papers* digital archive, 2003, https://profiles.nlm.nih.gov/ps/re trieve/ResourceMetadata/QQBCGF.

Larson, Ryan, Sarah Shannon, and Christopher Uggen. "6 Million Lost Voters:

State-Level Estimates of Felony Disenfranchisement, 2016." *Sentencing Project,* October 6, 2016, https://www.sentencingproject.org/publications/6-million-lost-voters-state-level-estimates-felony-disenfranchisement-2016/.

Lee, *Smoke Signals.*

Markel, Howard. "For Dostoevsky, epilepsy was a matter of both life and literature." PBS.org, November 10, 2017, https://www.pbs.org/newshour/health/for-dostoevsky-epilepsy-was-a-matter-of-both-life-and-literature.

McCurdy, Jesselyn, and Deborah Vagins. "Cracks in the System: 20 Years of the Unjust Federal Crack Cocaine Law." *ACLU,* October 2006, https://www.aclu.org/other/cracks-system-20-years-unjust-federal-crack-cocaine-law.

Open Line. "Dr. Paul Volberding on AIDS." KTVU, 1983. Courtesy of the Bay Area Television Archive at San Francisco State University, https://diva.sfsu.edu/collections/sfbatv/bundles/229303.

Open Line. "Silverman Closes San Francisco's Bathhouses." KTVU, September 23, 1984. Courtesy of the Bay Area Television Archive at San Francisco State University, https://diva.sfsu.edu/collections/sfbatv/bundles/229302.

Pogash, Carol. *As Real as it Gets: The Life of a Hospital at the Center of the AIDS Epidemic.* New York: Birch Lane Press, 1992.

"Poll Indicates Majority Favor Quarantine for AIDS Victims." *New York Times,* December 20, 1985.

Poole, *Dirty Poole.*

President Reagan's Remarks to the American Foundation for AIDS Research at the Potomac Restaurant in Washington, D.C., May 31, 1987. Reagan Library. Posted to YouTube on June 17, 2016, https://www.youtube.com/watch?v=UIi2kLGC44s.

"Race and the Drug War." *Drug Policy Alliance.* Accessed June 21, 2019, http://www.drugpolicy.org/issues/race-and-drug-war.

Rahamatulla, Altaf. "The War on drugs has failed. What's next?" *Ford Foundation,* March 23, 2017, https://www.fordfoundation.org/ideas/equals-change-blog/posts/the-war-on-drugs-has-failed-what-s-next.

Raphael, *Cash Crop.*

Rathbun and Peron. *Brownie Mary's Marijuana Cookbook & Dennis Peron's Recipe for Social Change.*

Reagan, Ronald. "The President's News Conference." Press conference, Washington, D.C., September 17, 1985. *The American Presidency Project,* https://www.presidency.ucsb.edu/documents/the-presidents-news-conference-951.

Rowe, Mona J., and Caitlin C. Ryan. "Comparing State-Only Expenditures for AIDS." *American Journal of Public Health* 78, no. 4 (April 1988): 424–29, https://ajph.aphapublications.org/doi/pdf/10.2105/AJPH.78.4.424.

San Francisco Chronicle, December 5, December 12, 1982; January 5 and July 21, 1983; August 17, 1985.

San Francisco Examiner & Chronicle, October 3, 1982.

"San Francisco General Hospital, AIDS Ward 5B/5A Archives, 1983–2003." Courtesy of the San Francisco Public Library, https://sfpl.org/pdf/libraries/main/sfhistory/archives-and-manuscripts/AIDS-Ward-5B-5A-finding-aid.pdf.

Schneider, Andrew and Mary Pat Flaherty. "Presumed Guilty." *Pittsburgh Press*, August 11–16, 1991.

Schneider, Keith. "Garberville Journal; Marijuana Once Reigned as the King." *New York Times*, January 26, 1988, https://www.nytimes.com/1988/01/26/us/gar berville-journal-marijuana-once-reigned-as-the-king.html.

Science Notes with Bill Skane. "GRIDS." KQED, 1982. Courtesy of the Bay Area Television Archive at San Francisco State University, https://diva.sfsu.edu/col lections/sfbatv/bundles/189618.

Shepard, Benjamin Heim. *White Nights and Ascending Shadows: An Oral History of the San Francisco AIDS Epidemic*. London: Cassell, 1997.

Shilts, *And the Band Played On*.

"A Timeline of HIV/AIDS." HIV.gov, last updated December 2018, https://www. hiv.gov/hiv-basics/overview/history/hiv-and-aids-timeline.

Skelton, Nancy, and Mark A. Stein. "Moscone-Milk Assassin Dan White Kills Himself in Garage of S.F. Home." *Los Angeles Times*, October 22, 1985.

Stein, Mark. "Nurses, S.F. Hospital Clash Over AIDS Danger." *Los Angeles Times*, August 23, 1985.

We Were Here. Directed by David Weissman and Bill Weber. Los Angeles: Red Flag Releasing, 2011.

When AIDS Was Funny. Directed by Scott Calonico. United Kingdom, December 2015.

White, Gilbert C. "Hemophilia: an amazing 35-year journey from the depths of HIV to the threshold of cure." *Transactions of the American Clinical and Cli matological Association*, 2010, https://www.ncbi.nlm.nih.gov/pmc/articles/ PMC2917149/.

Wilcox, Melissa M. *Queer Nuns: Religion, Activism, and Serious Parody*. New York: New York University Press, 2018.

Chapter 20: Ella-Vay-Shun

Abrams, Donald I., MD. "Letter From Dr. Donald Abrams." *Multidisciplinary As sociation for Psychedelic Studies*, April 28, 1995, https://maps.org/research-ar chive/mmj/abrams.html.

Abrams, Donald I., MD. "Medical Marijuana: Tribulations and Trials." *Journal of Psychoactive Drugs* 30, no. 2 (April–June 1998): 163–69, https://www.tandfon line.com/doi/abs/10.1080/02791072.1998.10399686.

Abrams, Donald I., MD. "Should Oncologists Recommend Cannabis?" *Current Treatment Options in Oncology* 20, no. 59 (July 2019), https://doi.org/10.1007/ s11864-019-0659-9.

Abramson, *For My Brothers*.

"Art Agnos visits San Francisco General Hospital." KPIX News, 1988. Courtesy of the Bay Area Television Archive at San Francisco State University, https://diva. sfsu.edu/collections/sfbatv/bundles/189408.

Balko, *Rise of the Warrior Cop*.

Brown, Joe. "The Quilt: A Battle Flag in the War on AIDS." *Washington Post*, Oc tober 2, 1988, https://www.washingtonpost.com/archive/lifestyle/1988/10/02/

the-quilt-a-battle-flag-in-the-war-on-aids/80faee08-9ffc-4541-93b9-48ac
94dd6d82/.

Gamson, *The Fabulous Sylvester.*

Hepler, Robert S., and Robert J. Petrus. "Experiences with Administration of Marihuana to Glaucoma Patients." *The Therapeutic Potential of Marihuana,* January 1976, 63–75, 10.1007/978-1-4613-4286-1_5.

"Interviews with AIDS patients and staff at SF General." KPIX News, December 1,
1988. Courtesy of the Bay Area Television Archive at San Francisco State University, https://diva.sfsu.edu/collections/sfbatv/bundles/189656.

Jones, Cleve, *When We Rise.*

Lee, *Smoke Signals.*

Morris, Charles E. III, ed. *Remembering the AIDS Quilt.* East Lansing: Michigan
State University Press, 2011.

Munson, A.E., L.S. Harris, M.A. Friedman, W.L. Dewey, and R.A. Carchman. "An-
ticancer Activity of Cannabinoids." *Journal of the National Cancer Institute* 55,
no. 3 (September 1975): 597–602, http://drugpolicycentral.com/bot/pg/can
cer/THC_cancer_sep_1975.htm.

Noyes Jr., R., S.F. Brunk, D.A. Baram, and A. Canter. "Analgesic effect of delta-
9-tetrahydrocannabinol." *Journal of Clinical Pharmacology 15,* nos. 2–3, February–March 1975, 139–43, https://www.ncbi.nlm.nih.gov/pubmed/1091664.

Pogash, *As Real as it Gets.*

Rathbun and Peron. *Brownie Mary's Marijuana Cookbook & Dennis Peron's Recipe for Social Change.*

San Francisco Chronicle, March 21, 1987; March 13, 1992.

San Francisco Examiner, January 8, 1995.

Shepard, *White Nights and Ascending Shadows.*

Shilts, *And the Band Played On.*

"A Timeline of HIV/AIDS." HIV.gov, last updated December 2018, https://www.
hiv.gov/hiv-basics/overview/history/hiv-and-aids-timeline.

We Were Here. Directed by David Weissman and Bill Weber. Los Angeles: Red Flag
Releasing, 2011.

Werner. *Marijuana: Gateway to Health.*

Chapter 21: The Wheel

"AIDS Surveillance Report." San Francisco Department of Public Health AIDS Office: AIDS Cases Reported Through December 1995.

Altman, Lawrence. "U.N. Reports 3 Million New HIV Cases Worldwide for '96."
New York Times, November 28, 1996.

Atakan, Zerrin. "Cannabis, A Complex Plant: Different Compounds and Different Effects on Individuals." *Therapeutic Advances in Psychopharmacology* 2,
no. 6 (December 2012): 241–54, https://www.ncbi.nlm.nih.gov/pmc/articles/
PMC3736954/.

Baum, *Smoke and Mirrors.*

Bay Area Reporter, February 2 and October 12, 1989; February 1, 1990; January 7, 1993.

Bonn-Miller, M. O., M. J. E. Loflin, B. F. Thomas, J. P. Marcu, T. Hyke, and R. Vandrey. "Labeling Accuracy of Cannabidiol Extracts Sold Online." *JAMA* 318, no. 17 (November 7, 2017): 1708–9, https://jamanetwork.com/journals/jama/full article/2661569.

"Cannabis and Cannabinoids (PDQ®) — Patient Version." NIH *National Cancer Institute*, updated June 3, 2019, https://www.cancer.gov/about-cancer/treat ment/cam/patient/cannabis-pdq.

Crimp, Douglas. "Before Occupy: How AIDS Activists Seized Control of the FDA in 1988." *The Atlantic*, December 6, 2011, https://www.theatlantic.com/health/ archive/2011/12/before-occupy-how-aids-activists-seized-control-of-the-fda-in-1988/249302/.

Doblin, R.E., and M.A. Kleiman. "Marijuana as Antiemetic Medicine: A Survey of Oncologists' Experiences and Attitudes." *Journal of Clinical Oncology* 9, no. 7 (July 1, 1991): 1314–19, https://ascopubs.org/doi/10.1200/JCO.1991.9.7.1314.

Doheny, Kathleen. "Marijuana, Hemp, CBD Oil: What's Legal and Where." *WebMD*, January 8, 2019, https://www.webmd.com/pain-management/news/ 20190108/marijuana-hemp-cbd-whats-legal-and-where.

France, David. *How to Survive a Plague: The Story of How Activists and Scientists Tamed AIDS*. New York: Alfred A. Knopf, 2016.

Hecht, Peter. *Weed Land: Inside America's Marijuana Epicenter and How Pot Went Legal*. Berkeley: University of California Press, 2014.

Hughes, Sallie, and Don Van Natta Jr. "Medical Necessity and Marijuana Use." *Washington Post*, November 20, 1990.

How to Survive a Plague. Directed by David France. Sundance Selects, 2012.

Jones, *When We Rise*.

Kolata, Gina. "AIDS in San Francisco Hit Peak in '92, Officials Say." *New York Times*, February 16, 1994.

Lee, *Smoke Signals*.

McCaffrey, Barry R. "The Administration's Response to the Passage of California Proposition 215 and Arizona Proposition 200." *National Criminal Justice Reference Service*, December 30, 1996, https://www.ncjrs.gov/txtfiles/215rel.txt.

National Academies of Sciences, Engineering, and Medicine. *The Health Effects of Cannabis and Cannabinoids: Current State of Evidence and Recommendations for Research*. Washington, D.C.: The National Academies Press, 2017, http://nationalacademies.org/hmd/reports/2017/health-effects-of-cannabis-and-cannabinoids.aspx.

"Protest Over AZT Price Led to the Arrest of 19." *New York Times*, February 9, 1988.

The Quake of '89: A Video Chronicle. KRON 4 archival news compilation, https:// diva.sfsu.edu/collections/sfbatv/bundles/189054.

Rathbun and Peron. *Brownie Mary's Marijuana Cookbook & Dennis Peron's Recipe for Social Change*.

San Francisco Chronicle, January 20, 26, and October 27, 1988; January 2, 30, February 1, September 18, October 7, 9, and 11, 1989; January 26 and August 6, 1990; March 13, July 23, August 5, 26, October 10, November 14, and December 16, 1992; August 5 and 6, 1996; January 15 and 16, 1997.

San Francisco Examiner, October 29, 1989; July 26, 1992.

Shepard, *White Nights and Ascending Shadows*.

Shilts, *And the Band Played On*.

"A Timeline of HIV/AIDS." HIV.gov, last updated December 2018, https://www. hiv.gov/hiv-basics/overview/history/hiv-and-aids-timeline.

Tom, Dara Akiko. "Grace and Fear Mark AIDS Epidemic in San Francisco." *Los Angeles Times*, October 30, 1994, https://www.latimes.com/archives/la-xpm-1994-10-30-me-56474-story.html.

Vandrey, R., J. C. Raber, M. E. Raber, B. Douglass, C. Miller, and M. O. Bonn-Miller. "Cannabinoid Dose and Label Accuracy in Edible Medical Cannabis Products." *JAMA* 313, no. 24 (June 23/30, 2015): 2491–93, https://jamanet work.com/journals/jama/fullarticle/2338239.

Velasquez-Manoff, Moises. "Can CBD Really Do All That? How One Molecule from the Cannabis Plant Came to be Seen as a Cure-all." *New York Times*, May 14, 2019.

We Were Here. Directed by David Weissman and Bill Weber. Los Angeles: Red Flag Releasing, 2011.

"Wrestling with AIDS." KQED Special Report, December 14, 1989, https://diva. sfsu.edu/collections/sfbatv/bundles/190109.

Epilogue: Licking the Spoon

Angell, Tom. "Marijuana Arrests Are Increasing Despite Legalization, New FBI Data Shows." Forbes.com, September 24, 2018, https://www.forbes.com/sites/ tomangell/2018/09/24/marijuana-arrests-are-increasing-despite-legalization-new-fbi-data-shows/#5f9de2dd4c4b.

"Race and the Drug War." *Drug Policy Alliance*, http://www.drugpolicy.org/issues/ race-and-drug-war.

Rahamatulla, Altaf. "The War on Drugs Has Failed. What's Next?" Ford Foundation, March 23, 2017, https://www.fordfoundation.org/ideas/equals-change-blog/posts/the-war-on-drugs-has-failed-what-s-next.

Rough, Lisa. "Can You Get a Cannabis Business License if You're a Convicted Felon?" Leafly.com, June 9, 2017, https://www.leafly.com/news/industry/can-convicted-felons-get-a-cannabis-business-license.

Schwartz, Matthew S. "San Francisco to Expunge Thousands of Marijuana Convictions." NPR.org, February 26, 2019, https://www.npr.org/2019/02/26/ 698045482/san-francisco-to-expunge-thousands-of-marijuana-convictions.

Witt, Emily. "How Legalization Changed Humboldt County Marijuana." *The New Yorker*, May 20, 2019.

READING GROUP GUIDE

1. Alia Volz introduces us to the "barge" in the prologue. She writes, "Equal parts therapist's couch, executive boardroom, and ladies' lounge, the barge was a place for sharing and intimacy" (xii). What did the barge represent to Alia? What role did it play within the larger cultural and political context of the story? What did the barge — or spaces like it — offer to people in the community? What have been the most treasured spaces in your own life?

2. What were some of the challenges the Sticky Fingers crew faced when beginning to make and sell magic brownies? How did these challenges change between the 1970s and '80s?

3. Alia describes an underground cannabis world powered largely by strong, ambitious women. How do the women in this story defy societal norms? In which ways do they conform?

4. Did this book change your understanding of the War on Drugs in the US? If so, in what way? Discuss its larger political and

social ramifications. What roles have race relations and politics played in drug enforcement over time? What connections can be drawn between the Nixon era and today's era of mass incarceration?

5. What were some of the social and political movements that took hold in San Francisco in the 1970s? How did Sticky Fingers interact with the activism of the day? Did that relationship evolve during the HIV/AIDS crisis?

6. Alia writes, "I grew up believing that I was made of my hometown, that there was no difference between me and the place I was born" (xii). Do you feel an elemental connection to your own hometown? Has that feeling changed over time?

7. Discuss the influence of the occult on Alia's family and Sticky Fingers Brownies. How did "magic," as Alia writes on page 22, infuse operations and decision-making? Meridy survived twenty-two years of illegal activity without an arrest. Was it because of street smarts, the occult, or something else?

8. Discuss Meridy and Doug's personal and professional relationship. What did they offer one another? What were some of their biggest disagreements? How did their personal relationship affect business, and vice versa? How does Alia approach her exploration of their relationship?

9. Discuss the illustrations Meridy and Doug created as packaging for Sticky Fingers Brownies, as featured at the beginning of each chapter. Which ones stood out to you and why? Discuss the ways that creativity and business acumen aligned for the Sticky Fingers crew. How did the illustrations promote

sales? How did they reflect the cultural and political changes in San Francisco?

10. Discuss how Alia balances history with memoir in her book. Do you think this approach is effective? Why or why not?

11. Meridy and Doug gambled with their freedom to operate an underground business. Why do you think they made those decisions? How does Alia feel about the risks her parents took?

12. Alia compares San Francisco in the 1970s and '80s with the city of today. She writes, "My parents belonged to the classic first wave of gentrifiers: white bohemians who moved into an inexpensive ethnic neighborhood and made it appear trendy." Now, with San Francisco serving as headquarters for powerful tech companies, the city has been "walloped by gentrification" (134). Talk about this change. What are the consequences of gentrification — both positive and negative? Do you see similar forces at work where you live? What is at stake?

13. Alia details how people showed up for one another at the height of the HIV/AIDS crisis (336–39). Discuss the role of community organizing in this history. How can we apply these strategies to the challenges of today?

14. Among other things, *Home Baked* is a portrait of an unusual mother-daughter relationship that weathers significant challenges. What strengths and weaknesses stand out to you?

15. Discuss the role of HIV/AIDS activism in paving the way for modern cannabis legislation and cannabusiness. Were you aware of these connections beforehand? Has this book altered your understanding of medical marijuana?

A CONVERSATION WITH THE AUTHOR

"Alia Volz on Her Personal History with Marijuana
& the LGBTQ Community"
by K. M. Soehnlein, *Lambda Literary*, May 10, 2020

Remember when "edible" was an adjective and not a noun? When selling pot could get someone sentenced as severely as selling heroin? (Prisons are still full of people, mostly people of color, serving out marijuana-related convictions.) The trajectory of how we got from then to now — with medical and/or recreational cannabis legal in twenty-two states — runs right through the queer liberation movement. Debut author Alia Volz gives this history the epic telling it deserves in her effervescent new memoir, *Home Baked: My Mom, Marijuana, and the Stoning of San Francisco*.

For Volz, who grew up in San Francisco in the eighties, marijuana was the family business. Her flame-haired, charismatic mother, Meridy, and her (not so) secretly bisexual father, Doug, ran Sticky Fingers Brownies, "the first known business of its kind to operate at that scale in California," she writes. At its peak, in the *Tales of the City* heyday, they baked ten-thousand pot brownies a month. The book is full of vivid scenes of the very *extra* Meridy (typical look: "a cobalt-blue turban, sparkling turquoise top, flowy blue harem pants, and Candie's mules") pushing baby Alia through the Castro in a stroller, making deliveries to Harvey Milk's camera shop or the apartment where disco legend Sylvester was sprawled on a divan.

Volz, an LGBTQ ally "raised by gay aunties," writes with a voice that is equal parts authoritative, mischievous, and moving. As she tries to unearth the facts behind her childhood as the daughter of the infamous Brownie Lady, she charts the larger story of the queer community under siege, turning to edibles for relief during the ravages of AIDS — and planting the seeds for the legal changes that bloomed into our cannabis-friendly world today.

Volz was kind enough to sit down for an interview and share some thoughts about her book. Below is an edited transcript of that conversation.

Your book tells the story of Sticky Fingers Brownies, your parents' wildly successful, underground marijuana brownie business. What led you to write it?

I grew up with these stories. My mom would hang out with her friends on her queen-sized bed, which we called "the barge," and as a little kid, I'd listen. After she had a bout of illness in 2006, it occurred to me to get her stories recorded in her own voice. The more I heard, the more questions I had about this really secretive world I grew up in. How did that fit into the larger world? What social pressures created it? When adult recreational use of marijuana was heading toward legalization, I became passionate that people understand where the right to consume marijuana comes from, and how the AIDS crisis was part of that. There's a debt of remembrance there.

The book is part memoir, but most of it takes place before you were born. How did you go about getting the story?

I started with the interviews. It's the nature of the beast — the nature of drug dealing — that the dealers led me to customers and growers, and customers led me to other customers. And then I went into the archives: the GLBT Historical Society archives, the history room at the SF Public Library, the *Bay Area Reporter* archives. The memoir is a Trojan horse. The story I wanted to tell was the social history of San Francisco in the '70s and '80s. I wanted to talk about the AIDS crisis and the bravery I witnessed as a child, the story of medical marijuana moving from party drug to panacea, the transition from dealer to healer. In the 1980s and 1990s, most medical-marijuana activists were also AIDS activists. The coauthor and driving force behind Prop 215 [which legalized medical cannabis in California in 1996 — the first in the nation to pass a statewide vote] had lost his lover to AIDS.

What surprised you the most about what you learned of your parents, their business, or the world they moved in?

When I started this project, I was estranged from my father. If we talked about the past, we'd end up in a fight. When I let him know what I was doing, he read some of my essays. He was hurt by some of it but also interested in sharing his side. He was as curious as I was to put together the person he used to be. We became very close through that process. That was really surprising to me. I was surprised by his bravery. His sexuality is exposed; his difficult temperament is exposed. There were things he doesn't remember — like the fact that he went to a gay bathhouse the day I was born — and he had to confront being represented on the page at a less flattering period of his life, when he was pretty young. It was very healing for us. He's now out of the closet and in love with this wonderful guy. They're such a nice couple, and it's changed his personality profoundly — it must be the shedding of shame.

Your mother is an amazing character. How do you think she managed to do something so original and unprecedented as start this business and grow it into what it became?

She's a very adventurous person. She's ballsy and never had a lot of fear. She would toss the I Ching before making any significant decision, and whatever it indicated, she would follow it. She would take these incredible risks but feel safe about it. She trusted her hippie oracles.

Your story moves along in time with the emergence of the LGBTQ community in San Francisco. Was there a point where you realized that the Castro would be like a character in your story?

It always was — it was a character in my memories. I was born in '77, and I started to have memories at about four years old, when my mother and I were living north of the city, and she would make monthly trips to San Francisco to sell brownies. We'd stay in Beck's Motor Lodge in the Castro! Her customers were mostly gay men, this parade of vibrant, exciting people with great hair and great outfits. As a kid, I was just in love — they were all so cool. We moved back to the city in '87; I was nine and was now seeing people who I thought of as surrogate aunties and uncles suffering so much, so ill, but also rising up. It really made an impression on me as a child — the love, loss, and bravery.

One of your mother's regular customers was Sylvester — how much of that story did you know about before you started the book?

I was lucky enough to remember Sylvester first-hand. My mom started selling brownies to him while she was pregnant with me and continued until he died in '88. She would sometimes take me with her. I remember his place on Twin Peaks — it had this amazing boudoir vibe, and he had a pool table, which absorbed my attention. When I was young, I identified really strongly with *Alice in Wonderland,* for obvious reasons — I was an only child always around stoned people, navigating these weird, drug-filled environments. Sylvester would wear turbans and caftans or flowy silk robes, and all this jewelry, and he would lounge on this velvet fainting couch, smoking a joint. He was the Caterpillar, right out of Wonderland. He was magical.

You've lived in San Francisco most of your life. You write, "I grew up believing that I was made of my hometown, that there

was no difference between me and the place I was born." Do
you feel that the spirit of freedom and adventure is alive and
well in San Francisco?

Oh, God no. It's been badly trampled. In more optimistic and
romantic moments, I can see it as cyclical. San Francisco has this
long history of recurring waves of mass migration—hundreds of
thousands of people come in, and in a very short time, displace
what was there before and create something new. The Gold Rush
displaced and massacred the Ramaytush Ohlone, who'd been there
for thousands of years. The hippies devastated Haight-Ashbury,
which was a thriving neighborhood with a large African American
population. The gay liberation activists transformed the city as a
whole. The techie tornado—a huge influx of people—have come
here to do this crazy thing, destroying what was there before. It's
a heartbreaker, but it also feels like it's part of the nature of this
place. I still feel a heart-connection that doesn't go away, even
though I am deeply disillusioned. I still feel that it's my town.

61. Chung Fu / Inner Truth

Sticky Fingers Brownies

Top right: Doug holding Alia Volz. *Bottom:* Meridy Volz

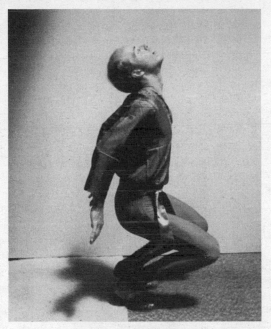

the sun

~Sticky Fingers Brownies~

the moon

~Sticky Fingers Brownies~

Top left: Doug Volz *Bottom right:* Meridy Volz as a mummy.

Top and bottom: Cheryl Beno

Top left: Barbara Hartman-Jenichen *Bottom right:* Alia (front) and Meridy Volz

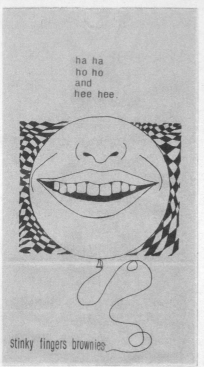

ha ha
ho ho
and
hee hee.

stinky fingers brownies

Top right: Alia Volz and Doug Volz in Willits, circa 1982 *Bottom:* Meridy Volz

Top left: Sticky Fingers Brownies *Bottom right:* Doug Volz

Top: Doug Volz (left), Meridy Volz, and Cheryl Beno *Bottom right:* Alia Volz, 2020